Advance praise for *Francis of Ass*

T0245541

"Howard Snyder weaves together in a fascin: creative, engaging, and contextualized story o. .... Assisi like no other account of this saint, and at the same time, an in-depth study of how renewal movements actually work. The final chapters of *Francis of Assisi, Movement Maker* then provide insightful comparisons with John Wesley, general patterns of renewal, and inspiring lessons and challenges for the church today."

— *Roger Schroeder*
Louis J. Luzbetak, SVD Professor of Mission and Culture
Catholic Theological Union at Chicago

"In a world where Christians all too often relegate monasticism to solitude and prayer, Howard Snyder provides a fresh and accessible introduction to St. Francis and St. Clare that reminds us of our missional call to vocation and service. Snyder incorporates both an introduction to the lives of these two saints, the movements they inspired, and the strength of their visions to inspire generations. Snyder also follows the Franciscan movement through ensuing years, helping the reader to understand the challenges movements face after the founder's demise, through periods of decline, and into times of needed renewal. A helpful reminder that lies at the intersection of piety and mission, in service for the sake of Christ."

— *Dean G. Blevins*
Nazarene Theological Seminary

"Howard Snyder brings his substantial and meticulous research skills and missiological acumen to focus on the life and ministry of Francis of Assisi in this riveting story of a 'wild and simple saint' who launched a remarkable movement. Drawing on Francis and his movement, Snyder's insights into the social and cultural dynamics and patterns of renewal movements are amazing, noting how such movements can experience mission drift over time, and how they must balance institutional structure with charismatic energy. This fascinating story of Francis and the movement he unleashed is as relevant today as it was 800 years ago, and invites us all, as followers of Jesus, to be inspired by Francis and to become lesser."

— *Darrell Whiteman*
Founder, Global Development, and Publisher
American Society of Missiology

"An admirably clear, detailed, and compelling account of Francis's life, which omits none of the charm of the contemporary stories."

— *Ann Wrote*
author, *Francis: A Life in Songs*

"Tradition is the charismatic memory of the Church. This is especially true when a biographer tells the story of a missionary and their movement together, illuminating insight both old and new from the Christian archive. It has been many years since we have had such a scholarly and lyrical portrait of a Christian saint in the context of his apostolate."

— *Tory K. Baucum*
Benedictine College, Atchison, Kansas

"Howard Snyder presents this most familiar of saints in a powerful and perhaps unfamiliar way, focusing on Francis's leadership. All who wish to ignite a Spirit-fueled movement today and into tomorrow do well to learn these lessons from the past."

— *Rev. Bruce N. G. Cromwell*
Free Methodist Church

"What a breath of fresh air! We Christians talk about aspiring to be like Jesus, but in Howard Snyder's book we look into the amazing lives of Francis and Clare and those who joined them, who made Jesus their pattern in every way. I'm inspired, challenged, and convicted of what it means for me to call myself a follower of Jesus in my time and place."

— *Linda Adams*
Bishop Emerita, Free Methodist Church USA

"Howard Snyder is one of the world's leading experts on church renewal, and in this book he uses his extensive knowledge and wealth of wisdom to explore the dynamics and enduring impact of the Franciscan movement. This illuminating study will both inform and inspire those who long to see God renew the life and mission of the church."

— *James E. Pedlar*
Bastian Chair of Wesley Studies and
Associate Professor of Theology, Tyndale University

"Dr. Snyder's exhaustive account of St. Francis and St. Clare's journeys from encounter, conversion, to ultimately becoming renewers of the Body of Christ is a convicting delight! Dr. Snyder's meticulous retelling of these saints' transition from the upper crust of Medieval Italy's wealthy class to the bowels of poverty and service feels like a joyful walk through the countryside surrounding Assisi. One leaves these pages personally convicted to follow Christ's own example more closely."

— *Deacon Nathan Gunn*
Young Life Northeast Division and
Global Cities Initiatives Coordinator

FRANCIS OF ASSISI,
MOVEMENT MAKER

The American Society of Missiology Book Series provides a platform for those engaged in the praxis of mission. Theologians, social scientists, historians, mission executives, missionaries, and activists from diverse religious traditions and cultures come together to form the American Society of Missiology. They reflect deeply on matters related to what can be discerned as God's redeeming activity in the world. This Series amplifies their voices for the renewal of the church, the transformation of the world, and the glory of God.

American Society of Missiology Series, No. 66

FRANCIS OF ASSISI, MOVEMENT MAKER

The Unconventional Leadership of a Simple Saint

Howard A. Snyder

ORBIS BOOKS
Maryknoll, New York 10545

Founded in 1970, Orbis Books endeavors to publish works that enlighten the mind, nourish the spirit, and challenge the conscience. The publishing arm of the Maryknoll Fathers and Brothers, Orbis seeks to explore the global dimensions of the Christian faith and mission, to invite dialogue with diverse cultures and religious traditions, and to serve the cause of reconciliation and peace. The books published reflect the views of their authors and do not represent the official position of the Maryknoll Society. To learn more about Maryknoll and Orbis Books, please visit our website at www.orbisbooks.com

Library of Congress Cataloging-in-Publication Data

Names: Snyder, Howard A., author.
Title: Francis of Assisi, movement maker : the unconventional leadership of a simple saint / Howard A. Snyder.
Description: Maryknoll, NY: Orbis Books, [2024] | Series: American Society of Missiology series ; no. 66 | Includes bibliographical references and index. | Summary: "An overview of the life of St. Francis of Assisi, the movement he founded, and lessons today for leadership and mission"— Provided by publisher.
Identifiers: LCCN 2023048047 (print) | LCCN 2023048048 (ebook) | ISBN 9781626985742 (trade paperback) | ISBN 9798888660300 (epub)
Subjects: LCSH: Francis, of Assisi, Saint, 1182-1226. | Clare, of Assisi, Saint, 1194–1253. | Christian saints—Italy—Assisi—Biography.
Classification: LCC BX4700.F6 S567 2024 (print) | LCC BX4700.F6 (ebook) | DDC 271/.302 [B]—dc23/eng/20240116
LC record available at https://lccn.loc.gov/2023048047
LC ebook record available at https://lccn.loc.gov/2023048048e

To my discipleship band brothers

Winfield

Steve

Jonathan

without whose encouragement, wisdom, and prayers

this book would never have been completed.

Contents

Preface to the American Society of Missiology Series xi

Preface xiii

Introduction xv

Part I
The Man—and the Woman

1. Unsaintly Francis 3

2. Assisi and Clare 14

3. Conversion: A Drama in Three Acts 19

4. Called to Mission 32

5. Birth of a Movement 44

6. Francis and the Pope 58

7. Epidemic of Peace 67

8. The Role of the Rule 90

Part II
The Movement and the Motives

9. Movement Dynamics 105

10. Clare Elopes 132

11. Francis's Muslim Mission 152

12. The First Manger Scene   174

13. Francis's Failing Health   180

14. Marks of the Cross   194

15. Song of the Creatures   202

16. Francis's Final Days   210

Part III
Movements of the Spirit

17. Francis Wins the Universities   227

18. New Age of the Spirit?   253

19. The Franciscan Story of Genghis Khan and
     Christopher Columbus   283

20. Patterns of Renewal   308

21. Lessons in Lesserness   332

Acknowledgments   353

Select Bibliography   355

Index   361

Previously Published in the American Society of Missiology Series 372

Preface to the American Society of Missiology Series

Beyond the bare-bones definition of missiology as the study of the church's worldwide mission, missiology explores the intersection of active faith and culture. As such, it is well positioned to provide invaluable resources for those who seek to understand the interaction between God, the engaged church, and the cultures of the world. The American Society of Missiology Book Series seeks to publish these resources and make them available for the wider church.

Missiology is interdisciplinary, intercultural, and international. Theologians, social scientists, historians, linguists, and other specialized disciplines have come together to form the American Society of Missiology (ASM). These scholars, who hail from their respective traditions and rich cultures, reflect on matters related to what can be discerned as God's redeeming activity in the world. This series amplifies their voices for the renewal of the church, the transformation of the world, and the glory of God.

Missiology can also be described as praxiological—that is, it is at once theoretical and practical. It was the Brazilian educator Paulo Freire who defined "praxis" as "action and reflection upon the world in order to transform it." Missiology is scholarship in the service of the church-in-mission, and vice versa: the practice of the church in the world serves missiological scholarship like nothing else can. Many mission executives, missionaries, and activists also belong to the Society. ASM is a rich community of scholar–practitioners who seek to make a contribution not only to the scholarly field of mission studies but also to the "trenches" where gospel bearers give of their blood, sweat, and tears for the sake of mission.

In collaboration with Orbis Books, whose commitment to praxis is core to its mission, the ASM Book Series seeks to make available relevant resources for both scholars and practitioners of *missio Dei*. We welcome your engagement and feedback; and should you feel inspired to contribute to this series, we also welcome your submissions.

Al Tizon, ASM Series Editor
Darrell Whiteman, ASM Publisher

Preface

I wrote this book because I want to see a deep movement of God's Spirit in our day. I pray for this. I believe Francis of Assisi and his movement point the way. I'm not sure when Francis first caught my interest. As a Methodist, I grew up hearing more about John Wesley and Francis Asbury than about Francis of Assisi. Studying at Notre Dame helped pique my interest, as did the movie *Brother Sun, Sister Moon*. But what really lit the flame was a visit Jan and I made to Assisi in the spring of 2003. Just two nights and one day, but I fell in love with the town, which still feels medieval. More deeply, I fell in love with Francis and his God-given vision for spiritual awakening that was also an awakening to our beautiful God-crafted world. I noted then in my journal that I hoped one day to write a book on *St. Francis's Way to Renew the Church*— something like my earlier book *The Radical Wesley and Patterns for Church Renewal*, but different.

Finally, here is the book. Dozens of books on Francis and two more visits to Assisi helped. My passion for a new spiritual awakening grows. In this book I distill key movement dynamics that still apply, and that I think the global church needs, and I believe longs for.

We look first at Francis and Clare themselves, then the amazing Franciscan movement, and finally the distilled truths *this* medieval phenomenon has for the twenty-first century church and world and for the earth.

Introduction

In the early days of his movement, Francis and his small band of brothers lived briefly in an abandoned shack along a stream in the valley below Assisi. It was summer. Francis and the brothers were walking along on a sunlit day.

Suddenly Brother Leo started feeling ill. A vineyard was nearby, so Francis gathered a few clusters of grapes and shared them with Leo and the others. Brother Leo immediately felt better. But then the vineyard owner came after Francis with a stick and began hitting him. As usual, Francis thanked God. The brothers went on their way, Francis singing,

> Leo had his grapes to eat;
> But poor Francis, he got beat!
> Leo had a choice tidbit,
> Brother Francis paid for it![1]

This was Francis—joyful, singing, spontaneous, sometimes funny, always watching out for his brothers.

In 1907, historian James Walsh published a provocative book, *The Thirteenth: Greatest of Centuries*. Walsh highlighted the many remarkable achievements of the 1200s: Rise of the first universities and Gothic cathedrals, age of the Troubadours, the art of Giotto and other masters, and in England, *Magna Carta* and the world's first Parliament (1215). This was the age of Thomas Aquinas (1225–1274) and of Dante Alighieri, the great Italian poet born in Florence in 1265 who later authored *The Divine Comedy*.[2]

All this in the thirteenth century. Yet the most famous person of the 1200s was a simple, lightly educated youth named Francis in the Italian

---

[1] Paraphrased from Omer Englebert, *Saint Francis of Assisi*, 2nd English ed., trans. Eve Marie Cooper (Chicago: Franciscan Herald Press, 1965), 124–25.

[2] James J. Walsh, *The Thirteenth: Greatest of Centuries* (New York: Catholic Summer School Press, 1907).

hill town of Assisi, a slight young man who embraced total poverty, wrote little, died in his forties—and has more books written about him than anyone else except Jesus. Thousands of young men flocked to follow Francis. A movement quickly sprouted. Franciscan brothers reawakened the church and would later make historic discoveries in astronomy, chemistry, physics, and other fields.[3] Charles Freeman, in his monumental *Reopening of the Western Mind*, credits Franciscan scholars, such as Roger Bacon, Bonaventure, John Duns Scotus, and William of Ockham, as among the intellectual influences that lead to the Renaissance and the Enlightenment.[4]

It's a puzzle. That puzzle, especially the puzzle of the movement itself, is the focus of this book. The key to the puzzle, I think, can help catalyze genuine movements of the Spirit today and can benefit each of us.

In some ways, the saint of Assisi was a failed leader. "Francis wasn't an organizer. He didn't strategize or plan. He was thoroughly Spirit-inspired in his approach to life."[5] Yet a movement sprang from his hands and heart that increasingly even today touches lives all around the globe.

In fact, Francis showed a kind of movement genius. There are different kinds of genius, as there are of intelligence. Francis's genius was more organic than organizational, more intuitive than cogitated, more spontaneous than studied. A little like Jesus, perhaps. In hindsight, Francis's leadership looks surprisingly shrewd.

Today, solid sources on Francis and his movement are rich and growing. The year 2026 will mark the eight hundredth year of Francis's death. Anticipating this, Franciscan scholars have issued a comprehensive three-volume set of newly translated and edited early sources and a companion volume on Francis's soul-friend, Clare: *The Lady—Clare of Assisi: Early Documents*.[6] One really can't write about

---

[3] Seb Falk, *The Light Ages: The Surprising Story of Medieval Science* (New York: W. W. Norton, 2020).

[4] Charles Freeman, *The Reopening of the Western Mind: The Resurgence of Intellectual Life from the End of Antiquity to the Dawn of the Enlightenment* (New York: Alfred A. Knopf, 2023).

[5] Jon M. Sweeney, *When Saint Francis Saved the Church: How a Converted Medieval Troubadour Created a Spiritual Vision for the Ages* (Notre Dame, IN: Ave Maria Press, 2014), 152.

[6] Regis J. Armstrong, OFM Cap., J. A. Wayne Hellmann, OFM Conv., and William J. Short, OFM, eds., *Francis of Assisi: Early Documents*, 3 vols. (New York: New City Press, 2001); Regis J. Armstrong, OFM Cap., *The Lady—Clare of Assisi: Early Documents*, 3rd ed. (Hyde Park, NY: New City Press, 2006).

the Franciscan movement without including Clare, so this book tells her story as well.

As I have dug into the earliest Francis sources, two things surprised me. First, I was surprised at the central place of the Bible in Francis's life and witness. Contrary to stereotypes of medieval Christianity, Francis knew the Bible very well indeed. He quoted it constantly. Second is the centrality of Jesus Christ. I knew Francis sought to imitate Jesus, especially in serving the poor and living simply. But I was surprised how much Francis, in his preaching and in guiding his poor brothers, constantly pointed to Jesus as example, Savior, and Lord in a fully orthodox sense.

Through the years, the most popular account of Francis has been *The Little Flowers of St. Francis*. This is a delightful collection of stories about the saint and his brothers, but it's often not historically reliable. So, I use *The Little Flowers* hardly at all. My book draws on many sources, but the foundational ones are the very first Francis biography, written by Thomas of Celano, and two accounts compiled by some of Francis's earliest brothers, now known as *The Anonymous of Perugia* and *The Legend of the Three Companions*.[7] I also use several sources that highlight the internal dynamics of the Franciscans as a movement of renewal.

Things New and Old?

Is there anything new to be learned from Francis? Of course! God still wisely brings "out of his treasure things new and old" (Matt. 13:42).

What can we learn?

- How Francis received and responded to God's grace—was awakened to Jesus, the world, and all its creatures.
- How the gospel, lived like Jesus, reshapes society, human culture, and personal lives—the very course of history.
- How renewal movements actually work.

Along the way, we should glance briefly at some other questions. Was Francis a forerunner of the Renaissance and Reformation, as some say? Was he trying to undermine church authority? Was he anticapitalist? Did he abuse his own body through his rigorous asceticism? Was he really up to leading the movement he birthed?

---

[7] Some of the key early accounts of Francis are called "legends," but that does not mean they are mere fables or myths. The word "legend" here simply translates the Latin word *legenda*, meaning an account to be read. The Latin verb meaning "to read" is *legere*.

This book explores these questions in three sections. *Part I* is all about Francis himself—how the son of a rich medieval merchant marked out a new way of life, becoming Francis of Assisi and birthing an unparalleled movement.

Part II uncovers the inner dynamics of this movement, the society of Franciscan Brothers (*fratres*, brothers, friars). Here we find system-shaking dynamics that resonate still.

Part III draws lessons for faith communities today and our own spiritual journeys. We are not Francis or Clare. But we learn by watching them as they humbly follow Jesus.

Some of this book's readers likely know a lot about Francis, while others know very little. So, I begin by telling Francis's own story, but always with an eye to the way Francis's life and calling birthed an amazing movement.

Francis is of course *Saint* Francis. But we aim here to see Francis not through the warm glow of sainthood, but rather to see sainthood through the glow of Francis. Francis, the fully human person, with his faith and failures, is quite fascinating and winsome enough. We don't need to supply a halo or multiply miracles. Francis simply wanted to follow Jesus simply, humbly, nakedly; in the flesh as much as in the Spirit; in the world with its marvelous creatures, even while already dwelling in heaven. This is what Francis did. We explore how a movement sprang up, seemingly spontaneously.

My aim here is to explain Francis as best I can as the maker of a movement, and to show the relevance of that for the church and Christian discipleship now. This means we must look closely at Francis's world, his context—not just religious but also political, economic, sociological, even geographical, realities that intertwine with and help us understand the Francis movement. I focus more on these contextual dynamics than do many books on Francis and his brothers. The goal is not just inspiration, but understanding. The story thus becomes immensely richer, yet all the more startling.

So here we look at the man and the woman (Francis and Clare), the movement and the motives, and the message and meaning for today.

Part I

The Man—and the Woman

1

Unsaintly Francis

On a fall morning in 1202, Francis woke up in jail. Just twenty years old, he was a prisoner of war in the city of Perugia, fifteen miles east of his hometown.

Perugia's militia captured Francis and other Assisi soldiers in the battle of Collestrada. The two armies clashed on a wooded hillside near the Tiber River on its winding way south to Rome.[1]

The battle occurred long before Italy became a unified nation. This was still the feudal age. Cities had their own militias and often were pawns in larger contests between rival kingdoms and princedoms. Perugia and Assisi were in fact ancient enemies. Perugians after all were Etruscans, their city tracing back well before Christ. Assisi was a Roman colony known earlier as Assisium.

Perugia declared war on Assisi in 1202 over a smoldering dispute. Francis joined other Assisi youth riding and marching forth to defend their home. As the son of a wealthy merchant, Francis would have had armor and a fine horse. Plated suits of armor were not yet in general use, so Francis likely wore a suit of closely linked chain mail, including hood and leggings. Over this he likely sported a colorful tunic of costly fabric from his father's shop.[2]

Parading out of Assisi, the soldiers probably filed past San Rufino Cathedral as they headed down to the city gate. Townsfolk cheered; bells rang. The troops included foot soldiers, archers, soldiers representing the town's various guilds; then finally the mounted troops.

---

[1] Omer Englebert, *Saint Francis of Assisi*, 2nd English ed., trans. Eve Marie Cooper (Chicago: Franciscan Herald Press, 1965), 424.

[2] Paul Moses, *The Saint and the Sultan: The Crusades, Islam, and Francis of Assisi's Mission of Peace* (New York: Doubleday Religion, 2009), 15–16.

On the other side of the valley, Perugia's troops marched out to meet Assisi's advancing army. Crossing the Tiber, they attacked Assisi's forces at Collestrada Hill. By late afternoon, Assisi was soundly beaten. Perugian soldiers chased the Assisians across the fields and cut them down in what contemporary sources called a massacre.[3] The captives were taken to Perugia. Francis was imprisoned along with the nobles in underground cells.[4]

Months passed. No release came. Francis met a fellow prisoner, a knight from Apulia, the southeastern region that forms the heel of Italy's boot. The knight had been in the service of the French Count Walter of Brienne, head of Pope Innocent III's papal militia. Walter was famous in battle and widely celebrated in Troubadours' songs. Francis already knew about him; he had heard of Walter's exploits, he and his soldiers with crosses on their chests, defending papal power.[5]

Before long, however, Francis fell ill. Eventually his father Pietro managed to negotiate his son's release, coming to terms on the ransom amount.[6]

But nearly a year had passed. Francis returned to Assisi ill and disillusioned, his dreams and his health shattered.

Francis's Roots

Francis was the son of Pietro di Bernardone and his wife Pica. The 1972 movie *Brother Sun, Sister Moon* pictures Pica as French. Quite possibly so, though the records are unclear. Pietro made frequent business trips north to France. Certainly, he could have met Pica there.[7]

Francis was born in 1181 or 1182, probably in late September and most likely in the Bernardone house, located on the Via Portica at the west end of the main town square, the Piazza del Comune.[8]

---

[3] Arnaldo Fortini, *Francis of Assisi*, trans. Helen Moak (New York: Crossroad Publishing, 1992), 155.

[4] Fortini, *Francis of Assisi*, 159.

[5] Fortini, *Francis of Assisi*, 161–63; Englebert, *Saint Francis*, 64.

[6] Fortini, *Francis of Assisi*, 165, 169.

[7] Fortini, *Francis of Assisi*, 89. Fortini viewed Pica's French background as certainly plausible; the name or nickname "Pica" likely "referred to her native land; and, in fact, the French word *pique* was used for inhabitants of Picardy," a region in France north of Paris. Several sources (though none from the time of Francis) say that "Francis's mother did indeed come from Picardy. Given the fact that it lay between Champagne and Flanders and so was a meeting place for the merchants of the world, it is certainly a possibility. The fact that the Bernardone son was called Francesco ('the Frenchman') gives the story additional weight," notes Fortini (89 n. m). My guess is that if Francis could be given a modern DNA test, his genetic code would show him to be between 30 and 50 percent French, primarily from the Provençal area.

[8] Fortini, *Francis of Assisi*, 89.

At baptism Francis was named Giovanni di Pietro di Bernardone—that is, John son of Pietro. Pietro was away on business; on returning, he promptly renamed his son Francesco, "little Frenchman"—a bit uncommon for an Italian boy. The name probably reflected Pietro's fondness for his French friends and business colleagues.[9]

Clearly there were French, especially Provençal, influences on Francis. He later called himself "God's Troubadour."

Francis's father Pietro, enterprising cloth dealer, was part of Assisi's rising merchant class. In his travels Pietro bought cloth from Flanders or Britain—fabrics "highly prized at the time" in Italy—and other goods.[10] In addition to selling a variety of textiles, he owned at least one olive grove and had property and flocks on the far side of Mount Subasio.[11]

In these days feudalism was giving way to the kind of interregional and international trade that in coming centuries would birth European capitalism. The social and economic ferment of the time grew partly out of the Crusades. Called by the popes and blending themes of pilgrimage and holy war, the Crusades sought to wrest control of the Holy Land from Islamic Turks who had captured Jerusalem in 637 CE, in the early days of Islam. Crusading quickly became a fundamental feature of European culture.[12]

In the first Crusade, French forces successfully recaptured Jerusalem (1099 CE). They promptly set up a string of "Christian" fortresses throughout the Holy Land. Muslim armies expelled the Crusaders some forty years later, though. This defeat lit the spark for the second and several later Crusades, none as successful as the first.[13]

Francis was in this sense a child of the Crusades. The third, fourth, and fifth Crusades all raged during his short lifetime. The Crusade movement

---

[9] Lawrence S. Cunningham, *Francis of Assisi: Performing the Gospel Life* (Grand Rapids, MI: William B. Eerdmans, 2004), 3; Fortini, *Francis of Assisi*, 88.

[10] Henri d'Avranches, *Versified Life of Saint Francis*, in *Francis of Assisi: Early Documents*, 3 vols., ed. Regis J. Armstrong, OFM Cap., J. A. Wayne Hellmann, OFM Conv., and William J. Short, OFM (New York: New City Press, 2001), 1:435 n. c. [hereafter FA:ED].

[11] Fortini, *Francis of Assisi*, 164, 175. Assisi's archives show that Pietro had "extensive holdings on Assisi's mount and plain," notes Fortini, including country houses where he and his family spent part of their time. Fortini, 114.

[12] James M. Powell, *Anatomy of a Crusade, 1213–1221* (Philadelphia: University of Pennsylvania Press, 1986), 59.

[13] Samuel Hugh Moffett, *A History of Christianity in Asia*, vol. 1, *Beginnings to 1500* (New York: HarperCollins, 1992), 393–94, gives a succinct summary. See also Jonathan Riley-Smith, ed., *The Oxford Illustrated History of The Crusades* (Oxford: Oxford University Press, 1995), "Chronology," 392–400.

in fact reached its zenith in Francis's day. Traveling Crusader armies unsettled much of Europe, contributing to the breakup of feudalism, stirring up anti-Semitism, but also spurring trade, travel, and learning.

The Crusading background helps explain Francis's later passion to reach Muslims—not with swords and spears, but with the peace and good news of Jesus.

For Francis's father though, Crusading was great for the pocketbook. Business was booming. His family was rich enough to have servants, just like the nobility. Pietro was part of the rising merchant class that was quickly gaining power vis-à-vis the older feudal aristocracy. During Francis's teen years, Assisi's citizens besieged Rocca Maggiore, the city's imposing hilltop citadel, and drove out the German garrison of the Holy Roman Empire. Leading Assisi merchants and others organized the town as a "commune" (municipality) and elected "consuls" as its chief officials. As a result, Assisi, largely liberated from the German-dominated Holy Roman Empire, came more directly under the sway of Rome and Pope Innocent III.[14]

Francis and Friends

As a teen, Francis was popular with his peers; sainthood was far from his mind. He probably did not yet know Clare, still a small child. Anyway, her family, the Offreduccios, were of noble class.

Growing up, Francis received a basic education. His heart language was of course Italian, a much-simplified version of earlier Latin. But in school he learned to read and write passable Latin. Later he would beautifully express his heart language in his moving poem, *Canticle of the Creatures.*

Francis also learned some French, including songs—perhaps those of the troubadours who periodically passed through Assisi, singing brightly of courtly love and chivalry.[15] For Francis always loved to sing. He likely learned some of the ballads based on popular tales such as *Reynard the Fox, The Romance of the Rose,* and *Knights of the Round Table.*[16]

---

[14] Cunningham, *Francis of Assisi,* 4–5; Ingrid J. Peterson, OSF, *Clare of Assisi: A Biographical Study* (Quincy, IL: Franciscan Press, 1993), 61; and other sources.

[15] The Provence region of France, along the Mediterranean, is about five hundred miles northeast of Assisi.

[16] These three books were, next to the Bible, the most popular and most read books of the thirteenth century. Francis would later describe his Lesser Brothers as his own "knights of the round table" who seek God and live lives of prayer and holiness. *Assisi Compilation,* FA:ED 2:208.

Francis's parish church, San Giorgio (St. George), near the Bernardone home, ran a school that Francis attended. Priests and perhaps nuns would have been his earliest teachers. In addition to learning to read and write Italian and some Latin, perhaps with a psalter as textbook, Francis also learned the legend of St. George and the dragon, depicted in fresco on one of the school walls.[17]

By this time the University of Bologna, 170 miles northeast of Assisi—the world's first university—had been functioning for more than a century. In Francis's day Bologna was emerging as a real university, branching into diverse fields of study. Francis though had no interest in academic study.

In his teens and early twenties, Francis enjoyed a lively circle of friends of his own class.[18] He was "naturally cheerful and jovial," according to *The Legend of the Three Companions*, and "courteous in manner and speech."[19] He loved stylish, colorful clothes, which he could easily afford. Early reports say he delighted in games and pranks, parties, and good food. It is easy to imagine Francis a popular, friendly figure among Assisi's youth.

Francis's earliest biographer, Thomas of Celano, says that Francis from childhood

> wasted and squandered his time almost up to the twenty-fifth year of his life. . . . He was an object of admiration to all, and he endeavored to surpass others in his flamboyant display of vain accomplishments: wit, curiosity, practical jokes and foolish talk, songs, and soft and flowing garments. Since he was very rich, he was not greedy but extravagant, not a hoarder of money but a squanderer of his property, a prudent dealer but a most unreliable steward.[20]

In other words, Francis did "all the things that adults deplore in the youth of today," Cunningham notes—"waste time and money; be preoccupied with fancy clothes which had to be of the latest mode; run around with the wrong crowd; chase after women; and take an interest

---

[17] Fortini, *Francis of Assisi*, 95.

[18] Editorial note: I am not fully consistent in the linguistic forms (Italian, Latin, French, English, etc.). I use for names of persons and places, including Francis's friends and early Franciscan brothers. I use the forms most familiar in the most common English texts. Thus, for example, I use "Bernardo" rather than "Bernard" but "Clare" rather than "Chiara," and "Bonaventure" rather than "Bonaventura."

[19] *Legend of the Three Companions*, FA:ED 2:70, 69.

[20] Thomas of Celano, *Life of St. Francis*, FA:ED 1:183.

in subversive music—in his case, the love songs *(chansons)* introduced from France."[21]

Earliest profiles of Francis suggest he possessed a natural affability, a sort of inborn charisma that attracted others—characteristics God's Spirit would in time transform and use.

The Call to Knighthood

Francis was about twenty-one when Pietro finally ransomed him from the Perugia prison. He returned home weak and ill.

Francis's illness, whatever it was, required months of rest. Days and nights turned into sober reflection and inner struggle. As he recovered strength, he began to walk about town with a cane. He gazed at "the beauty of the fields, the delight of the vineyards," the green-silvery olive groves stretching down the hills from Assisi—beautiful, yet they seemed now to hold little attraction. "He wondered at the sudden change in himself."[22]

This was a crisis of vocation, of life direction. Francis needed something higher and nobler—a life purpose.

God was calling, but Francis couldn't yet hear.

Then Francis learned that Count Walter of Brienne, the celebrated French nobleman he heard about in Perugia's prison, was recruiting soldiers for a big venture. Walter was in southern Italy, preparing a new expedition. One of Assisi's knights was about to go join him. This looked exciting. Perhaps Francis's new life was opening before him.

Francis decided to get serious about knighthood with its ideals of chivalry, honor, and romance and join Count Walter's forces. These were the hightide days of chivalry—the time when Christian ideals, aristocratic values and clout, and commercial interests all merged to reshape European society and excite many youth.

Shortly before Francis set out, though, he has a vivid dream. He sees a great Crusader fortress filled with armaments—a castle, a royal palace.[23] Its towers are festooned with banners. Atop the main tower a larger banner waves, bearing a bright Crusader cross. The gate is open. Francis walks in.

Spacious rooms and halls decorated with a vast array of arms come into view—swords and shields, spears and lances, helmets, axes, sparkling armor, coats of mail. "Crusader helmets with closed visors,

---

[21] Cunningham, *Francis of Assisi*, 7.

[22] Thomas of Celano, *Life of St. Francis*, FA:ED 1:185.

[23] Thomas of Celano, *Life of St. Francis*, FA:ED 1:186. Some sources say Francis saw these dream events occurring in his own house.

bejeweled helmets blazoned with coats of arms," all "ready for the use of an unknown army ... shouting a stirring war cry," suggests Fortini.[24]

Just ahead Francis sees a wide balcony and beyond that, the sea. A maiden, a princess, sits on a bench. Her long purple velvet dress contrasts with her white neck and face. Her beauty outshines the sunlit sparkle of the armaments.

The lovely maiden gazes far out over the blue sea. She seems to be waiting, perhaps for a message or for a ship to appear. Fortini writes, "She is the damsel that for so many years [Francis] has thought about, desired, loved, even though he has never known her. She is the chosen one. For her the banners are unfurled on top of the walls. For her the swords and the shields gleam, and for her exist the incomparable towers, the sky, the sea."[25]

Where is the knight who will lead warriors into battle, returning victorious to claim the princess, the castle? Again, a voice speaks: "*All this is for you* and for your knights."[26]

Francis's dream abounds with images and enchantments of the Age of Chivalry, the days of Crusader armies. It pictures the world of aspiring young knights, Francis's world.

In fact, the dream sets the stage for the conversion, the changes, the turnings Francis was entering now in his twenty-fourth year. There was indeed in Francis's future a castle, armaments, a youthful army. Additionally, there was also a mission and a battle, a crusade, a fair maiden—all contrasting sharply from Francis's imaginings.

A day or two later, new vigor stirring his blood and thoughts, Francis sets out on horseback with his new friend, the knight. They travel toward Apulia in southern Italy, where Count Walter then was, a region where Crusaders often set sail for the Holy Land.[27]

The two men ride as far as Spoleto, about thirty miles south, and spend the night. But then another surprise upsets Francis's plans. Perhaps word came that Count Walter had died. Or maybe Francis has another dream or vision, or maybe just second thoughts. Perhaps a relapse of his earlier illness. In any case, Francis abruptly changes his mind, gives up the idea of military glory, and returns home.[28]

---

[24] Fortini, *Francis of Assisi*, 184.

[25] Fortini, *Francis of Assisi*, 185.

[26] Fortini, *Francis of Assisi*, 185 (emphasis added).

[27] Paul Sabatier, *The Road to Assisi: The Essential Biography of St. Francis*, ed. Jon M. Sweeney (Brewster, MA: Paraclete Press, 2004), 10–12.

[28] Cunningham, *Francis of Assisi*, 8; Sabatier, *Road to Assisi*, 11. Fortini gives a

To forsake the career of a knight and potential Crusader and return home looked like failure, maybe cowardice. Yet this was another step in Francis's shift toward Christian discipleship and a much higher ideal of service and chivalry.

Back now in Assisi, Francis was again ill. Gradually his strength returned, but he was even less sure of his future than before. He took long walks in the countryside, sometimes with a friend. Sometimes he visited a rocky cave outside Assisi and there pondered his future. God began gently nudging his heart even before Francis knew it.

With his friend, Francis visited some shallow caves they likely had explored as children. Francis told his friend he was starting a great adventure but didn't explain. He wasn't quite sure himself. Francis seemed to be speaking in parables and puzzles. His castle dream was still on his mind. According to Thomas of Celano, Francis told his friends: "I will take a bride more noble and more beautiful than you have ever seen, and she will surpass the rest in beauty and excel all others in wisdom."[29]

Numerous caves or "grottos" are found around Assisi, especially further up Mount Subasio. Assisi tradition has long held that the cave where Francis now prayed and thought and sought out his future was among the cliffs and crags known as Sasso del Maloloco. Surrounded by evergreen oaks, ferns, and in spring flowering cyclamen, this is a picturesque spot where birds are often heard—an area of shallow caves known as the *Carceri* (literally, "prisons" or "cells") amid the forest, where a stream flows. Hermits had visited the area in earlier times, and a tiny oratory was there.[30]

Francis told his companion to wait outside while he meditated in the cave. He was there a long while, praying and struggling with his thoughts. When he finally emerged, he seemed different. He appeared drained and weak after an intense time of prayer. His friend could see Francis was troubled.[31]

Whatever happened in the cave, this was another step in Francis's turning. He was wrestling with himself, with God, his future. It was a time of doubt and suffering. According to Fortini, "More than ever the example of Christ, who also suffered, seemed the ultimate reality."[32]

---

more elaborate explanation, *Francis of Assisi,* 187–89, which refers to the earlier vision (183–85).

[29] Thomas of Celano, *Life of St. Francis,* FA:ED 1:188.

[30] Fortini, *Francis of Assisi,* 198; Englebert, *Saint Francis,* 153.

[31] Thomas of Celano, *Life of Saint Francis,* FA:ED 1:187–88.

[32] Fortini, *Francis of Assisi,* 199.

Beggar for a Day

Francis was feeling more and more drawn to the poor. He had always felt compassion toward poor and suffering folks, even during fun and frolic. Francis now "proposed in his heart, from [this point] on, never to deny alms to any poor person begging from him for God's sake, but rather to give more willingly and abundantly than usual. When away from home, if he could, he always gave money to any poor person requesting alms."[33]

He not only gave alms; he started listening to what poor folks said. He began to wonder what it would be like to *be* poor.[34]

Francis decided to join a pilgrimage headed for Rome. Many poor people lived there. Perhaps there Francis could find out what the life of a beggar was really like.

Arriving in Rome, Francis visited the church of Saint Peter. At Peter's tomb "he took a handful of coins from his money pouch, and threw them through a grating of the altar, making such a loud noise that all the bystanders were astonished at his generosity."[35]

Walking out the church doors, Francis found a crowd of poor beggars. He drew one aside and asked if he would switch clothes with him. The startled beggar was happy to do so! Francis donned the beggar's poor clothing, returned to the church steps, and began begging. As part of his disguise, Francis used Provençal French rather than Italian.[36]

The act seems impulsive, but Francis had already been pondering something like this.

Later he found the beggar again and switched back to his own clothes. He returned home to Assisi but told no one what he had done.

One day as Francis was praying, he felt God tell him, Francis, "What before seemed delightful and sweet will become unbearable and bitter; and what before made you shudder will offer you great sweetness and enormous delight."[37] And yet the way forward was still mist for Francis. Where and how was God leading?

---

[33] *Legend of the Three Companions,* FA:ED 2:72.

[34] *Legend of the Three Companions,* FA:ED 2:73.

[35] *Legend of the Three Companions,* FA:ED 2:73.

[36] *Legend of the Three Companions,* FA:ED 2:73. Thomas of Celano also recounts this incident in *Remembrance of the Desire of a Soul,* FA:ED 2:247. Thomas writes that after this, Francis "happily settled among the poor in the square in front of the church of Saint Peter, a place where the poor are abundant. Considering himself one of them, he eagerly ate with them. If his embarrassed friends had not restrained him, he would have done this many times."

[37] *Legend of the Three Companions,* FA:ED 2:74.

Lepers!

Soon something happened that turned Francis sharply in the right direction. Like most people of his day, Francis loathed lepers. He avoided them when he could. That was not easy, for Italy had many lepers and leper colonies. Some of the victims were suffering not from leprosy as we know it now, but rather from various other debilitating skin diseases such as elephantiasis or extreme psoriasis. Most victims, however, did suffer from real leprosy—now known as Hansen's disease, a chronic communicable infection with accompanying skin lesions and disfigurements. Only in the twentieth century was it discovered that leprosy's terrible disfigurements are caused not by the disease itself, but because lepers' nerves are so damaged, they don't feel injuries to their flesh.

Leprosy was widespread in Francis's day. Leper colonies dotted much of Italy. One estimate puts the number of leprosariums throughout all Christendom at nineteen thousand.[38] Medieval law required that lepers be isolated from other people as much as possible. They were forbidden to draw water from common wells or talk to children and were supposed to carry a bell or clapper. The Third Lateran Council (1179) required churches to provide lepers with separate chapels and cemeteries. The church showed compassion for lepers in various ways, remembering Jesus's example of touching and healing lepers. Medieval art sometimes even pictured Jesus himself as a leper.[39]

In the Assisi area, lepers lived in separate settlements outside the towns. An Assisi law specified, "No leper may dare to enter the city or walk around in it, and if any one of them shall be found, everyone may strike him with impunity."[40] Assisi had four or five leper colonies in its vicinity.[41]

Francis dreaded lepers. It is deeply poignant then that Francis in his *Testament* shortly before he died begins as follows:

> The Lord gave me, Brother Francis, thus to begin doing penance in this way: for when I was in sin, it seemed too bitter for me to see lepers. And the Lord Himself led me among them and I

---

[38] William H. McNeill, *Plagues and Peoples* (Garden City, NY: Doubleday, 1976), 175.

[39] Cunningham, *Francis of Assisi*, 10–11; Herbert Covey, "People with Leprosy (Hansen's disease) during the Middle Ages," *Social Science Journal* 38:2 (Summer 2001), 317–19.

[40] Fortini, *Francis of Assisi*, 211.

[41] Cunningham, *Francis of Assisi*, 10. In Francis's day, "Leprosaria were established outside thousands of medieval towns." McNeill, *Plagues and Peoples*, 175.

showed mercy to them. And when I left them, what had seemed bitter to me was turned into sweetness of soul and body. And afterwards I delayed a little and left the world.[42]

Francis's conversion was a process over time. It didn't happen all at once, as we see. But at the end, death drawing near, one thing shone most in Francis's memory: his encounter with lepers. Chesterton pictures it:

[Francis] was riding listlessly in some wayside place, apparently in the open country, when he saw a figure coming along the road towards him and halted; for he saw it was a leper. And he knew instantly that his courage was challenged, not as the world challenges, but as one would challenge one who knew the secrets of the heart of a man. What he saw advancing was not the banner and spears of Perugia, from which it never occurred to him to shrink; not the armies [of Walter of Brienne] that fought for the crown of Sicily, of which he had always thought as a courageous man thinks of mere vulgar danger. Francis Bernardone saw his fear coming up the road towards him; the fear that comes from within and not without; though it stood white and horrible in the sunlight. For once in the long rush of his life his soul must have stood still. Then he sprang from his horse, knowing nothing between stillness and swiftness, and rushed on the leper and threw his arms round him. It was the beginning of a long vocation of ministry among many lepers, for whom he did many services; to this man he gave what money he could and mounted and rode on. We do not know how far he rode, or with what sense of the things around him; but it is said that then he looked back, he could see no figure on the road.[43]

---

[42] Francis of Assisi, *The Testament*, FA:ED 1:124.

[43] G. K. Chesterton, *St. Francis of Assisi* (Garden City, NY: Image Books, Doubleday [1924], 1957), 52. See also Fortini, *Francis of Assisi*, 211. The principal early sources here are Thomas of Celano, *Life*, FA:ED 1:195; Thomas of Celano, *The Remembrance of the Desire of a Soul*, FA:ED 2:248–49; Bonaventure of Bagnoregio, *The Major Legend of Saint Francis*, FA:ED 2:533–34.

2

Assisi and Clare

Assisi rests on the slopes of Mount Subasio. This gently rising mountain, reaching 4,230 feet above the Adriatic Sea to the east, is part of the Apennine range that forms Italy's backbone. Assisi sits on the mountain's western flank overlooking the Umbrian valley below. The poet Henri d'Avranches in his life of Francis speaks of

> Assisi, in the upper reaches of Spoleto vale,
> With serried ranks of olive-trees
> All covered from head to toe.[1]

Assisi lies roughly halfway between Florence, one hundred miles to the northwest, and Rome, a hundred miles south. It shares Italy's Mediterranean weather—summers hot and dry; winters cool and often rainy, nights often below freezing, and occasional snowfalls.

Wandering through Assisi's narrow, winding streets, one easily feels transported back eight hundred years, half expecting to meet Francis around the next bend.

Over the centuries, local quarries gave the town most of its building blocks. The virgin stone has a pink hue, and even ancient buildings look newer than they are—especially now, since restorations and cleanings after the severe 1997 earthquake. The hills, plus the color of the stone and the valley view, give Assisi a pleasant loveliness.

---

[1] Henri d'Avranches, *Versified Life of Saint Francis*, in *Francis of Assisi: Early Documents*, 3 vols., ed. Regis J. Armstrong, OFM Cap., J. A. Wayne Hellmann, OFM Conv., and William J. Short, OFM (New York: New City Press, 2001), 1:429 [hereafter FA:ED]).

Francis's Assisi

Assisi is indeed an old town. Both Pliny the Elder and Ptolemy mention it in their geographies from the first and second centuries CE.[2] The old city itself, in contrast to the modern city in the valley below, is small, less than a mile long and about half as wide.

Assisi was pagan until it was evangelized by the Christian leader Rufino, bishop and martyr, in the third century CE. The city's cathedral, named for him, honors Rufino's life and witness. The cathedral was begun in 1140 and completed or renovated around the time of Francis's birth. Francis and Clare were baptized here, or possibly in Saint Mary Major, Assisi's older cathedral.[3]

Socially, Assisi was divided between the established aristocracy (the milieu of Clare and her family) and the rising merchant class (Francis's social set). Traditionally power and prestige were in the hands of the feudal lords and the bishop, allied with them, who together controlled the lion's share of land. But as newer merchants such as Pietro di Bernardone prospered, their political power grew. The town hall in the Piazza del Comune, rather than the cathedral, symbolized their growing influence and economic enterprise.

People with economic, political, and religious power in Assisi were the *majores*, the main or "major ones." They ran the city. But Assisi also had a large class of *minores*, the little or "minor ones," mainly day laborers, beggars, minor craftsmen and traders, herdsmen and farmers— and, of course, lepers. Francis would later call his spiritual brothers *fratres minores*, "little brothers" who identified mainly with the lowest of medieval society.[4]

The very geography of Assisi symbolized its power dynamics. High on the hill sits the Rocca Maggiore, the medieval fortress mentioned earlier. Lower down a steep hill is San Rufino Cathedral, traditional seat of ecclesiastical and aristocratic power. A few blocks down from the

---

[2] Henri d'Avranches, *Versified Life*, FA:ED 1:429 n. g.

[3] The question of where Francis was baptized is complex and disputed, partly because of the uncertainty of Francis's birth year. Today the baptismal font is in San Rufino, but it was in Saint Mary Major during the construction of San Rufino. The question is discussed in Thomas of Celano, *Remembrance*, FA:ED 2:241 n. b; Omer Englebert, *Saint Francis of Assisi*, 2nd English ed., trans. Eve Marie Cooper (Chicago: Franciscan Herald Press, 1965), 405; and Lawrence S. Cunningham, *Francis of Assisi: Performing the Gospel Life* (Grand Rapids, MI: William B. Eerdmans, 2004), 3–4. Fortini gives San Rufino as the baptismal site. Arnaldo Fortini, *Francis of Assisi*, trans. Helen Moak (New York: Crossroad Publishing, 1992), 85.

[4] Cunningham, *Francis of Assisi*, 3.

cathedral is the bustling town square, the Piazza del Comune, center of business and commercial interests and of the city government. Lower still—socially and much of the time physically—were the *minores*, the little ones who did most of the city's manual work.

Violence was a common fact of life in Assisi—"violence of vendettas, street brawls, warring families, grotesque forms of public torture or execution, and class struggles," notes Cunningham. "The grandees of the city would build towers at their homes not only to show power but also as fortresses to protect them when the inevitable vendettas would break out. It is against that aura of urban violence that we must understand the Franciscan cry of 'Peace!'"[5]

Assisi was pretty much a microcosm of what was happening across Europe. With the growth of trade and commerce, feudal villages were becoming organized cities, "communes" with their own laws, judges, militia, and their own coins—Florence's *florin* and Venice's gold *ducat* being some of the most widely circulated. Increasingly Assisi was a node in this larger network of change.[6]

Clare of Assisi

Among the children growing up in Assisi was a girl named Clare Offreduccio. Some twelve years younger than Francis, she was also of a different class. They would not have known each other, but perhaps knew *of* each other. The Offreduccio family may well have bought fine French or Persian fabrics at Bernardone's shop.

Like her mother and sisters, Clare was a devout Catholic who maintained regular spiritual disciplines. Years later when Clare was declared a saint, people who knew her as a young girl spoke of her simplicity, modest clothing, and her life of devotion and prayer. As a child, when she didn't have a rosary, she would count her Our Father prayers "with a pile of pebbles," according to *The Legend of Saint Clare*.[7] When she turned twelve her parents wanted her to marry, as was common. Clare firmly refused. She chose celibacy and a devotional life within her family and local community.[8]

---

[5] Cunningham, *Francis of Assisi*, 3.

[6] Michael G. Gable, "St. Francis of Assisi: A Prophet and Model for Social Justice and Peace," unpublished research paper, Maryknoll School of Theology, 1987, p. 8.

[7] *The Legend of Saint Clare*, in *The Lady: Clare of Assisi: Early Documents*, 3rd ed., ed. R. J. Armstrong, OFM Cap. (Hyde Park, NY: New City Press, 2006), 282.

[8] Englebert, *Saint Francis*, 161; Cunningham, *Francis of Assisi*, 37.

Clare, the firstborn, had two younger sisters, Catherine and Beatrice. Her parents, Favarone and Ortulana, were of the traditional nobility. Favarone was himself a count. His Offreduccio relatives included several wealthy knights and others of social influence. Clare's mother Ortulana went on long spiritual pilgrimages, sometimes taking Clare with her. Ortulana walked to Rome as well as all the way to the famous shrine at Santiago de Compostela in northwest Spain, some 1,300 miles east, thought to be the final resting place of the Apostle James (San Tiago). Once, at least, she walked to the famous shrine of Saint Michael the Archangel on Mount Gargano in southern Italy. Ortulana even made a pilgrimage to the holy sites in Palestine.[9]

Clare's biographer Ingrid Peterson notes, "Ortulana lived on the edge of great social and economic turmoil which empowered her. As other members of society began to gain freedom, so did women. Devotion to the humanity of Jesus changed both religion and culture. Ortulana's pilgrim journeys, her dominant position in a household of knights, and the vagueness of her husband's role indicate that she seized several new opportunities as a woman to become an individual person, rather than to assume the prescriptions for an aristocratic medieval woman. Clare later followed Ortulana's example." Yet "Ortulana's religious journeys to Rome, Jerusalem, and Saint Michael's ... indicate that she was not an ordinary woman of her culture. Although [some] medieval women did accompany men on the crusades, rarely did women travel as extensively as Ortulana."[10]

Ortulana means "gardener" in Latin, and *The Legend of Saint Clare* says "Ortulana, [who] would give birth to a fruitful plant in the garden of the Church, was herself overflowing with good fruits."[11] Ortulana "formed Clare from her childhood and nurtured her to be independent in spirit and action," but devoutly religious. Clare must "be considered in the context of the large cultural and religious movement of holy women of the Middle Ages, who were leading saintly lives in diverse places, many in their domestic settings. Clare was one of those holy women in an era known for the 'feminization of sanctity.'"[12] Even before entering her special vocation, following Francis and founding the Poor Clares,

---

[9] Cunningham, *Francis of Assisi*, 37; Ingrid J. Peterson, OSF, *Clare of Assisi: A Biographical Study* (Quincy, IL: Franciscan Press, 1993), 18.

[10] Peterson, *Clare of Assisi*, 49.

[11] *Legend of Saint Clare*, 280.

[12] Peterson, *Clare of Assisi*, 2.

Clare sought to lead a devout and holy life as understood in Roman Catholicism at the time. "The first women who [later] joined Clare" in her new community, Peterson notes, "were the women who had lived with her in her father's house" and knew her as a child and young teen.[13]

Clare lived virtually next door to Assisi's new Romanesque-style cathedral, San Rufino, a couple blocks up from the Piazza del Comune. The Offreduccio family had a large home facing the cathedral's piazza. Their house was said to be one of Assisi's grandest, likely "framed with large beams of oak placed at intervals" with stucco between the beams "somewhat in the manner of English Tudor buildings." The houses of Assisi's noble families, made of stone or brick, "were designed more as castles for protection than as the residential houses of the new towns."[14]

It was just a short walk from Francis's home by the Piazza del Comune up to Clare's house on the San Rufino piazza—ten minutes or so. But in another sense, the two homes were miles apart. The Bernardone and Offreduccio families were at opposite ends of the economic revolution happening in Assisi and across Europe. The later loving comradeship of Clare and Francis symbolizes the deep currents of peace and reconciliation their new paths of Christian discipleship embodied. As Assisi was a microcosm of wide-ranging changes in Europe, so Francis and Clare were a microcosm, an embryo and firstfruits of a renewal that shook the church and showed how to heal the world.

---

[13] Peterson, *Clare of Assisi*, 4.
[14] Peterson, *Clare of Assisi*, 56–57.

3

Conversion:
A Drama in Three Acts

It took Jesus three years to convert Francis—thoroughly to get his attention and win his full allegiance.

Francis says his encounter with the leper was decisive, life-changing. Yet it was only the beginning of the metamorphosis that would turn young Francis into a full-flowering Jesus follower.

One day Francis went to visit the nearby leper hospital at Arce in the valley below Assisi. Like many leprosariums, this one was called San Lazzaro after the poor beggar Lazarus, "covered with sores," of Jesus's parable (Luke 16:19–20).[1] Francis went there to leave a gift of money. The lepers lived in cells, a cross nailed to each door. Attendants called them together, and "to each of them [Francis] gave a piece of gold and a kiss on the lips."[2]

Francis was beginning his mission, exercising the most basic of rules: compassion. "To cleanse human beings from whatever leprosy

---

[1] This may have been one of many leprosariums run by the Order of Saint Lazarus, founded by Crusaders in Jerusalem after they won back the city from Muslim armies a century earlier. There is some dispute, however, about which leper hospital Francis now visited. See Thomas of Celano, *Life of St. Francis*, in *Francis of Assisi: Early Documents*, 3 vols., ed. Regis J. Armstrong, OFM Cap., J. A. Wayne Hellmann, OFM Conv., and William J. Short, OFM (New York: New City Press, 2001), 1:195 [hereafter FA:ED]); Arnaldo Fortini, *Francis of Assisi*, trans. Helen Moak (New York: Crossroad Publishing Co., 1992), 206.

[2] Fortini, *Francis of Assisi*, 212; see also Thomas of Celano, *The Remembrance of the Desire of a Soul* (The Second Life of Saint Francis), FA:ED 2:249.

contaminates them was the mission on which Francis embarked" that day at San Lazzaro. Much was still unclear to Francis, but his embrace of lepers was the first crucial turn in his conversion. More would come.[3]

San Damiano

Francis was now back in his father's home, back with Pietro and Pica and his family.[4] It was the summer of 1205.

Life with father was not easy. Francis had no interest in his dad's business. Pietro was embarrassed that Francis had abandoned the life of a knight and now rejected the life of a merchant. Even worse, Francis now embraced lepers! Pietro could "provide, without counting it, money to be swallowed up in dissipation so that his son might stand on an equal footing with the young nobles," wrote Paul Sabatier. "But he could never resign himself to see him giving [money] with lavish hands to every beggar in the streets."[5]

Francis was still seeking. He wondered and wandered the fields below Assisi. He often walked past the decaying small chapel of San Damiano, down the hill a short stroll from Assisi. His mother Pica watched, perplexed, like Mary storing up things, pondering them in her heart (Luke 2:19). Pietro, however, was increasingly disgusted and alienated from his wayward son.

Francis shared with various acquaintances his longings to find a new path—something that would flesh out what he had felt and sensed in his encounter with the leper and his earlier dream vision. He was changed, yet the future was foggy. He went to talk with Bishop Guido, but the bishop could not decipher Francis's rather vague dreams and desires.[6]

Francis told friends and acquaintances he was *not* going to follow his father's business and course of life. Some townsfolk thought he was mad, had lost his senses. He certainly was not mad, nor was he in doubt that he had started down a totally new path. But still he was seeking.

---

[3] Fortini, *Francis of Assisi*, 212.

[4] Francis had at least one younger sibling, Angelo di Pica, who became a merchant like his father. Fortini, *Francis of Assisi*, 89, 247, 475.

[5] Paul Sabatier, *The Road to Assisi: The Essential Biography of St. Francis*, ed. Jon M. Sweeney (Brewster, MA: Paraclete Press, 2004), 34.

[6] Sabatier, *Road to Assisi*, 34. This was Bishop Guido II, Assisi's bishop from 1204 until his death in 1228, two years after Francis's own death. A papal decree of 1198, during the tenure of Guido I, granted extensive episcopal privileges; "Guido II possessed broad powers in both the ecclesiastical and civil worlds." FA:ED 1:193, editorial n. a.

Francis had a special fondness for San Damiano—one of several small chapels in the area. His father had acquired extensive farmlands nearby in the fertile valley south of Assisi. The family owned property in the area called Fontanelle, the name referring to the land's many springs. "At this point their property became an extensive holding, rich in roads and water" in the valley below Assisi and extending up toward San Damiano.[7]

From boyhood Francis would have often walked past San Damiano going to or from his father's properties below. He may have stepped into the chapel from time to time. On this particular fall day in 1205, Francis turned aside, entered, and knelt and prayed before the crucifix.

"The church of San Damiano seemed to be collapsing from old age, already beyond repair, desolate, without devout worshippers and without prayers," writes Arnaldo Fortini.

> No one went down the worn staircase into the church. No lamp burned in front of its altar. Decrepit outer walls, cracked inner walls, crumbling bricks, worm-eaten beams, faded paintings. A low and smoke blackened vault, a narrow window, a holy water stoup covered with dust, an apse with vague vestiges of blue and gold, a cloister invaded by wild grass, a well without water. Silent, solitary, abandoned. On the [limestone lintel above] the door, the usual words so often found on the thresholds of ancient country chapels: *Domus mea*. My house. The House of God, tottering and derelict.[8]

Perhaps the chapel was not so bad as later legend pictures it, but it did need attention. The building was not totally abandoned. A poor old priest named Peter (Pietro) cared for it, ministering to people who occasionally stopped in. He lived in a small room adjoining the chapel. The edifice, at this time under the nominal supervision of Assisi's San Rufino Cathedral, dated back four or five centuries before Francis. It was dedicated to Saint Damian, a Christian physician in Syria who with

---

[7] Fortini, *Francis of Assisi*, 115. Based on his archival research, Fortini identifies additional Bernardone properties in the valley.

[8] Fortini, *Francis of Assisi*, 215. Fortini noted in 1959, the chapel "stood between a sea of olive trees and the ruins of a nearby Roman sepulcher, just as, after a thousand years, it does today. A little church, with a low vault, a narrow window like a slit in a fortress wall, a semicircular apse painted blue and richly adorned with stars, traces of which may still be seen" (Fortini, 29).

his brother Cosmas was martyred in 287 CE under Roman Emperor Diocletian.[9] But now the old Romanesque building with tiled roof badly needed fixing. The chapel was mostly empty, save for a plain masonry altar and behind it a faded ornamental screen, probably of wood, which served as an altarpiece.

But the chapel had one very special feature. Suspended above the altar was a large crucifix in Byzantine style. Influences from Eastern Orthodox Christianity were strong up and down the western coast of Italy—obvious still today in the architecture of Venice and Florence. Artistic, colorful Byzantine crucifixes were common throughout this area. The Crucifix of San Damiano would now play a crucial role in Francis's pilgrimage. Francis knelt, seeking guidance.

Go, Repair My Church!

Western Christians are familiar with spare, dark crucifixes depicting the agony of Jesus, eyes closed in death. Not so the San Damiano cross. The crucifix is a large colorful icon in reds and golds depicting Jesus crucified but with eyes wide open and a golden halo—Christ both crucified and risen! Other figures are ranged around the Christ figure: At the left, Virgin Mary and the Apostle John. On the right, Mary Magdalene, Mary the mother of James, and the centurion who begged Jesus to heal his servant. Saint Damian and Saint Rufino are two of several figures pictured below Jesus's feet. At the top, above Jesus's head, a small scene shows the risen Jesus, regally dressed, climbing from the tomb, surrounded by ten angels. At the very top, the hand of God extends over the head of the risen Christ—the blessing of God the Father on the sacrifice of Jesus.[10]

The entire crucifix, painted a century earlier by an unknown Syrian monk, is a large icon in Byzantine style. It tells the story of Jesus's life, death, and resurrection. The message: Jesus reigns from the cross. For Jesus had said, "And I, when I am lifted up from the earth, will draw all people to myself" (John 12:32).

Marc Picard, a Canadian Capuchin brother, deciphers the imagery in his book *The Icon of San Damiano.* It is "a Johannine icon," Picard says. All the imagery comes from John's Gospel. Jesus wears a crown of glory, not thorns. "Suffering and death are transformed.... The prayer of Jesus

---

[9] Giulio Mancini, *San Damiano: Recalling the Soul* (Assisi: Edizioni Porziuncola, 2009), 15 and other sources.

[10] Mancini, *San Damiano,* 15; Fortini, *Francis of Assisi,* 215.

is now answered: 'Father, glorify your Son' (Jn. 17:1)." The figures below Jesus all appear in the Gospel of John.[11]

Francis had seen this crucifix before of course, maybe many times. But today he was on a life-and-death quest. As he gazed at the open-eyed Jesus, God spoke. In his heart he clearly heard Jesus's words: "Francis! Go and repair my house, which as you see is falling into ruin!"[12]

Figure 3.1 San Damiano Crucifix (*author's photo of replica of crucifix*)

Francis rose, startled. He found Father Peter, the old priest-custodian. He gave the priest what money he had with him "so that he might relight the lamp before the crucifix," says Fortini.[13]

---

[11] Marc Picard, OFM Cap., *The Icon of San Damiano* (Assisi: Casa Editrice Francescana, 2000), 13–14, 38.

[12] Fortini, *Francis of Assisi*, 216. Today a small relief sculpture at San Damiano has the words in Latin: *Vade, Francisce, repara domum meam.*

[13] Fortini, *Francis of Assisi*, 216.

Francis then hurried up to his father's store. He took some expensive scarlet cloth and left immediately on horseback for Foligno, a larger market town nine miles away. There Francis sold both the cloth and the horse, then walked back to San Damiano. He planned to use the money straightaway to start repairing the old chapel. Jesus said, "Repair my house." Francis set out to do it.[14]

He tried to give the money to old priest Peter, but the priest, knowing who Francis was and his father's wrath, refused to take it. The priest was suspicious. What was Francis really up to?

Francis kept insisting the priest keep the money. Finally, Francis simply threw the money onto the chapel windowsill. Then he begged the priest to let him stay with him there at San Damiano. Seeing the youth's eager earnestness, the old priest agreed.[15]

Here is the second big step—the second key turning in Francis's conversion. Both, really, were revelations of Jesus, first through the leper, now through the cross.

The priest let Francis stay, but he had good reason to be wary. Youth of privilege sometimes ran away from home and sought church protection so as to escape prosecution. Yet the old priest saw something deep in Francis's appeal.[16]

Francis knew his father Pietro would be livid and might try to force him back home. When Pietro learned what Francis had done, he flew into a rage. His son had taken some of Pietro's valuable goods, plus one of his horses, sold them, and kept the money! Now he was hiding out at San Damiano.

But if Francis was under the protection of the church, his father must proceed cautiously. Pietro consulted some of his neighbors and fellow merchants. Finally, he determined to go down to San Damiano with some of his colleagues and try to persuade Francis to return home.[17]

Someone alerted Francis. In fact, Francis had already prepared. He knew his father might come for him, and he was determined he would not go back home. He had arranged an underground hideout in

---

[14] Fortini, *Francis of Assisi*, 216; Thomas of Celano, *Life of St. Francis*, FA:ED 1:188–89.
[15] Fortini, *Francis of Assisi*, 216–17; Thomas of Celano, *Life of St. Francis*, FA:ED 1:189–90.
[16] Whereas "others chose, for protection in case of need, well fortified churches such as San Giacomo and San Rufino, [Francis's] choice was the poorest and humblest church, with an obscure priest who certainly was not going to be able to protect him from the gathering storm." Fortini, *Francis of Assisi*, 217.
[17] Fortini, *Francis of Assisi*, 217; Thomas of Celano, *Life of St. Francis*, FA:ED 1:190.

a nearby house, so he fled there. The family owned a country home in Stradette, less than half a mile from San Damiano; Francis likely knew the caretaker. This may be where he hid, the caretaker his accomplice.[18] Someone apparently helped Francis hide and supplied him with food.[19]

And yet Francis was still seeking, wondering where God was leading. According to Thomas of Celano, Francis hid for a month. "Fasting and weeping, he earnestly prayed for the Savior's mercy, and lacking confidence in his own efforts, he cast his care upon the Lord. Though staying in a pit and in darkness, he was imbued with an indescribable happiness never before experienced."[20]

Summer was turning to autumn. Francis felt Jesus would now have him return to town. After weeks in hiding, he hardly looked himself. People in the streets wondered at first who he was, this pale figure with dirty clothes. Francis's biographers say that once the townspeople recognized him, they made fun of him; "they compared his latest circumstances with his former and they began to reproach him harshly," saying "he was insane and out of his mind." Some pelted him with mud and stones.[21]

Francis walked on up to the Piazza del Comune near his parents' home. Pietro di Bernardone was working in his shop when he heard the commotion. Just a madman in the streets, someone said. But then Pietro heard someone call Francis's name.[22]

Pietro rushed into the street. There was Francis, a crowd milling around him. Pietro "pounced on Francis like a wolf on a lamb and, glaring at him fiercely and savagely, he grabbed him and shamelessly dragged him home," says Thomas of Celano. Pietro "shut [Francis] up for several days in a dark place," determined to break his will.[23]

Pietro shouted abuse at his son, ridiculing his dreams and his senseless behavior. "He heaped upon the head of his son, one by one, all the outrages, the humiliations, the injuries" he felt he had received,

---

[18] The location of Francis's hiding place is not certain. Underneath San Damiano was a small crypt, a "subterranean pre-Christian cave," apparently a Roman burial site. This may have been where Francis hid. Ramona Miller, OSF, *In the Footsteps of Saint Clare* (St. Bonaventure, NY: Franciscan Institute, 1993), 57.

[19] Fortini, *Francis of Assisi*, 217–18.

[20] Thomas of Celano, *Life of St. Francis,* FA:ED 1:190–91. Thomas may exaggerate a bit here. See also Omer Englebert, *Saint Francis of Assisi,* trans. Eve Marie Cooper, 2nd English ed., rev. Ignatius Brady OFM and Raphael Brown (Chicago: Franciscan Herald Press, 1965), 76.

[21] Thomas of Celano, *Life of St. Francis,* FA:ED 1:191. See Fortini, *Francis of Assisi,* 219.

[22] Fortini, *Francis of Assisi,* 221.

[23] Thomas of Celano, *Life of St. Francis,* FA:ED 1:192.

exposing him to ridicule.[24] But Francis simply resolved even more to fulfill his new calling.[25] Pietro was within his paternal rights; the town's statutes permitted a father to confine in fetters a son who squandered the family wealth.[26]

Over weeks, Pietro tried repeatedly to dissuade Francis from his religious dreams and enter the family business. Francis wouldn't budge. Finally, Pietro decided he had better turn to the church. Bishop Guido held wide authority, and Francis seemed headed toward a religious vocation.

The time had come, however, for Pietro to make a business trip. Pica, Francis's mother, was distressed at her son's confinement. With Pietro gone, Pica freed Francis and comforted him. With gentleness and pleading she also tried to turn Francis away from his new sense of vocation—but in vain.[27]

Now free to leave the house, Francis returned to San Damiano, liberated and joyful. He could find and follow his calling. He spent hours meditating at San Damiano and in the surrounding countryside.

When Pietro returned, however, he was enraged to find Francis gone. He hurried to San Damiano, determined to bring his son back. Seeing him coming, Francis calmly walked out to meet his father. Francis's composure angered Pietro even more. He again poured out a torrent of abuse. Francis, now about twenty-five, said he would let God judge between him and his father.[28]

Pietro saw he could not dissuade his son. But what of the money? Francis had stolen a horse and valuable fabrics. He sold them and kept the money. This was a crime punishable by law. Pietro wanted his just payment. In Pietro's eyes, Francis was guilty of robbery and revolt. The legal penalty could be banishment from the city.

Pietro resolved to bring his son to trial before the city consuls, as prescribed by law. He did not realize that Francis had abandoned the money at the San Damiano window.

It was now early 1206. The weather had turned unusually cold, snow and ice mantling the olive trees along the path to San Damiano.[29]

---

[24] Fortini, *Francis of Assisi*, 221.

[25] Thomas of Celano says that although Pietro "badgered him, beat him, and bound him," "Francis became more fit and eager to carry out his holy plan. Neither the reproach of words nor the exhaustion of chains eroded his patience." Thomas of Celano, *Life of St. Francis*, FA:ED 1:192.

[26] Fortini, *Francis of Assisi*, 221.

[27] *Legend of the Three Companions*, FA:ED 2:79.

[28] Fortini, *Francis of Assisi*, 223; Thomas of Celano, *Life of St. Francis*, FA:ED 1:193.

[29] Fortini, *Francis of Assisi*, 225. Fortini gives the year as 1207; other sources as 1206.

Pietro di Bernardone went before Assisi's consuls and judge to present his case. "A son, in whom he had placed so many hopes, has revolted against him, plundered his shop, and left him at the mercy of public opinion," Fortini writes. "Now there is nothing to do but to declare the crime and inflict the penalties established by the statutes." Assisi's laws "considered with particular severity the case of a disobedient son who had squandered the family resources."[30] If found guilty, a dissolute son could be imprisoned for as long as his family felt necessary.

The judge that year, a man named Egidio, ordered that a summons be sent to Francis. A messenger carried the order to San Damiano, where Francis was again living with the elderly priest. Standing outside, the messenger cried out the summons, as the law required. Francis went out to meet him. The messenger gave Francis a warrant detailing the crimes Pietro accused him of.[31]

Francis had determined to place himself in the church's hands. He had a higher loyalty than his duty to his earthly father, for Jesus now called him. In the words of *The Legend of the Three Companions*, Francis "told the messenger that he had been made free by God's grace and, since he was a servant of almighty God alone, was no longer bound by the magistrates." The messenger reported back to the consuls, who concluded that because Francis was now "in the service of God, he no longer falls within our power."[32]

So, Pietro di Bernardone went to consult Bishop Guido and lodged his complaint. He wanted Francis brought to account, and he wanted his money. Bishop Guido agreed to intervene and sent a messenger to summon Francis. "I will go before the bishop," Francis said happily, "for he is the father and master of souls."[33]

Francis before the Bishop

Francis could claim the church's protection, since he was now living with a priest on church premises. This was consistent with ecclesiastical law. Violating the church's authority risked excommunication, as Pietro well knew.[34]

Saint Agatha's Day came, February 5th. Heavy snows had fallen, cloaking trees and houses in white. Francis walked up from San Damiano

---

[30] Fortini, *Francis of Assisi*, 224.
[31] *Legend of the Three Companions*, FA:ED 2:79; Fortini, *Francis of Assisi*, 225; Englebert, *Saint Francis*, 77.
[32] *Legend of the Three Companions*, FA:ED 2:79.
[33] Englebert, *Saint Francis*, 77.
[34] Fortini, *Francis of Assisi*, 226.

to the piazza of Santa Maria Maggiore (Saint Mary Major, Assisi's cathedral prior to the building of San Rufino and still the bishop's residence) for the decisive encounter with Bishop Guido.[35]

Pietro met his son and led him toward the bishop's palace. The proceeding probably occurred in the morning; such encounters usually were scheduled for 9:00 o'clock in the piazza before the bishop's residence. Many townspeople likely crowded around.

This was an ecclesiastical legal proceeding. Bishop Guido, with mitered head and wrapped in a blue velvet mantle secured with gold clasps, came forward, accompanied by the canons and acolytes of Santa Maria Maggiore, a notary, and other officials.[36]

Thomas of Celano says Pietro "led the son to the bishop ... to make him renounce into the bishop's hands all rights of inheritance and return everything that he had. Not only did [Francis] not refuse this, but he hastened joyfully and eagerly to do what was demanded."[37]

Seated on his bishop's seat (*cathedra*), Bishop Guido opened the proceedings and stated the case. Pietro then brought his complaint, accusing his son of wrongfully taking expensive cloth from his shop and selling it. Francis was wrong also to offer the money of the sold scarlet cloth and horse to the San Damiano priest.

Pietro vented his indignation. Francis must be punished according to the city's laws! Bishop Guido then spoke directly to Francis. We don't know his exact words, but the gist was this: "Put your trust in God, my son. If you wish to serve the church, well and good. But you have no right in the name of good works to use your father's property in this way. So return to your father what belongs to him, and he will be satisfied. God will find other ways to restore his church."[38]

Neither the bishop nor Pietro yet grasped what was really happening with Francis. "Lord Bishop," Francis said, "not only this money that I took from [my father] do I wish to restore to him, with all good will, but even the clothes that he has given me."[39] Thomas of Celano writes, "When he was in front of the bishop, [Francis] neither delayed nor

---

[35] Fortini, *Francis of Assisi*, 226–27. Santa Maria Maggiore was (still is) located about five blocks southwest from the San Rufino cathedral, just inside the Porta Moiano along the southern wall of the city.

[36] Fortini, *Francis of Assisi*, 227; Englebert, *Saint Francis*, 77. Fortini pictures the scene in considerable detail.

[37] Thomas of Celano, *Life of St. Francis*, FA:ED 1:193.

[38] See *Legend of the Three Companions*, FA:ED 2:80; Fortini, *Francis of Assisi*, 228; Englebert, *Saint Francis*, 77–78.

[39] See Fortini, *Francis of Assisi*, 228.

hesitated, but immediately took off and threw down all his clothes and returned them to his father. He did not even keep his trousers on, and he was completely stripped bare before everyone."[40] Francis laid all his clothes and money at Pietro's feet. "Up until today," Francis said, "I have called Pietro di Bernardone my father. From now on I shall say, 'Our Father, who is in heaven.'"[41]

The poet Henri d'Avranches a dozen or so years after Francis's death wrote: "Without a stitch, stark naked he stands, for all the world like Adam."[42]

Like Adam and Eve, Francis was "naked and unashamed" (Gen. 2:25) in his New-Creation life in God's garden. His Eve would be Lady Poverty. Knowingly or not, Francis's words echoed Saint Jerome centuries earlier: "Naked, I shall follow the naked Christ."[43] A later chronicler wrote, "By embracing the naked Christ on the cross, [Francis] was prepared to enter naked into wrestling with the naked devil."[44] Fortini calls this Francis's "great act of renunciation that freed him from all servitude to earthly things."[45]

Bishop Guido rose quickly and approached Francis. He wrapped his own rich outer cloak around the naked youth and embraced him.[46] The shocked crowd watched in disbelief. According to *The Legend of the Three Companions* Pietro di Bernardone, "overcome with unbearable

---

[40] Thomas of Celano, *Life of St. Francis,* FA:ED 1:193. See also Bonaventure of Bagnoregio, *The Major Legend of Saint Francis,* FA:ED 2:538. Numerous sources relate the story. Some say Francis went inside the bishop's residence to strip off his clothing, but this is unlikely. Thomas of Celano makes no mention of this, nor does Fortini. *The Legend of the Three Companions* says, "And going into one of the bishop's rooms, he took off all his clothes, and putting the money on top of them, came out naked before the bishop, his father, and all the bystanders"; and a few lines later (after Francis had given the money and clothes to his father), says, "At that moment, the man of God was found to be wearing under his colored clothes a hair shirt next to his skin" (FA:ED 2:80). These look like pious hagiographic comments added later to the manuscript. As will be noted further on, there is no credible evidence that Francis ever wore a hair shirt. See Fortini, *Francis of Assisi,* 229; Englebert, *Saint Francis,* 78; Sabatier, *Road to Assisi,* 39.

[41] Fortini, *Francis of Assisi,* 229; Englebert, *Saint Francis,* 78; Sabatier, *Road to Assisi,* 39.

[42] Henri d'Avranches, *Versified Life of Saint Francis,* FA:ED 1:449.

[43] Fortini, *Francis of Assisi,* 229; Lawrence S. Cunningham, *Francis of Assisi: Performing the Gospel Life* (Grand Rapids, MI: William B. Eerdmans, 2004), 20.

[44] *A Life of Saint Francis by an Anonymous Monk of a German Monastery* (c. 1275), FA:ED 3:842.

[45] Fortini, *Francis of Assisi,* 229.

[46] Fortini, *Francis of Assisi,* 230. Fortini adds, "Thus Francis married Lady Poverty." Sabatier writes, "the bishop was obliged to take under his mantle the poor Francis, who was trembling with emotion and cold." Sabatier, *Road to Assisi,* 40.

pain and anger, took the money and all the clothing. While he was carrying these home, those who were present at this spectacle were indignant at him, for he left nothing for his son to wear. Moved by piety [i.e., pity], they began to weep over him."[47]

With liberated spirit, Francis walked out of the square this cold morning, through the city gate, out of town, into his mission. He had returned Bishop Guido's cloak; "he took another one, poor and torn, from a farmhand" nearby.[48]

Lawrence Cunningham points to the symbolism embedded in Francis's dramatic act. "What one wore or dared to wear was a preoccupation in medieval and renaissance society," Cunningham notes, often regulated by law.[49] Issues of class and status were involved. Cunningham writes,

> One should not underestimate the symbolic power inherent in Francis's rejection. Pietro represented the rising new reality of late twelfth-century life: the rise of the money-earning entrepreneur whose skill in the making of money had given power to a new class of people. In early times it was the possession of physical power that counted; now it was the possession of wealth.... Francis's emphasis on poverty and non-possession was a prophetic rejection of the nascent capitalism of the late twelfth century symbolized by the success of his own father.[50]

Francis's renunciation of his father's authority and way of life was the third and final act in his drama of conversion. Jesus had spoken decisively to Francis three times, three ways. In the leper on the road, Jesus appeared to Francis as "the least of these." Jesus said in Matthew, "as you did it to one of the least of these who are members of my family, you did it to me" (Matt. 25:40). Then from the luminous San Damiano

---

[47] *Legend of the Three Companions*, FA:ED 2:80.

[48] Fortini, *Francis of Assisi*, 230. According to Fortini, "With chalk, [Francis] sketched on the back of [his mantle] a great cross, the knight's symbol that had appeared to him in his vision of the enchanted castle" (related in chapter 1). Fortini, 230.

[49] Cunningham, *Francis of Assisi*, 19.

[50] Cunningham, *Francis of Assisi*, 18. Cunningham also points to the theme of nudity in medieval religious literature and recalls New Testament themes such as Colossians 3:9–10 ("you have stripped off the old self with its practices and have clothed yourselves with the new self, which is being renewed in knowledge according to the image of its creator") and Ephesians 4:22–24 ("You were taught to put away your former way of life, your old self, corrupt and deluded by its lusts, and to be renewed in the spirit of your minds, and to clothe yourselves with the new self, created according to the likeness of God in true righteousness and holiness."). Cunningham, 18–19. On spiritual nudity as a theme, see Bonaventure, *Major Legend*, FA:ED 2:538 n. b.

icon, Jesus spoke to Francis as the crucified yet risen one, calling Francis to obey and live out the gospel. Now finally, as Francis stood before his father and Bishop Guido, Jesus spoke again to him, clarifying his vocation. He was to go forth into the world as Jesus had done. He had heard the gospel call.

Forth to a New Life

It was now nearly spring. Snow drifts remained in shaded areas the sun could not reach, but streams from melting snow swelled the small rivers below. Francis walked out of Assisi alone, "compelled to leave the city and go among persons who had never known him, so that he could rebuild his life." He set out for Gubbio, a town twenty miles north, a place he had visited before.[51]

Francis's liberated heart was full of joy. He began singing. He had always loved the songs of love and chivalry of the roaming French Troubadours. Continuing on his way, "he set out through the woods singing the Lord's praises in French at the top of his lungs."[52]

Francis now saw himself more as a troubadour than a crusader, a poet more than a soldier. But he was a troubadour with a song and story of liberation, deeper and more abiding than the armies of the Crusaders. Chesterton says Francis's new faith "was not a thing like a theory but a thing like a love-affair."[53]

In these days of chivalry, Fortini notes, "troubadours came down from their castles at the first hint of spring and travelled about celebrating the praises of the lady of their hearts on the public squares and in the courts." But now "Francis had his own love song, more ardent" than any troubadour's tune—"the most impassioned song on earth."[54] He was following Jesus.

But still he knew not where.

Francis's path led through a patch of forest. He went on singing. Suddenly a band of robbers rushed out and surrounded him. "Who are *you?*" they asked.

---

[51] Fortini, *Francis of Assisi,* 230.
[52] Englebert, *Saint Francis,* 79.
[53] G. K. Chesterton, *St. Francis of Assisi* (Garden City, NY: Image Books, Doubleday [1924], 1957), 16.
[54] Fortini, *Francis of Assisi,* 232.

4

Called to Mission

The bandits hear Francis singing. Someone they can rob! But when they see this character—poorly clad, no bag—they are puzzled and disgusted.

"Who are *you?*" the robbers demand, circling Francis.[1]

"I am the herald of the Great King!" Francis replies. "What is it to you?"

Irate, the bandits attack Francis, beat him up, throw him in a snow-filled ravine. "Lie there, you stupid herald of God!"[2]

Francis rolls around in the snow, perhaps chuckling, as the bandits move on. He jumps up, shakes himself off. Unhurt, he continues singing his French song—"he began in a loud voice to make the woods resound with praises to the Creator of all."[3]

On he walked to Gubbio. Francis knew of a Benedictine monastery there; perhaps he could spend the night. It was probably Santa Maria di Valfabbrica, located along the main road from Assisi to Gubbio.[4]

---

[1] "Francis opens up in song in the language of the French. | It resounds through the woods and reaches the ears of some robbers. | They leap forth and see a fellow with nothing. Their hopes disappointed, | They think they've been fooled and they throw out their query: | 'Who are you?'" Henri d'Avranches, *Versified Life of Saint Francis,* in *Francis of Assisi: Early Documents,* 3 vols., ed. Regis J. Armstrong, OFM Cap., J. A. Wayne Hellmann, OFM Conv., and William J. Short, OFM (New York: New City Press, 2001), 1:435 [hereafter FA:ED].

[2] Thomas of Celano, *Life of St. Francis,* FA:ED 1:194.

[3] Thomas of Celano, *Life of St. Francis,* FA:ED 1:194; see also Bonaventure, *Major Legend,* FA:ED 2:539.

[4] Arnaldo Fortini, *Francis of Assisi,* trans. Helen Moak (New York: Crossroad, 1992), 234, 242 n. s.; Thomas of Celano, *Life of St. Francis,* FA:ED 1:195. Possibly this was the monastery of Verecondo. Thomas of Celano says Francis was treated harshly here. "No mercy was shown him and he was not even able to get some old clothes" but

It was now nearly night. The Benedictine brothers took Francis in and gave him hospitality. He spent a few days there, working as a kitchen helper or scullery boy. But this was not his vocation. Besides, he needed clothes and wanted to return to San Damiano.[5]

Francis had a wealthy friend in Gubbio, someone he knew from the days he aspired to soldiering and knighthood. He found the friend's house and lodged there, apparently, for some weeks. His friend gave him a proper tunic to wear.[6]

While in Gubbio, Francis seems to have gone about ministering to lepers in the area. He decided to dress like a hermit: "he wore a sort of hermit's habit with a leather belt. He carried a staff in his hand and wore shoes" as hermits of the time often did.[7] "The hermit's life was a common form adopted by those who had left the world to take up a life of prayer and penance," Cunningham notes.[8] Francis would be one of them.

But God had told Francis, "Repair my church." What exactly did that mean? He was seeking guidance in "his still flexible plan to serve lepers, repair churches, and lead a life of prayer."[9]

Repairing San Damiano

It was now the warm summer of 1206. Francis longed to get back to Assisi, especially San Damiano. San Damiano cried out for repair. He remembered Peter, the old priest. Francis would go see him.

Peter again took Francis into his lodgings, and there he stayed for some days.

Occasionally Francis walked up to Assisi. In piazzas or open places, he would stop, perhaps sing a few songs, and announce his decision

---

was "covered with only a cheap shirt." So "forced by necessity, he moved on to the city of Gubbio." FA:ED 1:195.

[5] Thomas of Celano, *Life of St. Francis*, FA:ED 1:195.

[6] Thomas of Celano, *Life of St. Francis*, FA:ED 1:195; Omer Englebert, *Saint Francis of Assisi*, 2nd English ed., trans. Eve Marie Cooper (Chicago: Franciscan Herald Press, 1965), 79–80; Arnaldo Fortini, *Francis of Assisi*, trans. Helen Moak (New York: Crossroad Publishing, 1992), 242–43. Fortini identifies the friend as Frederico Spadalunga (Frederick Long-sword), a wealthy man Francis knew from the battle with Perugia, and who owned a substantial house on a main piazza of Gubbio. "Francis told [Frederico] all that had happened, all about his renunciation, his intentions. His friend listened to him, astonished. Despite all his efforts, he could not understand what Francis was talking about" (243). Fortini says Francis spent "a few months" with his friend (246).

[7] Thomas of Celano, *Life of St. Francis*, FA:ED 1:201.

[8] Lawrence S. Cunningham, *Francis of Assisi: Performing the Gospel Life* (Grand Rapids, MI: William B. Eerdmans, 2004), 23.

[9] Cunningham, *Francis of Assisi*, 24.

to repair San Damiano. Some townsfolk still thought him mad. Others were inspired and moved by his sincerity and the obvious changes in the young man.[10]

Francis wanted to get going with the repairs, but he had neither money nor materials. He went through Assisi's streets, begging for stones and other materials. Back and forth he went, carrying things down to San Damiano. Francis "became a new sort of beggar, reversing the parable; a beggar who asks not for bread but a stone," says Chesterton.[11]

Francis also begged for food. He wanted to live simply and not burden the old priest Peter. The priest was treating him more grandly than he should, Francis felt, giving him better meals than he deserved, better in fact than the priest could really afford.

Other people began helping Francis, and by spring the repairs were done. Francis was starting to fulfill his calling, he felt. "Rebuilding churches was a [traditional] medieval expression of piety," notes *Francis of Assisi: Early Documents*. In England Saint Wilfrid in the late 600s rebuilt a church edifice at York, plus another commemorating Saint Peter, and one named for Mary.[12] In a way it was the obvious thing: repair holy shrines.

Francis went on to repair other church buildings. The second was San Pietro della Spina (Saint Peter of the Thorn), a small chapel about two miles from San Damiano along an old road that descended through the valley.[13]

Also in the valley below Assisi stood the tiny chapel of Santa Maria degli Angeli (Saint Mary of the Angels). It also needed repair. The place was long known as the "Portiuncula," or "little portion," because of the small piece of land on which it was originally built. The chapel sat in thick woods of oak and evergreen holly oaks with a small garden in a clearing behind. It belonged to the Benedictines of Mount Subasio, but they had largely abandoned it.[14]

---

[10] Paul Sabatier, *The Road to Assisi: The Essential Biography of St. Francis,* ed. Jon M. Sweeney (Brewster, MA: Paraclete Press, 2004), 41.

[11] G. K. Chesterton, *St. Francis of Assisi* (Garden City, NY: Image Books, Doubleday [1924], 1957), 57.

[12] FA:ED, 1:197 n. a.

[13] Fortini, *Francis of Assisi,* 248. Fortini gives evidence for this identification rather than the larger Benedictine Church of San Pietro, sometimes identified as the second church edifice Francis repaired.

[14] Thomas of Celano, *Life of St. Francis,* FA:ED 1:201; Fortini, *Francis of Assisi,* 250–51; Englebert, *Saint Francis,* 84; Sabatier, *Road to Assisi,* 42–43.

Francis turned his attention to this little place—a spot that in a short time would become his base of ministry. He felt a special fondness for the Virgin Mary and was troubled to see the chapel in disrepair. The trees and garden plot added to the serene loveliness of the place. "To get on with the work as fast as possible, he moved into a [nearby] hut," notes Fortini.[15]

"Go Proclaim Good News!"

With the help of others, Francis worked through the fall and cold winter months. Fourteen-year-old Clare was among those who gave money to help fund the repairs.[16] By February 1208, Saint Mary of the Angels was ready for use.

In the church calendar, February 24 was the feast of Matthew the Apostle. That day a priest (likely a Benedictine from Mount Subasio) came down and celebrated the memorial Mass at the Portiuncula. This served in effect as the rededication of the chapel, and Francis was there.[17] Perhaps he and the priest were the only ones present.

The Gospel reading was Jesus's words to the Twelve:

As you go, proclaim the good news, "The kingdom of heaven has come near." Cure the sick, raise the dead, cleanse the lepers, cast out demons. You received without payment; give without payment. Take no gold, or silver, or copper in your belts, no bag for your journey, or two tunics, or sandals, or a staff; for laborers deserve their food. Whatever town or village you enter, find out who in it is worthy, and stay there until you leave. (Matt. 10:7–11)[18]

---

[15] Fortini, *Francis of Assisi,* 250. Thomas of Celano says Francis "had a warm devotion to the Mother of all good and he began to stay here [at that Portiuncula] continually." Thomas of Celano, *Life of St. Francis,* FA:ED 1:201.

[16] *Acts of the Process of Canonization* in Regis J. Armstrong, OFM Cap., *The Lady—Clare of Assisi: Early Documents,* 3rd ed. (Hyde Park, NY: New City Press, 2006), 193.

[17] Fortini, *Francis of Assisi,* 250. Fortini and Iriarte give the year as 1209, but according to most sources, it would have been 1208. Lazaro Iriarte, *Franciscan History: The Three Orders of St. Francis of Assisi,* trans. from Spanish by Patricia Ross (Chicago: Franciscan Herald Press, 1982), 5.

[18] The passage could have been Luke 9:1–2, but Fortini notes that "Only in the Mass for the Feast of Saint Matthias, in the missals of the time, is this selection from the Gospels to be found" (Fortini, 250 n.). However, Iriarte says "It seems certain that the gospel reading heard by Francis was Lk 10:1–8" (*Franciscan History,* 13, n. 9).

Francis was dumbfounded. Jesus was speaking right to him, giving next steps. He "humbly begged the priest after celebrating the solemnities of the Mass to explain the gospel to him. The priest explained it all . . . thoroughly line by line." Perhaps the priest also pointed Francis to similar passages in Mark 6:12 and Luke 9:1–2.[19]

"This is what I want!" Francis exclaimed excitedly. "This is what I seek, what I desire with all my heart." In his *Testament* Francis later said "no one showed me what I had to do, but the Most High Himself revealed to me that I should live according to the pattern of the Holy Gospel."[20]

Francis pledged on the spot to live Jesus's words to the letter. After nearly two years as a hermit, Francis was ready for his real calling.[21] "He flung away his shoes, put down his stick, and changed his belt for a cord," writes Fortini. "The uniform of the Friars Minor was complete. And Francis's days of indecision were over. He was ready to go forward, a perfect knight, to win the world for his lord."[22] Francis resolved ever after to live like Jesus, literally.

In the Bible, Jesus directs his words to his disciples—all Twelve, not just one. Francis sensed immediately that Jesus's call was not for him alone. Other youth would follow. Jesus had sent out many, not just one, "to proclaim the kingdom of God and to heal" (Luke 9:2).

Convergence and Commission

The threads of Francis's life were coming together, interweaving. His conversion was complete, though the road wasn't yet clear.

Francis was about twenty-seven. Looking back, we see the steps by which God led him.

Prison in Perugia after his first bitter taste of real battle jolted Francis from his carefree, rather flamboyant life. His months of illness at home led to days of reflection and questing.

Then suddenly the call to knighthood seemed to be the answer. Crusades! A noble chivalrous battle, good versus evil, it seemed. The struggle was between the church, embodied in Pope Innocent III, and

---

[19] Thomas of Celano, *Life of St. Francis*, FA:ED 1:201.

[20] Thomas of Celano, *Life of St. Francis*, FA:ED 1:201–2; Francis of Assisi, "The Testament," FA:ED, 1:125.

[21] "For two years he wore the habit of a hermit, but in the third year of his conversion he began the new Order of Lesser Brothers." Bernard of Besse, *A Book of the Praises of Saint Francis*, FA:ED 3:66. This is consistent with the chronology provided by Englebert, *Saint Francis*, 394.

[22] Fortini, *Francis of Assisi*, 251.

pagan powers. The papal military campaign in southern Italy looked like divine calling.

But then came Francis's strange dream, bathed in chivalry—a great castle, a Crusader fortress; a beautiful damsel, a young princess, chivalry embodied, implying a noble quest. This was a true call to noble knighthood.

But again, there was a relapse into illness, and more days and nights of questing and self-doubt. Yet this confusing trail led to the three decisive steps in Francis's conversion.

First, Francis's life-changing encounter with the leper on the road below Assisi. "The Lord Himself led me" to the lepers, Francis wrote. "I showed mercy to them. And when I left them, what had seemed bitter to me was turned into sweetness of soul and body."[23]

Then second, at San Damiano, God spoke to Francis through the Jesus icon: "Go, repair my church!" Francis sold his father's goods and horse for money to repair the chapel. Hiding from his father's anger led to his examination before Bishop Guido. Francis stripped off his clothes and set off nakedly to follow Jesus.

But follow where? What was the shape of his mission? Francis launched his mission by repairing two chapels, San Damiano and Saint Peter of the Thorn.

Then came the decisive climax just as Francis finished repairing Saint Mary of the Angels, the Portiuncula. As Francis watched the Mass, Jesus spoke straight to him from his Word: "Proclaim the good news! The kingdom of heaven has come near!" No gold, no provisions; just go and announce the gospel.

Francis's call and mission were complete, confirmed. He was certain Jesus had called him to go proclaim good news, certain he would have companions, certain God would work through him and his brothers. Francis now saw "the life of Jesus, who taught charity and love" as "the ideal to follow" (as Fortini puts it). Jesus was more than the object of doctrinal faith. "More than ever the example of Christ, who also suffered, seemed the ultimate reality."[24] In that light, only this looked bright. Everything else fades.

Francis was, however, still learning the meaning of faith. For a time, he struggled with "a very serious temptation of the spirit." The struggle

---

[23] Francis of Assisi, "The Testament," FA:ED 1:124.
[24] Fortini, *Francis of Assisi*, 197, 199.

continued for some years, despite all Francis's fasting and prayer and self-affliction.[25]

Then one day as Francis was praying at the Portiuncula, a voice spoke to him: "Francis, if you had faith like a mustard seed, you would tell the mountain to move from here, and it would move" (Matt. 17:20).

Francis replied, "What is the mountain that I could move?"

"The mountain is your temptation," the voice said.

Francis began to sob. *"Lord, let it be done to me as you have said!"*

At once the temptation was gone, and Francis was free.[26]

Francis was delivered by faith, not self-affliction. He went forth with new faith and renewed confidence, sure of his mission. A hundred years later one of Francis's most devout followers, Angelo Clareno, wrote, "Saint Francis himself used to say that the almighty power of God is made known and shines forth in the faith and endurance of the saints, because we have been saved by faith, and all the works of God are done in faith. 'Without faith it is impossible to please God' "[27]

In Francis's day, as in ours, faith was often misunderstood as merely affirming official doctrine. Francis of course affirmed and taught respect for the church and its doctrines. But he knew by experience that salvation comes by faith in God through Jesus Christ, not merely by right doctrine and church authority.

---

[25] *Remembrance of the Desire of a Soul*, FA:ED 2:324; Bernard of Besse, *A Book of the Praises of Saint Francis,* FA:ED 3:43. The *Assisi Compilation* says this temptation troubled Francis "day and night for more than two years" and that as a result Francis "could not be his usual cheerful self," and so he sometimes stayed apart from his brothers and refrained from talking as well as from food. "He would often go to pray in the woods near the church, so that he could better express his pain and could more abundantly pour out his tears before the Lord." *Assisi Compilation,* FA:ED 2:165.

[26] *Remembrance of the Desire of a Soul*, FA:ED 2:324; Bernard of Besse, *A Book of the Praises of Saint Francis,* FA:ED 3:43–44; *Assisi Compilation,* FA:ED 2:165–66; *Mirror of Perfection* (Sabatier ed.), FA:ED 3:346. Possibly this unspecified temptation was connected with Francis's concerns about the direction and leadership of the Order—Englebert, *Saint Francis,* 292–95. This incident is significant, given the medieval Christian world at this time, three hundred years before Martin Luther. The way of salvation had become so muddied by an over-emphasis on ascetic practices, church authority, and the misunderstanding of *repentance* (turning away from one's sins) as *penance* (actions and efforts to pay for sin) that the key truth of justification by faith, not works, was largely eclipsed.

[27] Angelo Clareno, *The Book of Chronicles or of the Tribulations of the Order of Lesser Ones,* FA:ED 3:392.

His First Sermon

Now Francis began to preach, proclaim—to announce good news the way Jesus did. The next morning after hearing Jesus's call at the Portiuncula, it seems, Francis walked up to Assisi.[28] He went to San Giorgio (Saint George), the parish church where he was first educated. How he was permitted to preach before the congregation, or whether perhaps he spoke to townsfolk gathered in the piazza before the church building, is unclear.

We don't know, but we do have an idea what Francis said in that first sermon. According to Thomas of Celano, Francis "began to preach penance to all with a fervent spirit and joyful attitude. He inspired his listeners with words that were simple and a heart that was heroic."[29] Penance here means *repentance*—a call to turn and follow Jesus truly, as Jesus announced in Matthew 4:17, "Repent, for the kingdom of heaven has come near."

The crowd was stirred by Francis's fervor and suddenly changed life. He seemed a different person from the youth they had known.

Francis now began a practice he followed all his life: Greeting everyone, "Peace!" He later wrote, "The Lord revealed a greeting to me that we should say: 'May the Lord give you peace.'"[30] Thomas of Celano notes, "At the outset of all his addresses, [Francis] proclaimed peace and prefixed all of his letters with a salutation using the word of peace."[31]

Francis was offering a new way of life, a new thing—an actual living-out of what Jesus did and taught. God had led him to an end and a beginning. Francis knew others would follow, but at first, he was alone.

---

[28] Sabatier, *Road to Assisi*, 45.

[29] Thomas of Celano, *Life of St. Francis*, FA:ED 1:202. Thomas continues, "His words were like a blazing fire, reaching the deepest parts of the heart, and filling the souls of all with wonder. He seemed entirely different from what he had been, and looking up to heaven he refused to look down upon earth. It is truly amazing that he first began to preach where he had learned to read as a little boy, and where at first he was reverently buried."

[30] Francis of Assisi, "The Testament," FA:ED 1:126.

[31] Thomas of Celano, *The Legend for Use in the Choir*, FA:ED 1:320. Henri d'Avranches: "His peace goes out to all. It becomes his mode of greeting, to | Good and bad alike, to citizen and pilgrim he announces it, | And for the faithful, both men and women, it is his prayer." *The Versified Life of St. Francis*, FA:ED 1:461.

Francis's Creaturely Friends

Yet Francis was not really alone. Jesus, he knew, was with him. Lady Poverty walked beside him, he might have said. And he was finding new companions in the created order.

Since hearing the gospel call, Francis's eyes—all his senses—were wakened to see and hear things he had missed. Not for another fifteen years would he write his *Canticle of the Creatures*, but even now he began to see all living things with new eyes. Like plants turning to the sun, birds and animals were drawn to Francis. They sensed his innocence, his warm affection, his fondness for all things living.

Long before his conversion, Francis was fond of earth's varied creatures. Throughout his preconversion soul-searching days he watched the world around him. When he began to look higher and beyond this world, he was looking for God, not for a route out of the physical world. For "the singular thing about Francis' turning toward religion" was that "it did not raise a barrier between him and the earth, but the earth itself became transformed in his sight and gave him a new joy," Brother Cuthbert wrote.[32]

In the days before his transforming encounter with the lone leper, Francis and a friend roamed around Assisi. Francis prayed alone in caves while his friend waited outside. Here, especially up the rocky slopes of forested Mount Subasio, Francis was surrounded by God's smaller creatures and all the varied beauties of creation.

Arnaldo Fortini sets the scene:

> [Mount Subasio] is a propitious place for dreaming. A dark forest of holm-oaks [evergreen holly oaks] spreads along the steep declivity in the rock. There is no stone so rough that it is not entwined by . . . tenaciously clinging roots, no crag so steep that its fissures do not bear a flowering of pale cyclamen, no convolutions of rock so harsh that they are not covered by spreading ferns.[33]

Francis could not fail to notice the birds and flowers—above all the birds, with their quick quirky ways. Francis warmly loved the Skylark because it dressed plainly, ate simply, and sang joyfully, ecstatically.

---

[32] Father Cuthbert, OFS Cap., *Life of St. Francis of Assisi*, 3rd ed. (London: Longmans, Green, 1948), 31.

[33] Fortini, *Francis of Assisi*, 198. Arnaldo Fortini, *Nova Vita de San Francisco* (Rome: Bibliotheca Fides, 1969), 1:251. Fortini says, "a propitious place to love and dream" (literal translation of the Italian).

In the wooded area of caves and cliffs Francis would have observed this "small creature friend ... whose voice seemed to Francis to be a revelation of things beyond human understanding," notes Fortini. The Skylark—"the humblest of all birds, since it rarely lives at the top of leafy green domes but walks, like all other troubled creatures, on the earth," seeking its food.[34]

"But suddenly it will rise up, dizzyingly, desperately, and fly higher, higher, enraptured with sun and blue sky, pouring out in the astonished silence a marvelous song, moving and exultant."[35] Wings beating wildly, a Skylark flies almost straight up, hovers a few minutes, then drops as quickly, singing all the while. For this reason, the Skylark has been a favorite of poets, Shakespeare included.[36] The poet Percy Shelley wrote his verses "To a Skylark," in the summer of 1820.

"Of all birds," notes the *Mirror of Perfection,* Francis "particularly loved a little bird called the lark."[37] Later Francis would say to his brothers,

> Sister lark has a capuche [cowl] like religious, and is a humble bird, because she gladly goes along the road looking for some grain. Even if she finds it in manure, she pecks it out and eats it. While flying, she praises the Lord very sweetly, like good religious looking down on earthly things, whose way of life is always in heaven and intention is always for the praise of God. Her clothes, that is, her feathers, resemble the earth and give an example to religious not to wear colorful and refined clothing, but those of a cheaper price and color, just as the earth is of little worth compared to the other elements.[38]

---

[34] Fortini, *Francis of Assisi,* 199.

[35] Fortini, *Francis of Assisi,* 200. The Skylark's song is a "protracted series of rapid chirps, whistles and trills, given from towering song-flights." Marianne Taylor and Daniele Occhiato, *Birds of Italy* (London: Bloomsbury Publishing, 2018), 108. Italy has several varieties of larks and also a number of kinds of warblers. The editors of *Francis of Assisi: Early Documents* note another common Italian bird that well fits Francis's description is the Blackcap Warbler (*sylvia atricapilla*), and this could be the bird Francis refers to. FA:ED, 3:362, n. a.

[36] William Shakespeare, *Cymbeline* II. iii. 21, cited in Edward A. Armstrong, *Saint Francis: Nature Mystic—The Derivation and Significance of the Nature Stories in the Franciscan Legend* (Berkeley: University of California Press, 1976), 89.

[37] *The Beginning of a Mirror of Perfection of the Status of a Lesser Brother* (Sabatier ed.), FA:ED 3:362. See also Fortini, *Francis of Assisi,* 200.

[38] *Mirror of Perfection,* FA:ED 3:362. See also Armstrong, *Saint Francis: Nature Mystic,* 90. Fortini also quotes this passage and adds in a footnote, "Those familiar with

Figure 4.1 Skylark *(Alauda arvensis) (Photo courtesy*
David Irving, used by permission)

Francis's depiction shows he did not merely notice small creatures in passing. He observed them closely. Animal stories of the time were commonly fables, interesting and morally instructive, but nonsense scientifically. Francis's "direct observation" of birds, however, was "exceptional in that age," notes ornithologist Edward Armstrong—pointing ahead to the time when "merely traditional descriptions of the appearance and behaviour of animals" would give way to empirical science.[39]

Assisi is an especially rich place to observe the beauty and bounty of creation. The town itself offers a magnificent view of the valley below and the hills and mountains beyond. From childhood, Francis roamed this physical world. Italy's countryside is rich in animal and plant life. In the town, swallows often built their clay nests under the eaves of large

---

Assisi territory know that one species of bird, the *allodola stazionaria,* is to be found only in the meadowlands of Mount Subasio." Fortini, *Francis of Assisi,* 200.

[39] Armstrong, *Saint Francis: Nature Mystic,* 90–91. See also Bret Thoman, OFS, *St. Francis of Assisi: Passion, Poverty, and the Man Who Transformed the Catholic Church,* 2nd ed. (Charlotte, NC: TAN Books, 2018), 142–50.

buildings, as their descendants do today. Evening skies are often filled with swooping swallows feasting on flying insects.[40]

Round about Assisi, in the valleys, rivers, and lakes and up the mountains, small creatures abound. Francis's stories tell of rabbits, fish, nightingales, even a wolf in the town of Gubbio.[41] In the valley along the streams and ponds one might see and hear a profusion of water birds— wild ducks, summer teal, bitterns, coots, plovers, cranes—at some seasons, an avian orchestra. There were also snipes, curlews, and waterhens.[42]

"Full of dove-like simplicity [Francis] exhorted all creatures to the love of their Creator. He preached to the birds and was understood by them."[43]

Francis observed the world around him, even bees and bugs. Thomas of Celano speaks of "the sweet tenderness [Francis] enjoyed while contemplating in creatures the wisdom, power, and goodness of the Creator ... he often overflowed with amazing, unspeakable joy as he looked at the sun, gazed at the moon, or observed the stars."[44]

Francis loved flowers. He noticed even the tiniest ones—white, blue, purple—common along the wooded footpaths then, as now. He noticed herbs as well—wild thyme, mint, balm. Francis later "ordered that some pieces of ground in the friars' garden always be used" for flowers, "these bearers of colour and perfume," and additional space for wild herbs.[45]

Francis's sensitivity to created things contrasted with the tendency of most church leaders and poets of his day (and since) to see the created order as always only pointing away to things spiritual; a mere shadow of more important truth. *Francis saw deeper.* Surely created things pointed to the Creator, but for that very reason, they were valuable and valued in their own right and in God's sight.

But now, in the year 1208, Francis had a mission to meet. Jesus had said, "Francis! Go and repair my house!" How, where, with whom? Yet he had no companions to help him.

---

[40] See Fortini, *Francis of Assisi,* 517; also Cynthia Hanson, "Bringing the Birds Back to Assisi," *Christian Science Monitor* (November 3, 1989), https://www.csmonitor.com/1989/1103/psong.html.

[41] Fortini, *Francis of Assisi,* 534–43.

[42] Fortini, *Francis of Assisi,* 439. See Taylor and Occhiato, *Birds of Italy.*

[43] Jacopo de Voragine, *The Golden Legend, Readings on the Saints,* FA:ED 2:798.

[44] Thomas of Celano, *Life of St. Francis,* FA:ED 1:250.

[45] Fortini, *Francis of Assisi,* 564. See *Mirror of Perfection,* FA:ED 3:366 and Thomas of Celano, *The Remembrance of the Desire of a Soul* (The Second Life of Saint Francis), FA:ED 2:353–54, for more details.

5

Birth of a Movement

Soon Francis did have companions. Young men joined him. He called them brothers.

If there is anything more astonishing than Francis himself, it is the speed with which young men flocked to him, birthing a movement.

It began of course with just a few. Two young men of Assisi had been watching Francis, puzzled but intrigued. Their names were Peter Catani[1] and Bernardo da Quintavalle. In the spring of 1208, they approached Francis. They wanted to follow him.[2]

Like Francis, Bernardo was from a wealthy merchant family. He had long known Francis. A thoughtful young man, he was intrigued by Francis's newfound life—his courage, sincerity, "his life of poverty and his industry in repairing deserted chapels."[3]

---

[1] The name is variously spelled as Peter of Catani or Catanii, Peter Cantani, Peter Catanio, and other variations.

[2] Here I follow mainly the account of John of Perugia, one of Francis's early brothers and thus an eyewitness of the community's early beginnings. He knew personally Bernardo, Peter, and other early brothers. His work, *The Beginning and Founding of the Order and the Deeds of Those Lesser Brothers Who Were the First Companions of Blessed Francis in Religion*, is best known as *The Anonymous of Perugia*, because John issued his narrative anonymously. It seems to have been written in 1240 or 1241, about fifteen years after Francis's death. Regis J. Armstrong, OFM Cap., J. A. Wayne Hellmann, OFM Conv., and William J. Short, OFM, *Francis of Assisi: Early Documents* (New York: New City Press, 2001), 2:34–58; editorial introduction, 31–33 [hereafter FA:ED].

[3] Father Cuthbert, OFS Cap., *Life of St. Francis of Assisi*, 3rd ed. (London: Longmans, Green, 1948), 62. Cuthbert notes that Bernardo "visited Francis secretly and then offered him the hospitality of his house," where Francis frequently spent the night and the two engaged in conversation. Bernardo thus "learned something of the secret of Francis' life," noting especially the time Francis spent in prayer and praise (62–63). See also Arnaldo Fortini, *Francis of Assisi*, trans. Helen Moak (New York: Crossroad, 1992), 266–68, and the sources Fortini and Cuthbert cite.

"What should we do?" Bernardo and Peter asked.

Francis replied, "Let's go and seek counsel from the Lord."

Next morning the three walked to St. Nicholas church on the Piazza del Comune to see what the Bible said. What did Jesus tell his disciples?[4] Francis knew what Jesus had told *him*. Would he tell his new companions the same thing?

At St. Nicholas, the "book of the Gospels lay near the altar that all might read who cared."[5] It was hard for Francis or Bernardo to read the Latin text, so they asked a priest's help.[6] Peter Catani was a scholar but was unfamiliar with the biblical text.

The priest opened the Gospels, apparently at random, and found these words: "If you wish to be perfect, go, sell everything you possess and give to the poor, and you will have a treasure in heaven; then come, follow me" (Matt. 19:21). Opening the book again, he read: "If any man wishes to come after me, let him deny himself and take up his cross and follow me" (Matt. 16:24). Then a third time, "Take nothing for your journey, neither staff, nor pouch, nor bread, nor money—not even an extra tunic" (Luke 9:3).[7]

When Bernardo and Peter heard this, they exclaimed, "This is what we want! This is what we were seeking." Francis said, "This will be our rule. Now go and fulfill the Lord's counsel as you heard it."[8] And so "God's Word makes a Rule," as Fortini adroitly puts it.[9]

---

[4] *Anonymous of Perugia*, 2:38; Fortini, *Francis of Assisi*, 268–69. *The Anonymous of Perugia* simply says "one of the city's churches"; *The Legend of the Three Companions* says it was St. Nicholas, as does Fortini. *Legend of the Three Companions*, FA:ED 2:85.

[5] Cuthbert, *Life of St. Francis*, 64.

[6] Fortini (*Francis of Assisi*, 269) says Francis "knew the priest well. He asked him to bring the book of the Gospels and put it, closed, on the reading stand on top of the altar" and that the priest proceeded to "open the Gospels three times." (Some sources say Francis himself opened the book and read the words.)

[7] *Anonymous of Perugia*, FA:ED 2:38; Cuthbert, *Life of St. Francis*, 64; Fortini, *Francis of Assisi*, 269–70. "It is very probable that the book consulted by Francis and his first companions is still in existence and is at the Walters Art Gallery of Baltimore," Maryland. Presumably this was a missal that included Gospel readings. "The words 'Gospels' and 'missal' were frequently used interchangeably at the time. It contains the passages that Francis took as the rule for his new order." Fortini, *Francis of Assisi*, 270, editorial n. g, by Helen Moak. See also Adrian House, *Francis of Assisi* (Mahwah, NJ: HiddenSpring [Paulist Press], 2001), 79, who traces the history of the missal. The missal can be viewed here: https://art.thewalters.org/detail/34845/st-francis-missal-2/.

[8] *Anonymous of Perugia*, FA:ED 2:38; Cuthbert, *Life of St. Francis*, 64; Paul Sabatier, *The Road to Assisi: The Essential Biography of St. Francis*, ed. Jon M. Sweeney (Brewster, MA: Paraclete Press, 2004), 46. See also *Legend of the Three Companions*, FA:ED 2:86.

[9] Fortini, *Francis of Assisi*, 269 (in the English translation by Helen Moak; the

The First Brothers

Peter and Bernardo promptly rid themselves of everything they owned. Bernardo "sold all his possessions, acquiring a large sum of money from the transaction," while Peter "dispose[d] of his more modest property."[10]

A few days later, a crowd of poor folk gathered in the Piazza of St. George. Bernardo handed out his money. Francis was there, "assisting at the distribution and singing aloud his praises to God." Townsfolk looked on, flabbergasted.[11]

In the crowd was an older priest named Sylvester, a canon at nearby San Rufino. According to *The Anonymous of Perugia*, Francis had bought stones from him to repair San Damiano. Seeing money flowing, Sylvester remembered the stones. "You didn't pay me much for the stones you got!" he told Francis. Francis smiled and said, "You will have your share, sir priest!" Francis gave him two handfuls of coins. "Enough?" he asked. Sylvester said it was and returned home.

But his conscience bothered him. He had a recurring dream of Francis and a dragon. A golden cross rose from Francis's mouth into the heavens, its arms stretching round the world. Sylvester reflected on the dream and on his actions. What Francis was doing seemed foolish. And yet, he realized, Francis was acting more like Jesus than he was.

Eventually Sylvester sought out Francis and himself joined his growing band of brothers—the first priest to follow Francis.[12] This did not happen, however, till about a year later after a dozen or so others had joined.

Meanwhile Bernardo and Peter—now Brother Bernardo and Brother Peter—followed Francis back to the Portiuncula. They were the first to adopt Francis's simple habit and, like Francis, walk barefoot. Three brothers: the first Franciscan community, embryo of a movement.

About a week later another Assisian, a youth named Giles, approached Francis. Kneeling, he asked if he could join the little band. Francis welcomed him with open arms. "And so the four of them"—Bernardo, Peter Catani, Giles, and Francis—"had boundless joy" together.[13]

Italian text has simply "The Word of God" [*il parola de Dio*], but with the sense of the Word as rule).

[10] *Anonymous of Perugia*, FA:ED 2:38 (first quote); Cuthbert, *Life of St. Francis*, 64 (second quote).

[11] Cuthbert, *Life of St. Francis*, 65.

[12] *Anonymous of Perugia*, FA:ED 2:38–39; Cuthbert, *Life of St. Francis*, 65, 69–70; Fortini, *Francis of Assisi*, 271–74. According to Cuthbert, Sylvester "became a lover of solitude, giving himself much to contemplation and prayer" (70).

[13] *Anonymous of Perugia*, FA:ED 2:40; see also Cuthbert, *Life of St. Francis*, 66.

Soon others joined Francis: Sabbatino, John of Cappella, Morico the Short. The little group took up life together at the Portiuncula, becoming the nucleus of the Franciscan community. Here they built a small dwelling or lodging place (*domunculam*, literally a lodge) as their home base.[14]

A few weeks later Francis and Giles set out for the coastal region east of Assisi, the Marches of Ancona.[15] As they walked along "they rejoiced enthusiastically in the Lord," Francis singing "with a loud and clear voice, in French, the praises of the Lord."[16] At the same time Francis apparently sent Bernardo and Peter off in another direction—their first mission.

As Francis and Giles walked along, Francis said, "Our religion [order] will be like a fisherman who casts his nets into the water catching a great number of fish, and, leaving the small ones in the water, he puts the large ones into his basket." Thus Francis "prophesied that the Order would expand."[17]

The Lord gave Francis "such certitude of the Order's spreading throughout the world, that he saw the future as though it were present," writes Bernard of Besse. Francis exclaimed, "I saw the roads filled with the multitude of those coming to us. They are coming from France; Spaniards are hurrying, German and English are running, and a huge crowd speaking other languages is rapidly approaching."[18]

---

[14] *Legend of the Three Companions,* FA:ED 2:87, ("a little hut"); Cuthbert, *Life of St. Francis,* 76 ("a small temporary shelter"). Moorman describes the early life of the community, including its simplicity and hardships, in some detail. John Moorman, *A History of the Franciscan Order: From Its Origins to the Year 1517* (Oxford: Oxford University Press, 1968), 22–23.

[15] Literally, the Borderland of Ancona, the region around and to the west of the coastal city of Ancona, which lies about eighty miles northeast of Assisi. It would take between twenty-five and thirty hours to walk from Assisi over the mountain all the way to the coast.

[16] *Legend of the Three Companions,* FA:ED 2:87. Fortini says it was "early June," and writes that Francis "improvised in Provençal, in spur of the moment inspirations that magnified God, Lord of heaven and earth, and exulted in works of His creation." Fortini suggests Francis chose the Marches of Ancona because it was safer than traveling in the vicinity of Perugia due to ongoing conflicts between Perugia and Assisi, and says Francis and Giles were along the Adriatic coast in July. Fortini, *Francis of Assisi,* 278–79.

[17] *Legend of the Three Companions,* FA:ED 2:88; see Cuthbert, *Life of St. Francis,* 72–73. In the 1200s, the term "religion," from the Latin *religio,* was commonly used in the sense of a religious order within the Roman Church. In the early 1300s, the word "order" became the more common term. See *Mirror of Perfection* (Sabatier ed.), FA:ED 3:260 n. a.

[18] Bernard of Besse, *A Book of the Praises of Saint Francis,* FA:ED 3:34.

At the Portiuncula, still more joined: Philip the Tall; Angelo Tancredi, a knight; Barbaro of Assisi; John of San Costanzo; Bernardo de Vigilante. Soon there were eleven, though authors debate just which brothers made up this first group. The stream was just beginning.[19]

Impossible Community

If the first secret of the Franciscan movement was Francis himself, here is the second: *community*. Community at its most elemental—shared life, meals together, body-and-soul fellowship, the sense of the New Testament word *koinonia*.

Things "moved rapidly" now, especially from "the morning when Bernard had distributed his goods to the poor.... From a recluse, Francis had been transformed into an apostle."[20]

Word spread. Other towns heard of this strange new group. Some folks thought they were crazy—certainly audacious, these formerly well-provisioned young men, now begging alms! But attitudes began shifting as people saw the character, the caring, the compassion of these brothers and their covenant commitment to each other. Someone in Assisi said, "Either they are saints or they are stark mad."[21]

Bishop Guido certainly wondered. He sent for Francis and asked him to reconsider living in absolute poverty. Francis replied, "Lord [Bishop], if we had any possessions, we would need arms to protect them because they cause many disputes and lawsuits. And possessions usually impede the love of God and neighbor. Therefore we do not want to possess anything in this world."[22]

This is one of the most profound things Francis ever said, especially given the growing commercialism of the time. Bishop Guido could hardly

---

[19] Fortini, *Francis of Assisi*, 286–87; Cuthbert, *Life of St. Francis*, 70, 89; Omer Englebert, *Saint Francis of Assisi*, 2nd English ed., trans. Eve Marie Cooper (Chicago: Franciscan Herald Press, 1965), 87. An account called *The Kinship of Saint Francis* by Arnald of Sarrant (1365) lists the first eleven brothers (before the Rule was approved) as "Brothers Bernard of Quintavalle, the first, and Peter Catanio, the second; the third was the most holy Brother Giles; the fourth Brother Sabbatino; the fifth, Brother Morico the Short; the sixth, Brother John of Capella; the seventh, Brother Philip the Tall; the eighth, Brother John of San Costanzo; the ninth, Brother Barbaro; the tenth, Brother Bernardo Vigilante or de Vida; the eleventh, Brother Angelo Tancredi, who was the first knight of the Order." Arnald of Sarrant, *The Kinship of Saint Francis*, FA:ED 3:681.

[20] Cuthbert, *Life of St. Francis*, 72.

[21] Cuthbert, *Life of St. Francis*, 73, based on *Legend of the Three Companions*, FA:ED 2:90.

[22] *Anonymous of Perugia*, FA:ED 2:41; also *Legend of the Three Companions*, FA:ED 2:89.

deny Francis's logic. He was satisfied for now, if not convinced. Guido knew from experience the constant church conflicts over property and possessions as well as between church and town and between nobles and merchants. He gave Francis his blessing.[23]

So, the new community formed its new life. Francis began shaping the brothers for mission. He sent Bernardo and Giles on their first tour. They walked a hundred miles northwest, down the hills to Florence in the Arno valley, about a three-day walk.[24]

Arriving late in the day, Bernardo and Giles went begging through the streets and seeking a lodging place, as the night was turning cold. They found a house with a portico on which was a bread oven. "We can stay here," they said.

They asked the lady of the house if she would welcome them for the night. Looking at the two vagabonds, she refused. "Can we at least sleep outside here, next to your oven?" She said yes, so they settled down to sleep.

A while later the woman's husband came home. When he saw the brothers, he said to his wife, "Why did you let these two rogues stay here?" She replied, "I didn't want to offer them hospitality in the house, but gave them permission to stay on the porch where they couldn't steal anything except the firewood." The husband, thinking the men likely were thieves, gave Bernardo and Giles nothing to cover themselves through the cold night.[25]

Early next morning, Bernardo and Giles walked to a nearby church for Matins. The lady of the house came in later for Mass. She was surprised to see the two brothers there, kneeling in prayer. "If these men were scoundrels," she thought, "they wouldn't be praying so fervently."

Just then a man came by, distributing alms to the poor. He offered coins to Bernardo and Giles, but they refused. "Why won't you accept the coins like other people?" he said. "I see you are just as poor and needy."

Bernardo replied, "Yes, we are poor, but our poverty is not as burdensome for us as it is for the other poor, for we have become poor by the grace of God and in fulfillment of his counsel."

The man was astonished. Had they ever possessed anything? Yes, they said, but for the love of God had given everything to the poor.

---

[23] *Legend of the Three Companions*, FA:ED 2:89; Cuthbert, *Life of St. Francis*, 75–76.

[24] Cuthbert, *Life of St. Francis*, 82. Cuthbert says Giles and Bernardo were "on their way to Spain."

[25] *Anonymous of Perugia*, FA:ED 2:43; *Legend of the Three Companions*, FA:ED 2:91.

The woman of the house where Bernardo and Giles had stayed saw all this. She told the brothers, "Christians, if you want to come back to my hospitality, I will gladly receive you into my home." Her husband agreed, telling the brothers, "Look, this is the lodging that the Lord has prepared for you. Stay here as long as you wish." Bernardo and Giles thanked God and their hosts. They stayed a few days, then continued on their way.[26]

In Florence and other places, people often took these early brothers as vagabonds, good-for-nothings. Some mocked; some threw mud or stones or roughed them up. According to *The Anonymous of Perugia,* "people considered them most despicable; that is why they nonchalantly and brazenly persecuted them as if they were criminals. In addition, they endured a great deal of hardship and suffering from hunger and thirst, from cold and nakedness." "They suffered all these things with constancy and patience, as blessed Francis had counseled them."[27]

When Giles and Bernardo got back to Assisi and joined Francis and the others at the Portiuncula, "their happiness was such that the evils they had endured were forgotten."[28]

The Portiuncula was now the geographical center of the embryonic Franciscan community, but Francis and the brothers were constantly on the move. "They went up and down the country, joyfully sowing their seed," writes Sabatier. The brothers' itinerant witness commenced at "the beginning of summer, the time when everybody" in the Umbrian valleys "is out of doors mowing or turning the grass." Often, they freely "passed a part of the day in aiding the peasants in their field work. They worked and ate together; field-hands and friars often slept in the same barn; and when at the morrow's dawn the friars went on their way, the hearts of those they left behind had been touched."[29]

What Is Happening Here?

It is time to pause and ponder what's going on here.

Assisi townsfolk knew about this little community forming down in the valley. Some of Assisi's best-known youth were there. What were Assisians to make of it? What did church officials think?

---

[26] *Anonymous of Perugia,* FA:ED 2:44; *Legend of the Three Companions,* FA:ED 2:91–92. Both sources say that afterward this man was very generous to the poor. See also Fortini, *Francis of Assisi,* 285.

[27] *Anonymous of Perugia,* FA:ED 2:45; see also *Legend of the Three Companions,* FA:ED 2:92.

[28] Fortini, *Francis of Assisi,* 286.

[29] Sabatier, *Road to Assisi,* 48–49.

Imagine this newborn little family.[30] Bernardo, a wealthy young merchant; Peter Catani, a well-respected young doctor of laws (attorney); Giles, "a passionate devotee of the ideals of chivalry," aspiring to win glory as a knight[31] but of no noble birth—rather "the son of a small farmer."[32] Sabbatino, about whom we know nothing except that he was born in Assisi and later was one of twelve brothers who set off with Francis on his mission to Muslims in Egypt.[33]

Next comes Morico the Short, also an Assisi youth about whom we know little. John de Capella was from another Assisi family; that's all we know except for his later history with the Franciscans. Angelo Tancredi was the first knight. Angelo was a near neighbor in Assisi who, like his wealthy family, early became enamored of the Crusades. Now he was a poor brother.[34]

We know little of Barbaro, another Assisian, though he, too, was among the brothers who departed on Francis's Muslim mission in 1219.[35]

Bernardo di Vigilante (the second Bernardo) seems to have been of a prominent Assisi family.[36] Philip the Tall also came from Assisi or its environs; he became a close associate of Francis and later served as Visitor (a sort of supervisor) of the Poor Clares.[37]

John of San Costanzo was likely from the nearby villa of San Costanzo.[38]

---

[30] See André Vauchez's summary in his *Francis of Assisi, the Life and Afterlife of a Medieval Saint*, trans. Michael F. Cusato (New Haven, CT: Yale University Press, 2012), 44–45.

[31] Fortini, *Francis of Assisi*, 274.

[32] Cuthbert, *Life of St. Francis*, 66.

[33] Fortini, *Francis of Assisi*, 395.

[34] Fortini, *Francis of Assisi*, 122, 287–91, 526, 529–30. Fortini provides considerable detail on Angelo Tancredi (Angelo di Tancredi, not to be confused with Angelo of Rieti) and his family. His name Tancredi celebrated Tancred (1075–1112), hero of the First Crusade. A younger cousin Ginevra (named for the famous Guinevere) later became Sister Benedetta, one of the early leaders among the Poor Clares.

[35] Fortini, *Francis of Assisi*, 286, 335, 395–96.

[36] Fortini, *Francis of Assisi*, 286.

[37] Philip later "served as Visitor of the Poor Ladies [Clares] of Saint Damian in 1219, and again from 1228 to 1246. He died in 1259." Thomas of Celano, *Life of St. Francis*, FA:ED 1:204 n. c. See also Fortini, *Francis of Assisi*, 278–80; Englebert, *Saint Francis*, 438–40, who gives a biographical sketch. Philip was called Philip the Long (*Filippo Longo*) but the designation may refer to his family line, not his physical characteristics, according to Fortini and Englebert. Thomas of Celano says the Lord gifted Philip to "speak of Him in words that were sweet and flowing with honey [*mellifluous*]" and to correctly interpret Scripture, though he had no formal training. Thomas of Celano, *Life of St. Francis*, FA:ED 1:204.

[38] Fortini, *Francis of Assisi*, 286. John likely got to know Francis and the other brothers when they began lodging at the Portiuncula.

A small community of twelve, counting Francis. All were local youth but of varying education, social status, interests, and gifts.

They were not unlike Jesus's first disciples.

Despite differences, these earliest brothers had key things in common. Above all, they were captivated by the spirit and vision of Francis. Chesterton said, "there was never a man who looked into those brown burning eyes without being certain that Francis Bernardone was really interested in *him*; in his own inner individual life from the cradle to the grave."[39]

None of the first brothers was poor. All were young, probably in their late twenties. (Later older men would join.) All were part of the rising generation shaped by the age of chivalry, growing prosperity and economic opportunity in the cities, the excitement and adventure of the Crusades, and the rise of universities. Francis took these dynamics and turned them upside down, focused them—the spirit of adventure, yes, but the pursuit of the lowly Jesus way, not of riches, fame, status. Most of the brothers were from the rising merchant or commercial class.

Some, like Bernardo da Quintavalle, were rich and would likely have become richer. Some, like Peter Catani, were well educated. Some, like Giles, aspired to knighthood. They varied mainly in wealth, social position, and in gifts and personalities.

All Francis's first dozen brothers would outlive him.

These young men were captivated by Francis—his radical upside-down, all-or-nothing commitment. And through Francis they were captivated by Jesus, the passion and focus of Francis's life. So, these youth left all, literally, and followed Francis.

This was of course the age of chivalry and romance, as we saw.[40] The rise of romantic love (as ideal and reality) in the eleventh and twelfth centuries goes some way toward explaining the rise of Francis in the thirteenth. Francis in fact embodied romantic love—passion turned not toward flesh-and-blood women, and not exactly toward God or Mary, but toward the great romance of denying self and all things in order to serve others. The romance of lesserness—serving Lady Poverty and in doing so, serving God and creation.

---

[39] G. K. Chesterton, *St. Francis of Assisi* (Garden City, NY: Image Books, Doubleday, [1924], 1957), 97.

[40] See especially C. S. Lewis, *The Allegory of Love: A Study in Medieval Tradition* (Oxford: Oxford University Press, 1936, 1959). Lewis gives a thorough analysis of the medieval romantic ideal.

Surprisingly, *this romantic ideal turned young men on*—all the energy and passion and virility of youth turned toward serving God and others and the creatures—turned not toward conquest of a virgin or an enemy Muslim or a heretic, but conquest of self in behalf of others.

In a sense, Francis was the true and great romantic of his age, and a true revolutionary.

Francis and his brothers "were filled with great joy, as if they had just acquired an immense treasure," wrote the early author John of Perugia. "They were able to rejoice so much because they had forsaken so much."[41]

What were they actually doing, this little community at the Portiuncula, now beginning to travel through fields and villages?

"Their days were spent in the service of others. If they were not on a journey bearing witness to the Gospel, they were tending the lepers in the hospitals or assisting the farmers in the fields or doing other menial service in return for their food."[42] At night they slept; they rose early to pray and praise. Francis began sending them out in pairs to visit surrounding towns.

> Wherever they went they had a care for the lepers they met on the way; they shared the labour of the poor; sought shelter at night in [out buildings] or in the servants' quarters or in the porches of houses or churches; begged their bread from door to door when they did not receive it in return for their work; exhorted [people] to good living and God-loving ways: but they would seek out solitary places for their hours of prayer.[43]

They were glad then to return to the Portiuncula and be reunited with Francis and the other brothers.

Francis himself consistently, repeatedly set the example of compassion for poor and suffering folks wherever he went.

> For though he was content with a ragged tunic, he often wanted to share it with some poor person. Sometimes during the coldest seasons, he used to approach rich people to lend him cloaks or furs. And as they responded ever more gladly to this, he used to say to them, "I accept this from you on this condition that you do not expect to have it returned." And when he would meet

---

[41] *Anonymous of Perugia*, FA:ED 2:40.

[42] Cuthbert, *Life of St. Francis*, 76.

[43] Cuthbert, *Life of St. Francis*, 78, summarizing material from several early sources.

someone who in his judgment was poorer, he would say to his companion, "We accepted this mantle on loan until someone poorer would come along to whom we could give it"; many times in cold weather he would deprive himself to help others who were in need.[44]

Francis "borrowed" from the rich and gave to the poor.

Francis was following the example of Jesus's early ministry in Galilee—both intentionally and, I think, almost unconsciously, instinctively. Jesus "went on through cities and villages, proclaiming and bringing the good news of the kingdom of God. The twelve were with him" (Luke 8:1). Francis and his brothers began traveling around Umbria, announcing the good news of the gospel, calling people to repent and turn to Jesus.

Neither Francis nor his brothers had permission to preach. Yet a movement was aborning. Francis said to his early followers, "God has mercifully called us not only for our own good but also for the salvation of many. Therefore, let us go through the world, encouraging and teaching men and women by word and example to [repent of] their sins and to remember the Lord's commandments, which they have forgotten for such a long time."[45] Francis drew comfort and confidence from Jesus's words: "Do not be afraid, little flock, for your Father delights to give you the kingdom" (Luke 12:32).[46]

Francis warned his companions of very mixed reactions. Some "faithful people—meek, humble, and kind . . . will receive you and your words with joy and love." Others will oppose and resist. "Therefore, resolve in your hearts to bear all these things with patience and humility."[47]

Here was Francis's mission. "For he knew that he was sent for this: to win for God souls which the devil was trying to snatch away," wrote Thomas of Celano.[48]

This was not of course the first or last time in history that a group of young men banded together radically to follow Jesus. Women did this as well, though with more restrictions, as Jo Ann Kay McNamara

---

[44] *A Life of Saint Francis by an Anonymous Monk of a German Monastery* (c. 1275), FA:ED 3:850. This unknown Benedictine author summarizes here from the two early Thomas of Celano biographies of Francis.

[45] *Anonymous of Perugia*, FA:ED 2:42. See similarly Thomas of Celano, *Life of St. Francis*, FA:ED 1:206–7.

[46] See *Anonymous of Perugia*, FA:ED 2:42.

[47] *Anonymous of Perugia*, FA:ED 2:42.

[48] Thomas of Celano, *Life of St. Francis*, FA:ED 1:214.

shows in *Sisters in Arms: Catholic Nuns through Two Millennia.*[49] Such movements have risen repeatedly through the whole span of Christian history. We may think of the earliest days of the Benedictines, or the first Cistercians who in turn rose reforming the Benedictines, or the first Ursuline Sisters, and others.[50] It is a story repeated in a long succession of radical movements that shook and brought new life to the body of Christ.

Are They Heretics?

As people in the Umbrian valleys watched the new community springing up around Francis, maybe they weren't totally surprised. Italians were accustomed to groups of monks and hermits traveling about. But this new movement did raise eyebrows. People knew about dangerous heretical groups around. Most troublesome were the Cathars (the anticlerical "purists" or "puritans" of the day) who denied the pope's authority and wanted to cleanse the church of its evil ways and bring renewal as they understood it. Denying the pope's supreme authority was heresy.

Waldensians, followers of Peter Waldo (Peter Valdes) in Lyons, France, were also troublesome.[51] The Roman Church considered them heretics; Protestants later saw them as early reformers. Cathars (also called Albigensians and Patarini) were most numerous in southern France, but in Francis's day, Cathar groups could be found in towns and cities throughout central and northern Italy—Florence, Siena, Spoleto, Bologna—and Waldensians existed in Milan, Genoa, and other towns.[52]

---

[49] Jo Ann Kay McNamara, *Sisters in Arms: Catholic Nuns through Two Millennia* (Cambridge, MA: Harvard University Press, 1996).

[50] On Angela Merici (1474–1540) and the Ursulines, see McNamara, *Sisters in Arms*, 459–61, 469–70.

[51] See Englebert, *Saint Francis*, 103; Howard A. Snyder, *Signs of the Spirit: How God Reshapes the Church* (Grand Rapids, MI: Zondervan, 1989), 10, 78, 174, 271. The Waldensians were initially called the *Vaudois* or "Poor Men of Lyons."

[52] "The rise of the city-states and the movement toward urbanization coincided with the heretical movements that began to appear in Western Europe.... At the onset of the thirteenth century, there were several heretical movements in Lombardy and the Italian Peninsula, the most significant being the Waldensians, and the Cathars.... The Catholic hierarchy perceived these movements as grave threats because they challenged the official Church authority.... Other heretical groups may have been present, and these two groups almost certainly had followers in many other cities [than those identified on Map 5, FA:ED, Appendix], but the historical evidence is missing." "Explanation of Maps," FA:ED 1:615.

The Cathars were severely persecuted by the official church. The last remnants in southern France were exterminated through an inquisition in 1320. The remaining Cathars were imprisoned or forced to wear big yellow crosses on the backs of their clothing; a few were burned at the stake. Emmanuel Le Roy Ladurie, *Montaillou, The*

Arnaldo Fortini wrote that "no other period was so afflicted by such a swarm of heresies" as were the days of Francis.[53] People of Assisi, especially church authorities, had reason to be concerned when any upstart group arose.

Were Francis and his brothers heretics? It soon became clear they weren't. Fools, maybe, not heretics. The group was spontaneous and strange but apparently harmless. Francis certainly had no authority yet to form a new order. In Assisi, Francis had some protection because people knew him, and Bishop Guido had informally given his blessing. But folks in other towns could easily mistake these brothers for heretics or dangerous vagabonds, seeing the brothers barefoot and poor and wearing their hooded earth-toned habits.

Francis knew he needed papal authorization if he was going to fulfill his mission. Thomas of Celano writes,

> When blessed Francis saw that the Lord God was daily increasing their numbers, he wrote for himself and his brothers present and future, simply and in a few words, a form of life and a rule. He used primarily words of the holy gospel, longing only for its perfection. He inserted a few other things necessary for the practice of a holy way of life. Then he went to Rome with all his brothers, since he greatly desired that the Lord Pope Innocent the Third confirm for him what he had written.[54]

Little Giovanni Is Healed

The pope did approve Francis's Rule. In just a few years Francis's brothers grew into a massive youth movement across Europe. Franciscan brothers would multiply in England and Scotland and in regions far beyond. The remarkable story provides us with part two of this book.

Meanwhile, in the year 1217, a boy named Giovanni di Fidanza was born in the hilltop town of Bagnoreggio, sixty miles southwest of Assisi. At about age ten, Giovanni fell deathly ill. By this time Francis himself had died and the Catholic Church had just proclaimed him a saint. So,

---

Promised Land of Error, trans. Barbara Bray (New York: George Braziller, 1978), vii–xvii. I discuss the Waldensians and their influence and similarities to the Franciscans in *The Radical Wesley: The Patterns and Practices of a Movement Maker* (Franklin, TN: Seedbed Publishing, 2014), 124, 145, 155, and in *Signs of the Spirit*.

[53] Fortini, *Francis of Assisi*, 253.

[54] Thomas of Celano, *Life of St. Francis*, FA:ED 1:210. See also *Anonymous of Perugia*, FA:ED 2:48.

Giovanni's mother prayed for her son's healing, making a vow to Saint Francis. Giovanni was healed. "I was snatched from the very jaws of death and restored to the vigor of a healthy life," he said.[55]

Later, at about seventeen, Giovanni entered the University of Paris. Soon he met Franciscan brothers and was fascinated. In 1243, he himself became a Franciscan, taking the name Bonaventure. Today we call him Saint Bonaventure, the best known and most influential Franciscan after Francis himself.[56]

---

[55] Bonaventure, *The Minor Legend of Saint Francis*, FA:ED 2:717. Similarly, Bonaventure, *The Major Legend of Saint Francis*, FA:ED 2:528.

[56] Ewert Cousins, ed. and trans., *Bonaventure: The Soul's Journey into God, The Tree of Life, The Life of St. Francis* (New York: Paulist Press, 1978), 1–6. The year 1221 has been traditionally considered Bonaventure's birth year, but 1217 "now is generally accepted by specialists," notes Cousins (2). In his own *Life of St. Francis* Bonaventure wrote, "For when I was a boy, as I still vividly remember, I was snatched from the jaws of death by [Francis's] invocation and merits.... I recognize that God saved my life through him, and I realize that I have experienced his power in my very person." Cousins, *Bonaventure*, 182; Bonaventure, *The Major Legend of Saint Francis*, FA:ED 2:528.

6

Francis and the Pope

A movement had begun, and Francis knew it. He had foreseen it, for Jesus revealed it to him. So, he wasn't surprised as so many others were.

It was now the spring of 1209.[1] Francis had only seventeen more years to live. But what happened in those years was phenomenal. It was spiritual and it was movemental, beginning an epidemic of peace.

Social Dynamics

The little community at the Portiuncula now numbered twelve. Lawrence Cunningham observes,

> With that number some need for structure was inevitable: when would the group gather for prayer? would they follow the canonical hours of the liturgy (Sylvester the priest would have had that obligation)? would they eat together? with what food and how supplied? As intuitive as Francis might have wished to stay, there was a certain inevitable need for a regularization of their life. That need became all the greater as the size of the fraternity increased in number.[2]

---

[1] Englebert makes a strong case for the year being 1209, though Fortini and some others hold the year was 1210. See Englebert's extended analysis; Omer Englebert, *Saint Francis of Assisi,* trans. Eve Marie Cooper, 2nd English ed. (Chicago: Franciscan Herald Press, 1965), 373–82. The editors of the *Francis of Assisi: Early Documents* volumes say the year was either 1209 or 1210. See Regis J. Armstrong, OFM Cap., J. A. Wayne Hellmann, OFM Conv., and William J. Short, OFM, eds., *Francis of Assisi: Early Documents* (New York: New City Press, 2001) [hereafter FA:ED].

[2] Lawrence S. Cunningham, *Francis of Assisi: Performing the Gospel Life* (Grand Rapids, MI: William B. Eerdmans, 2004), 31.

Cunningham speaks of Francis as "intuitive." Indeed. Francis knew two things immediately: the group *must* follow the example and command of Christ, and they must have some authorization from the church. According to *The Anonymous of Perugia*, Francis told his companions, "Brothers, I see that the Lord intends to make of us a large congregation. Therefore, let us go to our mother, the Roman Church, and inform the Supreme Pontiff about what the Lord is doing through us so we may continue doing what we have begun by his will and command."[3]

This meant a hundred-mile trek south to Rome. The twelve set off in pleasant weather in late spring. Most likely, Francis and the brothers followed the ancient Via Flaminia, which passed through Foligno, Spoleto, and other towns before ending in Rome.[4]

As they started out, Francis said, "Let us choose a leader whom we will obey as to the Lord. We shall take the roads he points out and lodge in the places he designates." Quite sensibly they chose Bernardo of Quintavalle, and their long walk went well. "Every night they found charitable people to give them lodging. Every day they went happily on, assured of success, for Francis had divulged a recent vision to them."[5]

Thomas of Celano describes the vision. As Francis was sleeping, he saw himself walking along a road. He came upon a very tall tree—"lovely and strong, thick and exceedingly high."

Francis walked up to the tree. He stood beneath it, looking up, admiring its grandeur. But then Francis himself grew so tall that he touched the treetop. He grasped it and "easily bent it to the ground." The dream foretold what Francis's encounter with the great Pope Innocent III would be like.[6]

Pope Innocent III

So, Francis and the brothers arrived in Rome. Their goal was to meet with Pope Innocent at the Lateran Basilica, the seat of the Roman pontiff.[7]

---

[3] *Anonymous of Perugia*, in FA:ED 2:48.

[4] The editors of *Francis of Assisi: Early Documents* provide a map of the likely route; FA:ED 1:210. The Via Flaminia was constructed about two hundred years before Christ.

[5] Englebert, *Saint Francis*, 107. The quote from Francis is Englebert's paraphrase of *The Anonymous of Perugia*: "Let us make one of us the leader and consider him the vicar of Jesus Christ for us. Wherever he wants to go, we will go; when he wants to rest, we will rest" (FA:ED 2:48); found also in *Legend of the Three Companions*, FA:ED 2:95.

[6] Thomas of Celano, *Life of St. Francis*, FA:ED 1:212.

[7] The basilica is also known as St. John Lateran. Located outside the Vatican, the Lateran Basilica is the cathedral of the Diocese of Rome. Dedicated to both John the

Francis simply wanted the pope to approve the Gospel-based covenant he had written for the brothers.

It wasn't that simple. Over the years, the papacy had become a formidable force. Papal power had grown markedly under Innocent III, who had been in power nearly a dozen years. At forty-eight, Innocent was at the height of his power—not the frail half-awake prelate played by Alec Guinness in *Brother Sun, Sister Moon.*

Innocent III is often called the most significant pope of the Middle Ages. Friedrich Gontard in *The Chair of Peter,* his history of the popes, describes the papacy during the reign of Innocent III as "the greatest power in the Western world."[8] "No Pope was ever closer to making the 'theory of the two swords' a triumphant reality" than Innocent III, notes Englebert. He could depose any king he felt was unworthy or disloyal. Innocent was the first pope to claim the title Vicar (earthly representative) of Christ, rather than Vicar of Peter, used by earlier popes.[9]

Lotario di Segni—the man who became Innocent III—came from an influential Italian family based near Rome, part of Rome's historic nobility. Innocent himself was the nephew of Pope Clement III. He had studied doctrine at the University of Paris under leading theologians, then canon law at the University of Bologna. One of his Paris classmates was Stephen Langton; later as pope, Lotario appointed Langton archbishop of Canterbury.[10]

While still in his twenties and not yet fully ordained a priest, Lotario served as an assistant to popes Lucius III, Gregory VIII, and Clement III. His reputation and influence grew. When elderly Pope Celestine III died on January 8, 1198, Lotario was unanimously elected the same day. At age thirty-seven he was one of the youngest popes ever and reigned for nearly two decades.[11]

Innocent was not shy about papal authority. The pope, he said in his coronation address, is the authorized "representative of Christ, the successor of Peter, the anointed of the Lord, . . . less than God but more

---

Baptist and the Apostle John, the Lateran is the oldest public church edifice in Rome (consecrated in 324 CE).

[8] Friedrich Gontard, *The Chair of Peter: A History of the Papacy,* trans. A. J. and E. F. Peeler (New York: Holt, Rinehart and Winston, 1964), 257.

[9] Englebert, *Saint Francis,* 100.

[10] Langton (c. 1150–1228) "is credited with the division of the Books of the Bible into chapters which, with small modification, is still in use." F. L. Cross and E. A. Livingston, *The Oxford Dictionary of the Christian Church,* 3rd ed. (Oxford: Oxford University Press, 1997), 950.

[11] Gontard, *Chair of Peter,* 258, 601.

than man, judging all other men, but himself judged by none." He wanted
to be clear: "The individual princes and kings have their own realms, but
Peter transcends them all in both the content and the extent of his rule,
for he represents him to whom belongs earth and all its glory."[12]

This is the man barefoot Francis and his poor brothers sought to win
with simple words.

Innocent was a reformer, but in a quite different sense from Francis.
Innocent believed God would hold him accountable for abuses in
the church if he didn't do all he could to correct them.[13] In 1215, he
convoked the influential Fourth Lateran Council. He had three big
conciliar objectives: reform the church, fight heresy, and launch a crusade
to reconquer the Holy Land (the Fifth Crusade, 1217–1229, after the
failure of the Fourth).[14]

Innocent told the two thousand or so bishops, abbots, priors,
cardinals, and others gathered at Lateran IV that this would be a council
of war: war against internal corruption, against infidels, against heretics.
And so it was. Jews and Muslims must henceforth be distinguished from
"Christian" society by their clothing. A crusade against heretics, especially
the Cathars (Albigensians) of southern France, was authorized.[15] Several
doctrines were defined. The first of its seventy-two canons (legal decisions)
gave formal definition to the doctrine of transubstantiation.[16]

---

[12] Gontard, *Chair of Peter,* 258. "Innocent III, whose faith was ardent and bold,
advocated a universal theocracy, with kings and peoples gravitating around it like
satellites around their planet." Arnaldo Fortini, *Francis of Assisi,* trans. Helen Moak (New
York: Crossroad Publishing, 1992), 294.

[13] Charles Edward Smith, *Innocent III: Church Defender* (Baton Rouge: Louisiana
State University Press, 1951), v.

[14] Many issues were in play at this time. In his biography of St. Dominic,
Marie-Humbert Vicaire writes, "At the council one could count three patriarchs,
four hundred and twelve bishops, more than eight hundred abbots and priors, the
representatives of those prevented from appearing in person, finally the ambassadors of
the majority of the Christian sovereigns. It was one of those rare moments in the history
of the world toward which all previous movements appear to converge. The problems
that Innocent had vigorously tackled from the beginning of his reign with varying results
were approaching their solution." M.-H. Vicaire, O.P., *Saint Dominic and His Times,*
trans. Kathleen Pond (New York: McGraw-Hill, 1964), 191.

[15] Gontard, *Chair of Peter,* 259–60, provides details.

[16] Gontard, *Chair of Peter,* 259. "Under Innocent III the conversion of bread and
wine into the body and blood of Christ through the words of the priest was made a
dogma.... This miracle arises from the ordination of the priest," ordination being one of
the authorized seven sacraments of the Roman Catholic tradition—baptism, confirmation,
the eucharist, penance, holy orders (priestly ordination), marriage, and extreme unction.
Lateran IV is important in fact in the historical development of the doctrine of seven
sacraments. "Innocent III formally incorporated the term *transubstantiation* in the decrees

Francis Faces the Pope

The Fourth Lateran Council was still six years off when Francis and his brothers arrived barefoot in Rome in 1209 for their papal appeal. Would Innocent III bend easily to the ground, as Francis had dreamed?

Legends aplenty surround Francis's papal encounter. One story has it that Francis, barefoot and ragged, walked right into Pope Innocent's presence and asked the pope to approve his rule. Francis looked so shabby that the pope pretended he was a poor swineherd. "Leave me alone with your rule!" he said. "Go find your pigs! You can preach all you want to them."

Francis promptly went out, found a pigsty, smeared himself with filth, and then returned. "My lord Pope," Francis said, "I have done as you said. Now please be good enough to grant my request." Taken aback by Francis's bold humility and sincerity, the pope reconsidered. After telling Francis to go wash up, he gave him a second hearing and approved his petition.[17]

Actually, when Francis and the brothers arrived in Rome, he unexpectedly ran into Bishop Guido, also visiting from Assisi. The bishop was surprised to see Francis, but he welcomed him and his companions. Why had they come? They weren't abandoning Assisi, he hoped, for Guido "greatly rejoiced to have such men in his diocese, for he relied most of all on their life and character," says Thomas of Celano.[18]

Francis explained. The bishop approved and said he would help Francis appeal to the pope. Guido was friends with Cardinal John of St. Paul, a Benedictine monk from Saint Paul's-Outside-the-Walls near Rome. John was a person of influence; he had recently been named Cardinal Bishop of Sabina in central Italy, was interested in the church's spiritual renewal, and was a confidant of Innocent III. Cardinal John welcomed Francis and gave him and the brothers lodging.[19]

---

of his Lateran Council." Adrian House, *Francis of Assisi* (Mahwah, NJ: HiddenSpring [Paulist Press], 2001), 253.

[17] Summarized from Englebert, *Saint Francis,* 108. Englebert notes that even if the anecdote is mere legend, it is not implausible, "either on the part of Francis, who sought out humiliation, or on the part of Innocent III, who sometimes used strong words when he was angry."

[18] Thomas of Celano, *Life of St. Francis,* FA:ED 1:210. See also *Anonymous of Perugia,* FA:ED 2:49.

[19] Thomas of Celano, *Life of St. Francis,* FA:ED 1:210; *Anonymous of Perugia,* FA:ED 2:49; Fortini, *Francis of Assisi,* 293. John was an influential member of the Roman Curia and "active in the apostolic movements of the period." FA:ED 1:210 n. b.

Cardinal John was impressed with the young men's fervor, their faith, and commitment. He advised Francis to adopt one of the existing monastic rules—perhaps the Benedictine one. But Francis had something more radical in mind, as his life already showed. John concluded that perhaps the Lord could actually use this new band of sold-out Jesus followers in reforming Christendom.

Cardinal John spoke with other cardinals and with Innocent himself about this surprising new group. Some objected. Living so simply, renouncing all possessions—this was beyond human capacity! John replied that to say Francis's way of life was impossible was to say the gospel itself was impossible.[20]

John set up an audience with Pope Innocent. Other cardinals present at the meeting were wary. Was this upstart from Assisi another Peter Waldo who had stirred up the so-called Poor Men of Lyons? Waldo had died four years earlier, but the church saw his growing body of followers (Waldensians) as troublesome heretics.

Francis and his brothers filed in to meet Innocent III. The pope was frankly impressed by Francis but also cautious. The life Francis proposed seemed "exceptionally hard and severe," Innocent said. He didn't question Francis's calling. But he said, "We must take into consideration those who will come after you lest this way of life seem too burdensome."

After hearing him out, the pope told Francis, "My son, go and pray that God will reveal to you whether what you ask proceeds from His will. In this way, knowing the Lord's will, We may accede to your desires."[21]

Early accounts say Francis went off to pray and ask the Lord to show the pope his will. In response, "the Lord spoke figuratively to [Francis] in spirit," as the *Legend of the Three Companions* puts it. It was a strange parable, and on their next encounter, Francis shared it with the pope. A poor but beautiful woman lived in the wilderness. A great king fell in love with her and married her. Later many handsome sons were born, though the woman and her sons continued to live poorly in the wilderness. When the sons were grown, the mother told them, "Go to the king, and he will provide for you."

So, the sons went to see the king. The king, "struck by their good looks," asked whose sons they were. When they told him who their

---

[20] Rosalind B. Brooke, *Early Franciscan Government: Elias to Bonaventure* (Cambridge: Cambridge University Press, 1959), 60.

[21] Quotations from *Legend of the Three Companions*, FA:ED 2:96–97. See also *Anonymous of Perugia*, FA:ED 2:49–50; Englebert, *Saint Francis*, 113.

mother was, the king "embraced them with great joy" and acknowledged them as his own sons. He took them in and fed them at his table.

"My lord," Francis said to the pope, "I am that little poor woman. The Lord has given me sons. The King of kings has assured me he will care for them."[22]

Hearing this (according to Thomas of Celano), Pope Innocent recalled a dream or vision he himself had a few days earlier. The Lateran Basilica was about to fall down, but a small, simple man propped it up. Here now before him, Innocent realized, was that simple man.[23]

Francis had not written a complete rule, only a simple summary of the Gospel texts through which Jesus had called him, with a few provisions added. Pope Innocent verbally approved this proto-rule, giving Francis and his little community provisional authority to preach and assist in Catholic parishes. Thomas of Celano in his earliest Francis biography writes,

> Exhorting and then warning them about many things, [the pope] blessed ... Francis and his brothers and said to them: "Go with the Lord, brothers, and as the Lord will see fit to inspire you, preach penance to all. When the almighty Lord increases you in number and grace, come back to me with joy, and I will grant you more things than these and, with greater confidence, I will entrust you with greater things."[24]

---

[22] Summarized from *Legend of the Three Companions*, FA:ED 2:97. See also *Anonymous of Perugia*, FA:ED 2:50. Francis's view of gender and the image of God was such that he could easily picture himself as either man or woman in his dreams and visions. Note also Francis's *Rule for Hermitages*—the interchangeable roles of "mothers" and "sons" (chapter 9).

[23] Thomas of Celano, *The Remembrance of the Desire of a Soul* (The Second Life of Saint Francis), FA:ED 2:256. Fortini discusses and recounts the dream in some detail; Fortini, *Francis of Assisi*, 298–300.

[24] Thomas of Celano, *Life of St. Francis*, FA:ED 1:212. "Penance" (*paenitentia*) here may be translated "penitence" or "repentance," or possibly "penance" in the sense of doing specific penitential acts. Here it is best translated "repentance," though the other meanings cannot be excluded, given Catholic understandings of the time. *Cassell's New Latin Dictionary* gives the classical meaning of *poenitentia* as "repentance, regret"; D. P. Simpson, *Cassell's New Latin Dictionary* (New York: Funk and Wagnalls, 1968), 419. Englebert says Francis and his brothers "were given the right to 'preach penitence,' i.e. to address moral exhortations to the people" (*Saint Francis*, 115). Certainly, that included repentance from sin. Francis lived during the period when the Catholic doctrine of penance was still being elaborated; it was further defined by the Fourth Lateran Council. The Council of Trent later confirmed the doctrine that penance was one of the official seven sacraments. Here the meaning certainly is not penance as a sacrament. Penance as a doctrine was one of the issues addressed by the Fourth Lateran Council in 1215.

This step was crucial. Official permission by Rome meant Francis and his brothers were not heretics. They had the right to travel and minister not only in Assisi but beyond, though as yet they had nothing in writing, no papal document to verify their status and claims. In this papal action, as Bret Thoman writes, "charism and institution ... joined hands in complementarity and mutuality to rebuild the church together."[25]

Francis and the brothers now first received the tonsure. The tops of their heads were shaved, leaving a circle of hair just above the ears. This signified their status as *clerics*—not priests or clergy, but people authorized by the church to form a community and preach and serve throughout the church. *The Anonymous of Perugia* says Pope Innocent "gave [Francis] authority to preach everywhere as the grace of the Holy Spirit was given him and that the other brothers were also to preach, provided that blessed Francis gave them the office of preaching." Cardinal John then "had all twelve of them given the tonsure."[26] From this point on, Francis's simple tunic and hood together with the tonsure identified him and his growing band as a distinctive community—then and still today. Other monks also were tonsured, but the Franciscans quickly became identifiable by their simplicity and manner of life as well as their appearance.

His first mission accomplished, Francis was ready to return to Assisi and pursue his major mission. After visiting the tombs of the Apostles, he and the brothers set off barefoot to return home. Full of joy from their welcome by Pope Innocent, "they set out without provisions, preaching in such places as they came upon along their route. People hastened from all

---

[25] Bret Thoman writes, "The encounter between Francis and Innocent was momentous. Francis—a relatively insignificant, highly charismatic, voluntary pauper ... met Pope Innocent III, an ecclesiastical bureaucrat who ruled over the powerful Catholic Church from a throne of opulence. Francis believed that the Holy Spirit was guiding him and would never fail him or his movement.... The pope believed in and worked within the institutional structures of the Holy See." Bret Thoman, *St. Francis of Assisi: Passion, Poverty, and the Man Who Transformed the Catholic Church*, 2nd ed. (Charlotte, NC: TAN Books, 2018), 139–40.

[26] *Anonymous of Perugia*, FA:ED 2:51; see also Lazaro Iriarte, *Franciscan History: The Three Orders of St. Francis of Assisi*, trans. from Spanish by Patricia Ross (Chicago: Franciscan Herald Press, 1982), 7. The word "tonsure" comes from the Latin word *tonsura*, meaning a clipping or shaving. Two other Latin words sometimes are translated "tonsure." The word *clerica*, which literally means "cleric" (from whence "clerk"), can, depending on context, be translated "one who is tonsured." The other term is *corona parvula* (literally, "small ring or crown"). *The Legend of the Three Companions* reads, "Francis and the other eleven brothers were given the tonsure [*tonsura*], as the lord cardinal [John] had arranged, wanting all twelve of them to be clerics" (FA:ED 2:98). See editorial notes, FA:ED 2:51, 98, 549.

parts to hear these preachers who were more severe upon themselves than on anyone else. Members of the secular clergy, monks, learned people, rich even, often mingled in the impromptu audiences gathered in the streets and public places," writes Paul Sabatier.[27]

"Visiting towns and villages, Francis began, with the authority now granted him, to preach passionately and to scatter the seeds of virtue."[28]

On their way back to Assisi the brothers stopped at Orte, a town where the Nera River joins the Tiber, roughly halfway between Rome and Assisi. Finding an ancient cave near the town, they lodged there for about two weeks—talking, reflecting back, looking ahead. They spent time in meditation and prayer. Each day, some would go to town and beg for food.

The brothers discussed their calling. Some wondered if they should focus primarily on a settled life of worship, like the Benedictines and other monastic orders who lived according to the Liturgy of the Hours. Francis discerned, however, that this would be a betrayal of their calling. "The poor knight of Christ must have no abiding place on earth, but wander through the world to win souls to God," as Cuthbert puts it.[29]

And so, the twelve walked on up to Assisi.

---

[27] Sabatier as edited by Sweeney, Paul Sabatier, *The Road to Assisi: The Essential Biography of St. Francis*, ed. Jon M. Sweeney (Brewster, MA: Paraclete Press, 2004), 56.

[28] Thomas of Celano, *Remembrance of the Desire of a Soul*, FA:ED 2:256. It is not totally clear from the sources whether Francis started preaching immediately on the way back to Assisi, or only after his return to Assisi.

[29] Father Cuthbert, OFS. Cap., *Life of St. Francis of Assisi*, 3rd ed. (London: Longmans, Green, 1948), 111.

7

Epidemic of Peace

Brother Thomas of Celano, Francis's first biographer, beautifully summarized the birth of Francis's movement:

> [The Lord] gave Francis companions and followers whom the blessed father formed with sound morals; he taught them to follow the way of evangelical perfection, to take up the title of complete poverty, and to walk the way of holy simplicity. He proclaimed the word of repentance to all and announced the word of God in simple words, but with great heart. At the outset of all his addresses, he proclaimed peace and prefixed all of his letters with a salutation using the word of peace. On account of these things, many people who had previously hated both peace and salvation, with the Lord's cooperation, came to embrace peace with all their heart; they became themselves children of peace and ardent seekers of eternal salvation. Thereafter many men—nobles and commoners, clergy and lay—clung to his footsteps and, rejecting all the world's false airs, they submitted their necks to the yoke of God.[1]

Thomas flags several things that marked the movement from its birth. First, the Lord himself gave Francis his companions. He did not ask people to join him. Young men, sometimes older ones, asked, becoming the first brothers. Some young women wished they could.

---

[1] Thomas of Celano, *The Legend for Use in the Choir*, in *Francis of Assisi: Early Documents*, ed. Regis J. Armstrong, OFM Cap., J. A. Wayne Hellmann, OFM Conv., and William J. Short, OFM (New York: New City Press, 2001), 1:320 [hereafter FA:ED]. See also *Anonymous of Perugia*, FA:ED 2:48.

Second, Francis "formed" these brothers "with sound morals." A process of discipleship, learning by word and example to live the Jesus way as Francis understood it. The brothers were instructed and socialized to be "lesser," learning by what they saw and what they did daily. This was radical, as radical as Francis himself: total poverty and holy simplicity. To Francis, this was "evangelical perfection."

Third, Francis and his brothers were not cloistered. They traveled about proclaiming the good news "in simple words, but with great heart." The brothers were not confined to monasteries, though they established many hermitages as refuges for rest and renewal. In an often-violent age, the age of the Crusades, the Franciscan message was *peace* because of Jesus: peace in and through Jesus.

Fourth, with this winsomeness many youth responded, embracing peace and earnestly seeking salvation. The response among common people was large, soon becoming a movement.

Finally, a remarkably mixed cross-section of people from many different regions became "lesser brothers." Thomas of Celano's comments flag two big social divides: nobles and commoners; clergy and nonclergy. New brothers "submitted their necks to the yoke" of Franciscan vows, rejecting worldly status, and all its "false airs." Francis struggled, however, to instill a sense of total equality among the brothers. Fortini says, "We should note that among [Francis's] first companions, those from the noble classes and from powerful families were predominant."[2]

Ripe for Renewal

Every social movement springs from both inner and outer factors; certainly that was true here. Francis and his little community tapped into an already rising spiritual fervor, a groundswell of spiritual hunger and thirst. Francis was unique, yes, but his movement was part of broader currents. The age was marked by "an emergent lay spirituality, which aspired to the monastic ideal of 'Imitatio Christi' [imitation of Christ] and its pursuit of the gospel-inspired *vita apostolica* [the life of Jesus's first apostles], with emphasis on evangelical poverty."[3]

Already in the century before Francis, renewal currents were stirring. Many longed for a return to the simplicity of early Christianity. This yearning grew into a self-conscious impulse toward reform that led to

---

[2] Arnaldo Fortini, *Francis of Assisi*, trans. Helen Moak (New York: Crossroad Publishing, 1992), 313.

[3] James M. Powell, *Anatomy of a Crusade, 1213–1221* (Philadelphia: University of Pennsylvania Press, 1986), 4.

what historian Marie-Dominique Chenu called "the evangelical awakening of the twelfth century,"[4] especially in the decades just before Francis.

Strange as it may sound to modern ears though, many Christians, led by the papacy and joined by both ecclesiastical and political leaders, viewed the Crusades as themselves pious forms of faithfully following Jesus—exercises in the imitation of Christ (*imitatio Christi*). Military campaigns to control the Holy Land claimed to be emulating Christ just as much as Franciscan and other renewal movements did. Clashing currents were stirring, a way of peace and a way of war, yet all embraced within the medieval understanding of Christian life and ethics. Crusade fervor and personal piety flowed together, sometimes clashing, yet often merged. In 1208, for example, Pope Innocent wrote a strongly worded letter telling Christians in northern Italy that they were guilty of enormous sin if they didn't support the Fifth Crusade.[5]

And Innocent III, the most powerful pope of the Middle Ages, supported Francis. The pope, as well as many bishops and cardinals, hoped the popular preaching of the Lesser Brothers would reignite spiritual fervor and counteract the growing influence of heretical groups like the Cathars.[6]

In short, several currents converged in the early 1200s, preparing the way for Francis's radically obedient Jesus following. The vital energy of the movement, however, came from Francis himself and the dynamism of radical community.

Be Fruitful and Multiply

In a few short years, the number of Franciscan brothers mushroomed from a dozen to thousands. The growth in numbers and geographic spread of Francis's *fratres minores,* "lesser brothers," astonishes. Other movements, particularly the Order of Preachers (Dominicans), which Pope Innocent approved six years after Francis's approval, grew and spread about the same time.[7] But really the church had never seen anything like the Franciscans.

Several critical currents converged that gave shape to Francis's movement. Francis sent teams of brothers into new areas, prompting

---

[4] Marie-Dominique Chenu, *Nature, Man and Society in the Twelfth Century*, trans. Jerome Taylor and Lester K. Little (Chicago: University of Chicago Press, 1968).

[5] Charles Edward Smith, *Innocent III: Church Defender* (Baton Rouge: Louisiana State University Press, 1951), 178, summarizing Pope Innocent's letter of December 1208.

[6] This point is brought out in the movie *Brother Sun, Sister Moon*.

[7] Dominic (1170–1221), a priest born in Spain, founded his order in France in 1215 to counteract the influence of the Cathars (Albigenses) and other heretical groups. Pope Innocent approved the order in 1216.

other youth to join. The Portiuncula remained the base, but gradually new communities of brothers formed elsewhere. Francis began holding periodic general meetings, "chapters," at the Portiuncula to maintain cohesion and give direction. Francis himself set out on his first mission to Muslims. In 1212 Clare of Assisi sought out Francis, asking to join. This led to the founding of the Poor Ladies of San Damiano, as we will see shortly.

Yet in these early years, the Franciscans were functioning with only the pope's verbal assent. That approval was of course known to cardinals, bishops, and most priests. A formally approved rule would not come for another dozen years.

When Francis and his brothers returned from Rome after receiving the pope's approval, they again made the Portiuncula near Assisi their primary base as they ministered throughout the area. Over the next months, the little community developed its pattern of shared common life.

As winter came on,[8] the brothers decided to move from the Portiuncula to an abandoned shack along the Rivo Torto, a few miles away, near the highway leading to Rome.[9] "It was too cold for the twelve companions to stay in the hut in the Portiuncula forest," says Fortini.[10] Rivo Torto ("twisting" or "tortuous stream") flows down into the valley below Assisi, not far from the Portiuncula. The shack was small for twelve men, but it was safe from rain, and the brothers made do. "Francis wrote their names with chalk on the beams so that when they wished to pray or rest, each might find his place."[11]

The brothers had no regular food source. They survived by begging from homes and farms. Sometimes their food was mainly turnips.[12] They spent their days helping farmers in their fields or visiting leper colonies. Evenings and early mornings they devoted to prayer together or separately. No doubt they also shared the day's experiences and discussed their life together, their mission, the meaning of discipleship. They got more fully acquainted and grew more deeply bonded.

---

[8] Late 1209, it seems.

[9] Paul Sabatier, *The Road to Assisi: The Essential Biography of St. Francis*, ed. Jon M. Sweeney (Brewster, MA: Paraclete Press, 2004), 57. Sabatier says the cabin "had served as a leper hospital." If so, it must have been a very small one. Vauchez calls it "a hovel." André Vauchez, *Francis of Assisi, the Life and Afterlife of a Medieval Saint*, trans. Michael F. Cusato (New Haven, CT: Yale University Press, 2012), 45.

[10] Fortini, *Francis of Assisi*, 291. Fortini pinpoints the location by means of maps and the Assisi archives.

[11] Omer Englebert, *Saint Francis of Assisi*, 2nd English ed., trans. Eve Marie Cooper (Chicago: Franciscan Herald Press, 1965), 117; see Thomas of Celano, *Life of St. Francis*, FA:ED 1:221.

[12] Thomas of Celano, *Life of St. Francis*, FA:ED 1:220.

Francis was teaching them what he himself was learning through prayer and their shared times of worship. Early biographers say that despite the hardships, these were some of the happiest days of the little community; "since they had nothing, they loved nothing; so they feared losing nothing."[13]

The brothers did suffer hardships, though. Francis taught them to welcome suffering as a blessing and a virtue. Sometimes the brothers took this too far, so Francis taught them balance. "He made it a rule for them not to chastize [sic] their bodies except when the body persisted in its laziness and negligence."[14]

One night as the brothers were sleeping, Francis was awakened by someone groaning. "I'm dying!" cried out a young brother.

Francis quickly got up, woke the others, and asked for a light. "Who is dying?" Francis asked.

"I am!" moaned the brother.

"What are you dying from?" Francis asked.

"Hunger!" the brother cried.

Francis quickly roused the others and told them to set the table and prepare a meal. "We can't let this 'dying brother' suffer alone or be ashamed to eat alone," Francis said. The brothers enjoyed a midnight meal together, and the "dying" brother was heartened. Francis warned the brothers not to try to imitate him in his fasting. "I have duties the rest of you don't," he said, "and besides, I simply need less food than you do."[15]

"Each of you must pay attention to his own nature," Francis added, "for some may be strong enough to thrive on less food than others. You are not bound to imitate those who need less. Let each give his body what it requires in order to be strong enough to serve the spirit. Beware of too much abstinence. It is just as much a sin to deprive the body of what it really needs as to be a glutton and eat too much. The Lord desires mercy and not sacrifice."[16]

Despite Francis's warnings, some brothers in their newfound zeal, and given current ideals of perfection and self-denial, did take things too far. Some "mortified their bodies excessively" by fasting, long vigils,

---

[13] Thomas of Celano, *Life of St. Francis*, FA:ED 1:218.

[14] Englebert, *Saint Francis*, 124.

[15] Summarized from *Assisi Compilation*, FA:ED 2:149; Thomas of Celano, *Remembrance*, FA:ED 2:259; Englebert, *Saint Francis*, 123; Father Cuthbert, OFS Cap., *Life of St. Francis of Assisi*, 3rd ed. (London: Longmans, Green, 1948), 120. Francis had doubtless reached a lower "set point" in his metabolism where he in fact felt less need for food.

[16] Paraphrased from *Assisi Compilation*, FA:ED 2:149; Thomas of Celano, *Remembrance*, FA:ED 2:259; Englebert, *Saint Francis*, 123; Cuthbert, *Life of St. Francis*, 120–21.

and cold temperatures. Some even wore iron rings or painful hair shirts (made of goat hair, horsehair, or rough cloth) next to their skin. The *Mirror of Perfection* reports, "Considering that the brothers could get sick because of this, and in a short time some were already ailing, [Francis] commanded in one of the chapters that no brother wear anything next to his skin except the tunic."[17]

This is significant. Some sources even today claim Francis himself wore a rough hair shirt at the time of his conversion and later. There is no credible evidence of this. The available evidence actually points in the opposite direction.

The early sources do report,

> We who were with him bear witness to this fact about him: from the time he began to have brothers, and also during his whole lifetime, he was discerning with the brothers, provided that in the matter of food and other things, they did not deviate at any time from the norm of the poverty and decency of our religion, which the early brothers observed. Nevertheless, even before he had brothers, from the beginning of his conversion and during his whole lifetime, he was severe with his own body, even though from the time of his youth he was a man of a frail and weak constitution, and when he was in the world [before his conversion] he could not live without comforts.[18]

One day in September 1209 while the brothers were staying at Rivo Torto, a big procession from Germany with thousands of knights passed nearby. This was the German King Otto IV and his entourage, on their way to meet Pope Innocent III in Rome. Otto, then about thirty-five, became sole king of Germany a couple years earlier. He expected to receive the pope's blessing and be crowned ruler of the whole Holy Roman Empire. In exchange, he promised the pope he would restore large areas of central Italy, including Assisi and the Umbrian Valley, to papal rule.[19]

Francis and the brothers heard the commotion. But Francis didn't want to see the spectacle. He sent one of the brothers to go and call out

---

[17] *Mirror of Perfection* (Sabatier ed.), FA:ED 3:279; similarly, *The Mirror of Perfection* (Lemmens ed.), FA:ED 3:234; *Assisi Compilation*, FA:ED 2:150.

[18] *Assisi Compilation*, FA:ED 2:150; *Mirror of Perfection* (Lemmens ed.), FA:ED 3:234; similarly, *Mirror of Perfection* (Sabatier ed.), FA:ED 3:279.

[19] This was all part of a very complex set of interactions and negotiations between Pope Innocent, Otto, Otto's uncle King John of England, and several rulers, cardinals, and others in positions of power. Various agreements were reached but not observed; promises were made, then broken.

to Otto that all this earthly glory was mere vanity and would not last.[20] This scene is hilariously portrayed in the movie *Brother Sun, Sister Moon.*

The brother's words to Otto proved prophetic. He was in fact crowned Holy Roman Emperor by Innocent III in October 1209, but the next year the pope excommunicated him for breaking his pledges. Innocent arranged for the young Frederick II (born in Italy and just fifteen at the time) to replace Otto as Holy Roman Emperor, as his father and grandfather (Frederick I) had been.[21]

As more and more youth joined the brothers, Francis assigned them to various places of service in the surrounding area. He would "clothe them with the habit and cord and then entrust them to some monastery or church, because the brothers as yet had no [adequate] place of their own to live. He would command such brothers to devotedly serve God and the church in which he had placed them, performing the tasks assigned to them, so as not to eat the bread of idleness."[22] Lesser Brothers must serve the church.

About this time the canons of Assisi's cathedral, San Rufino, invited Francis to preach. This may have been the first time. Soon he was preaching there regularly on Sunday mornings and occasionally in other churches as well. Typically, Francis walked up from Rivo Torto to Assisi on Saturday afternoons, about an hour's walk, and spent the night in a hut in the canons' garden next to the cathedral. Here he had time to meditate and prepare.[23] Then in the morning he preached in San Rufino, still a new building, bright with the rose-pink tinge of its stones from Mount Subasio.[24]

These were not the first times Francis preached in public, of course. As noted in chapter 4, Francis's first public sermon in or at a church

---

[20] Thomas of Celano, *Life of St. Francis*, FA:ED 1:221; Englebert, *Saint Francis*, 125; Fortini, *Francis of Assisi*, 295–96; Cuthbert, *Life of St. Francis*, 113. Some sources put this incident a year later, in 1210.

[21] Fortini, *Francis of Assisi*, 295–96, 309; Englebert, *Saint Francis*, 125. Frederick II was actually baptized in Assisi in a major ceremony in the San Rufino cathedral, and Fortini presents evidence that Frederick was in fact born in Assisi's Rocca Maggiore fortress. Fortini, 108–9.

[22] Thomas of Pavia, *The Deeds of the Emperors and Popes* (c. 1272–80), FA:ED 3:793. Thomas attributes this information to Brother Stephen, one of the early brothers. The editors of *Francis of Assisi: Early Documents* comment, "This information, related in no other early source, is of significant importance in understanding the very early years of the brotherhood." FA:ED 3:793 n. c.

[23] Bonaventure, *The Major Legend of Saint Francis*, FA:ED 2:551–52. Francis "one Saturday ... entered the city of Assisi to preach in the cathedral on Sunday morning, as was his custom," Bonaventure writes. Also Fortini, *Francis of Assisi*, 307; Englebert, *Saint Francis*, 133–34.

[24] Sabatier, *Road to Assisi*, 58.

building was at San Giorgio, his earlier parish church.[25] He had already started preaching out of doors. Still, this was a significant new step: preaching regularly before a Christian congregation in Assisi's cathedral, even though he was not a priest or trained Bible teacher or theologian. No doubt word of the pope's approval, amounting to a commission, had spread rapidly in Assisi and elsewhere.

Francis preached Jesus. His theme was always peace. Peace was especially relevant in these days of ongoing spats with Perugia and also between factions in Assisi itself: inner peace and outer peace, as Francis both taught and modeled.[26] "Those Sunday sermons in the Cathedral, backed by the life of the brethren at Rivo-Torto, were working their way into the conscience of the city.... Assisi was coming to acknowledge a prophet in its son and submit to his sweet guidance."[27] Some writers claim Francis's preaching was key to a peace pact between nobles and the town's leaders signed in Assisi on November 9, 1210. We lack clear historical evidence, though Francis's preaching doubtless had some pacifying effect on the town, as it did elsewhere.[28]

Meanwhile, Francis continued forming and teaching the brothers at Rivo Torto. His care for the brothers has often been described as maternal, mother-like. Francis himself often used the image. He seemed intuitively to read each brother's concerns, moods, even temptations. Francis was building community and mutual understanding and empathy—a spiritual, social, and economic formation. "The fraternity was [just] at the beginning of a corporate consciousness," as Cuthbert put it.[29]

But the brothers' stay at Rivo Torto was drawing to a close. One day a man showed up, leading a donkey. Coming to the cabin door, the man said to his donkey, "Get inside! Here's a good place for us!" Perhaps the man, a resident of the area, didn't like the brothers monopolizing the cabin and wanted them to leave.

In any case, Francis told the brothers they should go, leaving the cabin to the man and his donkey. The brothers returned to the Portiuncula, closer to Assisi.[30]

---

[25] Thomas of Celano, *Life of St. Francis*, FA:ED 1:202.

[26] Englebert rightly notes that the theme of peace "was timely, for more than ever, Assisians were at one another's throats and at sword's point with their neighbors." Englebert, *Saint Francis*, 134.

[27] Cuthbert, *Life of St. Francis*, 119.

[28] Fortini gives considerable background in *Francis of Assisi*, 309–15; see also Englebert, *Saint Francis*, 134–35.

[29] Cuthbert, *Life of St. Francis*, 121.

[30] Thomas of Celano, *Life of St. Francis*, FA:ED 1:222.

At the Portiuncula

Saint Mary of the Angels (the Portiuncula) was dear to Francis's heart. Not only had he repaired the chapel with his own hands. Even more significant was the fact that Jesus spoke to him here, clarifying the call to "Go, repair my house" he received at San Damiano. But Francis had no permission to stay at the Portiuncula or to turn it into a longer-term residence.[31]

Francis discussed the matter with Bishop Guido. Both the bishop and the San Rufino cathedral had several church buildings and properties under their jurisdiction. Neither Guido nor the cathedral was willing to offer property to Francis and his new community, however.

So, Francis walked further up Mount Subasio to the Benedictine monastery. Would the Benedictines grant Francis the use of the Portiuncula on an ongoing basis?

Saint Mary of the Portiuncula was "the poorest and smallest church that the monastery had under its jurisdiction."[32] The Benedictines agreed to give it to Francis for the brothers' extended use. Francis was overjoyed, for the place matched his own spirit and aims. He didn't want to accept the Portiuncula without some payment, though. So, he arranged to send the Benedictines a basket of fish annually on the feast of Saint Benedict. The Benedictines in turn said they would send a jar of oil in receipt.[33]

So, Francis and the brothers settled into the Portiuncula, the wooded property where Francis had stayed when he was rebuilding the structure. In addition to the small chapel, the property consisted of a thatched-roof cabin and several small clay-and-wattle huts, all surrounded by a hedge that enclosed also a small garden. The cabin served as the brothers' community house, a place to gather, converse, and share meals. Much of their time was spent working in the fields and, soon enough, on missionary journeys. But when at the Portiuncula, they followed the monastic practice of the Liturgy of the Hours, including the chanting of Psalms.[34]

According to *The Assisi Compilation*, "As soon as the brothers went to stay [at the Portiuncula], almost daily the Lord increased their number; and their fame and reputation spread throughout the whole valley."[35] The

---

[31] Thomas of Celano, *Life of St. Francis*, FA:ED 1:222. See chapter 4, above.

[32] Fortini, *Francis of Assisi*, 308.

[33] *Assisi Compilation*, FA:ED 2:154–55; Fortini, *Francis of Assisi*, 308; also Englebert, *Saint Francis*, 136.

[34] Englebert, *Saint Francis*, 137. "For shelter they built a few huts of mud and branches round the little chapel of Santa Maria degli Angeli." Lazaro Iriarte, *Franciscan History: The Three Orders of St. Francis of Assisi*, trans. from Spanish by Patricia Ross (Chicago: Franciscan Herald Press, 1982), 7.

[35] *Assisi Compilation*, FA:ED 2:155.

Portiuncula quickly became the center of the Franciscan movement; "the head and mother church of the entire Franciscan order."[36]

Daily, by word and example, Francis taught the brothers. Many did not yet know the set prayers of the church that made up the Daily Office, used in monasteries and in church services. When some of the brothers asked Francis how to pray, he told them, "When you pray, say 'Our Father' [that is, the Lord's Prayer] and 'We adore you, O Christ, in all your churches throughout the whole world, and we bless you, for by your holy cross you have redeemed the world.'"

Thomas adds,

> In this way holy simplicity filled them,
> innocence of life taught them,
> and purity of heart so possessed them
> that they were completely ignorant of duplicity of heart.
> For just as there was in them one faith,
> so there was one spirit,
> one will, one charity, continual unity of spirit,
> harmony in living, cultivation of virtues,
> agreement of minds, and loyalty in actions.[37]

This somewhat idealized portrait may be overstated, but it rings true to the experience of virtually all the early brothers.

The Character of Community

Church leaders, travelers, and scholars began noticing Francis's new community. Historian Lazaro Iriarte writes that "foreign chroniclers of the period" in their reports about these early Franciscans "emphasize the *novitas* [innovative novelty] of the movement initiated by Francis and the life style of his Order."[38] Iriarte adds,

> To [Francis's] personal spiritual experience was added his awareness as a founder, which came to him very clearly as soon as he was joined by companions. He did not draw inspiration from earlier forms of the religious life, nor did he need to be told by others what the group's way of life should be. Right until the end of his life he vigorously defended the originality of his

---

[36] Fortini, *Francis of Assisi*, 309.

[37] Thomas of Celano, *Life of St. Francis*, FA:ED 1:223. "Virtue" and the cultivation of the virtues and avoidance of vices is a frequent theme in the writings about Francis, reflecting the spiritualty and theology of medieval Christianity.

[38] Iriarte, *Franciscan History*, 9.

evangelical vocation against the claims of those who would have imposed alien patterns on him....

[Francis] was enabled by his instinct for following the Gospel to find a place within the social and religious framework of his time. For him, *leaving the world* ... did not mean shutting himself in a cloister, but offering to that society, which was engrossed in crafts and commerce, the living and immediate evidence of Christian conversion: a *penitential* presence. The Friars Minor would live among the people; they would become integrated with social reality by means of paid work, prayer with the Christian community, and preaching in the vernacular. And, in contrast with the new arbiters of society and their lust for gain, they would display total detachment, especially where money was concerned.[39]

Six marks, especially, distinguished the early Franciscan movement:

1. *Devout spirituality.* The Franciscans practiced inner and outward spiritual vitality and devotion, living out the medieval ideal of *pietas,* piety. Contemplation plus practical service set the rhythm of life together. The brothers sought in every way to follow Jesus, to be true and loving children of God, led by the Spirit. "Simplicity and joy were an essential part of the distinctively Christian tone of the brotherhood."[40]

The little community used simplified forms of traditional church practices. Most of the brothers "did not know the Church office," notes Thomas of Celano.[41] That is, they were unfamiliar with the church's daily set prayers marking the daily liturgical hours. Traditionally there were eight such hours: *Matins* (very early morning), *Lauds, Prime, Terce, Sext* (noon), *None, Vespers,* and *Compline,* just before retiring.[42] Under normal circumstances, the brothers were to observe all eight.

---

[39] Iriarte, *Franciscan History,* 9. The phrase "leaving the world" is from Francis's own *Testament,* his final personal testimony.

[40] Iriarte, *Franciscan History,* 10.

[41] Thomas of Celano, *Life of St. Francis,* FA:ED 1:222.

[42] As developed in Benedictine and other monastic orders from earlier precedents among the Desert Fathers, *Matins* (also called Vigil) occurred about 2 a.m.; *Lauds* (dawn prayer) about 5 a.m., but varying with the seasons; *Prime* (that is First Hour) about 6 a.m.; *Terce* about 9 a.m.; *Sext* ("sixth hour") at noon; *None* ("ninth hour") about 3 p.m.; *Vespers* (evening prayer) around 6 p.m.; and *Compline* just before retiring (about 7 p.m.). Benedict of Nursia (c. 480–c. 547), founder of the Benedictine Order, associated this practice with Psalm 119, verses 164 ("Seven times a day I praise you") and 62 ("At midnight I rise to praise you"). In monasteries this order of hours structured the entire day, as it still does in many.

Canonical Hours (Liturgy of the Hours, Divine Office)

Approximate Time	Name of Hour
2:00 a.m.	Matins
5:00 a.m.	Lauds (varies with the seasons)
6:00 a.m.	Prime (First Hour)
9:00 a.m.	Terce (Third Hour)
Noon	Sext (Sixth Hour)
3:00 p.m.	None (Ninth Hour)
6:00 p.m.	Vespers
7:00 p.m.	Compline (may vary with seasons)

"Seven times a day I praise you"—Psalm 119:164
"At midnight I rise to praise you."—Psalm 119:62

Priests who became brothers did of course know the prayers. Francis instructed the brothers who did not know them to pray the Lord's Prayer several times at each stated hour. The brothers' calling was to work and participate in society, however; they were not to lead a cloistered life. Liturgical prayers assisted the brothers in their various ministries but were not the central focus.

The brothers also practiced private prayer in ways that suited them, which might mean praying outside in nearby woods. They followed a modified fast during Lent and practiced the monastic Wednesday and Friday fasts. Beyond this there were no restrictions on diet; they could eat "whatever food was set before them."[43]

2. *Total poverty.* Francis embraced radical poverty and humility as essential to this renewed gospel life. "Poverty meant not only giving up material good and legal powers, but a total commitment to evangelical insecurity as a group" for the sake of loving and serving others.[44] The brothers were bound by rule and vocation to live "As pilgrims and strangers in this world [1 Pet. 2:11], serving the Lord in poverty and humility," seeking nothing except to love and serve, including caring for one another.[45]

---

[43] Iriarte, *Franciscan History,* 10.
[44] Iriarte, *Franciscan History,* 10.
[45] "The Later Rule" (1223), chap. 6, FA:ED 1:103.

Since the brothers did not live in monasteries, but rather in informal communities, their poverty did not mean uniformity in their life together. Consistent with Francis's original calling, their ideal was "the apostolic life." Their model was the apostles whom Jesus sent out to preach, heal, and serve lepers and the poor (Matt. 10:8–9; Luke 9:2). This way of life "gave the group as a whole complete release for the Kingdom," as Iriarte nicely puts it.[46]

3. *Brotherhood of equality*. From the first, Francis called the group a *fraternity*, brotherhood, a community of "lesser brothers" (*fratres minores*). "In this fraternity there was total equality among the brethren, without distinction of any kind, not even by virtue of holy ordination."[47] Francis himself simply *transcended* all the accepted social divisions, levels, stratifications of his day and culture.

This brotherly fraternity extended to all people, men and women, and in fact to the whole creation, all centered in Brother Jesus.

In practice, however, this ideal was hard to maintain.

4. *Minimal structure*. The Franciscan community was to be a close community, a fellowship, not a formally structured organization or hierarchy.

Francis had written in his first Rule, the one Innocent III originally approved orally, "let all the brothers not have power or control" over one another "for, as the Lord says in the Gospel: 'the rulers of the Gentiles lord it over them and the great ones make their authority over them felt; it shall not be so among the brothers. Let whoever wishes to be the greater among them be their minister and servant. Let whoever is the greater among them become the least.'" Rather, "through the charity of the Spirit, let them serve and obey one another voluntarily."[48]

As Iriarte notes, "The whole motive force of the fraternity flowed from the person of Francis, who was not so much the superior as the pattern and spiritual master of them all. Until the novitiate was introduced in 1220, new friars entered the Order [simply] by donning the habit with its [cord belt]; they gave proof of their evangelical vocation by giving up all their goods and ministering to lepers."[49]

---

[46] Iriarte, *Franciscan History*, 11.
[47] Iriarte, *Franciscan History*, 11.
[48] "The Earlier Rule" (1210–1221), chap. 5, FA:ED 1:67–68.
[49] Iriarte, *Franciscan History*, 11. See also Cajetan Esser, OFM, *Origins of the Franciscan Order*, trans. Aedan Daly and Irina Lynch (Chicago: Franciscan Herald Press), 24–26. From the beginning Francis understood his brothers to constitute an "order" within the church, though uniquely different from all existing ones because of its radical poverty and equality.

This equality and community was one of the things observers found most remarkable.

5. *Living by manual labor.* The brothers constantly engaged in physical work—helping farmers and others, caring for lepers, tending their garden, even hiring themselves out as day laborers, though always receiving payment in kind, never money.

If manual work did not produce enough food, Francis told them to go out begging, as he himself did. They should view begging as a grace, not a shame. Franciscans were not, however, to be a "mendicant" order, living exclusively or primarily by begging or by alms (the meaning of "mendicant").[50] Francis insisted on this. Iriarte notes,

> On entering the fraternity the brothers did not give up their former profession or craft [unlike other orders], but continued to practice it as a means of earning their bread and giving service. . . . For this purpose they were allowed to keep the tools or instruments of their trade. Others found work as servants or helped farmers in the fields. . . . The favorite occupation, however, was caring for lepers, with whom they shared whatever they obtained either by working or by begging. During the day they worked, preached, or asked for alms; at night they would take shelter at some hermitage, in a leper colony, or in church porches, unless some charitable person offered them hospitality.[51]

6. *Gospel proclamation, especially by example.* Preaching—most of all, by way of life—was essential. The goal of preaching was *conversion*, persuading men and women to turn from sin or careless living and be like Jesus. Brothers who were priests were allowed to do doctrinal preaching, but always with the deeper goal of Christian discipleship.

The brothers balanced their preaching and service in society with times of quiet contemplation—daily, of course, but also over longer periods. Francis modeled and taught the brothers to spend some time away in hermitages. There they would be among trees or flowers or along streams, together with birds and others of God's manifold creatures.

One time some brothers were staying at the hermitage of Monte Casale, about fifty miles northwest of Assisi. A band of robbers was active

---

[50] Historians often include the Franciscans among the church's mendicant orders, but this is misleading.

[51] Iriarte, *Franciscan History*, 12. In keeping with the vow of poverty, tools were not considered to be personal possessions but simply part of the community's necessary means of subsistence, like a gospel book or psaltery.

in the area, but they never attacked the Lesser Brothers, knowing they were very poor. Sometimes they did come to the hermitage, begging bread.

What to do? Some brothers said, "It is not right to give them alms because they are robbers and they do many very great evil things to people." Other brothers said, "Well, they beg humbly, and they're in great need." Sometimes the brothers would give them alms but always admonishing the robbers to repent and be converted.

About this time, Francis himself arrived. The brothers asked him what he thought.

Francis said, "If you do as I tell you, I trust in the Lord that you will win their souls." Francis told them to get some good bread and wine and take them to the robbers' hideout in the woods. Spread a tablecloth on the ground and put the food on it. Then call out, "Come, Brother Robbers, come to us, because we are brothers and we are bringing you some good bread and good wine." Then when they come, "humbly and joyfully wait on them." Afterward, the brothers should tell them the good news of Jesus. They should get the robbers to promise that they would never strike or injure anyone.

"Do not ask for everything at once," Francis advised, "or they will not listen. Because of the humility and love you show them, they will make the promise."

Do the same the next day, Francis said. Serve the robbers not only bread and wine, but also eggs and cheese. Again, the brothers should wait on the robbers as they eat.

After the meal, the brothers should say, "Why do you stay here all day long, dying of hunger, suffering many evil things and in your actions doing many evil things for which you will lose your souls unless you are converted? It is better to serve the Lord who will both supply your bodily needs in this world and save your souls in the end." Many will hear and convert, Francis said, because of the brothers' loving humility.

The brothers did as Francis said. God's grace settled on the robbers, and they did as they were urged. The robbers even started carrying wood to the hermitage. Many repented and began to live by the work of their own hands. Some even became Lesser Brothers.

The brothers were amazed at Francis—his spirit and advice, the fact that he had rightly foreseen how the robbers would respond, and how quickly the robbers did in fact convert to the Lord.[52]

---

[52] Summarized from *Assisi Compilation*, FA:ED 2:221–22; *The Mirror of Perfection* (Lemmens ed.), FA:ED 3:250–51; *Mirror of Perfection* (Sabatier ed.), FA:ED 3:310–11.

More and more, the active life of preaching and witness included missionary journeys not only within the church but to Muslims and nonbelievers in other lands. From the first, Francis understood that his Lesser Brothers must have a world mission.

Brother Giles later recalled, "When there were only seven of us in the Order," Francis gathered the brothers together in the woods at the Portiuncula and said, "I know, my dearest brothers, that the Lord has called us not only for our own salvation. Therefore, I want us to scatter among the nations, going about the world spreading the word of God and giving an example of virtue."[53]

In his thorough study *Origins of the Franciscan Order,* Franciscan scholar Cajetan Esser stresses the social uniqueness of Francis's community. Early reports note that "the Friars Minor came from all walks of life without distinction," Esser says. He adds,

> In the early Franciscan literature, no particular notice is taken of differences of origin on the basis of class or occupation. Whether nobles or peasants, rich or poor, learned or unlearned, cleric or laic, "let all in general be called Friars Minor."[54] In the new *fraternitas* of St. Francis, class and origin played no part. This attitude completely undermined medieval class-consciousness which regarded the existing social order as being ultimately of divine institution.[55]

Esser then quotes from Celano: "Francis and his brothers felt great gladness and unique joy whenever one of the faithful, led by the Spirit of God, came and accepted the habit of holy religion, whoever the person might be: rich or poor, noble or insignificant, wise or simple, cleric or illiterate, a layman of the Christian people."[56] Thomas "could hardly have given a more complete enumeration of class distinctions," Esser observes. "But all differences pale into insignificance before the one requirement that the newcomer should belong to the 'Christian people.' This alone is decisive for acceptance into the fraternity of the

---

[53] *A Book of Exemplary Stories* (c. 1280–1310), FA:ED 3:799–800.
[54] "The Earlier Rule," FA:ED 1:68. Esser's quotation comes from an older translation; the newer one in *Francis of Assisi: Early Documents* reads, "Let no one be called 'prior' but let everyone in general be called a lesser brother. Let one wash the feet of the other." Francis clearly refers to Jesus's words as found in Matthew 23:8, Luke 22:26, and John 13:14.
[55] Esser, *Origins,* 34.
[56] Thomas of Celano, *Life of St. Francis,* FA:ED 1:209.

Friars Minor, even though it gave cause for 'great wonder ... among people in the world.'"[57]

This, says Esser, was "the new concept of St. Francis and the Friars Minor," sharply contrasting with typical attitudes. Thomas of Celano noted, "No lowliness of birth, no weakness of poverty stood in the way of building up in God's work the ones God wanted to build up, a God who delights to be with the simple and those rejected by the world."[58] Esser concludes, "Here, the earlier social order is plainly characterized as deriving 'from the world'" and thus "an obstacle to God's free operation and contrary to the example Christ himself had given on earth. The *fraternitas* of St. Francis springs from the fundamental fact that with God there is no personal favoritism (Rom. 2:11)."[59]

Francis himself modeled this equality as best he could. All brothers were tonsured, but Francis refused to have the larger tonsure that signified priestly ordination. Thomas of Celano noted that whenever Francis had his head shaved, he would always tell the barber, "Be careful: don't give me a big tonsure! I want my simple [non-clergy] brothers to have a share in my head!" Francis wanted "the Order to be held in common by the poor and illiterate and not just by the learned and rich," Thomas notes. Francis would say, "With God there is no respecting of persons, and the Holy Spirit, the [true] general minister" of our Order "rests equally upon the poor and simple." Francis wanted to include these very words in the Rule, but the pope would not permit this when the Rule was finalized in 1223.[60]

Observers outside the Order found the social leveling of the Franciscan community remarkable, a surprising contrast with the prevailing social order.

Growth Brings Structure

News of the new community spread quickly. Youth from various lands— England, Spain, Germany, others—sought out Francis, asking to join his growing band. Early on God gave Francis a vision of the order's growth and diversity.

Statistics are imprecise, but clearly the "fraternity grew rapidly in the first decade of its life," notes Iriarte. At the community's general meeting in 1221 the brothers numbered somewhere between two thousand five

---

[57] Esser, *Origins*, 35 (the last phrase quoted from Thomas of Celano).
[58] Thomas of Celano, *Life of St. Francis*, FA:ED 1:209–10.
[59] Esser, *Origins*, 35.
[60] Thomas of Celano, *Remembrance*, FA:ED 2:371, cited also by Esser, *Origins*, 35.

hundred and three thousand. Just a year later, the fraternity had grown to between four and five thousand. This is not just growth; it is explosion. Such "uncontrolled growth," as Iriarte calls it, no doubt included some "indiscriminate admission of candidates." Rapid growth and issues of discernment became a huge challenge for Francis and for the Order, whose structures were just evolving.[61]

As the number of brothers grew, Francis sometimes cited the lives of his earliest converts as models of the ideal Lesser Brother. "The good Friar Minor," Francis said, "ought to love poverty like Brother Bernard and prayer like Brother Rufino, who prays even when he is asleep. He ought to be lost in God as [is] Brother Giles, as courteous as Brother Angelo, and as patient as Brother Juniper, that perfect imitator of Christ crucified. He ought to possess the purity and innocence of Brother Leo, the good manners and common sense of Brother Masseo, and finally, by his charity and detachment from the world, resemble Brother Lucido who never stays more than a month in the same place, asserting that we have no lasting home on earth."[62]

The more brothers, the more diverse they were. Not only the uneducated joined; increasing numbers of learned men became brothers. Francis told a parable about two brothers preaching before a large gathering of the Order. One was wise and learned; the other was simple and unlettered. Yet Jesus's spirit inspired both to preach edifying words of God.

Then Francis explained. Our fraternity has become large, he said.

> [It is now] like a general council gathered together from every part of the world under a single form of life. In it the learned can draw from the simple to their own advantage when they see the unlettered seeking the things of heaven with fiery vigor and those not taught by men knowing the spiritual things by the Spirit. In it even the simple turn to their advantage what belongs to the learned, when they see outstanding men, who could live with great honor anywhere in the world, humble themselves to the same level with themselves. Here is where the beauty of this

[61] Iriarte, *Franciscan History*, 15. Iriarte calls the estimates of three thousand in 1221 and five thousand in 1222 "doubtless exaggerated," yet notes that "Chroniclers from outside the Order also record this amazing expansion." Iriarte cites the work of Cajetan Esser.

[62] *A Mirror of the Perfection of the Status of a Lesser Brother* (1318; Sabatier ed., 1928), FA:ED 3:333, as paraphrased and condensed in Englebert, *Saint Francis*, 137.

blessed family shines; a diverse beauty that gives great pleasure to the father of the family.[63]

But more and more brothers, and Francis himself, started to see that some fixed organization and structure was necessary. Francis alone could not shepherd and guide a movement whose numbers were reaching into the thousands and who were scattered across regions speaking a mix of local languages.

Growth and the practical concerns of communication and coordination led to three strategic structural innovations between about 1217 and 1226, that is, beginning about five or six years after the brothers took up residence at the Portiuncula. Francis was adamant that he did *not* want his fraternity to become another traditional religious order, like the Cistercians or Benedictines. He wanted something much more mobile and dynamic, more radical, suited to the new age that was dawning. The Franciscans would not be cloistered or highly structured. But they would develop some functional forms. Three key innovations were adopted: periodic general meetings ("chapters"), geographic division into provinces, and a more fully elaborated and papally approved Rule.

Several of the heterodox movements of the day—especially the Waldenses and Cathars—preached a return to the simplicity and authenticity of the early church, as Francis himself did. But the Roman Church viewed these groups as dangerous heretics. Francis and his brothers pledged and lived out fidelity to the official church, including her doctrines and sacraments and the pope. For this reason, most church leaders viewed them favorably.

Annual Gatherings (Chapters)

For the first few years, Francis gathered all the brothers round him twice a year at the Portiuncula. They met at Pentecost and at the feast of Saint Michael the Archangel (Michaelmas, September 29). Almost from the beginning, Francis had started sending brothers out on missions of mercy and preaching, as we saw. Before long he wanted to see them again, hear how they were doing. This gave rise to reunions of all the brothers, usually at the Portiuncula.

These gatherings or family reunions were called chapters. As numbers grew, Francis reduced the gatherings to once a year, Pentecost only. From

---

[63] Thomas of Celano, *Remembrance*, FA:ED 2:370.

that point on, the Pentecost Chapter became the order's major annual celebration. Every brother attended who possibly could.

Chapters normally happened at the Portiuncula in the early years, though one of the earliest was held at the Benedictine monastery of San Verecondo near the town of Gubbio, about fifty miles north of Assisi—perhaps the same monastery where Francis spent a few days when he fled Assisi after renouncing his father's wealth. The Benedictine monks graciously hosted the brothers, who on this occasion numbered about three hundred.[64] An eyewitness reported that the Benedictine brothers "graciously provided them, as best they could, with the necessities of life ... there was plenty of barley and wheat bread, as well as millet and sorghum, pure water to drink, and apple wine diluted for the infirm," as well as "ample supplies of beans and peas."[65]

The main purpose of the chapters was to build unity and nurture their shared vision and mission.[66] French bishop James (Jacques) de Vitry, an eyewitness, reported early in 1216, "Once a year, in a place on which they agree, the men of this Order assemble to rejoice in the Lord and eat together; and they profit greatly from these gatherings. They seek the counsel of upright and virtuous men; they draw up and promulgate holy laws and submit them for approval to the Holy Father; then they disband again for a year and go about through Lombardy, Tuscany, Apulia, and Sicily."[67]

As the brothers gathered in the chapter, they would report their adventures and seek Francis's counsel. Francis in turn would share what he felt Jesus was continuing to teach him. Also, at the chapters new brothers assembling for the first time would witness firsthand the growth and dynamism of the movement.

"At the chapter," the *Anonymous of Perugia* reports, the brothers "would discuss how they could better observe the *Rule*. They appointed brothers who would preach to the people throughout each of the provinces, and assigned brothers" to their various places of service.[68] They gathered in order to be sent out again.

---

[64] Introduction to the *Passion of San Verecondo*, FA:ED 2:806; Englebert, *Saint Francis*, 476 n. 1.

[65] *Passion of San Verecondo*, FA:ED 2:807.

[66] "All attended, even novices, for the essential purpose of the meeting was to maintain the internal unity of the itinerant fraternity by contact between the brethren, and to keep alive its awareness of the common ideal." Iriarte, *Franciscan History*, 87.

[67] Quoted in Fortini, *Francis of Assisi*, 386 n. j. This contrasts with gatherings of dissenting groups like the Cathars who did not recognize or submit to the authority of the pope and the established church.

[68] *Anonymous of Perugia*, FA:ED 2:51, and similarly *Legend of the Three Companions*, FA:ED 2:100–1.

Chapters were times for Francis to teach, admonish, and correct the brothers as needed. "Everything, however, that he said in word, he would first, with eagerness and affection, show them in deed."[69] He taught them to respect priests and older folks and not to look down upon the wealthy or the nobility. They should not judge even those who ate or drank excessively or dressed extravagantly. Francis showed compassion especially to the poor and taught the brothers to do likewise. "In a word, he showed himself to be subject to all" as a true Lesser Brother.[70]

Francis modeled servanthood. He appointed one of the brothers his "guardian" to watch over him and to whom he pledged obedience. He taught them "to be attentive and devoted when hearing Mass" and honor the priests "who handle these tremendous and greatest sacraments." Francis said, "Let your way of life among the people be such that whoever sees or hears you will glorify and praise our heavenly Father."[71] The brothers were to be living embodiments of Jesus's Sermon on the Mount. He told them,

> As you announce peace with your mouth, make sure that you have greater peace in your hearts, thus no one will be provoked to anger or scandal because of you. Let everyone be drawn to peace and kindness through your peace and gentleness. For we have been called to this: to cure the wounded, to bind up the broken, and to recall the erring. Many who seem to us members of the devil will yet be disciples of Christ.[72]

When Francis saw that some brothers were taking self-denial to excess, he told them to be gentle with themselves, not to overdo fasting, vigils, or self-discipline. According to *The Anonymous of Perugia,* Francis "was so filled with the Savior's grace and wisdom, that he would make his admonition with kindness, his reprimand with reason, and his command with gentleness." So "he spoke to them compassionately, not as a judge, but as a father to his children and a doctor to his patient."[73]

Francis always delighted to welcome new brothers. The community celebrated whenever a new young man, "rich or poor, noble or insignificant, wise or simple, cleric or illiterate," joined them. So far as Francis was concerned, "No lowliness of birth, no weakness of poverty

---

[69] *Anonymous of Perugia,* FA:ED 2:52.
[70] *Anonymous of Perugia,* FA:ED 2:52.
[71] *Anonymous of Perugia,* FA:ED 2:52.
[72] *Anonymous of Perugia,* FA:ED 2:52–53.
[73] *Anonymous of Perugia,* FA:ED 2:53.

stood in the way of building up in God's word the ones God wanted to build up, a God who delights to be with the simple and those rejected by the world."[74]

Key decisions were made at the chapters. Missions beyond Europe were authorized. In 1221, the normal frequency of chapters was reduced to once every three years.[75]

Division into Provinces

The General Chapter of 1217, as the community was in its seventh year, divided the Order into *provinces*. This form of cell division and its geographic extent show how broadly the brotherhood had now spread. This was the second major structural innovation in the fraternity's life.

Creating provinces, Iriarte notes,

> was a most important step; it says a great deal for Francis' creative genius and his willingness to adapt to historical change that he introduced an organization which was entirely new to the monastic tradition, especially when it is remembered that, in these regional districts, the brothers continued to live without fixed abode. The province came to be the basic unit of the fraternity; it produced, as it were, a new type of itinerant community, which moved and acted in one region under the guidance of the "provincial minister."[76]

At first there were eleven provinces—six in Italy and one each in Germany, France, Spain, Syria, and Provence (later part of southern France, bordering Italy). Aquitaine was added in 1219 and England in 1224. (Aquitaine, on the Atlantic coast just north of Spain, was then ruled by England.)[77] Moorman notes, "Francis was still alive when, on September 10th, 1224, a party of nine of his disciples landed at Dover and set out to establish the Order in England. They appear to have been men after St. Francis' own heart, simple friars devoted to poverty, simplicity and humility untouched by the desire to modify the intentions of their founder."[78]

---

[74] Thomas of Celano, *Life of St. Francis*, FA:ED 1:209–10. "Cleric" here does not necessarily mean a priest; a "cleric" was a "clerk," that is, one who could read and write.

[75] Iriarte, *Franciscan History*, 16–20, 79–80, 87; Englebert, *Saint Francis*, 212–16.

[76] Iriarte, *Franciscan History*, 16.

[77] Iriarte, *Franciscan History*, 79.

[78] John R. H. Moorman, *The Grey Friars in Cambridge 1225–1538* (Cambridge: Cambridge University Press, 1952), 5.

As years passed, the number of provinces continued to grow. At Francis's death in 1226 provinces were "firmly established" throughout Europe and in Palestine. Most of the provinces were then subdivided in 1230. But the Chapter of 1239 reduced the number, realizing too many had been created. Under Bonaventure's leadership in 1263, Romania and Greece were added. Later the pope ruled that no new provinces could be formed without his consent.[79]

By 1266, four decades after Francis's death, the fraternity counted thirty-four provinces—seventeen south of the Alps and seventeen north ("ultramontane"). The southern provinces were mostly in Italy but included also Dalmatia, Greece, and the Holy Land. The northern group included three in Spain, five in France, four in Germany, plus those in England, Ireland, Denmark, Hungary, and Bohemia.[80] To make oversight easier, provinces were in time divided into smaller units called *custodies*, each with its *custos* (custodian, overseer). Some larger provinces eventually comprised as many as ten or twelve custodies.[81]

The General Chapter of 1221 made other important decisions, in addition to reducing the frequency of chapters. The Order had grown so large and widespread that it was now impractical to assemble everyone in one place. Thus, 1221 was "the last Pentecost Chapter at which all the brothers gathered together."[82]

Yet the question of a final, papally approved Rule was still far from settled. The role of the Rule—its contents and interpretation—created more and more debate and dissension in the Order.

---

[79] Iriarte, *Franciscan History*, 79–80.

[80] Iriarte, *Franciscan History*, 80. Although Spain and southern France are west, not north, of Italy, they are "beyond the Alps" (ultramontane) so far as Italy is concerned, the Alps being the major physical barrier between Italy and the rest of Europe.

[81] Iriarte, *Franciscan History*, 80. Iriarte provides further statistics, indicating that by 1282 the Franciscan Order counted 34 provinces, 171 custodies, and over 1,200 separate houses or communities. In addition, there were ten *vicariates*—essentially mission districts beyond the provinces. These included Scotland, Corsica, Bosnia, Russia, Tunisia, and China. Iriarte, 80–82.

[82] Introduction, "The Earlier Rule," FA:ED 1:63.

8

The Role of the Rule

Along with the development of provinces came other gradual organizational changes. The most important of these were embodied in the Rule that was officially approved by Pope Honorius III, the successor to Innocent III, in 1223.

The pope's approval of the new Rule was the third big structural marker in the Franciscan Order. Unlike the Earlier Rule, this Rule did receive the papal seal. It became known therefore as the *Regula bullata* (rule with the official papal seal) and the Earlier Rule as the *Regula non-bullata,* or "unsealed rule."[1]

At first the brothers functioned according to the simple Rule Francis drew up and Pope Innocent approved orally, as we saw. As the brothers continued to gather in chapter and discuss their shared life, they added to and revised their early Rule. The Rule "developed in light of the experiences of the brothers, the teaching of the Church, especially of the Fourth Lateran Council, and the teachings of Francis himself."[2]

The Fifth Crusade was raging. A large crusading army arrayed itself before the Muslim stronghold of Damietta in Egypt's Nile Delta. In 1219, Francis felt called to go there himself and proclaim the good news to the Muslim sultan. He and a few other brothers set sail from Ancona on Italy's east coast in June. By fall they were with the Crusade forces

---

[1] Lawrence S. Cunningham, *Francis of Assisi: Performing the Gospel Life* (Grand Rapids, MI: William B. Eerdmans, 2004), 66, 68. The Latin word *bulla* means "papal seal."

[2] Introduction, "The Earlier Rule," in *Francis of Assisi: Early Documents*, ed. Regis J. Armstrong, OFM Cap., J. A. Wayne Hellmann, OFM Conv., and William J. Short, OFM (New York: New City Press, 2001), 1:63 [hereafter FA:ED].

besieging Damietta.[3] Francis appointed two brothers, Matthew of Narni and Gregory of Naples, to supervise things while he was away.[4]

Francis's journey east kept him away from the Portiuncula for about a year. When he got back in mid-1220, several things upset him. As the Order continued its rapid growth, brothers were developing conflicting visions of what they should become. The "lack of organization in the Order and the increasing diversity of aims of its members" gave rise to considerable "dissension and dispute."[5] In response, some brothers pushed for much stricter rules and more elaborate organization. Otherwise, how could the leaders "govern an Order in which independence and even vagabondage were so esteemed?"[6]

The brothers Francis left in charge, Matthew and Gregory, had called a chapter to address these issues. They proposed adopting some of the regulations other orders had. Fast days and more practices of self-denial were added. Also, by now some brothers were raising substantial buildings as communal residences in various cities, something Francis strongly opposed. One provincial leader, Peter Staccia, established a Franciscan house of studies at Bologna, site of the increasingly influential Bologna University.[7]

Francis was eager to be home. But as he approached the Portiuncula, he was shocked to see a building that hadn't been there before. The town of Assisi had erected a large stone edifice near the Portiuncula to serve as a lodge for brothers who came to visit. This violated the Rule. Francis felt it undermined his vision of the Portiuncula as a model of humility and simplicity for the whole order.

Francis was angry. He and some other brothers climbed onto the roof and began throwing down the roof tiles. But town officials (including Francis's own biological brother Angelo, it is said) stopped him. "This building belongs to Assisi, not to you," they said. Francis had to give in.[8]

---

[3] Omer Englebert, *Saint Francis of Assisi*, 2nd English ed., trans. Eve Marie Cooper (Chicago: Franciscan Herald Press, 1965), 395. Ancona, about eighty miles away over the mountain, is the nearest major seaport to Assisi. See chapter 11 for the full story.

[4] John Moorman, *A History of the Franciscan Order: From Its Origins to the Year 1517* (Oxford: Oxford University Press, 1968), 48–49.

[5] Englebert, *Saint Francis*, 242.

[6] Englebert, *Saint Francis*, 243; see Moorman, *History of the Franciscan Order*, 53–54.

[7] Englebert, *Saint Francis*, 244; Sabatier, *Road to Assisi*, 119.

[8] *Assisi Compilation*, FA:ED 2:157; see *Mirror of the Perfection*, FA:ED 3:260; Arnaldo Fortini, *Francis of Assisi*, trans. Helen Moak (New York: Crossroad Publishing, 1992), 475. The *Mirror of Perfection* notes that Francis "feared that, upon seeing this house, the other brothers would build or have built great houses in the places where they

These changes brought Francis to a momentous decision. He would give up leadership of the brotherhood. "The direction of the Order was slipping from his hands into those of men who did not share his ideals" in the radical way he taught and lived, notes historian John Moorman.[9] Francis would turn the leadership over to a brother he deeply trusted.

Francis chose Peter Catani, an older man and one of the first four to join Francis. Peter was educated and for some time had been Francis's own vicar, the one appointed to watch over him and to whom he held himself accountable. Now at the Pentecost Chapter in September 1220 Francis cried out, "From now on, I am dead to you. But here you have Brother Peter Catani; let us all, you and I, obey him."

Francis prostrated himself before Peter. Then he stood and said, "Lord, I give back to You the family which until now You have entrusted to me. Now, sweetest Lord, because of my infirmities, which You know, I can no longer take care of them and I entrust them to the ministers."[10] Francis renounced his leadership as he had renounced his sonship with his father Bernardone fourteen years earlier.

This was a huge step, so different from other orders. Up to now Francis had been the undisputed head of the brotherhood. Now a different brother was given the official position of minister general.

Francis had led mainly by example. Now he would lead *only* by example. And by prayer and perhaps preaching. Francis once said, "In a prelacy [leadership office] there is a fall; in praise, a precipice; in the humility of a subject, profit for the soul."[11] Francis "intended, in his humility and his faithfulness to his own concepts, to remain always the *minore*, the least of all, the servant and subject of his brothers," notes Fortini.[12]

Two or three factors seem to have provoked this big step. First was the dissension among the brothers over the order's direction and structure. Another was a new papal requirement that all religious communities must institute a year-long novitiate and that a brother, once admitted, could

now stayed or where they would stay in the future. And especially [he opposed this new building] because he wanted [the Portiuncula] always to be a model and example for all the other places" where the brothers ministered. *Mirror of the Perfection,* FA:ED 3:260.

[9] Moorman, *History of the Franciscan Order,* 51.

[10] *Mirror of the Perfection,* FA:ED 3:287.

[11] Thomas of Celano, *Remembrance,* FA:ED 2:341. Fortini here renders the Latin (as translated from Italian to English by Helen Moak), "In office is found occasion for a fall. In praise, an occasion for complete destruction. In the humility of being a subject, an occasion for profit for the soul." Fortini, *Francis of Assisi,* 455. This is even more pointed and poetic in Thomas's Latin: *In proelatione casus, in laude praecipitium* [a precipice], *in humilitate subditi animae lucrum est.* Fortini, 455.

[12] Fortini, *Francis of Assisi,* 454.

never leave.[13] Perhaps even more decisive was Francis's poor health after his travels to the East. He simply lacked the stamina that the increasing weight of leadership demanded. Fortini points out that Francis "suffered from the inevitable contradictions between having to exercise authority as head of the order and his own need to make himself the least of all."[14]

Peter of Catani seemed a wise choice for leader. But he died unexpectedly the following March, 1221, just six months into his appointment. In what proved an even more momentous decision, Francis appointed Brother Elias as minister general, a decision further confirmed at the Chapter of 1221.[15] Francis chose Elias "for the role of mother to himself and had him made a father of the other brothers," as Thomas of Celano put it.[16]

Despite these big changes, Francis was still very active in the order's affairs. Especially, he was determined to confront the key organizational issues. He still had to get the brotherhood's Rule officially endorsed by the pope. And so, working with some brothers well versed in legal matters, Francis agreed to a number of revisions and additions to the Rule. The new version then received its final revisions at the Chapter of 1221.

This modified Rule of 1221 spelled out the brothers' common life in some detail. In a Prologue, Francis pledged his "obedience and reverence" to the pope. Chapter 1 then began, "The rule and life of these brothers is this, namely: 'to live in obedience, in chastity, and without anything of their own,' and to follow the teachings and footprints of our Lord Jesus Christ, Who says: 'If you wish to be perfect, go, sell everything you have and give it to the poor, and you will have treasure in heaven; and come, follow me.'"

Chapter 1 continues with similar quotations from or references to Jesus's words in Matthew 16:24 and 19:29, Mark 10:29, and Luke 14:26.[17] Francis was certainly not going to compromise on the central vision and covenant requirements of the movement.

The Rule's twenty-four chapters covered multiple aspects of the brothers' life together. In printed form today it runs to twenty-four

---

[13] It does not appear that Francis had envisaged such a legal requirement for his order.

[14] Fortini, *Francis of Assisi*, 455.

[15] Moorman, *History of the Franciscan Order*, 51; Fortini, *Francis of Assisi*, 476; Jon M. Sweeney, *The Enthusiast: How the Best Friend of Francis of Assisi Almost Destroyed What He Started* (Notre Dame, IN: Ave Maria Press, 2016), xxi, 163–72.

[16] Thomas of Celano, *Life of St. Francis*, FA:ED 1:267.

[17] Introduction, "The Earlier Rule," FA:ED 1:63–64. The statement quoted beginning "to live in obedience" is taken from a rule Pope Innocent had earlier approved (1198) for an order known as the Trinitarians. FA:ED 1:63 n. c.

pages.[18] It includes procedures for receiving new brothers after they had sold all possessions and given them to the poor. The first year then was probationary. The normal attire was "one tunic with a hood and, if it is necessary, another without a hood and a cord and trousers." The Rule adds, "Let all the brothers wear poor clothing and, with the blessing of God, they can patch them with sackcloth and other pieces, for the Lord says in the Gospel: 'Those who wear expensive clothing and live in luxury and who dress in fine garments are in the houses of kings' [Luke 7:25]. Even though [the brothers] may be called hypocrites, let them nevertheless not cease doing good nor seek expensive clothing in this world, so that they may have a garment in the kingdom of heaven."[19]

Chapter 3 specified that the brothers were to "recite the Divine Office, the praises and prayers." Brothers who were clergy should recite the prescribed prayers; for this they could "have only the books necessary to fulfil their office." Nonordained ("lay") brothers who could read were permitted a psalter. Brothers who could not read could have no books at all. In place of the prescribed prayers, they were to recite the Creed and specified numbers of repetitions of the Lord's Prayer for the eight canonical hours of the day (Matins, Lauds, Prime, Terce, Sext, None, Vespers, and Compline).[20]

These and similar provisions show how countercultural Francis and his brothers were in several respects—above all in their commitment to follow literally Jesus's words and deeds, and also in the ways the community included brothers of every class, from highly educated to some who were illiterate.

The Rule's fourth chapter speaks of "brothers who have been designated the ministers and servants of the other brothers" whose tasks included assigning "brothers in the provinces and places where they may be" and to visit and watch over them.[21] These provisions reflect the division into provinces in 1217 and show that the Order had found it necessary to appoint some brothers as "ministers" or supervisors.

Throughout this Earlier Rule, Francis returned repeatedly to the central focus on living and proclaiming the good news. Chapter 22 is Francis's admonition to the fraternity. "All my brothers," he wrote, "let us pay attention to what the Lord says: 'Love your enemies' and 'do good

---

[18] "The Earlier Rule (The Rule Without a Papal Seal) (1209/10–1221)," FA:ED 1:63–86.

[19] "The Earlier Rule," FA:ED 1:65.

[20] "The Earlier Rule," FA:ED 1:65–66.

[21] "The Earlier Rule," FA:ED 1:66.

to those who hate you' [Matt. 5:44] for our Lord Jesus Christ, Whose footprints we must follow, called His betrayer a friend and willingly offered Himself to His executioners." Francis went on, "Now that we have left the world, . . . we have nothing else to do but to follow the will of the Lord and to please Him." Quoting several Gospel passages, Francis admonished, "Let us, therefore, hold onto the words, the life, the teaching and the Holy Gospel of Him Who humbled Himself to beg His Father for us and to make His name known." Here Francis quotes much of Jesus's prayer in John 17 including the words, "As You [Father] sent me into the world, so I sent them into the world."[22] The parallel between Francis's fraternity and Jesus's first apostles could hardly be more explicit.

Francis concluded, "The brothers may have no other Rule." He ended with a Trinitarian doxology.[23]

Through the years, Francis's most devout brothers thought it "obvious that blessed Francis gave the very same rule to his brothers, as Christ gave to his followers."[24]

The Chapter of Mats

With the order's continuing growth, spread, and complexity (as Francis had foreseen) the community urgently needed to have the revised rule officially signed and sealed by the pope. Francis probably would have submitted the Rule of 1221, but a few brothers still disagreed on several points.

These issues came to a head at the important Pentecost Chapter of 1222. This was probably the celebrated Chapter of Mats, as it became known, when some five thousand brothers converged on the Portiuncula.[25]

Happily, the days were warm and pleasant. Brothers arrived on foot from all over Europe. They spread out over the plain before the Portiuncula, arranging themselves in groups by Franciscan province, like the tribes of Israel in the wilderness. When not all assembled the brothers spent their time in silent prayer, in assisting one another, or in quiet conversation, no doubt sharing their stories.[26]

---

[22] "The Earlier Rule," FA:ED 1:79–81.

[23] "The Earlier Rule," FA:ED 1:86.

[24] Arnald of Sarrant, *The Kinship of Saint Francis,* FA:ED 3:716.

[25] The date of the so-called Chapter of Mats is disputed. Some interpreters identify it with the Chapter of 1217 or a later one. Vauchez dates it as 1222, or possibly 1219. André Vauchez, *Francis of Assisi, the Life and Afterlife of a Medieval Saint,* trans. Michael F. Cusato (New Haven, CT: Yale University Press, 2012), 343. In fact, there may have been other chapters that fit the general description of this gathering.

[26] Englebert, *Saint Francis,* 212.

One of the brothers was António, a young Portuguese priest. He was so impressed by the Franciscans that he had felt called to join them. He became an outstanding Franciscan teacher, Bible scholar, and servant of the poor and sick. Within a year of his death, he was canonized as Saint Anthony of Padua, Italy, his last place of ministry. Francis was generally wary of theologians and scholars, but he was so impressed by Anthony's godly life and example that he wrote him a year or so later, "I am pleased that you teach sacred theology to the brothers providing that, as it is contained in the Rule, you 'do not extinguish the Spirit of prayer and devotion' during study of this kind." Anthony's was the kind of scholarship Francis could approve of.[27]

On Pentecost Sunday, Francis preached to the crowd as he felt led by the Spirit. Early in the morning, bells rang out calling the brothers together, "sounding out the joyous notes of a celebration." The field beyond the Portiuncula "was transformed into an immense temple, where the brothers prayed, mourned over their sins, and discussed the health of their souls."[28] Perhaps also they sang together. On their hearts also was the health and direction of their increasingly vast brotherhood.

The brothers were not alone that day. Word had spread, and many others "came to gape at the unaccustomed spectacle—noblemen, counts, knights, barons, priests, commoners," bishops, abbots of other orders.[29]

Francis began his sermon, announcing his theme: "My sons, we have promised great things to God; greater things are promised to us by God if we observe what we have promised Him: let us await confidently those promised to us. Brief is the delight of the world; but the punishment that follows is eternal. The suffering of this life is small, but the glory of the other life is infinite."

Francis elaborated on this theme. He comforted the brothers and encouraged them to obedience to the church, love for each other, prayer for all people, patience in hardships and temperance in prosperity, chastity, and peace with God, other people, and their own consciences. They must love and faithfully observe holy poverty. He concluded, paraphrasing Jesus and the Apostle Peter, "have no care or anxiety about what to eat or drink or other things necessary for the body, but . . .

---

[27] "A Letter to Brother Anthony of Padua," FA:ED 1:107; Cunningham, *Francis of Assisi*, 59–60; Fortini, *Francis of Assisi*, 476. Fortini calls Anthony "Francis's greatest disciple." Cunningham provides a sketch of Anthony's life and ministry, noting that in 1946 he was declared a Doctor of the Church.

[28] Fortini, *Francis of Assisi*, 475.

[29] Fortini, *Francis of Assisi*, 475.

concentrate only on praying and praising God; and leave all care for your body to Him, since He has a special care for you." The brothers received Francis's words joyfully, and when he finished all hurried off to pray.[30]

Several remarkable things happened at this important reunion. One was a visit from Dominic de Guzmán (St. Dominic, 1170–1221), the Spanish priest who founded the Order of Preachers (Dominicans). The order had been formed only recently; like the Franciscans, it was already growing rapidly. Dominic, while on his way from Burgundy to Rome with seven of his brothers, heard of the Franciscan gathering and decided to visit. Years later an elderly Franciscan, Raymond Barravus, told of twice hearing Dominic talk about attending a Franciscan chapter where he saw Francis and thousands of his brothers spread out over the plain.[31]

Though his own order was new, Dominic was a generation older than Francis. He would die in 1221. This means either that the Chapter of Mats occurred a few years before 1222, or (perhaps more likely) that Dominic visited an earlier but quite similar Franciscan chapter, perhaps in 1217.[32] In any case, we are told Dominic was astonished that Francis had not organized a system for supervising and caring for such a large assembly. Francis had not even given enough "care or concern for the things necessary for the body," Dominic felt.

But then people from the surrounding towns and villages—Assisi, Perugia, Spoleto, Foligno, others—started arriving with food and drink. When Dominic saw horses and donkeys and carts laden with provisions, he saw he had judged too hastily. Out from the towns came bundles of bread, cheese, other provisions, along with tablecloths, pots, dishes, cups, and utensils. God was providentially taking care of his poor, Dominic concluded.[33]

Disputing the Rule

More crucial for the Franciscan future was the presence of Cardinal Hugolino, a special friend and advisor to Francis who himself would

---

[30] *Little Flowers of Saint Francis*, FA:ED 3:596–97.

[31] Englebert, *Saint Francis*, 477.

[32] *Little Flowers of Saint Francis*, FA:ED 3:595, 597. Based on his research, Fortini concluded that Dominic's visit was in 1217. Fortini, *Francis of Assisi*, 476 n. o.; Cunningham, *Francis of Assisi*, 57. Vauchez dates the visit to 1218; Vauchez, *Francis*, 65.

[33] *Little Flowers of Saint Francis*, FA:ED 3:597. A number of writers describe this event. See Englebert, *Saint Francis*, 214; Lazaro Iriarte, *Franciscan History: The Three Orders of St. Francis of Assisi*, trans. from Spanish by Patricia Ross (Chicago: Franciscan Herald Press, 1982), 19. Iriarte places Dominic's visit in 1218.

shortly become pope.[34] Among the thousands gathered at the Chapter of Mats was a growing number of brothers who were scholars and teachers. Apparently unbeknown to Francis, some of these more learned brothers sought out the cardinal and asked him to persuade Francis to adopt one of the existing monastic rules for the new fraternity, as the Dominicans had recently done.

Hugolino discussed this with Francis. When the cardinal suggested that Francis and the brothers use one of the existing rules, Francis said nothing. Instead, he led Hugolino to the brothers' big assembly. Standing before the throng of brothers, Francis said,

> My brothers! My brothers! God has called me by the way of simplicity and showed me the way of simplicity. I do not want you to mention to me any *Rule*, whether of Saint Augustine, or of Saint Bernard, or of Saint Benedict. And the Lord told me what He wanted: He wanted me to be a new fool in the world. God did not wish to lead us by any way other than this knowledge, but God will confound you by your own knowledge and wisdom.[35]

Francis spoke so passionately that Cardinal Hugolino was shocked. He stood silent.[36] The brothers pushing for a different rule saw they could do nothing for the moment. Perhaps they could gently persuade Francis that the Rule needed to be rewritten now that the fraternity had grown so large and so difficult adequately to oversee.[37]

Francis was distressed over the growing dissension. He was still capable of simply imposing his own will, even though Brother Elias was now minister general. But Francis felt that making demands was contrary to the spirit of Jesus. He had once said, "There is no prelate in the whole world who would be as feared by his subjects and brothers as the Lord would make me feared to my brothers, if I wished. But the Lord gave me this grace: that I want to be content with all, as one who is lesser in the religion."[38] My task, Francis said, is "to overcome their vices and spiritually to correct them by my words and by my example."[39]

---

[34] *Little Flowers of Saint Francis*, FA:ED 3:595.

[35] *Assisi Compilation*, FA:ED 2:132–33; also *Mirror of the Perfection*, FA:ED 3:314; Moorman, *History of the Franciscan Order*, 55.

[36] *Assisi Compilation*, FA:ED 2:133.

[37] Moorman, *History of the Franciscan Order*, 55.

[38] *Mirror of the Perfection*, FA:ED 3:292.

[39] Moorman, *History of the Franciscan Order*, 56. This is Moorman's translation of Francis's words as quoted in *Mirror of the Perfection*, FA:ED 3:317, and *Assisi Compilation*, FA:ED 2:211.

Francis was open though to reworking the existing Rule sufficiently to bring peace and get the pope's seal. He would continue his leadership by word and example rather than demand. So, in the fall of 1222 Francis with two of his most trusted brothers, Leo (who was serving as Francis's secretary) and Bonizzo of Bologna, a brother trained in the law, set off for the hermitage of Fonte Colombo. This was a wooded place of solitude beside a mountain stream above the town of Rieti, a couple days' walk south of Assisi. It was named for the collared doves (*colombe*) that gathered there in fall and spring. Here Francis thought, prayed, conversed with some of the brothers, and then dictated to Leo a new Rule that he hoped would win general support.[40]

According to the *Mirror of Perfection* several discontented brothers, along with Elias, journeyed to the hermitage to try to sway Francis. They told Elias, "We heard that Brother Francis is making a new rule, and we fear that he will make it so harsh that we will not be able to observe it." If so, they would refuse to obey it. "Let him make it for himself and not for us."

"What do these brothers want?" Francis asked as he saw them approaching. When Elias told him, Francis raised his face to heaven and spoke directly to Jesus. "Lord! Didn't I tell you, they wouldn't believe me?"

Jesus replied in everyone's hearing: "Francis, nothing of yours is in the *Rule*: whatever is there is mine. And I want the *Rule* observed in this way: to the letter, to the letter, and without a gloss, without a gloss, without a gloss."

Jesus added, "I know how much human weakness is capable of, and how much I want to help them. Therefore, those who refuse to observe it should leave the Order."

Francis turned to the brothers and said, "Did you hear? Did you hear? Do you want me to have you told again?"

"Confused and terrified," the *Mirror of Perfection* says, these brothers "departed blaming themselves."[41]

Francis completed his draft of the new rule. He made some concessions to the dissidents' wishes, though none of great substance. He then delivered a copy to Brother Elias. Francis probably kept a draft himself. Somehow Brother Elias, however, "lost" (or more likely destroyed) the rule when the dissident brothers said it was intolerably

---

[40] Fortini, *Francis of Assisi*, 524; Moorman, *History of the Franciscan Order*, 372; Englebert, *Saint Francis*, 284.

[41] *Mirror of the Perfection*, FA:ED 3:253–54; Fortini, *Francis of Assisi*, 524.

strict. Not taking further chances, Francis himself then took the proposed new rule directly to Cardinal Hugolino in Rome.

But Cardinal Hugolino also felt the new rule was too strict, considering the order's wide expansion and growing diversity. Francis had to bow to the cardinal's authority, and thus further changes. The result was a modified rule not entirely to Francis's liking. Francis in fact had to give up much that he held dear.

With the changes required by the cardinal, the brothers approved the new Rule at the Pentecost Chapter of 1223. Then on November 29, 1223, Pope Honorius III himself confirmed the new Rule, giving it his seal.[42]

First, however, Pope Honorius himself insisted on more changes. Gone from the Rule in its final form were several of the more radical biblical texts, including the requirement that the brothers take nothing with them when they traveled. Gone was the requirement to own nothing and to travel only on foot. The key provision that new brothers must give all their belongings to the poor upon entering the community was undercut by adding, "If they cannot do this, their good intention may suffice."[43]

Although the new Rule was still quite demanding compared with other monastic rules, it opened the door to big changes over time. The new Rule did away with "almost everything . . . that commanded the Friars Minor to remain in the ranks of the truly poor," Englebert notes. From now on "the friars were engaged in elevating themselves to the social rank of other clerics and religious." The Rule no longer forbade the brothers to have books. Education and study became much more central. The vow of poverty was gradually interpreted more and more loosely—more "spiritually" and less literally. Not long after Francis's death, some brothers even became bishops.[44]

The Rule signed and sealed by Pope Honorius III in November 1223—the *Regula bullata*—is still the official Franciscan Rule to this day. Church historian Lawrence Cunningham summarizes its key points as follows:

1. The rule and life of the lesser brothers is to observe the gospel by living in obedience, without possessions of one's own, and in chastity [though as noted above, books were permitted].
2. Prospective members are to be observant Catholics. Regulations concerning disposition of personal wealth, the proper clothing

---

[42] Moorman, *History of the Franciscan Order,* 57; Fortini, *Francis of Assisi,* 524–25.

[43] "The Later Rule," FA:ED 1:100; Moorman, *History of the Franciscan Order,* 57–58.

[44] Englebert, *Saint Francis,* 288–89.

of postulants and professed members of the community, and simplicity of life are laid out.

3. Rules for liturgical prayer, fasting, and manner of going abroad in the world on mission.
4. The use of money is prohibited.
5. Obligation to work but without cash wages.
6. Necessity of dispossession of goods, the begging of alms, the care of sick brethren.
7. Penance(s) for errant brothers.
8. Rules for electing the minister general; the Pentecost Chapter.
9. Rules for preaching.
10. Admonition and correction of brothers.
11. Relationship with women and prohibition of entering convents.
12. Permission needed before going out to Saracens [Muslims] and other nonbelievers.[45]

Cunningham maintains that "the differences between the two rules is mainly (although not exclusively) an exercise in editing, pruning, and telescoping the text of the former [rule] into something that approached the canonical style of the latter." Scholars still debate how much the new Rule changed or compromised Francis's intentions. But it is clear "that the scriptural tone" of the Earlier Rule "disappeared in favor of a more precise legal statement." The underlying problem, Cunningham suggests, is

> the near impossibility of capturing in legal terms the esprit of a movement that was based on the intuitions of a singular religious genius. Attempts to sort out the legal issues concerning the Franciscan way of life would vex the Franciscan family long after [Francis's] death. . . . That being said . . . the emergence of some kind of structure, fortified by a rule of life, had a certain inevitability to it. Free-floating movements without structure have an almost inevitable tendency either to peter out or to turn into anarchic curiosities.[46]

Disputes and disagreements over the Rule were prompted by one underlying fact above all: the explosive growth of the Franciscan brotherhood. How and why did the Order grow so fast and expand so far, and so spontaneously? We will now try to understand the dynamics at work here.

---

[45] Cunningham, *Francis of Assisi,* 69. The full text is here: "The Later Rule," FA:ED 1:99–106.

[46] Cunningham, *Francis of Assisi,* 70.

We shall want to explore these issues further—the question of spirit versus structure, charism versus institution—when we ask what Francis and his brothers teach us today.

When Bonaventure wrote his major life of Francis some thirty years after Francis's death, he compared the writing and revising of the Rule to Moses receiving the Law on Sinai. In Bonaventure's retelling, Francis "went up to a certain mountain led by the Holy Spirit, with two of his companions, to condense [the Rule] into a shorter form." After a period of fasting, Francis "dictated the Rule as the Holy Spirit suggested to him."

After Francis's vicar, Elias, supposedly lost this version, Francis went back up the mountain (as Moses did in the Old Testament) and "rewrote it just as before, as if he were taking the words from the mouth of God."

According to Bonaventure, "Francis used to say that nothing of what he had placed [in the Rule] came from his own efforts but that he dictated everything just as it had been revealed by God." Bonaventure in fact viewed Francis's *stigmata* as "the seal of the Supreme Pontiff, Christ, for the complete confirmation of the Rule," for "only a few days had passed" from the time Francis finalized the rule until he received the *stigmata*.[47] In fact it seems Francis received the *stigmata* more than a year after finalizing the Rule.[48]

Bonaventure thus turns Francis into a second lawgiver, recalling Moses's experience as recorded in Exodus and Deuteronomy.[49]

---

[47] Bonaventure, *The Major Legend of Saint Francis*, FA:ED 2:558–59.

[48] On the chronology, see Englebert, *Saint Francis*, 395; Vauchez, *Francis*, 343; Sweeney, *The Enthusiast*, xxi.

[49] Exod. 19:20–25, 31:18, 34:1–28; Deut. 10:1–5.

Part II

The Movement and the Motives

Renewals in history arise from the convergence of three things: Prepared soil, fresh seed, and an inspired sower. A society or culture under stress and ready for change, plus a prophet who sees or senses what "new thing" will spark renewal, can change history, if the sower has the right seed.

II

The Movement and its Members

9

Movement Dynamics

In 2012 my wife Jan and I visited Waterford, Ireland's oldest city, on the Emerald Isle's southeast coast across from Wales. The city is still anchored by Reginald's Tower, dating back to Viking days in the 900s.

As we walked up into the city from the water's edge, lugging our suitcases, I was surprised to see a Franciscan chapel and friary. Franciscan Lesser Brothers had arrived here in Waterford in the mid-1200s, just a decade or so after Francis's death.

By the time Pope Honorius III approved Francis's revised Rule in November 1223, the brotherhood was a rapidly growing international network numbering something over five thousand brothers, as we have seen. Growth continued well beyond Francis's death in 1226 and his canonization two years later. Lazaro Iriarte in *Franciscan History: The Three Orders of Francis of Assisi* estimates conservatively that the brothers numbered thirty thousand in 1260 and forty thousand by 1300.[1]

Many eyewitnesses remarked on this surging growth. Already in 1220 one writer claimed the Franciscans had "spread throughout the whole world." They had "in a short time so multiplied in number that there is hardly a province in Christendom where they do not have some friars." Another chronicler said that "as the effect of God's power, scarcely a village throughout the whole world is to be found untouched by their sacred presence." Around 1230, the English chronicler Roger of Wendover wrote, "they fill the whole world."[2] By "world" these writers

---

[1] Lazaro Iriarte, *Franciscan History: The Three Orders of St. Francis of Assisi*, trans. from Spanish by Patricia Ross (Chicago: Franciscan Herald Press, 1982), 83.

[2] Cajetan Esser, OFM, *Origins of the Franciscan Order*, trans. Aedan Daly and Irina Lynch (Chicago: Franciscan Herald Press, 1970), 8–12, 37. Esser identifies and documents

of course meant primarily Europe and neighboring lands to the east, since the so-called New World was as yet unknown. Columbus set sail on his first voyage of discovery more than two centuries after Francis—with Franciscan help, as we shall see.

Thomas of Celano in his *Treatise on the Miracles of Saint Francis* also speaks of this rapid growth. "We then saw that vine spreading, in the briefest time, extending its fruitful branches from sea to sea. People came running from everywhere, the crowds swelled, and were quickly joined 'as living stones' to the grand 'structure of' this marvelous 'temple' [1 Peter 2:5; Mark 13:1]," the Franciscan brotherhood.[3]

Why? The young men who flocked to Francis quickly became an international youth movement—a starkly different sort of "crusade," armed not with swords but with the gospel of peace. How can this be explained—spiritually, sociologically, psychologically?

The meticulous German Franciscan scholar Cajetan Esser (1913–1978) thoroughly investigated these questions in his book, *Origins of the Franciscan Order.* Esser identifies multiple reasons for the remarkable Franciscan growth, factors both internal and external. The life of society and of the church were so organically intertwined at this time, though, that the internal–external distinction quickly loses meaning. We need to understand Franciscan growth *ecologically*—that is, by examining multiple interlaced factors and feedbacks—spiritual, political, anthropological, economic, though also recognizing that all causes do not have equal weight. As best we can, we will sort out the intertwining fibers of influence—cause and effect and feedback loops—in a way that clarifies the whole.

This chapter unpacks the dynamics that explain the Franciscan brotherhood *as a movement.* First, we examine eight factors that contributed to the order's expansion. In the second half of the chapter, we analyze eight innovations Francis introduced that strategically facilitated this growth, focusing especially on the key role of Franciscan hermitages.

---

all the sources mentioned here. Esser painstakingly compiled and analyzed witnesses from many early sources. I quote from him extensively in this chapter, supplementing the discussion with other sources. See the *Norman Chronicle* (1269–1272), which comments on the uniqueness and rapid growth and expansion of the Franciscans and also the Dominicans. *Norman Chronicle,* 3:825–26, in *Francis of Assisi: Early Documents,* ed. Regis J. Armstrong, OFM Cap., J. A. Wayne Hellmann, OFM Conv., and William J. Short, OFM (New York: New City Press, 2001) [hereafter FA:ED].

[3] Thomas of Celano, *The Treatise on the Miracles of Saint Francis,* FA:ED 2:400.

The Secret of Franciscan Growth

When Francis was converted, the soil for rapid growth of a new movement was already prepared. Francis's spiritual seed was sown in fertile soil. Had Francis been born a generation or two earlier, or a couple decades later, history would have been different.

Several key factors beyond the mere novelty of Francis's movement contributed to the order's growth and geographic spread. Together these dynamics help us understand how this spontaneous youth movement could grow so fast. Eight factors, especially, stand out.

1. *Francis's remarkable leadership by word and life.* To stress the obvious: there would have been no Franciscan movement without Francis. From the start, Francis's followers "felt the magnetism of the man and saint whose life they wished to imitate and to make their own," notes Esser.[4] Chesterton said simply, "men acted quite differently according to whether they had met [Francis] or not."[5]

We must start with the life, the singularity, the radicality, the personality, above all the spiritual authenticity and charism of Francis himself. Surely "in many respects," Esser writes, "the driving force in the early Franciscan movement was the living figure of St. Francis and his inspiring example. The very manner of his life was the model of the friars who followed him, his life the formative inspiration of theirs."[6] His transparent sincerity gave him moral authority.

Francis was a magnetic charismatic leader—not first as a great organizer, but by his own character, his authentic Jesus following. How do we explain Franciscan growth? First by looking at Francis's life and understanding it as best we can. Thus, the essential importance of Part I of this book. A Benedictine monk in Bavaria wrote, "the fame of [Francis's] virtue began to inspire many to contempt for the world and a desire for a better life."[7]

A particularly astute observer of the growing Franciscan movement was the French bishop and later cardinal, James de Vitry. As Esser notes, James "had come to know and admire the Order in Italy and in the Holy Land and understood its motives well, since he had left his own homeland

---

[4] Esser, *Origins*, 59.

[5] G. K. Chesterton, *St. Francis of Assisi* (Garden City, NY: Image Books, Doubleday [1924], 1957), 85.

[6] Esser, *Origins*, 39.

[7] Quoted in Esser, *Origins*, 39. "The world" here means contemporary society and its values, not the physical creation.

filled with like aspirations." James's writings "reveal how deeply the Friars Minor were linked in life and ideals with the already flourishing movement of the high Middle Ages to renew the life of the Gospel and the Church of the Apostles."[8] James reported in 1220, "The reason why this Order is spreading so rapidly over the whole earth is that it imitates so designedly the life of the primitive Church and in every way the life of the Apostles."[9] James later put it simply in a sermon to Franciscan brothers just after the saint's canonization: Francis "expressly followed Christ ... *for this reason* were his sons multiplied."[10]

Esser adds, "What fervent Christians of the time sought so ardently, but what unfortunately was so frequently lived in heretical fashion, was offered to them in Francis and his Order in a form that was at once orthodox and worthy of being followed. This was the reason ... why men the world over flocked to him." Esser explains, "In Francis we see the redeeming proof ... that one can live an apostolic life like the heretics ... and yet remain completely Catholic."[11]

The unique person of Francis in turn combined dynamically with several other key factors:

2. *Support of the papacy.* Unquestionably, the pope's support was a powerful factor in Franciscan growth.[12] Innocent III was a formidable figure, and the renewal of the church (as he understood it) was high on his agenda, as we saw in discussing the Fourth Lateran Council of 1215.

Innocent III was arguably the most powerful figure of the times, not only spiritually but also politically. He had considerable military and economic power at his disposal. The pope's ability and readiness to exercise the "two swords" of church and state and his promotion of the Crusades were major factors. Europe's various kings and princes may have had considerable power within their own regions, but only the pope had so many far-reaching levers of influence in his hands.

Pope Innocent was as sincere as Francis in his desire for church reform. But the two men understood reform and renewal quite differently. Innocent III was determined to stamp out corruption and unfaithfulness among the clergy and heresy among the people. Renewal for Francis

---

[8] Esser, *Origins,* 39.

[9] Quoted in Esser, *Origins,* 39. James wrote this from Damietta, Egypt, where he observed Francis's attempts to witness to Muslim leaders at the height of the Fifth Crusade.

[10] Quoted in Esser, *Origins,* 38, emphasis Esser's.

[11] Esser, *Origins,* 39, 52 n. 87.

[12] Esser, *Origins,* 38.

was something much more radical: an actual literal following of Jesus Christ, ministering to others in the spirit of Jesus. The pope was happy to endorse this as *part* of his overall agenda, his larger program of reform—which for him included backing crusades against heretics and Muslims.

The pope's support of Francis was crucial. In cities and parishes across Europe it meant two things: First, that the Franciscan brothers were themselves not heretics to be feared or persecuted. Second, that priests and bishops should welcome Francis's brothers. Priests should give them free reign to preach, teach, and serve others. Some church leaders did this reluctantly, fearing the Lesser Brothers would be disturbers of the peace with their radical gospel. But many priests and other clergy welcomed the Franciscans and their charismatic preaching and hands-on service to the poor, to lepers and others, seeing them as partners in their work. This was increasingly so as the Lesser Brothers spread and proved their worth.

Pope Innocent died unexpectedly in 1216 at age fifty. He was quickly replaced by Honorius III, an aged and infirm cardinal with a gentle spirit. The new pope's maxim was, "My rule will be lenient rather than stern."[13] Honorius III reigned for ten years, however, dying in 1227, a year after Francis's death. It was he who approved Francis's Later Rule (*Regula bullata*) in 1223.

Honorius III continued Innocent's policy of backing Francis and promoting the Lesser Brothers' expansion and ministry. The brothers are "sowing the seed of the word of God, after the example of the Apostles," Honorius said. Church leaders therefore should "let them go about by different places" (that is, travel about freely).[14]

Another influential supporter was Cardinal Hugolino (later Pope Gregory IX). Hugolino admired Francis's radical discipleship and call to poverty; Francis for his part valued Hugolino's upright life and his counsel. At Francis's request, Pope Honorius appointed Hugolino as a kind of advisor-overseer for the whole Order.

Thomas of Celano notes that Hugolino "was very anxious to establish" Franciscan communities "everywhere; and in far-off lands the illustrious reputation of [Francis's] yet more illustrious life secured for the Order the widest diffusion."[15]

---

[13] Friedrich Gontard, *The Chair of Peter: A History of the Papacy*, trans. A. J. and E. F. Peeler (New York: Holt, Rinehart and Winston, 1964), 273.

[14] Quoted in Esser, *Origins*, 54.

[15] Thomas of Celano, *Life of St. Francis*, FA:ED 1:269, 24, as translated by Esser, *Origins*, 38. Significantly, as Pope Gregory IX, Hugolino was "one of the most influential

3. *Francis's preaching.* Francis, it turned out, was a charismatic preacher in the most basic biblical sense. He preached in everyday Italian, not scholarly Latin.[16] Above all, his preaching was embodied and authenticated in his life.

Francis had a natural simple charism that attracted people, the fruit of the image of God in him. He spoke simply. These "natural" gifts were then inflamed by his conversion, his deep sense of God, and the way he saw God's glory reflected throughout the whole creation. "Praise be you, My Lord, through our Sister Mother Earth, who sustains and governs us, and who produces various fruit with colored flowers and herbs" (*Canticle of the Creatures*).[17]

Thomas of Celano tells how Francis in Italy, like Jesus in Galilee, "went around the cities and villages, proclaiming the kingdom of God and preaching peace and penance for the remission of sins, not in the persuasive words of human wisdom but in the learning and power of the Spirit."[18] Francis would at times speak "with such fire of spirit that he could not contain himself for joy. As he brought forth the word from his mouth, he moved his feet as if dancing, not playfully but burning with the fire of divine love, not provoking laughter but moving [his hearers] to tears of sorrow. For many of them were touched in their hearts, amazed at the grace of God" expressed through Francis.[19]

Francis called directly for conversion. Guided "by divine revelation, he chose to dwell among men for the edification of others, since [the brothers] had been especially sent by the Lord to convert many people."[20]

Bonaventure described Francis as "a great teacher. He spoke accurately about creation and the simplicity of eternal truths. But he did not have the required competence from himself, he was enlightened entirely from on high. He unraveled hidden mysteries."[21]

---

supporters of female religious movements during the Middle Ages," including the Poor Clares. Introduction in Regis J. Armstrong, ed. and trans., *The Lady: Clare of Assisi: Early Documents* (Hyde Park, NY: New City Press, 2006), 19.

[16] Stephen of Bourbon (a Dominican brother) in a tract of about 1255, FA:ED 2:789.

[17] See chapter 15.

[18] Thomas of Celano, *Life of St. Francis*, FA:ED 1:214–15; see Mark 9:15; Matt. 9:35; Acts 10:36; Mark 1:4; 1 Cor. 2:4.

[19] Thomas of Celano, *Life of St. Francis*, FA:ED 1:245.

[20] *A Life of Saint Francis by an Anonymous Monk of a German Monastery* (c. 1275), FA:ED 3:844. Similarly Bonaventure, *Major Legend*, FA:ED 2:551.

[21] Bonaventure, *The Evening Sermon on Saint Francis*, 1267, FA:ED 2:763.

The winsome simplicity of Francis's preaching is clear from contemporary accounts. His preaching power arose from his always pointing back to Jesus and the first Apostles. This was enriched by Francis's surprisingly wide knowledge of Scripture, both Testaments. Francis simply lifted Jesus, then pointed to people's lives and behavior now. The jarring contrast pricked ordinary folks' hearts and consciences, and sometimes those of the rich and powerful as well. Francis's charism was in turn multiplied in his brothers, many of whom, it turned out, also had preaching gifts.

An anonymous German monk wrote,

Though [Francis] often preached the Word of God among thousands of people, he was as confident as if he were speaking to a close friend. He used to view the largest crowd of people as if it were a single person, and he would preach fervently to a single person or to a few as if to a large crowd. He often uttered the most amazing things about which he had not previously thought. Sometimes when he could not remember what he had meditated about and did not know what to say, he would confess to the people without embarrassment that he had forgotten what he intended to say, would give a blessing to the people, and send them away. His eloquence was inflamed with zeal, moving the hearts of his listeners from the depths and ascending by the flame of compunction. Apostolic authority resided in him, and therefore he altogether refused to flatter the powerful of the world.[22]

We picture Francis, without notes, heartily preaching messages that he had prepared through meditation.

Bonaventure later summarized Francis's preaching:

Because he first convinced himself by action and then convinced others by word, [Francis] did not fear rebuke, but spoke the truth boldly. He did not encourage, but struck at the life of sin with a sharp blow, nor did he smooth over, but struck at the faults of sinners with harsh reproaches. He spoke with the same constancy of mind to the great and the small, and would speak with the same joy of spirit to the few as to the many.

[22] *A Life of Saint Francis by an Anonymous Monk of a German Monastery*, FA:ED 3:854–55. The author here draws on material from Thomas of Celano, *Life of St. Francis*.

People of all ages and both sexes hurried to see and hear this new man given to the world by heaven. Moving about through various regions, he preached the Gospel ardently, as the Lord worked with him and confirmed his preaching with signs that followed.[23]

On one occasion Francis was to preach before Pope Honorius III and his cardinals. Coached by Cardinal Hugolino, Francis prepared and memorized an appropriate sermon. But when he stood up to preach, his mind went blank. He admitted this to the august assembly, and asked for the Spirit's help. "Suddenly he began to overflow with such effective eloquence and to move the minds of those high-ranking men to compunction with such force and power that it was clearly evident it was not he, but the Spirit of the Lord who was speaking."[24]

Bonaventure mentions "signs that followed," a reference to Mark 16:20. Sometimes Francis's preaching, like Jesus's, was reinforced by physical healings. But the main power of his preaching was its passion and simplicity, accredited by Francis's life. Bonaventure notes that in Francis's view, preaching "should be done more by example than by word, more by tear-filled prayer than by long-winded sermons."[25]

One eyewitness, Thomas of Split, gives a poignant picture of Francis preaching before a large crowd at the town square in Bologna. This was in 1222, when Thomas was studying at Bologna's famed university. Thomas writes,

The theme of his sermon was: "Angels, People, Demons." He spoke so well and so clearly about these three kinds of rational creatures that this unlettered man's sermon became the source of not a little amazement for the many educated people who were present. He did not, however, hold to the usual manner of preaching, but spoke like a political orator. The whole tenor of his words concerned itself with abolishing hostilities and renewing agreements of peace. His habit was filthy, his whole appearance contemptible, and his face unattractive; but God gave his words such efficacy that many factions of the nobility,

[23] Bonaventure, *Major Legend*, FA:ED 2:626. Bonaventure here reworks Thomas of Celano's description of Francis preaching (FA:ED 1:215) and in the last sentence paraphrases Mark 16:20.
[24] Bonaventure, *Major Legend*, FA:ED 2:626; see also Thomas of Celano, *Life of St. Francis*, FA:ED 1:245.
[25] Bonaventure, *Major Legend*, FA:ED 2:587.

among whom the monstrous madness of long-standing enmities had raged uncontrollably with much bloodshed, were led to negotiate peace. There was such great popular reverence and devotion towards him, that a mob of men and women crowded in upon him, jostling about either to touch the fringe of his habit or even tear off a shred of his ragged clothing.[26]

Thomas of Celano writes that Francis "preached to the simple, in simple, concrete terms, since he knew that virtue is more necessary than words." But when he was "among spiritual people with greater abilities he gave birth to life-giving and profound words. With few words he would suggest what was inexpressible, and, weaving movement with fiery gestures, he carried away all his hearers toward the things of heaven."[27]

The French bishop James de Vitry believed Francis's preaching and that of other gifted Lesser Brothers was key to their rapid growth. He concluded (in a letter in 1216) that "before the end of the world, the Lord wishes by means of these poor and simple men to save many souls ... since the prelates are like 'dumb watchdogs unable to bark.'"[28]

4. *The powerful witness of Franciscan life and community.* The anonymous author of the *Normandy Chronicle* speaks of the "completely new form of life of the friars." Franciscan life together was a magnet that attracted youth especially, he noted. This author was unsympathetic toward the brothers, Esser notes, making his view of the Franciscans all the more poignant.[29]

Henri d'Avranches in his *Versified Life* speaks of Francis's appeal to all classes. Francis welcomed many young men into the community, irrespective of class or reputation: "the good, the bad, the high, the low, the rustic and the knight, commoner and man of noble blood, cleric and layman, the raw and the refined, the pauper, the rich man, the serf and freeman, the healthy and the sick. And Francis to one and all, a kind and loving welcome gave. The pattern he set attracted them, his exemplary, blameless life, all that lent authority to his words."[30]

James de Vitry was impressed "above all" that the Franciscans would "exclude no candidate from their community." Rather they would accept

---

[26] Chronicle of Thomas of Split, FA:ED 2:808.

[27] Thomas of Celano, *Remembrance*, FA:ED 2:318.

[28] Quoted in Esser, *Origins*, 37.

[29] Esser, *Origins*, 10, 37–38.

[30] Henri d'Avranches, *Versified Life of Saint Francis: Additions, Amplifications in Light of* The Major Legend, FA:ED 3:90–91 (reformatted from poetry to prose).

them "in full membership ... without any obstacle." James was astonished at the open equality of the Franciscan community where traditional social distinctions no longer applied. In fact, the Franciscans did not actually accept just anyone; every brother had to become poor and live the Rule. But social status, high or low, was no barrier.

The radical openness to all, combined with the radical commitment required to follow Francis, attracted youth who saw the world around them changing. Francis gave them a community and a cause. "Thus could the forces, aroused and enkindled by the religious movements of the high Middle Ages, flow freely into the Franciscan movement, just as the Lord guided them, without any 'worldly' barrier to hold them back."[31]

Cajetan Esser stresses this last point, especially. Francis and his brothers were not a revolt of one social class against another. Esser wrote,

> The members of this new Order come from all classes in Christendom, and no real importance is attached to differences of origin and birth. One should not regard the Order, therefore, as a reaction of a political or social nature, whereby the lower social strata sought to gain for themselves status in the Church and in society. In essence, the [brotherhood] is thoroughly Christian, based entirely on the Gospel. To that extent, even though this may not have been the founder's intention, it is actually a renewal of the "form of the primitive Church."[32]

In its early most dynamic days, the Order transcended the clergy/laity split: "cleric and laic are so united in one Christian fraternity, that all, whether cleric or lay, are *brothers* and 'members of one household.'" As the "Order of Lesser Brothers," the Franciscans "actually endeavored to replace the ancient feudal principle of class-distinction (accepted by most existing Orders) by the principle of evangelical brotherhood among its members. For this reason, this brotherhood ... is open to all classes of Christians. This aspect of the Order, which proved so attractive in those days, is not the least reason why the Order expanded so rapidly," writes Esser.[33]

In this sense—this truly fundamental sense—Francis and his brothers embodied a social revolution.

---

[31] Esser, *Origins*, 10, 37–38.
[32] Esser, *Origins*, 41–42.
[33] Esser, *Origins*, 42 (emphasis in the original).

5. The ferment caused by heretical movements. Religious movements such as the Cathars and Waldensians, seen as heretics, were greatly troubling the church. Or to reverse the argument: the Roman Church with its growing influence, abuses, political power, and authoritarian vertical hierarchy was prompting protests, resistance, and calls for renewal and deeper piety in many places across Europe. *Why,* these movements asked, was the church imposing unilateral authority and demanding unquestioning obedience to the pope and his cardinals and bishops rather than living and acting like Jesus? What had happened to the simplicity and spiritual dynamism of the early church? These oppositional groups were creating networks of communities of resistance, and many people were drawn to them.

Any movement that did not submit to the pope's authority was by definition heretical. There were big differences, however, between the Cathars, whose teachings clashed with Scripture at key points, and the Waldensians, who were seeking to renew the church and to follow Jesus free from the structure and trappings of a politically and economically powerful bureaucracy.

Francis and his brothers embodied a fresh and attractive solution, a way radically to follow Jesus that the Roman Church itself endorsed.

6. Spiritual decline of older monastic orders. One chronicler wrote that the older orders no longer had much impact because of the "inordinate manner of life" of their members. As Esser puts it, these orders "no longer attracted those who wished to leave the world" because they were not living what they preached.[34] The genuineness of the Lesser Brothers' visible witness shone even more brightly.

7. Francis's appeal to women as well as men. Thousands of women heard Francis preach. They saw their own sons or brothers going off to follow "the little poor man." Young women were moved by Francis's example and looked for ways to follow him. Above all was Clare of Assisi, whose remarkable story we will pick up shortly.

The early Lesser Brothers were of course that: brothers, not sisters. Observers were surprised therefore to see a women's movement also rising. Already in 1216, James de Vitry commented on women followers of Francis. Little communities of "Poor Ladies" sprang up near Assisi and

---

[34] Esser, *Origins*, 37. The quoted chronicler here is an unknown Premonstratensian monk based near Halle, Germany.

in other towns. These were women who followed Clare's example, giving up all possessions and forming convents (*hospitia,* they were called in Latin). These were the Poor Clares.

This parallel women's movement is often called the Second Order of Saint Francis—that is, the order founded by Clare under Francis's guidance. James de Vitry noted that these women led a fully communal life, having everything in common, which was not true of the Lesser Brothers.

Thomas of Celano himself documented this rising women's movement. Through Francis "the Church of Christ is being renewed in both sexes according to his form, rule and teaching," Thomas wrote, "and there is victory for the triple army of those being saved." By "triple army" Thomas means the Lesser Brothers, the Poor Ladies, and the so-called lay penitents—men and women who did not themselves enter orders, but whose lives were changed through Francis's life and teachings, and to whom Francis "gave a norm of life."[35] Such people were often called "tertiaries," meaning Third Order, men and women who, inspired by Francis, lived devout lives within everyday society.[36]

8. *Breakdown of feudalism.* The medieval system held firm for centuries but was now crumbling. Assisi itself was a microcosm of the transition from the older feudal order to the rising dynamism of commerce, regional trade, and municipal organization. The families of Francis and Clare themselves embodied the changes. Clare was raised in a traditional noble family whose influence was waning; Francis's father, a prospering cloth merchant, engaged in wide-ranging buying and selling.

The changing cultural context of Francis and his movement—religious, economic, political, social—opened the door to movements of various sorts—the Crusades; new business ventures; and new religious movements, heretical or otherwise. Commerce and the growth of craftsmen's guilds, increasing travel, and the rise of universities all played a role in Europe's social and cultural ferment. Thousands of young men flocked to centers of learning like Paris, Oxford, Bologna, Madrid, and others. University instruction was in Latin. Around the universities, students from various parts of Europe, speaking their own languages, grouped themselves into "nations" for mutual support. This in turn contributed to a sense of independence and self-government, suggests James Walsh, over time feeding social ferment across Europe. The various

---

[35] Thomas of Celano, *Life of St. Francis,* FA:ED 1:216–17.
[36] The key importance of these Third Order Franciscans (*tertiaries*) will be discussed in Chapter 20.

student groupings "represented the rise of that democratic spirit, which was to make itself felt in the claims for the recognition of rights for all the people in most of the countries [later] during the Thirteenth Century."[37]

Student communities at the universities constituted a ready-made entrée for the young Lesser Brothers who soon appeared among them. This in turn opened the door to the surprising impact the Franciscan brothers would have in all the major universities then forming and growing across Europe.

In sum, eight key factors help us understand the growth and dynamism of the Franciscan fraternity: (1) Most basic was the impact of Francis's own life. Added to this was, (2) the backing of the papacy, (3) Francis's preaching, (4) the dynamism of Franciscan community, (5) ferment sparked by heretical movements, (6) spiritual decline of older orders, (7) Francis's appeal to women as well as men, all in the context of (8) the breakdown of feudalism.

But we must dig deeper. This is not the whole story. If these eight factors explain the Franciscan Order's mushrooming growth, we are still left with *how* and *why* questions. How did a simple, lightly educated youth from Assisi unleash such dynamism? Answering this requires looking more closely at the innovations Francis introduced.

Francis's Innovations

Compared to Saint Benedict of Nursia (c. 480–547), founder of the Benedictines, or Ignatius Loyola (1491–1556), founder of the Jesuits centuries later, Saint Francis was no great organizer, so it seems. He wrote little; his Rule was simple and mostly Bible quotes; he established nothing like Loyola's *Spiritual Exercises* or Benedict's detailed *Rule*. Franciscans were racked by disputes and divisions shortly after Francis's death, and even before.

It is therefore easy to misread or underestimate Francis's organizational genius. But genius there was—genius of a different sort. Francis wanted minimal structure, maximal flexibility; minimum formality, maximum informality; little mandate, much personal responsibility; no

---

[37] James J. Walsh, *The Thirteenth: Greatest of Centuries* (New York: Catholic Summer School Press, 1907), 77. Walsh notes that the students' "very struggle to maintain [independence from university authorities] ... was of itself a precious training against the usurpation of privileges that was to be of great service later in the larger arena of national politics, and the effects of which can be noted in every country in Europe, nowhere more than in England, where the development of law and liberty was to give rise to a supreme heritage of democratic jurisprudence for the English speaking peoples of all succeeding generations" (77). Walsh is probably at least partially right here.

status-seeking, great humility. In short, there was more living organism than formal organization.

Francis perhaps reminds us of Jesus, who left no book, no doctrinal creed, no organizational chart—but plenty of inspiration and a perfect example and access to the Holy Spirit.

Just as Francis wanted to be like Jesus, so he wanted the brothers to be like the first disciples. He took seriously Jesus's words:

> You know that the rulers of the Gentiles lord it over them, and their great ones are tyrants over them. It will not be so among you; but whoever wishes to be great among you must be your servant, and whoever wishes to be first among you must be your slave; just as the Son of Man came not to be served but to serve, and to give his life a ransom for many. (Matt. 20:25–28)
>
> But you are not to be called rabbi, for you have one teacher, and you are all students. And call no one your father on earth, for you have one Father—the one in heaven. Nor are you to be called instructors, for you have one instructor, the Messiah. The greatest among you will be your servant. All who exalt themselves will be humbled, and all who humble themselves will be exalted. (Matt. 23:8–12)

The stir that the earliest Franciscan community provoked, and the things observers most remarked upon, offer clear testimony to Francis's innovative genius. From the earliest days, observers commented on the Franciscan community's novelty, its innovations.

Other religious orders were very well known, of course. Especially the Benedictines and Cistercians—the latter an order of monks and nuns that arose as a renewal within the Benedictine Order a century before Francis. The key figure in the rise and rapid spread of the Cistercians was Bernard of Clairvaux (1090–1153), canonized less than a decade before Francis was born. By Francis's day, Saint Bernard was famous. Cistercians had founded monasteries throughout much of Europe, from Italy and Spain to Scotland and Ireland. Living in cloistered communities, both Benedictines and Cistercians engaged in manual labor, especially agriculture, and had a large influence on both church and culture.[38]

---

[38] Through their financial transactions and agricultural innovations, the Benedictines and Cistercians also had a significant impact on the economy and on the rise of capitalism. See Rodney Stark, *The Victory of Reason: How Christianity Led to Freedom, Capitalism, and Western Success* (New York: Random House, 2005, 2006), esp. 55–61.

But the Franciscans embodied a different reality, something unique. New wine was being poured into new wineskins. As a new order, the Franciscans "represented something completely new in the religious life of the Church," states Esser.[39]

First and foremost, the Franciscans were not cloistered. A distinct order, yes, but highly mobile. This required "new forms of discipline . . . to bind together this community, which from the outside seemed so loosely knit, and permit it to take on the form of a common life, with certain new features."[40]

Francis was adamant: he did not want his brothers to be elaborately organized with a highly structured way of life, like other orders. So, Francis introduced several creative innovations that enabled the Lesser Brothers to thrive with minimal formal structure. In fact, Francis was not really trying to organize anything or invent anything. He simply wanted to do what Jesus did—he himself, and all his brothers.

Francis introduced eight structural novelties: (1) *a common covenant,* expressed in the Rule; (2) *common clothing,* the Franciscan habit; (3) teams of *traveling preachers*; (4) brothers *sent on mission*; (5) a fraternity *living homeless lives*; (6) *annual chapter gatherings*; (7) *the bond of common prayer*; and (8) *a vital network of hermitages.* These were the sinews that held the brotherhood together. On the surface, they seem like other orders. But eyewitnesses saw something new here and in the way these ties interconnected.

1. *Common covenant.* The brothers were bound together willingly by shared covenant, the Rule Francis himself wrote. At the beginning, when Peter Catani and Bernardo da Quintavalle first joined him, Francis wrote down a simple Rule based on Jesus's words to his first Galilean followers when he sent them out. The Rule bound the brothers together, not in a legal or contractual sense, but as a relational bond by which they pledged themselves to Francis and to the shared life of poverty he modeled. This was powerful. It was not so much a covenant of word as of act and whole-person lifestyle. The Rule gave the brothers their *forma vitae,* their form of life.

Early observers did not fully grasp the import of the brothers' Rule. The point they mainly stressed was that this new community was approved by the pope. But for the brothers themselves, the more

---

[39] Esser, *Origins,* 53.
[40] Esser, *Origins,* 53.

important point was that they were bound in covenant to Francis, to one another, and above all to Jesus Christ and his example.[41]

Other orders had their rules or constitutions, of course. But Francis insisted that his brothers *not* adopt one of these earlier rules. That was not what Jesus had said to do. Existing rules were both too strict and too lenient—too strict in the ways they regimented members' daily lives and too lenient—not radical enough—in the life to which the brothers were called. Francis "sought to embody in a form binding on his friars the great desire of his [own] heart, namely, a way of life according to the Gospel."[42]

2. *Common clothing: the Franciscan habit.* Here again the point was to follow Jesus as simply as they could. Their habit was like the way Jesus's first apostles were generally visualized in the High Middle Ages. The brothers' common clothing gave visible witness to their common calling.[43]

Early observers of the Franciscans commented on their habit. Some were surprised or dismayed at the brothers' poor clothing, what one called the "rough sackcloth" the brothers wore. A monk named Richerius described Francis this way: "He wore a kind of tunic on which there was a capuche [hood], but of the very poorest cloth, and girded himself with a knotted cord, and so, shoeless and tonsured, he went forth."[44] Buoncompagni the Rhetor noted in 1220 that the Franciscan brothers followed Jesus in simple clothing and bare feet. In England at the renowned Benedictine Abbey of St. Albans, Roger of Wendover commented with some admiration, "In food and clothing they display the most extreme poverty, walking barefoot, giving to all the greatest example of humility."[45]

Also in England, the eminent Benedictine artist and chronicler Matthew Paris wrote that the brothers "go barefoot, girded with ropes, wearing grey tunics, patched and reaching to the heel, with a capuche sewn on."[46] (Franciscan tunics might be brown or grey, depending on the cloth available in the regions where they lived. In England the Franciscans were commonly called Greyfriars due to the color of their habits.)

James de Vitry reported that many young men "put on the habit of the Friars Minor, that is, the mean and shabby tunic which they wear and

---

[41] See Esser, *Origins*, 84–96.
[42] Esser, *Origins*, 87.
[43] Esser, *Origins*, 96–97.
[44] Quoted in Esser, *Origins*, 97.
[45] Both are quoted in Esser, *Origins*, 97, with sources specified.
[46] Matthew Paris, *Historia Anglorum*, quoted in Esser, *Origins*, 98.

the rope with which they are girded." The brothers "wear neither furs nor linen, but only woolen tunics fitted with a capuche; they have no capes, mantles, or [other] hoods, nor any other piece of clothing."[47]

The Franciscan habit was so distinctive that the brothers were instantly recognized as they traveled about. "Plain and simple," the Lesser Brothers' clothing "hardly differed at first from the dress of other poor people, yet within a few years it became the *signum distinctivum* [distinctive sign] whereby the Friars Minor were set off from their contemporaries and recognized as such. Men of that time soon came to see it as a true religious habit."[48] The brothers sometimes patched their tunics inside and out, not only because of wear but to add warmth in cold weather. Francis wrote in his *Testament* that the brothers were "content with one tunic, patched inside and out, with a cord and short trousers."[49] In some circumstances, however, they did in fact wear shoes or sandals.[50]

3. *Traveling preachers.* The most striking thing about the Franciscans was how the brothers went "through the world calling people everywhere to repentance and proclaiming the Kingdom of God." Such a way of life "made the stable, cloistered life unthinkable," notes Esser.[51] This starkly contrasted with the traditional monastic way. Benedictine monks for example took a "vow of stability," committing themselves for life to their particular monastery.

In 1216, James de Vitry noted that after their annual gatherings, the brothers scattered: "Throughout the year they are dispersed through Lombardy, Tuscany, Apulia, and Sicily."[52]

4. Brothers *sent on mission.* Francis's brothers did not travel about randomly (as some alleged). They were *sent*—commissioned by Francis himself.

The missionary impulse was part of Francis's own calling. As soon as the brothers numbered eight (including Francis himself), he commissioned them, wrote Julian of Speyer: "calling them all together and pairing them two-by-two," he "sent them forth into the diverse parts of the world." Francis "earnestly explained many things to them about the reign of God and contempt of the world and of self," and especially "about patience

---

[47] Quoted in Esser, *Origins*, 98, with source noted.
[48] Esser, *Origins*, 99.
[49] Francis, *The Testament*, FA:ED 1:125.
[50] Esser, *Origins*, 100.
[51] Esser, *Origins*, 54.
[52] Quoted in Esser, *Origins*, 54.

and humility." Following Jesus as literally as he could, Francis "provided them not with an extra coin in their belts, but with a heart free of worry for tomorrow."[53]

As the brothers' numbers grew, Francis continued sending them in pairs or small teams into different countries and cities. Bishop James de Vitry noted in 1220, the brothers "are sent out two by two throughout the world."[54] Roger of Wendover reported that the Franciscan brothers traveled from town to town "in groups of ten or seven to preach the word of life."[55]

Some churchmen disapproved, naturally. One complained that the Franciscan brothers wandered through towns and cities "without discretion."[56] Another chronicler, probably thinking of the many established monasteries of other orders, wrote that the Franciscan brothers were "running about everywhere."[57] By this time the new Order of Preachers (Dominicans) was also sending out preachers. But the Dominicans focused on combatting heresy and false doctrines. The Franciscan passion was preaching repentance to all and teaching everyone the day-by-day following of Jesus.

5. A brotherhood *living homeless lives*. Describing early Franciscan ministry in some detail, James de Vitry was struck above all by their homelessness. "By day [the brothers] go into the cities and villages to win souls to God, dedicating themselves to the active ministry; at night, however, they return to deserted or remote places to give themselves to contemplation." The early Franciscans lived without fixed dwellings or assured means of support. "They have no monasteries or churches, fields or vineyards or animals, houses or other property where they may lay their heads," James noted, unlike other orders. Esser comments, "The monastery of the Friars Minor, if we may thus phrase it, is the wide world."[58] Like Francis, the brothers were wholly committed to Lady Poverty. "The contrast between the homeless friars and the other religious orders" could not be clearer, Esser writes. "Their 'cloister' is the wide world, where they seek to serve the Kingdom of God by a life of poverty."[59]

---

[53] Julian of Speyer, *The Life of Saint Francis*, FA:ED 1:381. Bonaventure renders Julian of Speyer's text: "[Francis] revealed his proposal to send them to the four corners of the world." Bonaventure, *Major Legend*, FA:ED 2:546.

[54] Quoted in Esser, *Origins*, 54.

[55] Esser, *Origins*, 54.

[56] Esser, *Origins*, 54, quoting Buoncompagni the Rhetor in about 1220.

[57] Esser, *Origins*, 54.

[58] James de Vitry in Esser, *Origins*, 55; Esser, *Origins*, 55.

[59] Esser, *Origins*, 57.

"Then as later," Esser notes, "anxiety about a fixed place to live seems never to have worried these wandering preachers."[60] Thomas of Celano wrote,

> Disturbed by no fears, distracted by no cares, they awaited the next day without any worry. Though frequently on hazardous journeys, they were not anxious about where they might stay the next day. Often they needed a place to stay in extreme cold, and a baker's oven would receive them; or they would hide for the night humbly in caves or crypts.[61]

At other times the brothers might lodge as guests in the homes of church leaders or friends. This form of life marked the Lesser Brothers of the first generation. Esser notes that "in the first decades of the Order's existence, the Friars Minor, as true religious and yet free from all ties of monastic stability, went through the world on apostolic journeyings," following "the example of Christ and his Apostles."[62] This began to change, however, even before Francis's death in 1226.

6. *Annual chapter gatherings.* Not long after the first small group of brothers joined Francis, he began sending them out on missions, as we saw. But before long Francis yearned to see them again, and they wanted to see him.

Esser puts it this way: "When the friars were only eight in number, Francis sent them by the 'mandate of holy obedience' to the four points of the compass, two by two, to preach" the good news. "Soon, however, he longed to see them all, and prayed to God to bring them back once more. Thus they soon found themselves together again."[63] And so began the Franciscan chapters (assemblies), usually held annually. These reunions became a major feature, a key punctuation point, in the Franciscan way of life. None of the more traditional orders did this. These reunions were key in kindling and renewing the Francis spirit and ethos, especially as the number of brothers grew into hundreds, then thousands.

Coming together again, the brothers shared their adventures, reported to Francis, confessed failings, prayed, and received Francis's correction and teaching. Like Jesus, Francis was always teaching the brothers the meaning of their way of life, often drawing on Scripture, especially

---

[60] Esser, *Origins*, 57.
[61] Thomas of Celano, *Life of St. Francis*, FA:ED 1:218.
[62] Quoted in Esser, *Origins*, 58.
[63] Esser, *Origins*, 71. Thomas of Celano provides more details, *Life of St. Francis*, FA:ED 1:207–9.

the gospels. Three elements—recounting experiences, confession, and instruction—became the pattern of chapter assemblies.[64]

Esser summarizes: "During these reunions [the brothers] experienced in holy joy a sense of their oneness and community, and, through the meal they all shared in, a sense of belonging together. The days of Chapter became a happy means of manifesting outwardly the bond of brotherhood which inwardly welded them into a community." As Francis and the brothers met together, they also discussed strategy and the challenges they faced, and they made decisions for the future. Thus, the chapter took on an organic legislative function.[65]

Most of the early chapters were held at the Portiuncula near Assisi, but with time they were held in other places, as noted earlier. The chapters lasted several days, sometimes a week or more.[66]

James de Vitry noted, "After the Chapter, [the brothers] are sent by [Francis], in groups of two or more, into the different regions, provinces and cities."[67] As the number of brothers multiplied in other countries, smaller regional chapters were held (provincial chapters) in addition to the annual chapter (General Chapter). As early as about 1228, provincial chapters were being held in London or Oxford and at various places on the Continent.[68]

Chapter gatherings—reunions, much like early Methodist camp meetings centuries later—were thus a key unifying bond as the brotherhood expanded. These were supplemented also by personal visits that Francis, and with time other leaders, made to the brothers in their various places of ministry. Francis gave the brothers freedom to appeal to him in any time of great difficulty. He sometimes appointed "vicars" to travel around in his stead and see how the brothers were doing and console or comfort them as might be needed. The Earlier Rule instructed, "Let all the brothers who have been designated the ministers and servants of the other brothers assign their brothers [to their missions] in the provinces and places where they may be, and let them frequently visit, admonish and encourage them spiritually."[69] The Later Rule (*Regula bullata*) had a similar provision.

---

[64] Esser, *Origins*, 71.
[65] Esser, *Origins*, 72–73.
[66] Esser, *Origins*, 75, 78, citing James de Vitry.
[67] Quoted in Esser, *Origins*, 73.
[68] Esser, *Origins*, 78–80.
[69] "The Earlier Rule," FA:ED 1:66.

7. *The bond of common prayer.* All men and women in monastic orders lived a life of prayer, of course, their days ordered by the hours of the Divine Office. The Franciscans also followed this practice (as noted above in chapter 7). But whereas the Dominicans and some other orders developed their own patterns of prayer, the Franciscans used the same Liturgy of the Hours as did the church in Rome. Francis himself insisted that the brothers maintain the same pattern of worship everywhere. Esser remarks, "That an Order should thus introduce uniformity of worship throughout the whole community was something completely new in the history of liturgy!"[70] This uniform practice of prayer daily bound the brothers not only to God and each other but also to the church.

In England, the chronicler Thomas of Eccleston, himself a Franciscan, commented on the prayer life of the Lesser Brothers. About 1258, Thomas completed his chronicle, *The Coming of the Lesser Brothers to England.* Thomas told how the brothers sang together the prayers of the canonical hours. Thus "on the main feast days they sang with such great fervor that at times their vigils continued throughout the night; and even if there were no more than three or four, or at most six, they sang solemnly with music."[71]

The brothers recited "intercessory prayers for the friars living and dead, which gave the fraternity an increased sense of community," Esser notes.[72] In this way the brothers gradually developed their own poetic liturgies for remembering departed brothers and for commemorating special days in the life of the Order.

The Breviary. Fairly early, Franciscans started using *breviaries,* handbooks containing the prayers for the canonical hours. Breviaries first appeared in the Roman Church at the same time that the Franciscan brotherhood was emerging. Pope Innocent III authorized their use, probably in connection with the reforms introduced by the Fourth Lateran Council (1215). The breviary was (as the name suggests) a small "brief" one-volume abridgement of the Liturgy of the Hours (Canonical Hours).[73]

---

[70] Esser, *Origins,* 106.

[71] Thomas of Eccleston, *The Coming of the Friars Minor to England,* in *XIIIth Century Chronicles,* trans. Placid Hermann, OFM (Chicago: Franciscan Herald Press, 1961), 117–18.

[72] Esser, *Origins,* 106.

[73] Esser, *Origins,* 105. Esser notes that "under Innocent III—probably in 1215 in connection with the Fourth Lateran Council—an abridged, comprehensive book of the Canonical Hours was compiled in one volume, namely, the Breviary."

Pierre Salmon notes, "The Friars Minor adopted this breviary in 1223 and became its propagators."[74] The Later Rule (*Regula bullata*) specified that the Franciscan brothers were to "recite the Divine Office," and for this reason "they may have breviaries."[75] Through their travels, Franciscans spread thousands of these hand-copied Roman handbooks, written in Latin, across Europe and even beyond. By 1230, the brothers were also using *antiphonaries* (choir books) showing the brothers how to sing (chant) the antiphons (verses from the Psalms) that were used as responses in the Liturgy of the Hours.[76]

A breviary still preserved at the Saint Clare Basilica in Assisi contains an inscription by Brother Leo from about 1257. It reads,

> Blessed Francis acquired this breviary for his companions Brother Angelo and Brother Leo, and when he was well he wished always to say the Office, as is stated by the Rule. At the time when he was sick and not able to recite it, he wished to listen to it. And he continued to do this for as long as he lived. He also had the Book of the Gospels copied, and whenever he would be unable to hear Mass due to infirmity or any other manifest impediment, he had that Gospel read to him, which on that day was read at Mass in Church.[77]

The small hand-copied Latin Breviary became, in effect, the Franciscan's Book of Common Prayer. Its widespread use had two or three effects. It bound the brothers together in common prayer; it gave the Franciscan communities a recognized place within the larger liturgical structure of the church; and it became a means through which the brothers shared their life of prayer, praise, and good works with the life of local parishes, the "laity." The brothers maintained a sort of rhythmic interplay between their own common life and the life of the Catholic congregations in the areas where they ministered. This was in a sense a three-way flow, three forms of community: the local parish

---

[74] Dom Pierre Salmon, *The Breviary through the Ages*, trans. Sister David Mary (Collegeville, MN: Liturgical Press, 1962), 116. "Innocent III (1198–1216), a man of action with a talent for organization, must have naturally been led to get up a less cumbersome, handier and more convenient breviary" than anything then existing (Salmon, 116, quoting Le Carou). This was consistent both with Innocent's reform agenda and with the growth of the Franciscan brotherhood.

[75] "The Later Rule" (chap. 3), FA:ED 1:101.

[76] Esser, *Origins*, 108.

[77] Inscription of Brother Leo, FA:ED 2:773.

church, the Franciscan brothers together, and the "tertiaries" (third-order brothers and sisters and families living their normal day-by-day lives in the world). Powerful!

Each Lesser Brother knew and felt their common unity, especially in the first decades during and then beyond Francis's own lifetime. Their life was a spiritual and social ecosystem consisting of the various elements just noted: common covenant, common clothing, teams of preachers sent out on mission, shared homelessness, annual chapter reunions, and the bond of common prayer and liturgy.

8. *A vital network of hermitages.* The Franciscan life of prayer and mission was deepened by the Order's hermitages, the network of retreat houses the brothers founded. Lesser Brothers must not have homes or established centers, but they *were* to have hermitages and to use them often.

Typically, the hermitages were located in remote places—the term "hermitage" is rooted in the Latin word for "desert"—and were quite simple. They were not walled, but were often surrounded by a hedge. Cells were humble, made of clay or wood or branches or of small natural caves or grottos.[78] Often hermitages were sited in hills or mountains at higher elevations above towns and cities. The Franciscan author Ignatius Brady writes, "Francis himself constantly felt the need for periods of solitude and inner prayer in out-of-the-way places. And as a result, it was not long before the Order, which was not supposed to own the property, nevertheless acquired the use of *many* solitary places for the pursuit of deeper prayer and penance."[79]

One of Francis's earliest writings is in fact his *Rule for Hermitages,* a short set of instructions written about 1217. Francis probably composed this while he himself was on retreat at LaVerna, the mountain where he later received the *stigmata.*[80] "Names of hermitages are spread throughout the early biographies of the saint."[81] Spending time apart in prayer and reflection was a key element in Franciscan life from early on.[82]

---

[78] Cajetan Esser, OFM, "The *Regula Pro Eremitoriis Data* of St. Francis of Assisi," *Franciscan Solitude*, in André Cirino, OFM, and Josef Raischl (St. Bonaventure, NY: The Franciscan Institute, St. Bonaventure University, 1975), 184.

[79] Ignatius Brady, OFM, "A 'Rule for Hermitages,'" in Cirino and Raischl, *Franciscan Solitude*, 196 (emphasis added).

[80] The full text is given (in English) in FA:ED 1:61–62, and (in Latin and English) in Cirino and Raischl, *Franciscan Solitude*, 142–44.

[81] Introduction, *A Rule for Hermitages,* FA:ED 1:61.

[82] There is now a considerable literature on Franciscan hermitages. See especially Cirino and Raischl, *Franciscan Solitude*.

Hermitages were a common feature of medieval spirituality, of course. They were not unique to Franciscans. But Francis turned them into something "distinctly Franciscan."[83]

A fascinating feature of hermitage life is the way Francis employed mother–child and Mary–Martha dynamics. Here Francis reveals once again his feminine side as well as his creativity. Franciscan hermitages blended solitude with intimate community so that time alone was enriched by time shared.

About 1365, Brother Arnald of Sarrant, France, wrote *The Kinship of Saint Francis.* Arnald traced nine "conformities" between Francis and Jesus. He noted, "Just as Christ had many hermits and anchorites, so Francis established many hermitages in which he wanted some to live the life of Martha, and others that of Mary."[84]

In his *Rule for Hermitages* Francis wrote,

1. Those who wish to dwell in a religious way in hermitages may be three brothers or, at the most, four; let two of these be the "mother" and have two "sons" or at least one.

2. Let the two who are "mothers" keep the life of Martha and the two "sons" keep the life of Mary (cf. Lk 10:38–42) and have one enclosure in which each one may have his cell in which he may pray and sleep.[85]

3. And let them always recite Compline of the day immediately after sundown; and strive to maintain silence, recite their Hours, rise for Matins; and seek first the Kingdom of God and His justice (Mt 6:33).

4. And let them recite Prime at the proper hour and, after Terce, they may end their silence, speak with and go to their mothers.

The "sons" normally would eat with their "mothers," then return to their cells to complete the rest of the canonical hours as part of their prayer time, then retire.

Francis specified that no one else was permitted "to enter or eat in the enclosure" of the hermitage. The "mothers'" role was to "protect

---

[83] Introduction, *A Rule for Hermitages,* FA:ED 1:61.

[84] Arnald of Sarrant, *The Kinship of Saint Francis,* FA:ED 3:696.

[85] Appropriating the Mary–Martha roles was not wholly unique to the Franciscans, but Francis's adoption and adaptation of this dynamic shows "how very much Francis wishes to be formed by the gospel." Esser, "The *Regula,*" 183.

their 'sons'" from other people so that their prayers and silence would be undisturbed. The "sons" were to speak to no one other than their "mothers," or perhaps with a supervising brother, should one come to visit.[86] Francis specified finally,

> 10. The "sons," however, may periodically assume the role of the "mothers," taking turns for a time as they have mutually decided. Let them strive to observe conscientiously and eagerly everything mentioned above.[87]

Francis carefully crafted these simple rules to nourish close community and informality—in sharp contrast with the established hierarchical clergy–laity roles. Brothers on retreat in the role of "sons" were to "speak with and go to their mothers"—"speak with," not "confess to." Periodically reversing the mother–son and Mary–Martha roles, the brothers mutually built up one another as the Apostle Paul exhorts in Ephesians 4 and other places. Everything here works against hierarchy and fixed distinctions, even though the Franciscans existed as an order within a highly structured hierarchical church.

In his detailed analysis of *The Rule for Hermitages,* Cajetan Esser notes that the document is "of great significance for the early history of [Francis's] Order."[88]

In some ways the Portiuncula itself was the forerunner of the hermitages. Early on, the community built a separate house near the Portiuncula where brothers could go for solitude and recite their hours (according to some sources). In December 1224, Pope Honorius III specifically permitted the Franciscans to have their own oratories and hermitages.[89]

Esser notes that the Franciscan hermitages "never were supposed to become large, as eventually among the Carthusians" and other orders. "Francis saw the poverty of his Order better preserved in small fraternities." It was in fact the small number of brothers in each hermitage "that distinguishes the Franciscan hermitage from the numerous contemporary forms of this sort," notes Esser. Francis did not want any of

---

[86] Summary of items 5–9.

[87] Quotations of the *Rule for Hermitages* from Cirino and Raischl, *Franciscan Solitude,* 142–44. The text in FA:ED 1:61–62 is virtually identical.

[88] Esser, "The *Regula,*" 150. Esser notes that later editions of the Rule improved the Latin; "the Latin style of Saint Francis" was known "to have been clumsy and often incorrect" (164).

[89] Esser, "The *Regula,*"166.

the brothers to become permanent hermits "living by themselves, but as brothers in a genuine fraternity." Time away in a hermitage "was designed to be voluntary"; it was recommended but not mandated.[90]

Hermitages were thus designed to deepen the bonds of the entire Order, not divide the community between active members and solitary saints. Time in hermitages was a way to deepen identity with the whole scattered Franciscan brotherhood, each brother understanding that his brothers in other lands were following the same pattern. "The brothers in the hermitages are not segregated from the whole brotherhood of the Order."[91]

Life in the hermitages was structured around the canonical hours, as Francis's instructions make clear. The brothers probably prayed some of the hours together rather than alone, though this is not specified.

One of Francis's early brothers, Stephen, spent some months in a hermitage that Francis sometimes visited. Francis assigned Stephen to serve as cook and care for the kitchen while the other brothers spent time in prayer and silence. At the proper hour, Stephen would bang on a pan, calling the brothers to dinner.

Sometimes Francis would come out of his cell in the morning at Terce (about 9 o'clock), and if the kitchen fire wasn't yet lit, he would go pick some greens and bring them to Stephen. "Cook up these greens," Francis would say, "and it will go well with the brothers."

Stephen occasionally cooked eggs or prepared cheese for the brothers. "Francis would be totally happy, eating with the others and praising the skill of his cook." But then Francis would say, "Brother Stephen, you made too much food today! Don't cook anything tomorrow."

Brother Stephen was a little fearful of Francis, so next day he made no food. Francis then complained, "Brother Stephen, why haven't you made us a meal?"

"Because you told me not to," Stephen replied.

Francis responded perhaps with a sly smile, "Discretion is a good thing, for we shouldn't always do what the superior says!"[92]

Francis's *Rule for Hermitages* shows again his organizational genius—his gift for minimal structure to nourish maximal spiritual impact. Here as elsewhere we see that "Francis does not 'regulate' so much, but gives free elbow-room for the brothers' own judgment," Esser

---

[90] Esser, "The *Regula*," 181–82.
[91] Esser, "The *Regula*," 183.
[92] Summarized from an account of Thomas of Pavia, FA:ED 3:795–96.

comments. Here "lies the difference between the life in hermitages of the Lesser Brothers and that of the other contemporary forms of this life outside the Order. Francis truly knew how to integrate into the spirit and life of the Order" the growing popularity of spiritual retreats.[93]

* * *

The explosive growth of the Lesser Brothers in the two decades before and after Francis's death in 1226 at first seems mystifying. Yet viewing the Franciscan movement in its historical setting reveals the intertwining strands that largely explain not only the movement's growth but also the remarkable impact the Franciscans would have through the 1300s and beyond—an impact that continues, globally, even today. In chapter 20 we will go deeper into the dynamics of spiritual movements to glean pertinent insights for today's church and our own lives.

Meanwhile in Assisi, a parallel movement to Francis's little community was growing, birthed and led by a woman, Clare of Assisi.

---

[93] Esser, "The *Regula*," 192. Esser provides considerably more information and analysis of the Franciscan hermitages, especially in the earliest period.

10

Clare Elopes

In 1212 Clare of Assisi made up her mind to follow Francis's lead and enter a life of total discipleship. She would become a Franciscan brother as much as a woman could.

G. K. Chesterton tells how Clare did it. "Francis helped her to escape from her home and to take up the conventual life. If we like to put it so, he helped her to elope into the cloister, defying her parents as he had defied his father. Indeed the scene had many of the elements of a regular romantic elopement; for she escaped through a hole in the wall, fled through a wood and was received at midnight by the light of torches."

Chesterton adds, "A girl of seventeen in the thirteenth century was certainly old enough to know her own mind."[1] Clare eloped to find a better life, a holy and devout path full of light and meaning.

Clare had watched Francis. She was fascinated to see his little community down at the Portiuncula, now just two years old, growing and flourishing. She had heard Francis preach in Assisi, probably many times.

A sense of call from God grew within Clare. Francis's words "fell on good ground," Ingrid Peterson writes. "The message of the Gospel—not as it was being lived in the church, but in its possibilities for human life as exemplified by Jesus—was what Francis preached, and that is exactly what Clare ... [was] seeking even before [she] met Francis."[2]

---

[1] G. K. Chesterton, *St. Francis of Assisi* (Garden City, NY: Image Books, Doubleday [1924], 1957), 110–11.

[2] Ingrid J. Peterson, OSF, *Clare of Assisi: A Biographical Study* (Quincy, IL: Franciscan Press, 1993), 9.

Clare had grown into a beautiful young woman with blonde hair. Lord Ranieri di Bernardo of Assisi repeatedly asked her hand in marriage, as did other wealthy knights. She refused them all.[3]

Raised in a wealthy noble family, Clare could read and write Latin much better than Francis. She loved music. She would have heard the minstrels and troubadours who periodically came through Assisi with their songs of chivalry and romance and adventure. She could speak and write well; her writing "is colored by the vocabulary of the literature of chivalry," wrote Englebert.[4]

"I want to follow Francis and his way of life," Clare felt. She wanted to join his fraternity. But as a woman, how could she?

Meanwhile Francis had heard of Clare's dedication to a life of holiness and wanted to meet her. And Clare, having watched the changes in Francis and his conversion a few years earlier, wanted to meet him. Like him, Clare had compassion for the poor and did what she could to help them. Their mutual commitment to a life of deeper discipleship was a magnet between them.

Clare took the initiative and arranged to meet Francis secretly. Over a period of months, they met repeatedly, Francis accompanied by Brother Philip the Long.[5] Lady Bona, who often accompanied Clare, said that "many times [Clare] went secretly" to meet Francis "so as not to be seen by her parents."[6]

Together Clare and Francis dreamed up a plan for her to join the brothers. His community was still in its early stages, and "Francis may well have thought that some way would be found whereby a woman could be attached to the community, accept the same standards of poverty, and assist in the more practical work such as the care of the lepers. This certainly seems to have been what Clare wished," notes Moorman.[7]

---

[3] Regis J. Armstrong, ed., "Introduction," in *The Lady: Clare of Assisi: Early Documents* (New York: New City Press, 2006), 15; Peterson, *Clare of Assisi*, 19. Later during the canonization process, Ranieri di Bernardo gave personal testimony to Clare's holiness; *The Lady: Clare of Assisi*, 193–94.

[4] Omer Englebert, *Saint Francis of Assisi*, 2nd English ed., trans. Eve Marie Cooper (Chicago: Franciscan Herald Press, 1965), 161.

[5] *The Acts of the Process of Canonization* (1253), in *The Lady: Clare of Assisi*, 168 n. a.

[6] Testimony of Lady Bona, *Process of Canonization*, 192; see John Moorman, *A History of the Franciscan Order: From Its Origins to the Year 1517* (Oxford: Oxford University Press, 1968), 32.

[7] Moorman, *History of the Franciscan Order*, 33. Bishop Guido was aware of these discussions, according to Moorman.

Palm Sunday Flight

Clare made her decision. She would leave her family forever and devote her life entirely to a religious vocation, just as Francis had. He would be her guide.

March 18, 1212, Palm Sunday, was the date she chose.[8] That bright Sunday Clare went with her family and crowds of others to the service. Traditionally at this service, young virgins processed to the front to receive an olive branch from Bishop Guido.[9]

The assembled townsfolk went forward, each to receive their branch. The young maidens, dressed in white like brides, filed to the altar, each for her branch.

All except Clare. She sat still in her pew. Bishop Guido came down the sanctuary steps and handed Clare her branch.[10]

The rest of Palm Sunday Clare waited quietly for night to come. Then in the darkness she crept downstairs. She didn't use the main door that opened onto the piazza by the cathedral, knowing it would be guarded by the family's man-at-arms standing outside. But there was another door, rarely used, leading to a side street. Lady Cristiana, an older friend of the family who later herself became a Poor Clare, gave this sworn testimony after Clare's death:

> Because she did not want to leave through the usual exit, fearing her way would be blocked, she went out by the house's other exit that had been barricaded with heavy wood beams and an iron bar so that it could not be opened even by a large number of men. She alone, with the help of Jesus Christ, removed them and opened the door. On the following morning, when many people saw that door opened, they were somewhat astonished at how a young girl could have done it.

How did she know this, Cristiana was asked. She said she herself was in the house at the time.[11]

---

[8] Moorman, *History of the Franciscan Order*, 33; Englebert, *Saint Francis*, 394. Some scholars believe the date was March 28, 1211 (Palm Sunday). See *The Lady: Clare of Assisi*, 145 n. b; Arnaldo Fortini, *Francis of Assisi*, trans. Helen Moak (New York: Crossroad Publishing, 1992), 338.

[9] Palms are not common in Assisi but olive trees are plentiful, so olive branches served instead.

[10] *The Lady: Clare of Assisi*, 285–86; Peterson, *Clare of Assisi*, 111; Fortini, *Francis of Assisi*, 339; Englebert, *Saint Francis*, 162.

[11] *Process of Canonization*, 185. Clare was either seventeen or eighteen at this time.

Clare's flight was carefully planned. On the side street she rendezvoused with Pacifica, her older friend and "second mother," who had helped Clare prepare. Pacifica agreed to accompany Clare to the Portiuncula to meet Francis.[12]

The pair made their way the dozen blocks down steep streets to the nearest city gate. Then on down to the plain and across to the Portiuncula—about a two-mile walk.[13]

Francis was expecting them. When Clare and Pacifica arrived "the brothers, who were observing sacred vigils before the little altar of God, received the virgin Clare with torches," says *The Legend of Saint Clare*.[14]

Safe with Francis

Francis welcomed Clare into the community of brothers. First, he cut her hair, giving her a tonsure much like his. "There, her hair shorn by the hands of the brothers, she put aside every kind of her fine dress."[15] There "before the altar of the blessed Virgin," Clare "the humble servant was married to Christ."[16]

But Clare could not stay with the brothers without causing scandal. Her family would probably soon come for her. Francis and the brothers had to take her somewhere else temporarily. Fortunately, the Monastery of Saint Paul, a community of Benedictine nuns, was nearby in the town of Bastia. The monastery was authorized to shelter people in danger. Over many years, it had grown rich and influential, and in 1198 the pope himself granted it the right of asylum. Francis called brothers Bernardo and Philip the Long, and together they took Clare there for temporary refuge.[17]

---

[12] Fortini, *Francis of Assisi*, 340.

[13] *Legend of Saint Clare*, in *The Lady: Clare of Assisi: Early Documents*, 286.

[14] *Legend of Saint Clare*, 286. Today a series of colorful recent murals along a hallway at the Portiuncula depicts Clare's arrival and Francis's reception of her.

[15] *Legend of Saint Clare*, 286. This scene has been repeatedly pictured in art, from the small relief at the Saint Clare Basilica in Assisi to a contemporary painting at the Portiuncula to the romantic imagined riverside scene beautifully portrayed in the movie *Brother Sun, Sister Moon*.

[16] *Legend of Saint Clare*, 287. Lawrence Cunningham comments that Clare "came to the Portiuncula with a strong sense of Christian discipleship and a formed spiritual maturity beyond her years. Clare thus underwent two conversions. She turned from an already pious life of Christian observance in a domestic setting toward the new vision that Francis and his companions offered." Clearly Clare was influenced by her mother, Ortulana, who "seems to have been an inveterate pilgrim who had visited the famous shrine of Compostela and also the holy places in Palestine" (as noted earlier). Lawrence S. Cunningham, *Francis of Assisi: Performing the Gospel Life* (Grand Rapids, MI: William B. Eerdmans, 2004), 37–38.

[17] Peterson, *Clare of Assisi*, 114; Fortini, *Francis of Assisi*, 341–42; *The Lady:*

The next morning Clare's family, finding the secure door unbarred and Clare gone, was shocked and distraught. Uncle Monaldo and other male family members said Clare was dishonoring her family. *Vilitas* means cheapness, baseness—that was the term they used (think of the English word "vile"). The news spread. Monaldo and others ran to the Portiuncula to bring Clare back. Higher-class families often opposed their young women entering the religious life. It lowered prospects for a suitable marriage that might enhance family prestige.[18] The family menfolk were determined to bring Clare home by persuasion or even by force if need be. Bring her to her senses. But arriving at the Portiuncula, they were frustrated to discover Clare gone.

Off they went to the Benedictine monastery. Clare met them in the chapel, but she was adamant in her commitment. The *Legend of Saint Clare* says,

> They employed violent force, poisonous advice, and flattering promises, persuading her to give up such a worthless deed that was unbecoming to her class and without precedent in her family. But, taking hold of the altar cloths, she bared her tonsured head, maintaining that she would in no way be torn away from the service of Christ.[19]

Her hands on the altar, Clare was claiming the right of sanctuary. So the men did not force her, though the family still tried to dissuade her and bring her home. Clare was steadfast. The family finally gave up and accepted her decision.[20]

Clare of Assisi, 168 n. a. The Monastery of Saint Paul "had been placed under the jurisdiction of the bishop of Assisi by a papal bull of 1198, which had also threatened with excommunication anyone who used violence on lands subject to the bishop. Also, the Benedictine monasteries for women, organized on the feudal pattern, had armed forces at their disposal and were themselves capable of making violators pay most dearly." Fortini, *Francis of Assisi*, 345 editorial n. h.

[18] *Legend of Saint Clare*, 287; also Fortini, *Francis of Assisi*, 344. Helen Moak in her English translation of Fortini elaborates: "The violence of the reaction of Clare's family to this rebellious girl must be understood against the medieval concept of honour, in which criticism or infamy brought on by the deeds of any one member of a family or clan was held to be equally shared by all. What women did was held to be an especial threat to the family honour." Moak quotes Antonio Pertile, *Storia del diritto italiano dalla caduta dell'Impero Romano alla codificazione*, 2nd ed. rev. (Turin, Italy, 1892–1903), 238: "For that reason one maintained guardianship over them so long as they remained at home and saw to their proper marriage or placement, for the double considerations of providing for their material support and guaranteeing the honour of the house." Fortini, *Francis of Assisi*, 345n h.

[19] *Legend of Saint Clare*, 287.

[20] *Legend of Saint Clare*, 287.

Clare had already sold her family inheritance, preparing for her new vocation. This meant she lacked the necessary dowry to join the sisters at the Saint Paul Monastery. She would have to go elsewhere.[21] A few days later Francis, together with brothers Bernardo and Philip the Long, escorted her on foot to another community of nuns, the monastery of Sant'Angelo di Panzo up the slopes of Mount Subasio. Clare was now tonsured and clad like a Franciscan, so the four walking together would appear to any passersby as simply another small band of traveling Lesser Brothers.

Clare's younger sister Catherine, a girl of about fifteen, came to visit Clare the week after Easter. The two were very close; one can imagine their intimate conversations. Catherine soon felt drawn to join Clare.[22] Her decision was in effect the birth of a new community of women pledged to the same radical commitment that Francis and his brothers were living at the Portiuncula in the valley below. Recalling the renowned third-century virgin martyr Agnes of Rome, Catherine took the same name. She would be Sister Agnes.[23]

But Clare was not happy at Sant'Angelo. This was not the life she dreamed of, longed for. She "implored Francis to take her away and allow her to start a new way of life, the kind of life which they had discussed in those long talks."[24] So now Francis took Clare and Agnes to San Damiano, the place Francis had foreseen such an order. Here Clare would freely build her community, raise her family of newborn sisters.

Sisters of San Damiano

From this point on, San Damiano was home—in effect the motherhouse of the Poor Clares. Clare was devoutly Christian well before she met Francis. What she wanted was a more radical discipleship like his. Now she was beginning. With her birth sister, now Sister Agnes, Clare formed a new community at San Damiano, the very place where Jesus spoke to Francis through the death-and-resurrection crucifix icon: "Go and rebuild my church."

In Assisi, news of Clare's radical conversion spread like fire. Women talked of it and wondered what it might mean for them or their daughters

---

[21] Clare at about age eighteen "sold all her inheritance and gave it to the poor," as all Francis's brothers who had inheritances had done. *Process of Canonization*, 195.

[22] "Sixteen days after the conversion of Clare, Agnes, inspired by the divine spirit, ran to her sister, revealed the secret of her will, and told her that she wished to serve God completely" as Clare was doing. *Legend of Saint Clare*, 303.

[23] Peterson, *Clare of Assisi*, 115; Fortini, *Francis of Assisi*, 348.

[24] Moorman, *History of the Franciscan Order*, 34.

or sisters. More women joined Clare, resolutely walking down the path to San Damiano just over a mile beyond Assisi's southeastern gate. It was "as if a magnet had been placed in San Damiano."[25]

As word spread, women from surrounding towns in the Spoleto Valley went to San Damiano and joined Clare in her new community.[26] Lady Pacifica, Clare's close confidante, came almost immediately. Several noblewomen from Clare's own extended family, older than herself, soon joined Clare in her new sisterly society. Before long Clare's own mother Ortulana came, too.[27] Others kept coming, in time so many that Clare had to start more communities elsewhere.[28]

The sisters did not of course condemn others who didn't join. They just wanted to serve them. "Their primary intention was to follow in the footsteps of Jesus in poverty and humility."[29]

Clare's example and dedication sparked a women's movement paralleling Francis's movement of men. The Poor Clares were both like and unlike their Franciscan siblings. Like their brothers, the Poor Clares grew, though more slowly. By 1228, fifteen years after their founding, the Clares had communities in Perugia, Foligno, Spoleto, Florence, Siena, Milan, Padua, Trent, Verona, Pamplona (Spain), and at least a dozen other places.[30] When Clare died in 1253, the number of Poor Clare monasteries was at least one hundred ten.[31] Pope Innocent IV later wrote that in Clare "the modest virgin was united to the desired embraces of the virgin Spouse [Christ], and from the bed of irreproachable virginity, a progeny came ... [and] spread through almost every part of the world like a heavenly plant abundantly fruitful for God."[32]

---

[25] Peterson, *Clare of Assisi*, 141.

[26] "The *Acts of the Process of Canonization* shows that almost half of the community at San Damiano did not come just from Assisi, but from the Spoleto Valley," which included several towns "as far as the Tiber Valley, and beyond." *Legend of Saint Clare*, n. a.

[27] *Process of Canonization*, 146; Fortini, *Francis of Assisi*, 338, 352. Perhaps Clare's father had died, but this is uncertain.

[28] Fortini lists about two dozen others by name, giving information on several. Fortini, *Francis of Assisi*, 350–53.

[29] Ramona Miller, OSF, *In the Footsteps of Saint Clare* (St. Bonaventure, NY: Franciscan Institute, 1993), 49.

[30] "Other Decrees of Pope Gregory IX," in *The Lady: Clare of Assisi*, 365; Letter of Cardinal Rainaldo dei Conti di Segni, in *The Lady: Clare of Assisi*, 133. Cardinal Rainaldo names twenty-two cities in addition to San Damiano.

[31] "Notification of Death," in *The Lady: Clare of Assisi*, 135–38. In the male-dominant culture of the time, women's religious communities could not grow as rapidly as did the Franciscans. Given the cultural limitations, the growth of the Poor Clares was remarkable.

[32] "Prologue," in *Process of Canonization*, 142.

The New Form of Life

Clare and her sisters were organized informally at first, figuring out day by day how to function as community. Yet they had no rule or constitution. All looked to young Clare as their leader, even though most of the women were older. From the first, Clare showed herself a gifted guide. Much of that skill flowed from her own humility, love, and Christ-likeness.

But how would they live? They couldn't go out begging, like their Franciscan brothers. People voluntarily gave them supplies, but that was undependable. They raised herbs and vegetables, which helped supply their meager diet. Franciscan brothers (called "questors" for this purpose) gave support by begging for them.[33] Clare "received with great joy the fragments of alms and the scraps of bread that the questors brought and, as if saddened by whole [loaves of] bread, she rejoiced more in the scraps."[34]

In 1241, Pope Gregory IX gave the Poor Clares explicit permission to rely on their Franciscan brothers for needs they couldn't supply for themselves. Designated Franciscan priests were permitted to enter the sisters' monasteries to provide maintenance, protection, the sacraments, and burials.[35] In terms of movement dynamics, this broad papal provision nurtured the *symbiosis,* mutuality, between the Poor Clares and the Franciscans, as well as with their Third Order followers out in society who drew life from the Franciscans and Clares.

San Damiano itself was more than the small chapel Francis had restored. Its connected structures included several rooms with small windows and other space. The grounds had once been a Roman cemetery. A small chapel built of local stone had been erected four or five centuries earlier. Sometime in the previous century or two a hospice and priest's residence were added.[36]

Quite near and yet well outside Assisi, San Damiano was an ideal place for Clare to begin her community. She and her sisters adapted

---

[33] *Process of Canonization*, 148, 157. This was suggested by Clare in her *Form of Life*, chap. 12 (*The Lady: Clare of Assisi*, 125). Brother Bentevenga, who was once cured by Clare, was one of these begging brothers. In the early years, several brothers lived near San Damiano for this purpose (*The Lady: Clare of Assisi*, 148, 157, 170 n. b).

[34] *Legend of Saint Clare*, 300.

[35] Gregory IX, *Vestris piis supplicationibus* (May 31, 1241), addressed "to His beloved daughters, all the abbesses and enclosed nuns of the monasteries of the Order of Saint Damian," in *The Lady: Clare of Assisi*, 363–64.

[36] Giulio Mancini, *San Damiano: Recalling the Soul* (Assisi: Edizioni Porziuncola, 2009), 11.

and modified the structure, fashioning a refectory. A cloistered garden of flowers and herbs alongside but lower than the chapel became a favorite spot for Clare, a place of peace and meditation.

"Life at San Damiano was a pilgrimage of poverty; the journey progressed from poverty to humility to charity climaxed in mysticism," as Sister Ramona Miller puts it.[37] Clare considered herself now to be unconditionally wed to Jesus Christ through the Holy Spirit. She was a true bride. Her passion, she said, was to serve and follow him who "though more beautiful than the children of men became, for [our] salvation, the lowest of men, was despised, struck, scourged untold times throughout His entire body, and then died amid the suffering of the Cross."[38]

In organizing their life together, Clare and her sisters had the church's liturgical patterns to guide them. The Liturgy of the Hours provided the structure, and prayer was the heart. Daily life at San Damiano was a rhythm of shared and private prayer, as it was among Francis and his brothers—except that Clare and her community lived a cloistered life.

The community's times of prayer were interspersed with practical tasks of sustaining their shared life and serving lepers and poor folk as they were able. Some of the sisters were allowed to leave San Damiano in pairs or small groups to serve others outside the cloister. These Poor Clares were the "serving sisters."[39] Also, from time to time, people from Assisi or the surrounding area came to San Damiano to be healed.[40]

Clare was so severe with herself, especially in fasting, that the sisters worried. According to Sister Pacifica, Clare "kept vigil so much of the night in prayer, and kept so many abstinences that the sisters lamented and were alarmed." She "was so very strict in her food that the sisters marveled at how her body survived."[41] Clare was eating nothing at all on Mondays, Wednesdays, and Fridays. Francis and Bishop Guido saw Clare was harming her health, and they intervened. She must eat "at least half a roll of bread" on those days, they said.[42] After she became ill, Francis

---

[37] Miller, *In the Footsteps of Saint Clare*, 65.

[38] Clare, *The First Letter to Agnes of Prague* (1234), in *The Lady: Clare of Assisi*, 49.

[39] Clare called sisters who served out in the community or villages "serving sisters." These sisters, as Armstrong notes, were "not bound to the law of enclosure and [enjoyed] certain mitigations" because of their assigned ministries. *The Lady: Clare of Assisi*, 150 n. b.

[40] Peterson, *Clare of Assisi*, 256. There was an area at San Damiano where visitors could speak with the sisters. *The Lady: Clare of Assisi*, 167.

[41] *Process of Canonization*, 146.

[42] Testimony of Sister Pacifica, in *Process of Canonization*, 146.

also told Clare she must stop sleeping on her bed of twigs and use a bed made of a sack of straw.[43]

Clare seemed to gain such joy and nourishment from her extended prayer times that she hardly felt the need for physical food. This was an important element in her life and influence—yet it seriously weakened her body. She did in fact eventually impair her health through her severe austerity.

At first Clare and her new community were not officially authorized by the church. Francis himself wrote them a simple Rule. Clare later said in her *Testament*: "I, together with a few sisters whom the Lord had given me after my own conversion, willingly promised [Francis] obedience, as the Lord gave us the light of His grace through [Francis's] wonderful life and teaching." Clare says Francis "frequently examined us according to the example of the saints and his brothers" and "greatly rejoiced in the Lord" when he saw that the sisters "did not shirk deprivation, poverty, hard work, trial, or the shame or contempt of the world" but rather "considered them as great delights." Francis "bound himself ... always to have the same loving care and special solicitude for us as for his own brothers."[44]

Clare's central focus, however, was not Francis; it was Jesus. She calls herself "a handmaid of Christ and of the poor sisters of the Monastery of San Damiano ... and the little plant" of Francis. She writes at the beginning of her *Testament,* "The Son of God has become for us the Way that our blessed father Francis, His true lover and imitator, has shown and taught us by word and example."[45]

Clare's focus was Jesus Christ and his poverty, sufferings, and service to others. Her focus was Jesus, but primarily the suffering Jesus of the cross. There is relatively little focus on the risen Jesus. Here of course both Clare and Francis were typical of their time. Focus on Jesus's sufferings and poverty paralleled and prompted the focus on extreme self-denial and self-imposed suffering through fasting and a range of ascetic practices.

Unlike Francis, Clare sometimes wore a hair shirt. She did this over a substantial period of years. One she wore is still among the relics at the Basilica of Saint Clare in Assisi. In the documents assembled for the process of canonization, Sister Benvenuta testified that "Clare at one time had a certain shirt made of boar's hide. She wore it secretly under her

---

[43] Testimony of Sister Agnes (daughter of Assisi's mayor), in *Process of Canonization,* 170.

[44] Clare, *The Testament,* in *The Lady: Clare of Assisi,* 61.

[45] Clare, *Testament,* 62, 60.

woolen tunic with the skin and bristles close to her skin. Likewise, another time, she had another shirt made of horsehair, knotted with certain cords. She tied it around her body, and thus afflicted her virgin flesh." When Clare was ill, however, her sisters "took the shirt, rough as it was, away from her."[46] Wearing hair shirts "was such a severe practice," notes Sister Ingrid Peterson, "that Clare easily withdrew it from her sisters."[47] She didn't want her sisters to use hair shirts, even if she often did.

Clare suffered from serious illness for years. "Since the strength of her flesh had succumbed to the austerity of the penance [she had practiced] in the early years, a harsh sickness took hold of her ... [for] twenty-eight years."[48] Several of the San Damiano sisters in fact suffered from illnesses. Regis Armstrong comments on "the difficult, constricted quarters of San Damiano, the poor diet and rigorous fasting of the Poor Ladies, and the inevitable sicknesses, especially tuberculosis and malaria, to which they were susceptible."[49]

These circumstances raise questions. Were Clare and Francis and their communities so extreme in their self-denial as to harm themselves and in some ways impair their witness? It is clear that Clare, and Francis as well, harmed their own physical health through the severity of their disciplines.

Several of the San Damiano sisters in their testimonies said they couldn't explain Clare's holiness. They thought it was the most perfect ever seen on earth, next to that of the Virgin Mary. What did this holiness consist of? What was the evidence, the sisters were asked. Sister Lucia said Clare's holiness was seen "in great punishment of her flesh and in great harshness of her life." Clare "tried to please God and to teach her sisters in the love of God. She had great compassion for the sisters, both for their body and soul."[50] For Sister Lucia, "punishment of the flesh and harshness of life" were key marks of holiness—showing again how holiness was understood at the time. Other sisters put the accent more strongly on Clare's love, care, and compassion. But nearly all mentioned her severe asceticism.

Clare led her community for forty-two years.[51] At first the San

---

[46] Sister Benvenuta, in *Process of Canonization*, 151. Clare once lent her hair shirt to Sister Agnes (not Clare's biological sister). Agnes testified that she wore it for three days, but that "while she was wearing it, it seemed very rough to her, so she could in no way stand it." Testimony of Sister Agnes, in *Process of Canonization*, 178.

[47] Peterson, *Clare of Assisi*, 204.

[48] *Legend of Saint Clare*, 313.

[49] Regis Armstrong, *The Lady: Clare of Assisi*, 394 n. d.

[50] *Process of Canonization*, 174.

[51] Peterson, *Clare of Assisi*, 147.

Damiano sisters were known as Damianites (or Order of Saint Damian), then in time as the Poor Clares or Order of Poor Ladies. After Clare's death they would become, officially, the Order of Saint Clare. They are often called the Second Order of Saint Francis.[52]

In her *Testament*, Clare expressed clearly her goal and passion. She felt "the Lord Himself has placed us as a model, as an example and mirror not only for others, but also for our sisters whom the Lord has called to our way of life as well, that they in turn might be a mirror and example to those living in the world.... [We] are greatly bound to bless and praise God and to be strengthened more and more to do good in the Lord."[53] Clare and her sisters were living not mainly for themselves.

This helps us understand Clare's asceticism. She saw her self-imposed sufferings in the sense of the Apostle Paul's words: "I am now rejoicing in my sufferings for your sake, and in my flesh I am completing what is lacking in Christ's afflictions for the sake of his body, that is, the church" (Col. 1:24). Clare suffered not from guilt or to gain forgiveness; she was interceding for others and for the world. Her suffering was intercession, identifying with Jesus. She suffered more so that others might suffer less.

The Rule of Clare and the Privilege of Poverty

The story of the official Rule of Clare is complicated. Clare had trouble convincing the pope and Roman Curia to permit her and her sisters to live the life they felt certain God had called them to.

For three years, from 1212 to 1215, the San Damiano sisters lived under the "Form of Life" Francis gave them. But then the Fourth Lateran Council (1215) forbade the formation of new orders, unless by special papal permission. From that point, the Poor Ladies lived under the much older Rule of Saint Benedict (the constitution that governed the Benedictines). This served for a while as the "Rule of Saint Clare."

Clare believed that the most faithful way she and her sisters could honor Francis was to live the very same life of total poverty Francis did—to follow his Rule.[54] This was virtually unheard of for women.

---

[52] Clare and her sisters were known first, officially, as the Order of St. Damian. In 1263, about eight years after Clare was declared a saint, Pope Urban IV changed the name to the Order of Saint Clare. Introduction to Bonaventure, "The Morning Sermon on Saint Francis," FA:ED 2:747.

[53] Clare, *Testament*, 61.

[54] Peterson writes, "Women talk to each other, and in so doing, discover and nourish hope, destroy demons and dark fears. Women talk about things of the heart, and for Clare the burning project of her heart was to be poor like the poor Jesus.... The Privilege

No other female religious community had such an extreme rule.[55] Other monasteries and convents asked the pope for "special privileges to safeguard their vast possessions," notes Fortini, but Clare "asked Pope Innocent III to grant them the privilege of possessing nothing." Never had Innocent received such a request![56]

It seems Innocent III did grant Clare's wish, however, issuing "The Privilege of Poverty" in 1216. This brief document placed Clare and her sisters directly under the pope's jurisdiction rather than under the bishops.[57] The declaration begins by acknowledging that Clare had "renounced the desire for all temporal things" and had "sold all things and given them to the poor" (Luke 18:22), and grants Clare the "privilege" she asked. Pope Innocent wrote,

> [You] propose not to have any possessions whatsoever, clinging in all things to the footprints of Him, the Way, the Truth, and the Life, Who, for our sake, was made poor. Nor does a lack of possessions frighten you from a proposal of this sort; for the left hand of the heavenly Spouse is under your head [Song of Solomon 2:6] to support the weakness of your body.... He Who feeds the birds of the heavens and clothes the lilies of the field will not fail you in either food or clothing, until He ministers to you in heaven.... Therefore, we confirm with our apostolic authority, as you requested, your proposal of most high poverty, granting you by the authority of this letter that no one can compel you to receive possessions.[58]

But Clare ran into a roadblock just three years later. Cardinal Hugolino, with the pope's permission, issued a "Form and Manner

---

of Poverty was worth talking about, and eventually Clare talked about it to Francis, to the Poor Ladies, and to the *parade of popes* who passed through the papacy during her lifetime." Peterson, *Clare of Assisi,* 3 (emphasis added).

[55] "The Privilege of Poverty, a community living without corporate ownership, was unheard of in a monastic foundation." Peterson, *Clare of Assisi,* 321.

[56] Fortini, *Francis of Assisi,* 360; see also Peterson, *Clare of Assisi,* 184.

[57] Peterson, *Clare of Assisi,* 20.

[58] Introduction, "The Privilege of Poverty of Pope Gregory IX," in *The Lady: Clare of Assisi,* 86 n. b. Scholars today question whether Innocent III actually did issue such a "privilege" to Clare and her sisters, as the documentary evidence is meager, and Innocent III died suddenly in 1216. Cunningham says "it was not until 1228, two years after the death of Francis, that his 'privilege of poverty' ... for three convents in Assisi was granted by the pope" (Cunningham, *Francis of Assisi,* 38). In any case, the San Damiano sisters and the new communities they formed were fully committed to absolute poverty. See Introduction, "The Privilege of Poverty of Pope Gregory IX," in *The Lady: Clare of Assisi,* 86.

of Life" for the Poor Ladies that required Clare and her sisters to live strictly by the Rule of St. Benedict.[59] That rule, though certainly austere, permitted the sisters to own property. This undercut Clare's passion and sense of call. The Benedictine rule "remained in effect for all the new monasteries of Poor Ladies until 1253," notes Peterson. Yet it is precisely this rule that "Clare labored the remainder of her lifetime to change"— finally succeeding only just before her death.[60] Clare was determined "to have her own Rule with its insistence upon poverty and mutual charity officially recognized by the Church," Armstrong writes.[61]

Pope Innocent III died suddenly in 1216 and was succeeded by Honorius III. Then when Honorius passed in 1227, eighty-year-old Cardinal Hugolino himself became pope, taking the name Gregory IX. As Cardinal Hugolino, he had been a key friend and protector of Francis. He was especially close to Clare. He had great confidence in Clare's prayers and as pope often solicited her prayerful intercession.[62]

Gregory IX served fourteen years (1227–1241), becoming "one of the most influential supporters of female religious movements during the middle ages."[63] In September 1228, a year after his election and two years after Francis's death, Gregory finally acceded to Clare's wish and officially granted her and her sisters "The Privilege of Poverty," essentially reinstating the provision Innocent III seems to have granted a dozen years earlier.[64] Sister Filippa testified that when Clare "learned a brother had come with the letters bearing the papal bull, she reverently took it even though she was close to death and pressed that seal to her mouth in order to kiss it." Clare died the next day.[65]

---

[59] Peterson, *Clare of Assisi*, 322; *The Lady: Clare of Assisi*, 73.

[60] Peterson, *Clare of Assisi*, 322.

[61] Armstrong, Introduction to "The Form and Manner of Life of Cardinal Hugolino," in *The Lady: Clare of Assisi*, 74.

[62] *Legend of Saint Clare*, 304–5. The volume of early documents pertaining to Clare includes two letters to Clare from him, one when he was still a cardinal (previous footnote), and one as Pope Gregory IX, dated October 30, 1228 (*The Lady: Clare of Assisi*, 346–47).

[63] Armstrong, "Introduction," in *The Lady: Clare of Assisi*, 19. The text of Gregory IX's "Privilege of Poverty" is virtually identical to that of Innocent III in 1216. See "The Privilege of Poverty of Pope Gregory IX," in *The Lady: Clare of Assisi*, 87–88. Peterson says the earlier (1216) Privilege of Poverty was revoked by Pope Gregory IX in 1227, but Clare protested so vigorously that he restored it in September 1228 (Peterson, *Clare of Assisi*, xxv). Citations from the Song of Solomon (such as here) are frequent in the spiritual literature of the Middle Ages and in much of the literature on Francis and Clare.

[64] Peterson, *Clare of Assisi*, 326.

[65] *The Acts of the Process of Canonization* in *The Lady: Clare of Assisi*, 162.

Pope Gregory later tried to get Clare and her sisters to lessen the severity of their life. Concerned for her health and welfare, the pope tried to persuade Clare to "accept some goods that would allow her and her companions to live without anxiety for the future." This amounted to failure to trust wholly in God's providence, Clare felt. She "objected with a ferocity unimaginable in a creature so sweet and delicate." She told the pope, "Holy Father, release me from my sins, but not from the vow to follow our Lord Jesus Christ."[66]

When Gregory IX wrote a stirring letter praising Clare for the contribution her prayer life made to the whole church, Clare used her favor with the pope to press her case for absolute poverty. Peterson writes, "Clare, an astute politician, knew how to capitalize upon her worth and used the only power she had, which was the power over her own body. She staged a hunger strike, threatening to starve herself" to safeguard the right to poverty. "The pope relented. Clare had won a battle for the Privilege of Poverty."[67]

As we will see later, however, what the papacy gave with one hand it took away with the other, insisting that the Poor Ladies must live a more conventional, more cloistered, less severe kind of community life. But for now, the community of Poor Ladies at San Damiano could live completely possession-less, relying solely on God's grace and providence.

Clare herself had a remarkably deep prayer life, often accompanied by "torrents of tears that burst forth in her" and inspired her sisters' prayers. *The Legend of Saint Clare* elaborates, speaking of "how much strength [Clare] received in her furnace of ardent prayer, how sweet the divine goodness was to her in that enjoyment. For when she returned with joy from holy prayer, she brought from the altar of the Lord burning words that also inspired the hearts of her sisters. In fact, they marveled that such sweetness came from her mouth and that her face shone more brilliantly than usual."[68]

Following Clare's example, in coming decades many new communities of Poor Ladies sprang up in Italy and around Europe, as noted. Like Francis, Clare's example and way of life sparked a new movement—a movement of women rather than men. In Chesterton's words, Clare "became the foundress of a great feminine movement which still profoundly affects the world; and her place is with the

---

[66] Fortini, *Francis of Assisi*, 361.
[67] Peterson, *Clare of Assisi*, 21.
[68] *Legend of Saint Clare*, 298, 299.

powerful women of history."[69] Cuthbert notes, "There were times indeed when Clare envied the [Franciscan] brethren their opportunities of spending themselves in carrying the Gospel to [people] who knew not Christ; and perhaps had she lived in other days, she might have been the foundress of a body of missionary women."[70] I think this is an astute observation.

Clare as Abbess

Throughout her decades as abbess, Clare was the spark and anchor of the community at San Damiano. She was abbess, "mother" of the community, though beginning at a young and inexperienced age. Clare "knew how to read the heart of each like an open book," Fortini says.[71]

During the canonization process, several sisters testified to their life with Clare and under her supervision. Sister Pacifica said, "When she ordered her Sisters to do something, she gave the order with much timidity and humility, and most of the time she would more readily do something herself than order others to do it." Sister Amata said, "When [Clare] returned from prayer, her face seemed more luminous and more beautiful than the sun. And her very words had in them such sweetness that her life seemed entirely celestial."

Sister Filippa testified, "She despised herself above all and made herself the inferior of all the other Sisters, serving them, giving them water for their hands and washing the toilet chairs for the sick Sisters with her own hands, and even washing the feet of the servant Sisters."

Sister Agnes, daughter of Assisi's mayor, said Clare "had a straw mat for a bed, and a bit of straw under her head, and with this bed she was content.... After she was sick, on the order of Saint Francis she had a large sack of straw."[72] Sister Angeluccia added that whenever Clare sent "serving sisters outside the monastery, she reminded them to praise God when they saw beautiful trees, flowers, and bushes; and, likewise, always to praise Him for and in all things when they saw all peoples and creatures."[73] Clare shared Francis's love of the good earth and its creatures, and she probably yearned for Francis's freedom of travel.

---

[69] Chesterton, *St. Francis of Assisi*, 112.
[70] Father Cuthbert, OFS Cap., *Life of St. Francis of Assisi*, 3rd ed. (London: Longmans, Green, 1948), 169.
[71] Fortini, *Francis of Assisi*, 354.
[72] These testimonies (Pacifica, Amata, Filippa, Agnes) quoted from Fortini, *Francis of Assisi*, 354–55. See *Process of Canonization*, 141–90.
[73] *Process of Canonization*, 189.

When Clare became too ill to rise from bed, Sister Pacifica testified, "she had herself raised to sit up and be supported with some cushions behind her back. She spun [thread and] from her work she made corporals and altar linens for almost all the churches of the plains and hills around Assisi." These then were hand delivered by Francis's brothers.[74]

Often there were difficult days. The sisters' life at San Damiano certainly should not be idealized. Trials and tribulations were constant, Sister Ingrid Peterson notes.

Near the end of her life, Clare wrote several instructions and admonitions for her sisters. Wherever the sisters might spread after her death, Clare wrote, let them "not acquire or receive more land" around their dwelling "than strict necessity requires for a garden and for raising vegetables." If they need more land to protect "the integrity and privacy of the monastery ... beyond the limits of a garden, let no more be acquired or even accepted than strict necessity demands. This land should not be cultivated or planted but remain always fallow and uncultivated."[75] Clare knew how convents of other orders often acquired more and more land over time through bequests or gifts of people seeking merit from God.

Clare exhorted her sisters, present and future, "to strive always to imitate the way of holy simplicity, humility and poverty and also the integrity of our holy way of living, as we were taught from the beginning of our conversion by Christ" and by Francis. For "not by any merits of ours but solely out of the largesse of His mercy and grace, the Father of mercies has spread the fragrance of a good reputation, both among those who are far away as well as those who are near," Clare wrote, recalling the words of 2 Corinthians 1:3 and 2:15. "And loving one another with the love of Christ, may you demonstrate without in your deeds the love you have within so that, compelled by such an example, the sisters may always grow in the love of God and in mutual charity."

The Legend of Clare and Francis

Countryfolk around Assisi would tell this story:

Francis and Clare were walking along opposite sides of a river in flood. Francis wanted to try to cross the river but was impeded

---

[74] *Process of Canonization*, 147. As we saw, at the beginning when her kin tried to force Clare to return home, she took "hold of the altar cloths [and] bared her tonsured head, maintaining that she would in no way be torn away from the service of Christ" (*Legend of Saint Clare*, 287). Altar cloths had special meaning for Clare, it would seem.

[75] Clare, *Testament*, 63–64.

by the powerful, eddying current. He was troubled because treacherous water kept him from joining the sister after his own spirit. But suddenly Clare threw her mantle on the water, stepped on it, and in an instant walked across the river. The blessed Francis, full of awe and devotion, said, "See, Sister, you are more in favour with God than I am."[76]

Genesis 2:18 reads, "Then the Lord God said, 'It is not good for man to be alone; let us make him a helper like himself.'" Regis Armstrong writes, "God has repeated those words from time to time during the course of history. One day God said: It is not good for Francis to be alone; let us make him a helper like himself. And in this way Clare was created. Clare truly was a helper 'like himself' for Francis, having the same nature, of the same mettle as he, in the truest sense a 'twin soul.'"[77]

But their friendship "was not exclusive. It did not exclude the others, those brothers of Francis or those sisters of Clare, but rather overflowed onto them. Francis is the brother and father of all the sisters; Clare is the sister and mother of all the brothers. When a friendship between a man and a woman is of this quality—non-possessive sharing—it becomes a reminder of creation; it returns us to relationships of original innocence."[78]

"Instead of looking at each other, Clare and Francis looked in the same direction," at Jesus, "poor, humble, crucified," notes Armstrong. Seeing Jesus "from slightly different angles" and "with the gifts and sensitivities of a man and of a woman," Clare and Francis offer us a fuller image of the incarnate Jesus.[79]

Invaders at the Gate

Clare was fearless when she needed to be. One Friday in September 1230, when Clare was thirty-five, a band of Muslim soldiers (Saracens, as they were often called) arrived at the gate of San Damiano.[80] This was not a Muslim army; it was a brigade of mercenaries in the employ of

---

76 Fortini, *Francis of Assisi*, 359–60.
77 Armstrong, "Introduction," in *The Lady: Clare of Assisi*, 9.
78 Armstrong, "Introduction," in *The Lady: Clare of Assisi*, 10.
79 Armstrong, "Introduction," in *The Lady: Clare of Assisi*, 10.
80 Regis Armstrong notes that this occurrence "is one of the few incidents that can be dated with certainty: a Friday in September, 1230, at about the hour of Tierce." Clare's sisters frequently mentioned it later when testifying during the canonization process, though no other sources record the event. Editorial notes, *The Lady: Clare of Assisi*, 154, 360.

Frederick II (1194–1250), king of Sicily and Germany and nominally a
Christian. In 1220, he was declared Holy Roman Emperor.[81] Frederick
attempted forcibly to control much of Italy, battling the papal forces.
His mercenaries arrived in the Spoleto Valley intending to force Assisi
and other towns to submit. His army included an "array of soldiers
and Saracen archers swarming like bees at the imperial command to
depopulate [Spoleto Valley] villages and to spoil its cities."[82]

Saracen soldiers came upon San Damiano as they were attacking
Assisi. The sisters felt vulnerable; they knew well the common threat
of violence and rape at the hands of soldiers. Clare had assured them
though, "My sisters and daughters, do not fear because the Lord will
defend you. I wish to be your ransom; if it should happen that the
enemies come down to the monastery, place me before them."[83]

The soldiers did come in, scaling the wall. Clare was sick in bed.
Sister Benvenuta said the Saracens "climbed down into the part within
the cloister of San Damiano." Clare "got up from her bed and called
her sisters, comforting them not to be afraid."[84] Clare asked the sisters
to sing a hymn, then went to prayer, appealing to God for his help and
protection.

Clare then went down to the entrance to the refectory, which faced
the open cloister where the Saracens were gathering. Sister Francesca,
who like Benvenuta, Filippa, and Amata was there, described the scene:
"Throwing herself prostrate on the ground in prayer, [Clare] begged
with tears, saying among other things: 'Lord, look upon these servants
of yours, because I cannot protect them.'" Some of the nearby sisters
said they heard "a voice of wonderful sweetness" assure Clare, "I will
always defend you!" Clare prayed the Lord would protect Assisi as well,
and again the voice responded, "The city will endure many dangers, but
it will be defended."[85]

The soldiers were taken aback at this unexpected scene, and a bit
bewildered. They soon left, doing no harm.

---

[81] Though German, Frederick inherited the Kingdom of Sicily through his mother.
He viewed himself as standing in the line of the ancient Roman emperors. The pope
excommunicated him three times; Gregory IX called him an Antichrist.

[82] *Legend of Saint Clare*, 300.

[83] Sister Amata's testimony, in *Process of Canonization*, 164.

[84] Benvenuta's testimony, in *Process of Canonization*, 154.

[85] Testimony of Sister Francesca, in *Process of Canonization*, 174–75. Some of the
sisters who heard the voice said Clare later told them not to tell anyone while she was
still alive. Peterson, *Clare of Assisi*, 224.

Clare lived to nearly sixty, surviving Francis by twenty-seven years. The incident of the Saracen soldiers invading San Damiano in 1230 was her sole direct encounter with Muslims. With Francis, however, Muslim encounter came earlier. Ten years before this, Francis set out to witness directly to Muslims in Egypt.

11

Francis's Muslim Mission

The year 1219 was a most unusual one for Francis and his brothers. It was a year of expanding missionary work beyond Italy but also of growing tensions within the Order. Above all, this was the year Francis met Muslim Sultan Malik al-Kamil in Egypt and told him about Jesus.

The clash between the way of Francis and the way of the world appears most starkly in Francis's encounter with Muslims during the Fifth Crusade. Here we see the real upside-down power of the Francis movement.

Francis spent time alone on retreat early in 1219, it seems, before participating in the General Chapter at the Portiuncula in May. Like other General Chapters, this one featured a good deal of discussion about ongoing issues in the growing Order: leadership, recruitment, liturgical practices, possible revisions to the Rule. The most important issue, however, was international missions—sending teams of brothers all over the world. Francis had a global vision from day one, as we saw earlier. By now the Order had spread throughout Europe but not much beyond.

The Chapter of May 1219, probably at Francis's urging, decided to send missionary teams into all the world. Jesus had said, "Go into all the world and proclaim the good news to the whole creation" (Mark 16:15); "make disciples of all nations" (Matt. 28:19). As the movement expanded internationally, "Francis rejoiced in spirit upon hearing" of "holy brothers in faraway lands ... who, by word or deed, led sinners to the love of Christ," wrote Bonaventure.[1]

---

[1] Bonaventure, *The Major Legend of Saint Francis*, in *Francis of Assisi: Early Documents*, ed. Regis J. Armstrong, OFM Cap., J. A. Wayne Hellmann, OFM Conv., and William J. Short, OFM (New York: New City Press, 2001), 2:588 [hereafter FA:ED].

The 1219 Chapter formed new bands of brothers for Hungary and Germany and other parts of Europe but also for other lands beyond. The port city of Naples on Italy's west coast, more than a hundred miles beyond Rome on the "shin" of Italy's boot, became an important transit point for Franciscan brothers in their missionary travels. "Many brothers from other places" would come together at the Franciscan convent in Naples "on their way to different parts of the world," notes Thomas of Celano.[2]

Brother Giles set out for Tunis, almost directly across the Mediterranean from Sicily. More than a hundred brothers went to Spain, and some traveled on to Morocco.[3] It was in Muslim Morocco that the first Franciscan brothers died as martyrs: Berardo, Peter, Adiuto, Accursio, and Otto.[4]

Francis himself had long wanted to witness to the Muslim world— the lands and peoples who were the targets of the Crusades. At the 1219 Chapter, Francis said he planned to go to Syria to preach Jesus to the Saracens (Muslims). Moorman notes, "After months of prayer [Francis's] mind was made up and no power on earth could stop him. He had always longed to die as a martyr; this time he fully intended to achieve his ambition."[5] His motive was not masochistic. His passion was to be faithful to Jesus in both life and death.

Journey to the Holy Land

Francis set out for the Holy Land in early June, a few weeks after the chapter meeting. He walked to Ancona on the Adriatic Sea, about eighty miles northeast of Assisi. From this port, ships often carried Crusaders to the Holy Land.

---

[2] Thomas of Celano, *Treatise on the Miracles of Saint Francis*, FA:ED 2:447. In contemporary English "convent" usually means a nunnery, but during Francis's day, the term (deriving from the verb "convene") was applied to religious communities of both men and women, as well as the buildings that housed them.

[3] John Moorman, *A History of the Franciscan Order: From Its Origins to the Year 1517* (Oxford: Oxford University Press, 1968), 48, 71; Omer Englebert, *Saint Francis of Assisi*, 2nd English ed., trans. Eve Marie Cooper (Chicago: Franciscan Herald Press, 1965), 233–34. This was not the first time Franciscan brothers had been in Spain (Francis himself had visited), but the work had not prospered.

[4] Moorman, *History of the Franciscan Order*, 36, 71–72, 229; Englebert, *Saint Francis*, 238; Lawrence S. Cunningham, *Francis of Assisi: Performing the Gospel Life* (Grand Rapids, MI: William B. Eerdmans, 2004), 59.

[5] Moorman, *History of the Franciscan Order*, 48. Cardinal Hugolino had earlier kept Francis from leaving Italy; he felt Francis's personal presence in Italy was crucial to the new order's life and development. "To anyone who did not know Francis, his decision to undertake a mission to the infidels at this critical juncture would surely seem but another indication of his lack of common prudence. In truth it was the highest wisdom." Father Cuthbert, *Life of St. Francis of Assisi*, 3rd ed. (London: Longmans, Green, 1948), 273.

Other brothers wanted to go with him. Several of them accompanied Francis to Ancona, too many for the mission. Their ship could accommodate a dozen at most in addition to Francis. Francis didn't want to prefer some over others. So he called a young boy playing at dockside and asked him to pick twelve brothers randomly. Thus the missionary band was providentially selected, Francis felt: Peter Catani, Illuminato of Rieti, Leonardo, Barbaro, Sabbatino, Caesar of Speyer, and six others— twelve in all. Some, like Peter Catani, were well educated. At least two were former knights.[6] Some had been among Francis's first companions in Assisi, so they knew him especially well. Elias was not among them; in fact, he was already in the Holy Land, heading up a Franciscan mission in Acre. He later joined the brothers at Damietta.

Twelve poor brothers: Francis's idea of a true crusading army.

The ship transporting Francis and his brothers carried a good many Crusader soldiers. The vessel embarked for the Holy Land on June 24, 1219. It docked at the Crusader fortress of Saint John d'Acre (today part of Israel) about three weeks later. Acre was a Christian stronghold built by the Knights Hospitaller (Order of Knights of the Hospital of Saint John of Jerusalem), an early Catholic military order founded a century earlier to care for poor and sick pilgrims to the Holy Land.

The ship soon continued, arriving at Damietta, Egypt, in the Nile delta, a few days later.[7]

Damietta was the focal point of the Fifth Crusade, which lasted about five years. Pope Innocent III himself called the crusade in 1213, promoted it vigorously, and helped organize its armies. By the authority of Christ and Peter (so he claimed) the pope promised eternal salvation to all who personally joined the Crusader army or who paid for others to go in their place.[8] Francis himself may have heard the pope preach the crusade on one of his visits to Rome.

As always, the crusade's big goal was to free Jerusalem from the Muslims—"a goal on which Innocent III had set his heart," Fortini notes.[9]

---

[6] Englebert, *Saint Francis*, 234; Moorman, *History of the Franciscan Order*, 48–49; Cuthbert, *Life of St. Francis*, 275–76; Arnaldo Fortini, *Francis of Assisi*, trans. Helen Moak (New York: Crossroad Publishing, 1992), 395–96; Thomas of Celano, *Remembrance*, FA:ED 2:265 n. c.

[7] Englebert, *Saint Francis*, 234; Fortini, *Francis of Assisi*, 396.

[8] J. Hoeberichts, *Francis and Islam* (Quincy, IL: Franciscan Press, 1977), 11–12. The pope ardently promoted the Fifth Crusade to raise such a large force that it could overrun Muslim armies.

[9] Fortini, *Francis of Assisi*, 397 n. e.

But at this point the main Christian and Muslim forces were facing off not at Jerusalem but in Egypt. The strategy was to defeat the Muslim army at Damietta, move on south a hundred miles and conquer Cairo, then turn east and liberate Jerusalem. "If the Moslems could be driven out of the Nile valley, not only would they lose their richest province, but they would be unable to keep a fleet in the Eastern Mediterranean; nor could they hold Jerusalem long against a pincer attack coming from Acre and from Suez," notes historian Steven Runciman.[10] Capturing Damietta was key.

The Battle of Damietta

Damietta was (and is still) located at a bend in the main branch of the Nile River, about four miles in from the Mediterranean coast. It was a substantial city of about eighty thousand. The population included a significant number of Christians of the Melkite Rite—an ancient branch of the Christian faith that had maintained friendly relations with Rome.[11] The Muslim armies set up camps just north and south of the city, while the city itself was well fortified.[12]

Figure 11.1 Siege of Damietta—Cornelis Claesz van Wieringern, 1627

About June 1, 1218, the first Crusader ships arrived at Damietta. The Crusaders set up their base unopposed along the Nile about two miles north of the city and began preparing a siege. Before long, some sixty

---

[10] Steven Runciman, *A History of the Crusades,* vol. 3, *The Kingdom of Acre and the Later Crusades* (Cambridge: Cambridge University Press, 1954, 1987), 150.

[11] Paul Moses, *The Saint and the Sultan: The Crusaders, Islam, and Francis of Assisi's Mission of Peace* (New York: Doubleday, 2009), 79, 103.

[12] Map in Moses, *The Saint and the Sultan,* xii.

thousand Crusaders had assembled.[13] The Nile River floods annually, reaching its lowest level in June before rising rapidly in mid-July. It continues rising more slowly until October, then subsides gradually until June, when the cycle starts over. Both Muslims and Crusaders used the river's flood cycle to their advantage when they could. Intentionally or not, the Crusaders arrived when the Nile was at its lowest.[14]

The sprawling Crusader encampment consisted not only of soldiers and their officers but also church officials and hundreds of civilians, men and women, who helped support the Crusader effort. Linda Bird Francke describes the scene:

> Many of the English, French, Spanish, Germans, and Italians were military men—knights, archers, foot soldiers, Levantine mercenaries—but as many as twenty thousand more were civilian camp followers, including pilgrims, servants, merchants, cooks, some of the knights' families, and several shiploads of French prostitutes. Many among the military men were indeed carrying the banner of Christ, but a sizable number were atheists or profiteers looking to scavenge the riches of Egypt.[15]

The Crusaders built a huge portable catapult capable of lobbing large rocks over the walls into the city. When a full lunar eclipse occurred, Crusaders took it as a prophetic omen. Had not Jesus himself said the following?

> [They] will fall by the edge of the sword and be taken away as captives among all nations; and Jerusalem will be trampled on by the Gentiles, until the times of the Gentiles are fulfilled. There will be signs in the sun, the moon, and the stars, and on the earth distress among nations confused by the roaring of the sea and the waves. People will faint from fear and foreboding of what is coming upon the world, for the powers of the heavens will be shaken. Then they will see "the Son of Man coming in a cloud" with power and great glory. Now when these things begin to take place, stand up and raise your heads, because your redemption is drawing near. (Lk. 21:24–28)

---

[13] Linda Bird Francke, *On the Road with Francis of Assisi* (New York: Random House, 2005), 155.

[14] Reminding us perhaps of Jeremiah 46, "Who is this, rising like the Nile, like rivers whose waters surge? Egypt rises like the Nile, like rivers whose waters surge. It said, Let me rise, let me cover the earth, let me destroy cities and their inhabitants" (Jer. 46:7–8).

[15] Francke, *On the Road with Francis*, 156.

Sultan Malik al-Kamil, ruler of Egypt at this time, held power over the Holy Land with the exception of the small Crusader enclaves along the Mediterranean coast. Al-Kamil was a nephew of the great Saladin (1138–1193), the first Sultan of Egypt and Syria. Saladin successfully united Muslim forces against the Crusaders, wresting Jerusalem from Christian control in 1187 and turning it into an Islamic state.[16]

Sultan al-Kamil was in Cairo when the Crusaders reached Egypt. Carrier pigeons flying in from Damietta alerted him that Crusader forces had landed. He hurried north to Damietta with additional troops to reinforce the stronghold.[17] He encamped at Fariskur, about six miles south of Damietta, a safe distance from the Crusaders but sent large numbers of troops north to defend the city.

Many of the Crusaders were excited to be in the land of the Bible. A popular legend held that Damietta was the place where Pharaoh's daughter had plucked baby Moses from the bulrushes along the Nile.

After settling in to their camp, the crusading armies mounted their siege. Fortini calls the siege of Damietta "one of the most dramatic events of the thirteenth century." He quotes the account of an unknown crusader who wrote of "the joys, the tribulations, the passions, the abandonments, the various torments, borne by the militant Christians" of the Crusader armies.[18]

The Crusaders were hardly a glorious holy host. Fortini notes,

Adventurers of every race had come, and murderers, to gain absolution for frightful crimes. [Pirates] and grasping merchants were found shoulder to shoulder with proud and austere men, in a heterogeneous throng perennially animated by piety and ambition, heroism and jealousy, holiness and brutality. There were bishops, princes, Templars, Hospitallers, priests, dukes, counts, marquises, men-at-arms of the land and of the sea.

... banners of every imaginable kind fluttered from the masts of ships: pennants, ensigns, flags of every pattern and colour, flags of France, Germany, Brittany, Spain, Frisia, Holland. Companies, knights, and infantry of the Italian republics were there, equal in arms and courage to the most powerful kingdoms: [Venice,

---

[16] *Chronicle of Ernoul*, FA:ED 1:605 editorial n. e. Saladin, a Sunni Muslim of Kurdish descent, founded the Ayyubid dynasty, which was dominant in Muslim lands throughout the twelfth and thirteenth centuries.

[17] Bonaventure, *Major Legend*, FA:ED 2:602 n. a; Moses, *The Saint and the Sultan*, 81–82.

[18] Fortini, *Francis of Assisi*, 397.

Genoa, Pisa, Bologna; even] a company of Crusaders of the Spoleto Valley.[19]

Whatever the nationality, all shields, ships, armor, flags, even war horses, were emblazoned with the Crusader emblem: bright red cross on a white background, the cross of St. George. Altogether, an impressive Crusader army numbering in the hundreds of thousands.[20]

The Crusaders launched several futile attacks on Damietta and the Muslim encampments. The city with its many castles and other buildings was strongly defended and well stocked to withstand a two-year siege. The landward sides were "surrounded by three walls, each higher than the other, with a moat between the first and second"; the middle wall had twenty-eight watchtowers.[21] In total, the city numbered more than a hundred red ocher towers and was defended by hundreds of archers, crossbowmen, and infantry. Just outside the walls, a heavy chain stretched across the river to a strong tower near the opposite bank to prevent hostile ships from proceeding further upstream toward Cairo. Just beyond the chain lay a bridge of boats.[22]

The Crusader generals decided they must capture the river tower and break the chain to gain a foothold south of the city. They launched attacks by ship in late June and early July 1218. Crusaders tried at first to breach the tower with siege ladders. But with the waters surging near the tower base and Muslim soldiers' arrows, javelins, stones, and flaming oil from above, the first attacks failed miserably. Ships were destroyed and many soldiers drowned, weighed down by their heavy armor.

But the Crusaders tried again in late August. This time they lashed two ships together and built a high tower of beams and poles with upper and lower platforms to attack the stone tower at its upper levels. A long ladder extended forward so the Crusaders could quickly reach the fortress. Some three hundred soldiers managed to maneuver the attack ship upstream to the Muslim tower and lash it to the tower itself.

A bloody battle raged for hours. Muslim catapults sent a torrent of stones against the Crusaders, while Muslim defenders in the tower

---

[19] Fortini, *Francis of Assisi*, 398. "The license and disunity reigning in this army was sufficient explanation of its previous failures," suggests Englebert. *Saint Francis*, 234.

[20] John (Jean) of Brienne, brother of Walter of Brienne and king of Acre, was at Damietta with a force of 100,000 warriors, notes Fortini. *Francis of Assisi*, 399.

[21] James M. Powell, *Anatomy of a Crusade, 1213–1221* (Philadelphia: University of Pennsylvania Press, 1986), 140.

[22] Runciman, *History of the Crusades*, 3:152; Fortini, *Francis of Assisi*, 399; Francke, *On the Road with Francis*, 158.

attacked with arrows and lances and "Greek fire," a chemical compound that ignited on contact with water. The Crusaders persisted, however. After some twenty-four hours, they won possession of the tower. They managed to cut the chain across the Nile, force their way upstream, and establish a beachhead above the city.[23]

God had come to their aid, the Crusaders felt. There were even rumors of mysterious white-clad warriors led by a captain in red armor.[24]

Thus the situation remained for about three months. But then both Crusaders and Muslims suffered a near disaster. It was now late November 1218. The Nile was still at flood stage. Suddenly a fierce gale blew in from the Mediterranean, pushing the Nile waters into a surge that inundated the Crusader camp. "Every tent was flooded and the stores were soaked," writes historian Steven Runciman. "Several boats were wrecked and others driven across to the Moslem camp. Horses were drowned. When the flood subsided, there were fishes lying about everywhere, a delicacy, says the chronicler Oliver of Paderborn, that everyone would gladly have forgone."[25]

A stalemate now ensued through the winter months. The weather turned unusually cold, the temperature likely dipping down into the forties Fahrenheit. Lacking fruit and vegetables, soldiers became ill with scurvy. Men suffered from swollen and bleeding gums, lost teeth, loose fingernails, painful legs and feet, and the reopening of earlier wounds. About a fifth of the army died. Thousands more gave up and sailed back to Europe, discouraged and disillusioned.[26]

The siege continued, however, with periodic attacks and counterattacks. As the weather warmed, the Crusaders launched a major assault on Palm Sunday—March 31, 1219. Fortini reports that "there was bitter fighting from dawn until late at night. The women in the camp were on the field of battle with the Crusaders, taking them water, wine, bread, and stones for their weapons. Priests followed to recite the prayers of the day while bandaging and blessing the wounded." The chronicler Francesco Pipino wrote that "on that holy day the only palms carried by the Christians were crossbows and bows, arrows and lances, swords and shields." Reports said the Muslims lost thirty ships and five thousand fighters.[27]

---

[23] Moses, *The Saint and the Sultan*, 82–85.
[24] Fortini, *Francis of Assisi*, 400.
[25] Runciman, *History of the Crusades*, 3:156.
[26] Moses, *The Saint and the Sultan*, 89.
[27] Fortini, *Francis of Assisi*, 401.

Francis on the Nile

About four months later, in August 1219, Francis and his brothers arrived. A year had passed since the Crusaders had captured the river tower. Francis and Brother Illuminato surveyed the scene. Beyond the Crusaders' camp and remote from the siege, Francis must have been struck by the varied plants and wildlife in this region of rivers and lakes—an abundance of birds and fish; gardens, orchards, and pasturelands.[28]

Large Lake Manzala, just east of Damietta, sits on a major flyway for migrating water birds. "Millions of birds pass through Egypt annually seeking food, shelter, and rest," notes Mona Ahmed.[29] Lake Manzala is a strategic wintering area for hundreds of thousands of waterfowl. Marshes around the lake annually draw massive numbers of migrating ducks, teal, flamingos, herons, pelicans, coots, gulls, and other birds.[30] Franciscan sources don't tell us whether Francis went out and talked with the congregating waterfowl, as he often did in Italy. But one wouldn't be surprised.

Francis soon learned that the Crusaders were about to launch a fresh attack. Their forces now controlled the western bank of the Nile both above and below the city. With the Nile in front and Lake Manzala at its back, Damietta was virtually surrounded.

But Francis was troubled. To attack at this time was not God's will, he felt. He told one of his brothers, "If the battle happens on this day the Lord has shown me that it will not go well for the Christians. But if I say this, they will take me for a fool, and if I keep silent my conscience won't leave me alone. What do you think I should do?"

Francis's companion replied, "Father, don't give the least thought to how people judge you. This wouldn't be the first time people took you for a fool. Unburden your conscience, and fear God rather than men."

Francis "leapt to his feet, and rushed to the Christians crying out

---

[28] Powell, *Anatomy of a Crusade*, 140; Francke, *On the Road with Francis*, 158.

[29] Mona Ahmed, "Egypt Is Perfect Transit for Migrating Birds," https://www.egypttoday.com/Article/6/33773/Egypt-is-perfect-transit-for-migrating-birds.

[30] Kamal H. Shaltout and Tarek M. Galal, "Ecosystem of Lake Manzala" (2007). "A waterfowl census in 1990 showed that more than 574,000 water birds wintered in the Egyptian wetlands; of which over 234,000 birds wintered in Lake Manzala (40.7% of the total). This census included approximately 256 grebes, 22,500 cormorants, 2,330 herons, 333 flamingos, 19,000 ducks, 175 raptors, 436 rails and coots, 42,500 waders, 106,000 gulls, and 39,400 terns." https://www.researchgate.net/profile/Kamal_Shaltout/publication/280597558_Ecosystem_of_Lake_Manzala/links/55bc9b2208ae9289a09593b3/Ecosystem-of-Lake-Manzala.pdf.

warnings to save them, forbidding war and threatening disaster," reports Thomas of Celano. The Crusaders "took the truth as a joke. They hardened their hearts and refused to turn back."[31]

The army attacked on August 29, advancing against the Muslim forces by land and ship. They fell into a trap. The Muslims fell back, feigning flight. When the Crusaders, led by the Knights Templar, the Teutonic Knights and the Hospitallers, advanced near enough, the Muslims counterattacked. The Crusaders fled, suffering major losses. Sultan al-Kamil sent troops directly against the Crusader encampment, nearly overrunning it and endangering Francis and Illuminato themselves.[32]

"The massacre was so great that between the dead and the captives the number of our forces was diminished by six thousand," writes Thomas.[33] Historian James Powell in *Anatomy of a Crusade* comments, "It was a disaster that fully justified the prediction of Francis."[34]

Francis continued six months with the Crusaders, observing the siege, caring for the sick and wounded, praying with them—meanwhile seeking some way to cross over to see the sultan. Brother Illuminato and another brother or two were with him. Some Crusaders viewed Francis as a prophet, since he had predicted defeat in the battle at the end of August. Meanwhile the unhealthy conditions of the camp seem to have affected Francis's fragile health. It may be here that Francis first developed the eye ailment, maybe trachoma, that bothered him the rest of his life.[35]

By this time James de Vitry had been named bishop of Saint John d'Acre, the Crusader outpost along the Mediterranean coast that Francis visited on his way to Egypt. James visited Damietta several times and in his writings comments on Francis's being there. Francis "is so amiable that he is venerated by all," James wrote. He so impressed the Crusader

---

[31] Thomas of Celano, *Remembrance*, FA:ED 2:265–66.

[32] Powell, *Anatomy of a Crusade*, 158–59.

[33] Thomas of Celano, *Remembrance*, FA:ED 2:266. See also Francke, *On the Road with Francis of Assisi*, 160.

[34] Powell, *Anatomy of a Crusade*, 158–59. "The Muslims compounded their victory by beheading fifty knights from each of the [three main] military orders and displaying the heads on wooden stakes along the way to Fariskur," writes Francke, *On the Road with Francis*, 161. Adrian House reports the beheadings but not the display of the heads. Adrian House, *Francis of Assisi* (Mahwah, NJ: HiddenSpring [Paulist Press], 2001), 209.

[35] Francke writes, "The hot and squalid camp was thick with flies, which spread disease from one to the next, and Francis was not spared. He developed an eye infection, thought to be trachoma, which led to chronic watering of his eyes, painful sensitivity to light, and clouding of his vision. He became jaundiced and, for the rest of his life, is thought to have suffered from hepatitis." Francke, *On the Road with Francis*, 159.

soldiers and priests that some actually joined the Franciscans. James names three: "Colin, the Englishman, our clerk," plus Master Michael and Dom Matthew—all clergy, apparently.[36] The Lesser Brothers are "multiplying rapidly on all sides because [their order] imitates the primitive Church and follows the life of the Apostles in everything," James said.[37]

Time passed. The siege continued, punctuated by occasional skirmishes. Inconclusive peace talks dragged on between the sultan, the Crusade's military leaders, and Cardinal Pelagius, representing Pope Innocent.[38] Shiploads of Crusaders left; others arrived. "These were dark days for the Christians," says Fortini. "A deep exhaustion weighed upon the solders of the faith, who by now were sure that the war was lost and that the Crusade had ended miserably."[39]

Meanwhile Sultan al-Kamil sought to drum up support among Muslims elsewhere for the defense of Egypt. He sent heralds throughout Muslim lands. "He who wishes to acquire Christian slaves, come join the ranks!" the Sultan said. "Let it be known to everyone that almost all the Christians are dead or have fled! Those who remain cannot in any way escape from the hands of the sons of Mohammed!"[40] Meanwhile Al-Kamil continued sending envoys to the Crusaders, trying to arrange peace.

During this lull in fighting, Francis watched for an opportunity to cross over to the Muslim camp. He had long dreamed of seeing a Muslim leader embrace the Christian faith and of winning peace between Muslims and Christians.

Finally at the end of September, Francis decided to act. He explained his plan to Cardinal Pelagius, who must have thought Francis was crazy. Pelagius at first refused to give permission, fearing for Francis's life. But Francis kept urging, and finally the cardinal agreed.[41]

---

[36] Englebert, *Saint Francis*, 235.

[37] Paul Sabatier, *The Road to Assisi: The Essential Biography of St. Francis*, ed. Jon M. Sweeney (Brewster, MA: Paraclete Press, 2004), 102.

[38] Cardinal Pelagius, a Spaniard, arrived at Damietta in mid-September, about three months after the first Crusaders' arrival. "His coming to Damietta at once caused trouble," for John of Brienne, now Crusader king of Acre, "had been accepted as leader of the Crusade." Pelagius, however, as the pope's official representative, insisted on calling the shots. Runciman, *History of the Crusades*, 3:155.

[39] Fortini, *Francis of Assisi*, 410.

[40] Fortini, *Francis of Assisi*, 411.

[41] Powell, *Anatomy of a Crusade*, 159.

Francis Sees the Sultan

Francis and Illuminato set out from the Christian camp, planning to cross to the east side of the Nile and walk south across no-man's-land past Damietta to the sultan's site at Fariskur.[42] Presumably the two brothers crossed the river on a makeshift pontoon bridge of boats roped together.[43]

As the pair set out, they saw two lambs in the field, Bonaventure says. "Trust in the Lord, brother," Francis told Illuminato, "for the Gospel text is being fulfilled in us: 'Behold, I am sending you forth like sheep in the midst of wolves.'" So on they went, singing the Twenty-third Psalm, "The Lord is my Shepherd. . . . Even though I walk through the darkest valley, I fear no evil; for you are with me; your rod and your staff, they comfort me."[44]

Francis knew the risks. The sultan had promised a gold *bezant*—a valuable Byzantine gold piece, common currency at the time—to anyone who would bring him a Crusader's head. Francis had long before decided that his final calling might be martyrdom, and he was ready.[45]

Neither Francis nor Illuminato, unarmed and in simple habits, looked much like real Crusaders. The two brothers, wrote James de Vitry, "set out for the camp of the Sultan of Egypt, fortified only with the shield of faith."[46] On the way they probably saw and smelled the rotting corpses of men and horses from the fierce battle not many days earlier.[47]

Seeing the two poor friars approaching, Muslim sentries quickly apprehended them. "I am a Christian," Francis said. "Take me to your master." The pair were probably taken into custody at Damietta, then conducted on to Fariskur.

One of the earliest reports, the *Chronicle of Ernoul,* says that when the Muslim sentinels saw the two men approaching, they assumed they either were messengers or Crusader soldiers who wanted to convert to Islam. There is some evidence that during the lull between fighting, men from both sides crossed over to join the faith of the other.[48] Historian Runciman comments, "The Moslem guards were suspicious at first

---

[42] As a strategic move, al-Kamil had "set up his camp at Fariskur, some six miles south of Damietta, ready to attack the Crusaders in the rear should they try to assault Damietta." Runciman, *History of the Crusades,* 3:159.

[43] Moses, *The Saint and the Sultan,* 126.

[44] Bonaventure, *Major Legend,* FA:ED 2:602.

[45] Bonaventure, *Major Legend,* FA:ED 2:602.

[46] James de Vitry, *Historia Occidentalis* (c. 1221/25), FA:ED 1:584.

[47] Moses, *The Saint and the Sultan,* 127.

[48] *Chronicle of Ernoul* (1227/29), FA:ED 1:605.

but soon decided that anyone so simple, so gentle and so dirty must be mad, and treated [Francis] with the respect due to a man who had been touched by God. He was taken to the Sultan al-Kamil, who was charmed by him and listened patiently to his appeal."[49]

Later accounts (including that of Bonaventure) say the two brothers were severely beaten, insulted, and chained. Early sources make no mention of this. The *Chronicle of Ernoul,* considered one of the most reliable accounts, merely says the Muslim sentries "seized [the pair] and led them to the Sultan."[50]

The sentries first asked the two uninvited guests what they wanted. Francis responded that he was a follower of Jesus and wished to speak with the sultan. The Muslim soldiers assumed that meant that the two men had a message for the Muslim leader, perhaps a response to a peace proposal.

So, Francis and Illuminato were brought to Fariskur. "What Francis saw was a sea of earth-colored tents in al-Kamil's almost one-mile-square camp."[51] Eventually Francis and Illuminato were brought before Sultan Malik al-Kamil himself. It was a unique historical encounter, often colorfully imagined by artists. What must the sultan, leader of vast Muslim forces in the Middle East, have thought of this small figure Francis and his companion?

Francis was sure of his mission and undaunted in meeting the sultan. He and al-Kamil were about the same age—the sultan thirty-nine and Francis a year or two younger. Francis "had no fear of anyone's status, rather he spoke calmly to the wise and the uneducated, to the great and the small," wrote Julian of Speyer.[52] He simply hoped to persuade al-Kamil to become a convinced disciple of Jesus Christ.

As always, Francis began, "May the Lord give you peace." The sultan responded similarly, perhaps with the traditional Arabic greeting, "Peace be upon you." He asked why Francis had come. Did Francis have some message for him, or did he and his companion want to become Muslims? The sultan had had personal experience of Egyptian Christian monks who had embraced Islam.[53]

No, Francis said, they certainly did not want to become Muslims. They indeed had a message, but not from the Crusader army. They were messengers from the true Lord God, telling him to give his soul to God.

---

[49] Runciman, *History of the Crusades,* 3:160.
[50] *Chronicle of Ernoul,* FA:ED 1:606.
[51] Francke, *On the Road with Francis,* 163.
[52] Julian of Speyer, *Life of Saint Francis,* FA:ED 1:409.
[53] Moses, *The Saint and the Sultan,* 129.

Bonaventure writes that Francis told al-Kamil "with an intrepid heart that he had been sent not by man but by the Most High God in order to point out to him and his people the way of salvation and to announce the Gospel of truth. He preached to the Sultan the Triune God and the Savior of all, Jesus Christ, with such great firmness, such strength of soul, and such fervor of spirit that the words of the Gospel appeared to be truly fulfilled in him: 'I will give you utterance and wisdom which all your adversaries will not be able to resist or answer back.'"[54]

We don't know Francis's exact words, but typically Francis preached the New Testament kingdom of God "not in the persuasive words of human wisdom but in the learning and power of the Spirit," as Thomas of Celano wrote, paraphrasing the Apostle Paul. Francis spoke confidently and directly, not using "fawning or seductive flattery."[55]

The *Chronicle of Ernoul* summarizes Francis's message this way:

> If you wish to believe us, we will hand over your soul to God, because we are telling you in all truth that if you die in the law which you now profess, you will be lost and God will not possess your soul. It is for this reason that we have come. But if you will give us a hearing and try to understand us, we will demonstrate to you with convincing reasons, in the presence of the most learned teachers of your realm, if you wish to assemble them, that your law is false.[56]

"*If* you wish to believe us," Francis had said. Sultan al-Kamil was intrigued. Clearly these poor men were no threat. They had come in peace, ready to dialogue. Al-Kamil was accustomed to discussion and debate. James de Vitry wrote that the sultan was delighted with Francis's words and spirit and "became sweetness itself."[57] Bishop James, who by this time had had considerable contact with Muslims, wrote that the sultan "recognized [Francis] as a man of God and changed his attitude into one of gentleness, and for some days he listened very attentively to Francis as he preached the faith of Christ to him and his followers." In fact, wrote James, most Muslims "willingly listen to all these Lesser Brothers when they preach about faith in Christ and the Gospel teaching," as long as they don't criticize or condemn Mohammed.[58]

---

[54] Bonaventure, *Major Legend*, FA:ED 2:602–3 (quoting Luke 21:15).
[55] Thomas of Celano, *Life of St. Francis*, FA:ED 1:215.
[56] *Chronicle of Ernoul*, FA:ED 1:606.
[57] Quoted in Moses, *The Saint and the Sultan*, 131.
[58] James de Vitry, *Historia Occidentalis* (c. 1221/25), FA:ED 1:584.

Accounts of this encounter speak of Francis preaching to the Sultan and his court. It seems to have been more of a dialogue over several days than a series of sermons. Probably Francis gave an initial presentation of the good news, much as he often did in his preaching throughout Italy, though adapted to his audience. Did Francis speak in Latin, in which he wasn't very fluent? The sultan perhaps could understand it. Or did Francis speak in his native Italian, an interpreter translating into Arabic? This seems more likely.

Al-Kamil was a learned man—a true Arabic sultan, a well-educated scholar more than a warrior, though he was both. At home in Cairo, he often sat with Muslim scholars and sages on Friday nights and had lively exchanges.[59] The sultan sometimes dialogued with Sufis, Muslim mystics who emphasized prayer and piety and often dressed simply. Sufis saw Jesus as a true man of God, though not the Messiah. Al-Kamil loved the poetry of the contemporary Sufi mystic Ibn al-Farid. He may well have viewed Francis and Illuminato as in effect Christian Sufis.[60]

Julian of Speyer wrote that "with great steadiness [Francis] withstood the sultan and with great eloquence he neutralized the arguments of those railing against the Christian faith." This certainly suggests lively dialogue and debate. "The sultan accepted [Francis] with enormous honor and offered him many precious gifts." When Francis flatly refused them, al-Kamil "was even more amazed at this man unlike any other, and listened more intently to his words"—though the sultan, like King Agrippa hearing the Apostle Paul, was not ready to embrace this new faith.[61]

Dialogue continued for several days. "In a tent populated with brilliant, sophisticated religious thinkers and poets, Francis held his own," writes Paul Moses. Though we have no firsthand accounts, we know for sure that "in the worst of times, a Christian and a prominent Muslim engaged in reasoned public discussion about their religious differences" and about their faiths—on one side a learned Muslim sultan with his subjects and scholars and attendants; on the other, two poorly clad Christian brothers who were simply trying to honor Jesus.[62]

---

[59] Moses, *The Saint and the Sultan*, 140.

[60] Moses, *The Saint and the Sultan*, 137–39. Moses details the sultan's interest in Sufism and its influence on him and his court. The *Qur'an* itself speaks positively of Jesus, though denying the incarnation and Jesus's resurrection. See A. H. Mathias Zahniser, *The Mission and Death of Jesus in Islam and Christianity* (Maryknoll, NY: Orbis, 2008).

[61] Julian of Speyer, *Life of Saint Francis*, FA:ED 1:395.

[62] Moses, *The Saint and the Sultan*, 141.

James de Vitry's chronicle says al-Kamil listened intently to Francis. It was an "astonishingly peaceful scene of a monk preaching the Christian faith to the enemy's monarch in the middle of a war," notes Paul Moses.[63] Sultan al-Kamil himself was a firm Sunni Muslim, not likely to adopt the Christian faith. Though a benefactor to his people who had established religious schools, he was genuinely curious about Francis and his faith. More pressingly, he needed to make peace with the Crusaders. Damietta, under siege for more than a year, was suffering from famine and disease. The city was desperate for relief. Al-Kamil knew that even now more Crusader ships might well be on their way from Europe. If Francis could be a bridge to peace, that would be victory itself.

Earliest accounts of Francis with the sultan picture a peaceful and cordial encounter, no ugly conflicts or challenges. Later versions say the Muslims threatened Francis and Illuminato with death, the sultan's advisors insisting the sultan was duty-bound to cut off the heads of the infidels for preaching against Islam.

One story has it that the sultan wanted to test Francis's devotion to Jesus and his cross, so he laid out a beautiful multicolored carpet "almost entirely decorated with a geometric pattern of crosses." Then he summoned Francis. To enter the room, Francis would have to tread on the crosses. But if he refused to do so, he would be insulting the sultan.

Francis entered and crossed the carpet without hesitation. "How dare you tread on the crosses?" the sultan asked.

Francis replied, "You should know that two thieves were crucified with Jesus. We Christians possess the cross of Christ, and surround it with devotion. But you have been left with the crosses of thieves. I am not afraid to walk on the crosses of the thieves."[64]

Al-Kamil provided abundant food and comfortable lodging for Francis and Illuminato within his encampment. He conversed with the brothers on multiple occasions, it seems. According to the *Chronicle of Ernoul*, the sultan invited Francis and Illuminato to remain with him, and he would provide them a home. When Francis saw, however, that al-Kamil was not going to convert to Jesus, he told the sultan that he and Illuminato would return to the Crusaders' camp, if he would let them.[65]

Al-Kamil agreed. Francis refused the sultan's gifts of "gold, silver, and silk garments," for he was wed to Lady Poverty. Just a little food, Francis

---

[63] Moses, *The Saint and the Sultan*, 132, referencing James de Vitry's report.

[64] Summarized from *A Book of Exemplary Stories* (c. 1280–1310), FA:ED 3:798–99. It is not possible to document this story from the earliest sources.

[65] *Chronicle of Ernoul*, FA:ED 1:607.

said, and they would be on their way. "The Sultan gave them plenty of food to eat, whereupon they took their leave of him, and he had them escorted safely back to the Christian army."[66]

Four decades after Francis's death, when Bonaventure wrote his account of these events, he turned Francis's encounter with the Muslims into a trial by fire, literally. Bonaventure says Francis told the sultan:

> If you wish to be converted to Christ along with your people, I will most gladly stay with you for love of him. But if you hesitate to abandon the law of Mohammed for the faith of Christ, then command that an enormous fire be lit and I will walk into the fire along with your priests so that you will recognize which faith deserves to be held as the holier and more certain.

The sultan refused, according to this account, saying his Muslim leaders would never agree. In that case, Francis said, "if you wish to promise me that if I come out of the fire unharmed, you and your people will come over to the worship of Christ, then I will enter the fire alone. And if I shall be burned, you must attribute it to my sins. But if God's power protects me, you will acknowledge Christ the power and wisdom of God as the true God and Savior of all." Al-Kamil said he wouldn't dare accept this, though he admired Francis.[67]

There are several problems with Bonaventure's version. For one thing, the Fourth Lateran Council had condemned trial by ordeal just four years earlier, in 1215. Also, this seems inconsistent with the manner of Francis, who always stressed loving enemies in the spirit of Jesus. Bonaventure's version of the story became embodied in art and architecture, however. "This colorful scene of Francis standing beside a blazing fire, with a horrified Illuminato close by and the concerned sultan before him on a marble throne," notes Paul Moses, "is the enduring image of the encounter between saint and sultan."[68] One of the earliest and popular such versions is that of the artist Giotto in the Basilica of Saint Francis in Assisi.

The truth seems to be rather that Francis carried on an animated and respectful exchange over a period of a week or more during a lull in the fighting as peace negotiations proceeded. Thomas of Celano in his brief account says Sultan al-Kamil "honored [Francis] as much as he could,

---

[66] *Chronicle of Ernoul*, FA:ED 1:607.
[67] Bonaventure, *Major Legend*, FA:ED 2:603.
[68] Moses, *The Saint and the Sultan*, 134.

offering him many gifts, trying to turn his mind to worldly riches. But when he saw that he resolutely scorned all these things like dung, the Sultan was overflowing with admiration and recognized him as a man unlike any other. He was moved by his words and listened to him very willingly."[69]

From what we know of al-Kamil, it seems unlikely that he wanted to turn Francis's mind to "worldly riches," but rather simply wished to show appreciation and appropriate hospitality.

Bishop James de Vitry reports that at the end of their dialogue, al-Kamil "privately asked [Francis] to pray to the Lord for him, so that he might be inspired by God to adhere to that religion which most pleased God."[70] Such a request could well be a courtesy offered by a convinced Muslim. The *Qur'an* after all speaks positively of those People of the Book (Jews and Christians) who "are believers" and not "evil-livers." They "recite the revelations of Allah in the night season" and "believe in Allah and the Last Day, and enjoin right conduct and forbid indecency, and vie with one another in good works. These are of the righteous.... Allah is Aware of those who ward off (evil)."[71]

Al-Kamil had certainly witnessed more than he wanted of People of the Book who were "evil-livers." As Paul Moses writes, "Al-Kamil had seen the worst face of Christianity: the face of invaders pressing forward, wielding the True Cross like a weapon.... He knew the avarice of the Christian merchants with whom he once negotiated trade treaties" and who now wanted to control Damietta as a key trading post. "Francis had shown Sultan al-Kamil what it meant to be a true Christian, a holy person who truly believed Jesus' call to love the enemy."[72]

Francis refused the sultan's lavish gifts, but he may have accepted one small item as a token of friendship. Francis was nothing if not courteous—a prime virtue with him in this, the age of courtly ("courteous") chivalry. Today among the relics in Assisi's Saint Francis Basilica is a silver-and-ivory horn, about ten inches long, said to be the sultan's parting gift. Doubtful legend has it that Francis later used the horn to summon people to his preaching.[73]

In keeping with traditional Egyptian hospitality, Francis and al-Kamil likely shared a final meal together, as we noted. Paul Moses comments,

---

[69] Thomas of Celano, *Life of St. Francis*, FA:ED 1:231.
[70] James de Vitry, *Letter VI* (1220), FA:ED 1:581.
[71] *Qur'an* 3:110, 113–15.
[72] Moses, *The Saint and the Sultan*, 145.
[73] Francke, *On the Road with Francis*, 144.

"This scene of Francis peacefully breaking bread at a banquet with Sultan Malik al-Kamil, his supposed enemy, could not differ more" from later Christian iconography. "Their meal ought to have been the enduring image of the encounter between the saint and the sultan, printed in bright colors on cathedral walls."[74] Linda Francke comments, "The sultan called him Brother Francis and admired him for his bravery and the depth of his religious conviction. Francis, in turn, admired the sultan for his reason and humanity," even though Francis was unable to bring the sultan to faith in Jesus Christ as Lord and Savior.[75]

Al-Kamil gave Francis one other parting gift, according to some accounts: permission for him and his brothers to visit Jerusalem's Holy Sepulcher free of the normal tribute charge. With that, Muslim soldiers under the sultan's command escorted Francis and Illuminato safely back to the Crusaders' camp.[76]

Arnaldo Fortini reflects on the wonder of Francis's encounter with Sultan al-Kamil. What fascinates us, writes Fortini, is simply

> the meeting of these two great and noble spirits, and the fact that at the very time Christian and Moslem armies were engaged in trying to annihilate each other, the barriers between these men fell forever and they came to understand and love one another.
>
> One can hardly imagine the amazement and admiration of the Crusaders when, after nearly a month, they saw Francis and Illuminato reappear in Damietta, with an escort of Saracen knights sent by the sultan to protect and honour them, [an escort] as large as those provided for emperors.[77]

The Fall of Damietta

Things now moved swiftly. People in besieged Damietta were starving. Peace talks had stalemated. More Crusader ships could arrive any day. And other pressing issues, including a possible coup, were calling al-Kamil back to Cairo.

On September 26, 1219, the sultan launched a direct attack. Taking advantage of the Nile's rapidly rising current, he sent a squad of galleys floating north to the Christian camp. Muslim soldiers landed out of

---

[74] Moses, *The Saint and the Sultan*, 146–47.

[75] Francke, *On the Road with Francis*, 165.

[76] Angelo Clareno, *Book of Chronicles or of the Tribulations of the Order of Lesser Ones*, FA:ED 3:398; Moses, *The Saint and the Sultan*, 145.

[77] Fortini, *Francis of Assisi*, 433, citing the *Chronicle of Ernoul*, 1:12.

range of the Crusaders and began hurtling huge rocks into the Crusader compound, using catapults. The Muslims then tried to storm the Christian defenses. They were repulsed, for during the lull in fighting the Crusaders had strengthened their defenses, and fresh French troops had arrived. The Muslim forces had to retreat.

Cardinal Pelagius and the Crusader commanders realized the Muslim situation was now desperate. An initial contingent of Crusaders managed to cross Damietta's moats, burn the wooden gates, and raise the Crusader flag on one of the city's twenty-eight towers.

The next day Crusader forces fully breached the city, scaling its walls without opposition. The sultan's forces had withdrawn further south, leaving the city nearly defenseless. The English chronicler Roger of Wendover describes the scene:

> [The Crusaders] found the streets strewed with the corpses of the dead, and were met by an intolerable stench from them and the most squalid-looking human beings. The dead had killed the living; husband and wife, father and son, master and servant, had perished from the stench of one another. And it was not only the streets which were full of the dead, for corpses were lying about in houses and bedchambers; boys and children had asked for bread, and there was no one to break it for them; infants hanging at the breasts of their mothers were rolling over the bodies of the dead; the pampered rich died of hunger.[78]

Muslim sources say that when the remnant of Damietta's residents realized the sultan's forces were not going to rescue them, they agreed to surrender. They would give up the city provided the Crusaders allowed them to leave unharmed with whatever they could carry. Nevertheless, some Crusaders raped Damiettan women and killed or enslaved some of the people, according to the Arab chronicler Abu Shama.[79]

Of Damietta's eighty thousand inhabitants, only about three thousand remained alive. Most of the survivors were near death. Francis himself entered the city and must have been deeply grieved and repulsed by what he found. Cardinal Pelagius and the Crusader soldiers rejoiced, however. Pelagius sent a report to Pope Honorius III; the pope likened the victory to Joshua's conquest in the Old Testament when the walls of Jericho came

---

[78] Roger of Wendover, *Flowers of History*, 423–24, quoted in Moses, *The Saint and the Sultan*, 149.

[79] Abu Shama, *The Book of the Two Gardens*, cited in Moses, *The Saint and the Sultan*, 149–50.

tumbling down.[80] Meanwhile the Crusaders converted Damietta's grand mosque—Egypt's second oldest—into a cathedral dedicated to Virgin Mary. Francis was probably still in Damietta when the cathedral was officially dedicated on February 2, 1220.[81]

Despite the victory at Damietta, the Fifth Crusade ended badly. For months, the Crusaders awaited the arrival of King Frederick II of Germany, newly crowned Holy Roman Emperor, with his army. But Frederick never came. Attacks by al-Kamil's soldiers weakened the Crusade forces. Finally in 1221, Cardinal Pelagius ordered the Crusaders to move south and conquer Cairo. But the attempt failed, and in the end the Crusaders had to abandon Damietta and evacuate Egypt altogether.[82] "It was with shame that was bitter and well-earned that the soldiers of the Cross sailed back to their own countries." So ended the Fifth Crusade; "nothing had been gained and much lost, men, resources and reputations," writes Runciman.[83]

Return to Assisi

Meanwhile Francis was eager to get back to Italy and his brothers at the Portiuncula. Other brothers had now arrived in Damietta; he left them there to minister, forming a small Franciscan convent. Francis then sailed away to his homeland the first chance he got.

Francis perhaps traveled home by way of the Holy Land and a visit to the Church of the Holy Sepulcher in Jerusalem.[84] He apparently spent some months at Acre, ministering and preaching Jesus in areas controlled by Crusaders. He was suffering from the eye infection which he likely contracted at Damietta; his weeks in Acre may have been a time of convalescence. According to the *Assisi Compilation*, "From the time when he was overseas to preach to the Sultan of . . . Egypt, he had a very severe eye disease, caused by the hardship and fatigue of travel, as he endured the extreme heat both in coming and going. . . . Because of the sufferings and bitter experiences of Christ, which He endured for us, [Francis] grieved and afflicted himself daily in body and soul to such a degree that he did not treat his own illnesses."[85]

---

[80] Moses, *The Saint and the Sultan*, 149–51.

[81] Moses, *The Saint and the Sultan*, 149–51; Francke, *On the Road with Francis*, 166–67; Runciman, *History of the Crusades*, 3:165.

[82] Fortini, *Francis of Assisi*, 434 n. q.

[83] Runciman, *History of the Crusades*, 3:170. Runciman gives a full account of the Crusade's end, 165–70, as does Powell, *Anatomy of a Crusade*, 175–91.

[84] Moses, *The Saint and the Sultan*, 151–52.

[85] *Assisi Compilation*, FA:ED 2:180.

During this time Francis got the news of the beheading of the brothers sent to Morocco to preach to Muslims.

Francis had now been away from the Portiuncula—the center of Franciscan community and decisions—for more than a year. It was time to go home.

Dante in his *Paradiso* decades later summarized Francis's Muslim mission this way:

> And after, in his thirst for martyrdom,
> within the presence of the haughty Sultan,
> he preached of Christ and those who followed Him.
>
> But, finding hearers who were too unripe
> to be converted, he—not wasting time—
> returned to harvest the Italian fields.[86]

---

[86] Dante Alighieri, *The Divine Comedy*, *Paradiso* Canto XI, 104–5, quoted in FA:ED 3:885.

12

The First Manger Scene

Nativity scenes (or manger scenes, creches) are found worldwide at Christmas time, even in lands where there are few if any Christians.

It wasn't always so.

Christians have of course celebrated Christmas from the church's earliest days. Christian tombs sometimes depicted a stable or cave where Jesus was born. Over the centuries as the faith spread and local Christians started acquiring church buildings, they sometimes pictured the manger scene there in various ways.[1]

But never the way Francis of Assisi did.

Christmas was extra special to Francis. He seems to be the first to come up with the idea of reenacting the Nativity scene using live animals. Francis was a born dramatist. Maybe the best drama he created was the live manger scene in the small forested hill town of Greccio, sixty miles by foot south of Assisi, in 1223, three years before his death.[2]

It had been a stressful year for Francis. The winter weather was severe. At the end of November, the Franciscan's final Rule, the *Regula bullata*, was finally approved in Rome. That done, Francis and Brother Angelo walked back to Assisi. Francis would never see Rome again.[3]

---

[1] Lawrence S. Cunningham, *Francis of Assisi: Performing the Gospel Life* (Grand Rapids, MI: William B. Eerdmans, 2004), 76.

[2] The story is that the name Greccio derives from a group of Greek refugees who founded the city centuries before.

[3] Omer Englebert, *Saint Francis of Assisi*, 2nd English ed., trans. Eve Marie Cooper (Chicago: Franciscan Herald Press, 1965), 298.

Greccio, Christmas Eve

Two weeks before Christmas, Francis contacted his friend John Velita, a prominent nobleman of Greccio who loved Jesus and cared for the poor. "I want to have a special Christmas Eve celebration of Jesus's birth," he told John, "and I would like you to make the preparations."

Why Greccio? Probably because of Francis's friendship with John, John's character and resources, and his prominence in the town. The Lesser Brothers already had a hermitage there that Francis liked to visit. Greccio rests on a forested mountain spur overlooking the Rieti Valley, and the mountainside has many caves. John's property included a hillside grotto that Francis thought would be perfect for a live Nativity drama.[4]

Francis's first biographer, Thomas of Celano, may himself have participated in these events. He gives what sounds like an eyewitness account. According to Thomas, Francis told his friend John, "If you desire to celebrate the coming feast of the Lord together [with me] at Greccio, hurry before me and carefully make ready the things I tell you. For I wish to enact the memory of that babe who was born in Bethlehem: to see as much as is possible with my own bodily eyes the discomfort of his infant needs, how he lay in a manger, and how, with an ox and an ass standing by, he rested on hay."[5]

Francis wished to mount a memorable festival that dramatized Jesus's radical good news. He "wanted everyone to share in the joy of this 'feast of feasts.' He wanted the poor and the hungry to sit at the tables of the rich, and oxen and asses, the humble beasts who had warmed the cold body of the baby Jesus with their breath, to be given more than the usual amount of grain and hay."[6]

Quickly John set about making arrangements. People offered to share the needed animals and supplies. Francis invited all the Lesser Brothers from the surrounding area. Word spread throughout Greccio and neighboring towns.

---

[4] Englebert, *Saint Francis*, 300. Englebert says Francis had cleared this idea with Pope Honorius in advance because he intended to use live animals, because the event would include a Christmas Mass outdoors rather than in a chapel, and perhaps also "to avoid any friction with the local pastor or ordinary." Englebert, *Saint Francis*, 488 n. 8.

[5] Thomas of Celano, *Life of St. Francis*, in *Francis of Assisi: Early Documents*, ed. Regis J. Armstrong, OFM Cap., J. A. Wayne Hellmann, OFM Conv., and William J. Short, OFM (New York: New City Press, 2001), 1:254–55 [hereafter FA:ED]. Some accounts say Francis while in the Holy Land had visited Bethlehem, and that inspired the reenactment at Greccio.

[6] Fortini, *Francis of Assisi*, 531.

So, on Christmas Eve, the people came—many from Greccio, others from the countryside round about. "Winding up the mountain, the procession wended its way toward the spot where—between a great ox and a little donkey—the Crib was set up."[7]

Thomas of Celano writes:

> As they could, the men and women of that land with exultant hearts prepare candles and torches to light up that night whose shining star has enlightened every day and year. Finally, the holy man of God comes and, finding all things prepared, he saw them and was glad.
>
> Indeed, the manger is prepared, the hay is carried in, and the ox and the ass are led to the spot. There simplicity is given a place of honor, poverty is exalted, humility is commended, and out of Greccio is made a new Bethlehem.[8]

For Francis, the focus is the baby Jesus, symbolized by the manger, and the animals standing near. The accounts do not mention people enacting the parts of Mary, Joseph, shepherds or wise men, or a real baby. Francis wanted animals to receive special attention at Christmas.

"The forest amplifies the cries and the boulders echo back the joyful crowd," writes Thomas. The Lesser Brothers begin singing, "giving God due praise, and the whole night abounds with jubilation."[9]

Francis has donned a deacon's robe to assist the priest.[10] He sings out the Gospel lesson: "She gave birth to her first-born son and wrapped him in swaddling clothes and laid him in a manger."[11] Francis is visibly stirred as he gazes at the manger and the scene—"filled with heartfelt sighs," Thomas of Celano says, "overcome with wondrous joy."[12]

---

[7] Englebert, *Saint Francis*, 300.

[8] Thomas of Celano, *Life of St. Francis*, FA:ED 1:255.

[9] Thomas of Celano, *Life of St. Francis*, FA:ED 1:255.

[10] Thomas of Celano says Francis was "dressed in the vestments of the Levites" (that is, a deacon, not a priest) in order to assist the priest in the Mass. *Life of St. Francis*, FA:ED 1:256.

[11] Fortini, *Francis of Assisi*, 533.

[12] Thomas of Celano, *Life of St. Francis*, FA:ED 1:255–56. Thomas adds, "Over the manger the solemnities of the Mass are celebrated and the priest enjoys a new consolation." Does this perhaps refer to one of the later annual commemorations of this event? The editors of *Francis of Assisi: Early Documents* note, "This text could be a description of the ceremony repeated each Christmas at Greccio in memory of Francis's actions." FA:ED 1:255 n. a.

Francis then preaches a sermon as people crowd around in the midnight air. His voice strong and clear but wavering with emotion, he tells the story of the birth of the "babe from Bethlehem," emphasizing the phrase and the name "Jesus." Townsfolk in whose hearts "the child Jesus [had] been given over to oblivion" are reawakened.[13]

Eventually the celebration draws to a close. People return home with joy.[14]

Francis was delighted. This is what he wanted. A Nativity drama honoring the Nativity animals was such a fine idea, he thought, that he would like to start a new tradition of special care for animals, birds, and the poor at Christmastide. Companions of Francis often heard him say, "If I ever speak to the emperor, I will beg him, for the love of God and by my entreaties," to enact a law requiring "people each year on the Nativity of the Lord to scatter wheat and other grain along the roads outside towns and villages, so that all the birds, but especially our sister larks, may have something to eat on such a solemn feast."[15]

Remembering the gift of the newborn Jesus and his mother Mary, everyone should "give brother ox and brother ass a generous portion of fodder on that night," and "all the poor should be fed their fill by the rich."[16]

These would be true signs of God's kingdom, Francis felt.

For Francis, "the pain of human beings and the pain of animals are not divisible; we, too, must feel what they have to bear."[17]

Nativity Scenes and Mystery Plays

Francis's Nativity drama in 1223 took place just at the time mystery plays—public enactments of scenes from the Bible—were becoming popular throughout Europe. Eventually mystery plays were performed throughout the year by various town guilds. These were not associated primarily with Christmas, however. Typically, they presented a cycle of stories from the Old Testament (Creation, Adam and Eve, Noah and

---

[13] Thomas of Celano, *Life of St. Francis*, FA:ED 1:256.

[14] Thomas of Celano, *Life of St. Francis*, FA:ED 1:256.

[15] Arnaldo Fortini, scholar and former mayor of Assisi who died in 1970 at age eighty, embeds the Greccio nativity scene in the middle of his long chapter, "Love of all Creatures" (in Italian, "L'amore di tutte le creature"). In this chapter he tells stories of swallows and other birds and creatures and Francis's interactions with them.

[16] *Assisi Compilation*, FA:ED 2:129–30. See also Thomas of Celano, *The Remembrance of the Desire of a Soul* (The Second Life of Saint Francis), FA:ED 2:375. The reference here is to the Holy Roman Emperor—at this time, Frederick II.

[17] Fortini, *Francis of Assisi*, 539.

the Ark, and so forth) and on through the New Testament Nativity narratives. They often included Last Judgment scenes also, featuring "hell-mouth, a favorite property of the ancient English stage" consisting of "a huge face constructed of painted canvas exhibiting glaring eyes and a red nose of enormous dimensions; the whole so contrived with movable jaws of large, projecting teeth, that, when the mouth opened, flames could be seen within the hideous aperture."[18] Quite a contrast, in other words, to Francis's Nativity drama.

Mystery plays sometimes became controversial because of the liberties actors occasionally took and because of their growing popularity. The rise and spread of mystery plays—for example in England, the land of Shakespeare—is part of the background history of drama and theatre in our day.[19]

There is no direct link between Francis's Nativity "play" in Greccio and the mystery plays, but the growing popularity of dramatizations and mystery plays at this time helps set the stage for Francis's dramatic initiative.

The first live Nativity drama in Greccio was eight centuries ago. Recently a curious journalist, Linda Bird Francke, visited Greccio at Christmas and reflected on her experience:

> Francis must have been ecstatic to have re-created the birth of Jesus for so many people. Little did he know that he had started a tradition that would be celebrated all over the Christian world for centuries to come—and continues at Greccio to this day. That same Nativity scene is reenacted four times during the Christmas season and draws some thirty thousand people carrying candles and singing. It is also memorialized on the rough cave wall of the Chapel of the Crèche with two beautiful side-by-side frescoes, one of Francis at the Nativity in Greccio, the other of Mary and Joseph with the baby in Greccio's twin city of Bethlehem. The still-vibrant thirteenth-century frescoes are the work of the Giotto School and rival those in the basilica at Assisi.[20]

---

[18] James Orchard Halliwell-Phillipps, "The Life of William Shakespeare," in *The Works of William Shakespeare*, 10 vols. (New York: P. F. Collier & Son, 1912), 1:17.

[19] James J. Walsh, *The Thirteenth, Greatest of Centuries* (New York: Catholic Summer School Press, 1907), 136, 238–53. Walsh argued that "St. Francis may be considered in one sense as the father of the modern drama," and describes the Nativity scene at Greccio (239).

[20] Linda Bird Francke, *On the Road with Francis of Assisi* (New York: Random House, 2005), 191.

No surprise, really, that Francis's live Nativity drama became an annual event, drawing more and more people, especially after Francis's death three years later. Thomas of Celano notes, "At last, the site of the manger was consecrated as a temple to the Lord. In honor of the most blessed father Francis, an altar was constructed over the manger, and a church was dedicated."[21] Soon miracles stories sprang up. Hay preserved from the manger cured animals, helped women suffering in hard labor give peaceful births, and others be healed of "an assortment of afflictions."[22]

The annual Nativity celebration still draws crowds of tourists and local folk up the winding road to the site. If you visit Greccio today, try to go during Christmastide.

Thomas of Celano ends his first book on the life of Francis here, with the live Nativity celebration and a short hymn of praise.[23]

All of us today who at Christmas display a manger scene (creche, presepio, crib, Nativity display) in our homes, or who see one in front of a church building or in a town square, owe something to the lowly Francis.

---

[21] Thomas of Celano, *Life of St. Francis*, FA:ED 1:257.
[22] Thomas of Celano, *Life of St. Francis*, FA:ED 1:256–57.
[23] Thomas of Celano, *Life of St. Francis*, FA:ED 1:257.

13

Francis's Failing Health

Francis is as famous for his death as for his life. The marks of the crucified Jesus he received in his body (the *stigmata*) and his final hours were of a piece with his life.

Here again Francis much resembled the one whose footsteps he followed.

Francis was never robust, physically speaking. His initial calling came through sickness. Later he fell ill several times. Gradually he developed chronic conditions that progressively worsened. The most aggravating ongoing problem concerned his eyes.

Omer Englebert wrote,

> Few men have suffered more than St. Francis. In addition to the infirmities due to his continuous state of poor health and the mysterious tortures of the stigmata, he constantly afflicted his body with fasting and vigils, with fatigue, penances, and mortifications of every sort. He habitually treated "brother ass" [his body] with such harshness that before leaving it, he felt the need of a reconciliation.[1]

Lawrence Cunningham notes similarly that Francis was "in shockingly bad health in general since, as Bonaventure says, he treated his body as an overworked slave."[2]

---

[1] Omer Englebert, *Saint Francis of Assisi*, 2nd English ed., trans. Eve Marie Cooper (Chicago: Franciscan Herald Press, 1965), 292.

[2] Lawrence S. Cunningham, *Francis of Assisi: Performing the Gospel Life* (Grand Rapids, MI: William B. Eerdmans, 2004), 109.

Francis does seem to have experienced some inner conflict over the way he abused his body. He was caught between two ideals: the ideal, often exaggerated during the Middle Ages of denying and even abusing the flesh, and the ideal of respecting and caring for the good creation.

Behind this paradox lies a question already identified: How does Jesus actually want us to glorify God through our bodies (1 Cor. 6:20)? What does bodily discipleship really mean?

Thomas of Celano wrote, "Francis, the herald of God, put his footprints on the ways of Christ through innumerable labors and serious diseases, and he did not retreat until he had more perfectly completed what he had perfectly begun. When he was exhausted and his whole body completely shattered, he never stopped on the race of his perfection and never allowed relaxing the rigor of discipline. For even when his body was already exhausted he could not grant it even slight relief without some grumbling of conscience."[3]

But is this really what Jesus called Francis to do? And should it be celebrated?

How should we treat "Brother Body"? How fully in fact should we draw the line between body and spirit? According to the *Mirror of Perfection,* Francis would say, "In eating, sleeping, and fulfilling other bodily needs, a servant of God must satisfy his body with discernment. In this way Brother Body cannot grumble, saying: 'Because you do not satisfy my needs, I cannot stand up straight and persevere in prayer, or rejoice in tribulations, or do other good works.'" But "if a servant of God, with discernment, has satisfied his body well enough, but Brother Body wants to be lazy, negligent, and sleepy in prayer, vigils and other good works, then he should punish it like any wicked and lazy beast of burden, because it wants to eat but refuses to work and carry its weight."[4]

Here Francis reflects the spirituality of his age more than the teachings of Jesus. Yet Francis did frequently return to the example of Jesus's own sufferings. If a servant of God does not or cannot have his bodily needs met, "then let him patiently bear this for the love of God Who also 'suffered want and found not one to comfort' him. If he bears

---

[3] Thomas of Celano, *Remembrance,* in *Francis of Assisi: Early Documents,* ed. Regis J. Armstrong, OFM Cap., J. A. Wayne Hellmann, OFM Conv., and William J. Short, OFM (New York: New City Press, 2001), 2:382 [hereafter FA:ED].

[4] *Mirror of Perfection* (Sabatier ed.), FA:ED 3:344.

this need with patience, the Lord will credit it to him as martyrdom."[5] Francis really could not in his time grasp the intimate interconnection and interdependence of body and spirit.

Thomas of Celano records a conversation Francis had with a brother whose counsel he especially valued. Francis was troubled that "even against his will it was necessary to smear medical remedies on his body" to get relief. "What do you think of this, dear son?" Francis asked. "My conscience often grumbles about the care of the body. It fears I am indulging it too much in this illness, and that I'm eager for fine lotions to help it. Actually, none of this gives it any pleasure, since it is worn out by long sickness, and the urge for any savoring is gone."

The Lord gave the unnamed brother the right words. "Tell me, father, if you please, how attentively did your body obey your commands while it was able?"

"It was obedient in all things," Francis said. "It did not spare itself in anything, but almost rushed headlong to carry out every order. It evaded no labor, it turned down no discomfort, if only it could carry out commands." He and his body were completely agreed, said Francis, "that we should serve the Lord Christ without any objection."

"Well, then, my father, where is your generosity?" the brother asked. "Where is your piety and your great discernment? Is this a repayment worthy of faithful friends: to accept favors gladly but then not to give anything in return in time of need? To this day, what service could you offer to Christ your Lord without the help of your body? Haven't you admitted that it exposed itself to every danger for this reason?"

"I admit, son, this is nothing but the truth," Francis said.

The brother replied, "Well, is it reasonable that you should desert a faithful friend in great need, who risked himself and all that he had for you, even to the point of death? Far be it from you, father, you who are the help and support of the afflicted; far be it from you to sin against the Lord in such a way!"

"Blessed are you also, son," Francis responded. "You have wisely given me a drink of healing medicine for my disquiet!" Then Francis said jokingly to his flesh, "Cheer up Brother Body, and forgive me; for I will now gladly do as you please, and gladly hurry to relieve your complaints!"[6]

---

[5] *Mirror of Perfection* (Sabatier ed.), FA:ED 3:344. Francis is here quoting from Psalm 69:20–21. See similarly *Mirror of Perfection* (Lemmens ed.), FA:ED 3:233.

[6] Thomas of Celano, *Remembrance,* FA:ED 2:382–83.

And Francis went on with his ministry. The words of the Apostle Paul in 2 Corinthians 11 could well be applied to Francis: "on frequent journeys, in danger from rivers, danger from bandits, danger from my own people, danger from Gentiles, danger in the city, danger in the wilderness, danger at sea, danger from false brothers and sisters; in toil and hardship, through many a sleepless night, hungry and thirsty, often without food, cold and naked. And, besides other things, I am under daily pressure because of my anxiety for all the churches. Who is weak, and I am not weak? Who is made to stumble, and I am not indignant? If I must boast, I will boast of the things that show my weakness" (2 Cor. 11:26–30).

Francis's Early Illnesses

As a youth in Assisi, Francis was popular, a favorite of his friends. But he was small and always a bit frail.

Francis was not prepared for Assisi's battle with Perugia, which we read about in chapter 1. After nearly a year in prison, likely in unhealthy underground conditions, Francis returned home weak and ill. His gradual recovery, and the questioning that went with it, led finally to his conversion.

During the twenty years from his conversion to his death, Francis suffered two main ailments. The first one concerned his stomach, the other, his eyes. Through all the years, travels, victories, praises, and trials of Francis's ministry, illness and pain were often his companions. Without some grasp of his physical condition, we don't fully understand him or his movement.

Over the years many scholars, physicians, and Franciscan brothers have tried to get a clear picture of Francis's maladies. Though mystery remains, with time a sharper image emerges. Careful examination of the Francis sources combined with advances in medical science have led to new insights.[7]

In the 1970s a Swiss Capuchin brother named Octavian Schmucki (1927–2018) thoroughly researched the question of Francis's illnesses.

---

[7] See especially Octavian Schmucki, OFM Cap., "The Illnesses of St. Francis of Assisi before His Stigmatization," trans. Sergius Wroblewski, OFM, *Greyfriars Review* 4:3 (1990), 31–61; Octavian Schmucki, "The Illnesses of Francis during the Last Years of His Life," trans. Edward Hagman, OFM Cap., *Greyfriars Review* 13:1 (1999), 21–59. Perhaps the first medical doctor to study Francis's illnesses was Albert Bournet who in 1893 published (in French) a book on *St. Francis of Assisi: A Social and Medical Study* (Lyons, France). See Schmucki, "The Illnesses of Francis," 21. Schmucki reviews several studies and proposed diagnoses.

Schmucki noted the need for an interdisciplinary approach (both history and science), and acknowledged in Francis's case the inherent complexities of the body–soul connection. Schmucki's writings, together with the early Francis sources and the work of later researchers, help us better understand the physical ailments Francis endured.

The earliest writings on Francis agree that his health was never strong. The *Assisi Compilation* says that "Francis was always sickly. Even in the world he was by nature a frail and weak man, and he grew more sickly until the day of his death."[8] The same source states that "from the time of his youth he was a man of a frail and weak constitution."[9] Francis himself told a brother, "I was ill from the beginning of conversion to Christ."[10]

Many Francis sources tend toward hagiography—idealizing him, exaggerating his saintly qualities, including his endurance of physical weakness and illness.[11] Despite this, the sources incidentally give key clues. Schmucki notes that "the extraordinary and converging number of relevant details mentioned for no particular reason" in the sources provide "a rare level of historical credibility" regarding Francis's physical condition.[12] The sum of comments from multiple sources gives us "one of the most detailed medieval medical 'case histories' that survive," one author notes.[13]

Stomach Issues: Chronic Malaria

Francis's health was first impaired by his months-long imprisonment in Perugia at age twenty. Once back home, it took him another year or so to recover. There are good reasons to think that Francis contracted malaria from mosquito bites during this time and that its effects continued for some time, even after his seeming recovery. Malaria was then widespread in Italy and could lead to long-term weakness.

Francis's symptoms as described in the sources are consistent with a diagnosis of chronic malaria. He would experience both "the burning heat of fever" and a "freezing sensation" from time to time.[14] He is

---

[8] *Assisi Compilation*, FA:ED 2:225. "Sickly" here probably has the sense of "frail" or "infirm" (*infirmitius*). Schmucki, "Illnesses of Francis" (1999), 25.

[9] *Assisi Compilation*, FA:ED 2:150.

[10] *Assisi Compilation*, FA:ED 2:211.

[11] Hagiography, from the Greek word for saint, *hagios*.

[12] Schmucki, "Illnesses of Francis" (1999), 25.

[13] K. Haines, "The Death of St. Francis" (1976), quoted in Schmucki, "Illnesses of Francis" (1999), 25–26 n. 19.

[14] Henri d-Avranches, *The Versified Life of Saint Francis*, FA:ED 1:432.

sometimes described as having "quartan fever," that is, a fever that comes and goes over periods of about four days. This would typically be the case with malaria. Today *quartan malaria* signifies intermittent malarial fever usually accompanied by seizures or convulsions every four days.[15] The *Assisi Compilation* notes, "For a long time even until the day of his death, blessed Francis suffered ailments of the liver, spleen, and stomach."[16] These could well be related to malaria.[17]

Most people who contract malaria fully recover. But malaria can become chronic, affecting a patient's stomach, liver and spleen, and general health, especially if it remains untreated.[18] The book *Disease and History* notes, "Untreated quartan or tertian malaria rarely kills by its own direct action; it is a chronic infection that causes increasing ill health and renders the sufferer more liable to attack by other diseases and less able to resist them." The main cause of the ongoing effects is chronic anemia due to destruction of hemoglobin in the red blood cells.[19] Francis did not take care of his body, and this description fits his chronic condition precisely.

Schmucki, concurring with doctors who have examined Francis's symptoms, notes that Francis's health "after his conversion did not take long to deteriorate, because of the very harsh treatment that he subjected his body to by prolonged fasts, vigils, and other mortifications of the same kind."[20] Added to the austerity of Francis's life is thus the likelihood of continuing low-grade chronic malaria and also, relatedly, a gastric ulcer. Sources often mention Francis suffering "ailments of the liver, spleen, and stomach" over a period of years and even until his death.[21] The complex of malarial factors very likely led to a persistent stomach ulcer (an infection and open sore on the inner lining of the stomach).[22]

It would have been difficult if not impossible for Francis or his companions to distinguish precisely between pain in the stomach,

[15] Clayton L. Thomas, ed., *Taber's Cyclopedic Medical Dictionary*, 18th ed. (Philadelphia: F. A. Davis, 1997), 1,155.
[16] *Assisi Compilation*, FA:ED 2:211.
[17] See Schmucki, "Illnesses of St. Francis" (1990), 31–35; Schmucki, "Illnesses of Francis" (1999), 21–26.
[18] https://jamanetwork.com/journals/jamainternalmedicine/article-abstract/545282.
[19] Frederick F. Cartwright, with Michael D. Biddiss, *Disease and History* (New York: Thomas Y. Crowell, 1972), 142.
[20] Schmucki, "Illnesses of St. Francis" (1990), 35.
[21] *Mirror of Perfection*, FA:ED 3:339.
[22] Thomas, *Taber's Cyclopedic Medical Dictionary*, 2,023; Schmucki, "Illnesses of St. Francis" (1990), 40.

liver, or spleen. Given all Francis's various reported complaints and symptoms, the likelihood of a stomach ulcer deriving principally from chronic malaria and poor diet seems very strong. Schmucki notes, "Medical writers who have tried to interpret the pathological symptoms described in the early sources tend to say that [Francis] developed a gastric ulcer quite soon. It was an inevitable result of his superhuman activity as an itinerant preacher and was aggravated by an inadequate and unhealthy diet."[23]

For years Francis's life was one of travel, preaching, and counseling others, punctuated by retreats at various hermitages. In 1214 or 1215, Francis, Bernardo, and some other brothers made a strenuous trip on foot to Spain. He and his companions likely visited the famed pilgrimage site of Santiago de Compostela in northwest Spain, thought to be the burial place of James the Apostle.[24]

Francis's aim in going to Spain, however, was to travel on to Morocco to witness to Muslims. Illness prevented him from going. He suffered complete physical collapse, even losing his speech for some days.[25] Schmucki concludes that this episode was "either because of a particularly severe case of gastric dyspepsia [burning pain or heartburn in the upper abdomen] or an attack of intermittent fever."[26] In either case, the underlying cause would have been chronic malaria. Francis was forced to return home.

Later in Italy, Francis again became quite ill, suffering from a fever. Bishop Guido urged him to lodge at the bishop's palace in Assisi for a period of rest and recovery, and Francis agreed.[27] He gradually recovered and soon resumed his travels.

It appears that Francis suffered the direct and indirect effects of chronic malaria from the time of his conversion till his death. At times the symptoms were quite mild; at other times more severe. His level of energy varied accordingly. With his profound joy in the Lord, identification with Jesus's life and sufferings, and total dedication to his calling, throughout

---

[23] Schmucki, "Illnesses of Francis" (1999), 26.

[24] Schmucki, "Illnesses of St. Francis" (1990), 38; Vera and Hellmut Hell, *The Great Pilgrimage of the Middle Ages: The Road to St James of Compostela* (New York: Clarkson N. Potter, 1966), 20.

[25] Thomas of Celano, *Life of St. Francis*, FA:ED 1:230; Thomas of Celano, *Miracles*, FA:ED 2:416.

[26] Schmucki, "Illnesses of Francis" (1999), 26–27; see also Schmucki, "Illnesses of St. Francis" (1990), 38–41.

[27] Schmucki, "Illnesses of St. Francis" (1990), 41–43; Schmucki, "Illnesses of Francis" (1999), 27.

most of his twenty years of active ministry his spirit was able to rise above even the pains of his body.

At the Pentecost Chapter of 1220, Francis resigned his leadership of the brothers (as noted in chapter 8). The weight of worsening health and impaired energy, together with unlimited expansion of the Order and the push of some brothers to relax the Rule, were too much for Francis. The Lord assured him, he felt, that from this point on his leadership would be solely by example, prayer, and preaching.[28]

Eye Disease: Trachoma

The Francis sources frequently mention eye problems. Francis had an eye condition that, like his stomach issues, became chronic, varied in intensity, and at times became quite severe.

The *Assisi Compilation* reports, "From the time when [Francis] was overseas to preach to the Sultan of Babylon and Egypt, he had a very severe eye disease." His brothers and others urged him to seek treatment. He refused. "What was bitter to his body he accepted and considered sweet on account of the sweetness and compassion that he drew daily from the humility and footprints of the Son of God."[29]

In his book on Saint Francis, Lorenzo Gualino, a physician, details Francis's symptoms: "During the last years of his life, Francis of Assisi suffered from grave ophthalmitis, which affected, although not with the same seriousness, both eyeballs, and was characterized by acute pain (we are not sure whether of the eyes or of the head), by photophobia or difficulty in bearing intense light, and by a progressive loss of sight, with stages of remission and recrudescence, until he was totally blind."[30]

This sounds like progressive trachoma. Francis probably contracted trachoma while he was in the Middle East, most likely when he was in Egypt at the time of the Fifth Crusade. We noted in chapter 11 that the hot weather and unhealthy conditions in the Crusader encampments along the Nile damaged Francis's health. Linda Bird Francke writes, "The hot and squalid camp was thick with flies, which spread disease from one to the next, and Francis was not spared. He developed an eye infection,

---

[28] *Assisi Compilation*, FA:ED 2:142; Thomas of Celano, *Remembrance*, FA:ED 2:340–41.

[29] *Assisi Compilation*, FA:ED 2:180. The *Mirror of Perfection* speaks of "very severe pain in his eyes." FA:ED 3:339.

[30] Lorenzo Gualino, *L'uomo d'Assisi*, 90; quoted in Schmucki, "Illnesses of St. Francis" (1990), 48. Gualino ruled out glaucoma as a possible diagnosis.

thought to be trachoma, which led to chronic watering of his eyes, painful sensitivity to light, and clouding of his vision."[31]

Bonaventure and others attributed Francis's eye problems to his excessive weeping, his frequent flow of tears. That is pious gloss, however; "the flow of tears, prolonged and abundant though they might be, does not cause blindness."[32] More likely, Francis suffered from conjunctivitis—inflammation of the conjunctiva, the mucous membrane between the eyelids and the eyeball. Trachoma is in fact "a chronic contagious form of conjunctivitis" that can lead to blindness.[33] It is caused by a bacterium (*chlamydia trachomatis*) easily transmitted by infected body fluids. Though various diagnoses of Francis's eye problems have been proposed, including glaucoma, trachoma best fits all the evidence.

Trachoma was common in Egypt where Francis was living with or near the Crusader troops. Schmucki cites an Italian medical dictionary's description of trachoma as

> a serious inflammation of the conjunctiva, which lines the inner surface of the eyelids and is reflected over the eyeball. It is the most serious and dangerous form of conjunctivitis, because of its high degree of contagiousness, because it is a chronic disorder, and because of the frequent gravity of its effects. Trachoma, which usually attacks both eyes, takes hold especially in individuals who are weak, anemic and malnourished.... Flies, traveling from infected ... to healthy eyes, are one of the most frequent sources of infection.... [As the disease progresses, it attacks the cornea.] The patient complains, especially in the initial period, of burning or soreness in the eyes, an intolerance to light (photophobia), and more or less abundant lachrymal secretions [eye waterings] that are very contagious.[34]

Francis increasingly suffered from all these symptoms. Chronic malaria would have made him both more susceptible to trachoma and more seriously ill, if he got it.

---

[31] Linda Bird Francke, *On the Road with Francis of Assisi* (New York: Random House, 2005), 159.

[32] Schmucki, "Illnesses of St. Francis" (1990), 44.

[33] Thomas, *Taber's Cyclopedic Medical Dictionary*, 1,979.

[34] Schmucki, "Illnesses of St. Francis" (1990), 47. Schmucki quotes from Segatore and Poli, *Dizionario Medico* [1954], 1163ab.

Schmucki says rightly that "it is not up to us to make a definitive judgment on the profound nature of the Poverello's eye trouble." Nevertheless, trachoma is the most probable. That disease, Schmucki writes,

> easily concurs with what the sources say about the time and place of its appearance (Egypt), with the previous disposition of the subject (extreme corporal feebleness), with the simultaneous ailments of both eyes, with the flow of tears, with the chronic return of the illness, with the pain, with the sensitivity to light, and with the progressive loss of vision. At least this is certain— that since his sojourn in the Orient, 1219–20, the saint suffered a grave organic infection of the eyes.[35]

Treatment: Cauterization

Both Francis's brothers and church officials began insisting that Francis get medical help. Cardinal Hugolino out of compassion and concern told Francis, "Brother, you do not do well in not allowing yourself to be helped with your eye disease, for your health and your life are of great value not only to yourself but also to others." You are compassionate to your own brothers, Hugolino said; now be merciful with yourself; "you must not be cruel to yourself in such a serious and manifest need and illness." Exercising his church authority, the cardinal *ordered* Francis to get medical help.[36]

On a visit to San Damiano in the winter of 1224–1225 to talk with Clare, Francis's eyes grew much worse. He could barely see. He stayed in a small cell at or near the chaplain's house. Brother Elias (serving as general minister at this time) ordered Francis to see an eye doctor, as the cardinal had also ordered. Elias wanted to be with Francis, he said, so he could arrange for his care and comfort him, since Francis was in great pain. The weather was very cold, however, so the treatment was postponed.[37]

Eye doctors had a recommended treatment for this kind of eye problem: cauterization. This "remedy" had been used for such eye disease for centuries and was employed also for headaches. Cardinal Hugolino and Francis's own brothers virtually insisted, out of compassion for Francis, that he undergo this recommended treatment.

---

[35] Schmucki, "Illnesses of St. Francis" (1990), 49.
[36] *Assisi Compilation*, FA:ED 2:184; also *Mirror of Perfection*, FA:ED 3:339.
[37] *Assisi Compilation*, FA:ED 2:184; Englebert, *Saint Francis*, 395.

Thomas of Celano writes that Hugolino "tried to find a way for [Francis] to regain the earlier health of his eyes." Neglecting his eyes would be sinful, Hugolino told Francis, not virtuous. So, Francis complied. "From then on he more carefully and freely did what was needed for his treatment."[38]

Francis prepared for the cauterization ordeal. His "illness had grown so bad," Celano reports, "that any relief at all required the greatest expertise and demanded the most bitter medicine. This is what was done: his head was cauterized in several places, his veins opened, poultices applied, and drops poured into his eyes. Yet he had no improvement but kept getting steadily worse."[39]

A well-known eye doctor from Rieti, about sixty miles south of Assisi, was engaged to perform the cauterization. Several brothers helped Francis travel to the hermitage of Fonte Colombo, near Rieti, in order to see the doctor.

The Assisi Compilation describes the treatment in some detail:

[Francis] was wearing on his head a large capuche [hood] the brothers had made for him, with a piece of wool and linen cloth sewn to [it], covering his eyes. This was because he could not look at the light of day because of the great pain caused by his eye disease. His companions led him on horseback to the hermitage of Fonte Colombo....

When the doctor arrived there, he told blessed Francis that he wanted to cauterize from the jaw to the eyebrow of the weaker eye.[40]

The doctor lit a fire and heated his cauterizing iron. Francis spoke to the fire and the glowing instrument. "My Brother Fire," Francis said, "noble and useful among all the creatures the Most High created, be courtly to me in this hour." In words recalling his *Canticle of the Creatures* Francis said, "For a long time I have loved you and I still love you for the love of that Lord who created you. I pray our Creator who made you, to temper your heat now, so that I may bear it." Then he made the sign of the cross.[41]

---

[38] Thomas of Celano, *Life of St. Francis,* FA:ED 1:271.
[39] Thomas of Celano, *Life of St. Francis,* FA:ED 1:271.
[40] *Assisi Compilation,* FA:ED 2:189.
[41] *Assisi Compilation,* FA:ED 2:190.

Chesterton remarks, "If there be any such thing as the art of life, it seems to me that such a moment was one of its masterpieces. Not to many poets has it been given to remember their own poetry at such a moment, still less to live one of their own poems."[42]

The scene was more than some of the brothers could take. Off they ran. "The surgeon takes in his hands the red-hot glowing iron.... The hissing iron sinks into the tender flesh, and the burn is extended slowly straight from the ear to the eyebrow,"[43] about two and a half inches. "The burn was a long one," reports *The Assisi Compilation,* "because, day and night for years fluid had been accumulating in his eyes. This is the reason, according to the advice of the doctor, for cauterizing all the veins from the ear to the eyebrow, although, according to the advice of other doctors, it would be very harmful. And this proved to be true, since it did not help him at all. Similarly, another doctor pierced both his ears, but to no avail."[44]

Here was the medical theory: Sealing off the veins to the eyes by cauterization would prevent fluid from pooling in the eyes. This was an unhappy misdiagnosis. The infection was in the eyes themselves, not elsewhere in the body.[45]

Francis said he felt no discomfort and chided the brothers for running off. "You, faint-hearted, of little faith," Francis said, "why did you run away? I tell you the truth: I felt no pain or even heat from the fire. In fact, if it's not well cooked, cook it some more!"[46]

The flabbergasted doctor decided he had witnessed a miracle. "I tell you the truth," he said, "and I speak from experience: I doubt that a strong man with a healthy body could endure such a severe burn, much less this man, who is weak and sick."[47]

---

[42] G. K. Chesterton, *St. Francis of Assisi* (Garden City, NY: Image Books, Doubleday [1924], 1957), 94–95.

[43] Thomas of Celano, *Remembrance,* FA:ED 2:355.

[44] *Assisi Compilation,* FA:ED 2:190–91.

[45] Schmucki documents and explains the various treatments recommended for eye disease at this time. Different doctors advised different things, including bloodletting. One medic, Vincent of Beauvais (c. 1190–c. 1264), a French Dominican friar, wrote as follows: "When it is necessary to treat by cauterizing in places where there is excessive harmful fluid, drying and burning agents are not enough to drive out the fluid; hence fire must be applied, for its end is to dry and to burn.... Extreme putrefaction and an overabundance of fluid render such treatment necessary." Quoted in Schmucki, "Illnesses of Francis" (1999), 40.

[46] *Assisi Compilation,* FA:ED 2:190.

[47] *Assisi Compilation,* FA:ED 2:190.

The treatment did no good. Francis continued to suffer from trachoma the rest of his life. The main symptoms he daily endured were pain and watering in the eyes, extreme sensitivity to light, and near blindness.

Of the thousands of portraits of Saint Francis, only one shows his eye disease. It is in the town of Greccio, site of the first manger scene. Linda Bird Francke described it as part of her journey retracing Francis's travels:

> His deteriorating condition is captured in a haunting portrait at the sanctuary in which he is wiping his weeping, diseased eyes with a white cloth. It is the only image, anywhere, of Francis and his eye affliction and was commissioned before his death by Lady Jacopa de Settesoli, the pious widow of Rome who is now buried near him in Assisi. The original painting was lost, but this fourteenth-century copy shows Francis, sadly, as he actually was toward the end of his life.[48]

Figure 13.1 Francis wipes ailing eyes *(Located in a church in Greccio, Italy)*

---

[48] Francke, *On the Road with Francis*, 190.

At this distance in time, we cannot be fully certain about Francis's illnesses and ailments. Cunningham says, however, "One thing is certain: any 'medical' treatment given in his day was at best useless and quite likely dangerous. In fact, what we know about what was done to him [to alleviate illnesses] seems more like well-meaning torture than treatment. The cauterization of his temples with white hot irons, ... and a subsequent treatment that consisted of piercing his ears to relieve his eye problems are examples of the state of 'medical' care in this period." Cunningham adds, "However ill he may have been, his pains did not touch his soul."[49]

---

[49] Cunningham, *Francis of Assisi,* 109–10.

14

Marks of the Cross

The Gift of Mount LaVerna

The image of Francis wiping his eyes, reproduced in the previous chapter, shows the *stigmata*—the marks of the crucified Jesus in Francis's foot and open hand.

Francis received the *stigmata* at the Franciscan retreat site high on Mount LaVerna, seventy miles northwest of Assisi. Located in the Tuscan Apennines about 3,700 feet above the valley in central Italy, LaVerna was a favorite retreat spot for Francis. The *stigmata* event occurred in late 1224, nearly a year before Francis's cauterization treatment, narrated above. We must tell the story here.

Francis walked to LaVerna some weeks after the General Chapter in June 1224. This was the last chapter he attended and also the last of six visits to LaVerna.[1]

The site—the whole mountain, in fact—had been given to Francis and his brothers eleven years earlier. Wealthy Count Orlando dei Catani, moved by a sermon Francis preached, donated the place to the brothers on May 8, 1213.[2] Orlando told Francis, "I have a mountain in Tuscany, which is very solitary and wild and perfectly suited for someone who wants to do penance in a place far from people or who wants to live a

---

[1] Omer Englebert, *Saint Francis of Assisi*, 2nd English ed., trans. Eve Marie Cooper (Chicago: Franciscan Herald Press, 1965), 303.

[2] Mount LaVerna was conferred to Francis and his brothers orally in 1213 and later, in 1274, legally confirmed by Count Orlando's sons in an official document. See "Donation of La Verna (1274)," in *Francis of Assisi: Early Documents*, ed. Regis J. Armstrong, OFM Cap., J. A. Wayne Hellmann, OFM Conv., and William J. Short, OFM (New York: New City Press, 2001), 3:801–3 [hereafter FA:ED], which includes the text of the document.

solitary life. It is called La Verna. If that mountain should please you and your companions, I would gladly give it to you for the salvation of my soul."[3]

Francis welcomed the gift. He sent some brothers to confirm the mountain's suitability for retreats. The legal deed specified that the donation included "all the forest land, the rocky lands and the meadowlands, without any limitation, from the top of the said Mountain all the way to its base."[4] Much of the mountain is covered by forest, but at its top is a high cliff that Dante later described in his *Paradiso* as "the rocky crest" between the Tiber and Arno rivers, whose sources lie in this area.[5]

LaVerna is a place of surpassing beauty about midway between Italy's east and west coasts. It is a place of grassy meadows; birds singing; wooded hills of beech, oak, and pine; odd-shaped rock outcroppings; and broad vistas of Italy's hills and valleys—or at other times lost in clouds. Pleasant in summer, it can be snowbound in winter.

Geologically LaVerna, with its huge split and tumbled rocks, suggests the early violent history of Earth when mountains were thrust up by earthquakes and shifting tectonic plates. The rocks are not volcanic, but rather similar in composition to those found along the coast where it curves around toward France. In the Middle Ages, Christian legend claimed that the mountain was created by earthquakes at the moment Jesus died on the cross.

The *Stigmata*

Here on Mount LaVerna, the marks of Jesus's crucifixion were imprinted in Francis's flesh. It happened on Saturday, September 14, 1224, the feast of the Exaltation of the Holy Cross. Francis was thirty days into a forty-day fast from the feast of the Assumption of Mary (August 15) to Michaelmas (the feast of St. Michael the Archangel) on September 29.[6]

---

[3] Arnaldo Fortini, *Francis of Assisi*, trans. Helen Moak (New York: Crossroad Publishing, 1992), 551, thus implying works' righteousness or salvation by good works. Similarly, Ugolino Boniscambi of Montegiorgio, *The Deeds of Blessed Francis and His Companions*, FA:ED 3:453.

[4] Fortini, *Francis of Assisi*, 547–48 n. c.

[5] Speaking of Francis's *stigmata*, Dante writes, "Twixt Tiber and Arno on the rocky crest / From Christ's own hand the final seal he won, / Borne for two years upon his limbs impressed." Dante Alighieri, *The Divine Comedy*, trans. Melville Best Anderson (New York: Heritage Press, 1944), *Paradiso*, Canto XI, 106 (p. 325). *Francis of Assisi: Early Documents* translates this as "there, on the naked crag between the Arno / and Tiber, he received the final seal / from Christ; and this, his limbs bore for two years." FA:ED 3:885.

[6] Fortini, *Francis of Assisi*, 553.

Lawrence Cunningham highlights the liturgical significance of September 14—"the day that marks the beginning of the season of abstinence and fasting for monks and nuns as an observant anticipation of the joyous days of the Christmas season. The liturgical office of that day is replete with the imagery of the cross and the other elements attendant upon it. The experience of the stigmata cannot be seen apart from the emphases that fill the liturgical offices of that day."[7]

Francis had set out from the Portiuncula with three brothers, Masseo, Angelo Tancredi, and Leo, "a man of the greatest simplicity and purity, because of which St. Francis loved him very much and used to reveal nearly all his secrets to him."[8] The four spent the first night at a Franciscan hermitage and the second in an abandoned church building. The third day they ascended LaVerna.[9]

But Francis was too weak to climb the mountain. According to a story in *The Considerations of the Holy Stigmata,* his brothers found a poor local farmer and asked him to lend Francis his donkey.

"Are you friars of that Brother Francis of Assisi about whom people say so much good?" he asked.

"Yes," they said.

The man happily saddled his donkey, led it to Francis, "and with great reverence helped him get into the saddle."

The poor man followed as Francis and the others ascended. After a bit, he said to Francis, "Tell me, are you Brother Francis of Assisi?"

"Yes," Francis said.

"Well then," said the man, "try to be as good as everyone thinks you are, because many people have great faith in you. So I urge you: never let there be anything in you different from what they expect of you."

---

[7] Lawrence S. Cunningham, *Francis of Assisi: Performing the Gospel Life* (Grand Rapids, MI: William B. Eerdmans, 2004), 108.

[8] *The Considerations of the Holy Stigmata,* in Raphael Brown, ed. and trans., *The Little Flowers of St. Francis* (New York: Doubleday, 1958), 174. On the nature and sources of *The Considerations,* see John V. Fleming, *Introduction to the Franciscan Literature of the Middle Ages* (Chicago: Franciscan Herald Press, 1977), 64–66. "The five 'considerations' ... attempt to give a precise and ordered account of the exact circumstances under which Francis received the stigmata," notes Fleming. "It is a work which deserves to be better known" (65–66).

[9] According to *The Considerations of the Holy Stigmata,* Francis endured a fierce battle with devils during the second night. He went out into the forest and appealed for Jesus's help. Christ came and strengthened him. "And so he spent that whole night in holy contemplation without sleeping," which left him exhausted the next morning. *Considerations,* 176.

Francis was delighted with the man's bluntness. He dismounted, knelt before him, kissed his feet, and thanked him for the kind warning. The farmer and brothers helped Francis back up and onto the donkey again.

So they continued climbing. The August sun grew hot, the path steep, and the farmer got very thirsty. He called out to Francis, "I am dying of thirst. If I don't have something to drink, I'll suffocate in a minute!"

Francis again got off the donkey and knelt in prayer. He lifted his hands to God. God heard his prayer. Francis told the man, "Run quickly to that rock, and there you will find running water which Christ in His mercy has just caused to flow."

The man ran to the spot and found clear water flowing. He drank heartily and was refreshed. The account adds, "neither before nor afterward was any spring ever seen there or anywhere nearby."[10]

Francis and the brothers continued up the winding path as the day drew on. At one point they stopped to rest under a large oak. The *Considerations* says that as Francis looked around and admired the view, "a great number of all kinds of birds came flying down to him with joyful songs, and twittering and fluttering their wings." Some settled on his head and shoulders, others on his arms and lap and around his feet. They seemed to be celebrating, welcoming Francis to the site.

It's good we're here, Francis told the others; "our little brothers and sisters the birds show such joy over our coming."

Continuing on a bit further, the small company came to a place Francis's brothers had prepared for him—a beautiful spot with a little hut made of tree branches.[11]

Brothers Masseo and Angelo with the farmer and his donkey returned to the valley below. Leo remained to care for Francis. Francis asked Leo to bring him a little bread and water once a day. Also, Leo was to take care that no one disturbed Francis.[12]

And Francis began his forty-day fast.

According to *The Assisi Compilation,* each day began with birds:

In early morning at dawn, while [Francis] stood in prayer, birds of various kinds came over the cell where he was staying. They did not come altogether, but first one would come and sing its

---

[10] *Considerations,* 177. All direct quotes are from this source, 176–77. Whether or not the story of the farmer and his donkey is precisely accurate historically, it certainly breathes the spirit of Francis.

[11] *Considerations,* 177–78.

[12] *Considerations,* 178.

sweet verse, and then go away, and another one come and sing and go away. . . .

Francis was very happy at this and received great consolation from it. But when he began to meditate on what this might be, the Lord told him in spirit: "This is a sign that the Lord will do good for you in this cell and give you many consolations."[13]

The scene of the *stigmata* is one of the most celebrated ones in Christian art. The earliest written record, however, comes from Thomas of Celano. In Thomas's telling, Francis received a mysterious vision. Before him was "a man, having six wings like a Seraph, standing over him, arms extended and feet joined, affixed to a cross. Two of his wings were raised up, two were stretched out over his head as if for flight, and two covered his whole body," like the seraphs in Isaiah 6:2.

"When [Francis] saw these things," Thomas continues, "he was filled with the greatest awe, but could not decide what this vision meant for him. Moreover, he greatly rejoiced and was much delighted by the kind and gracious look that he saw the Seraph gave him. The Seraph's beauty was beyond comprehension, but the fact that the Seraph was fixed to the cross and the bitter suffering of that passion thoroughly frightened him."

What did this mean, Francis wondered. Then he saw his own flesh start to change. "Signs of the nails began to appear on his hands and feet, just as he had seen them a little while earlier on the crucified man hovering over him.

"His hands and feet seemed to be pierced through the middle by nails, with the heads of the nails appearing on the inner part of his hands and on the upper part of his feet, and their points protruding on the opposite sides. Those marks on the inside of his hands were round, but rather oblong on the outside; and small pieces of flesh were visible like the points of nails, bent over and flattened, extending beyond the flesh around them. On his feet, the marks of nails were stamped in the same way and raised above the surrounding flesh. His right side was marked with an oblong scar, as if pierced with a lance, and this often dripped blood, so that his tunic and undergarments were frequently stained with his holy blood."[14]

This account, written just four or five years afterward, is consistent with other descriptions. Lesser Brothers who reported seeing the *stigmata* later at the time of Francis's death or shortly before give similar reports.

[13] *Assisi Compilation*, FA:ED 2:227.
[14] Thomas of Celano, *Life of St. Francis*, FA:ED 1:263–64.

The accounts make clear that the nail formations were actually hardened dark projections of Francis's own flesh (perhaps like the material of fingernails).

After this visitation, Francis continued his fast for the remaining ten days till Michaelmas, September 29. Now it was time to make his way back to the Portiuncula before snows made the roads around Mount LaVerna impassable. With the help of a donkey and his brothers, Francis returned to St. Mary of the Angels, the Portiuncula.[15]

No one witnessed the imprinting of the *stigmata*, and Francis refused to talk about it. He hid the marks as best he could, often pulling his sleeves down so only his fingers showed. Thomas of Celano writes, "He hid those marks carefully from strangers, and concealed them cautiously from people close to him, so that even the brothers at his side and his most devoted followers for a long time did not know about them."[16] Much of the time Francis was alone in prayer and contemplation, either at the Portiuncula or at one of the Franciscan hermitages. Comparatively few saw him during this period.

Some brothers eventually convinced Francis that for the sake of his witness, he should tell what happened. Thus, we have the story. Some brothers meanwhile discovered the marks by accident. One day Brother Rufino, for example, as he was rubbing Francis's chest, inadvertently touched the scar on Francis's side. Francis winced. He pushed Rufino's hand away, crying out in pain.[17]

Several other accounts mention the *stigmata*—the earliest ones, only briefly. *The Anonymous of Perugia* (written about 1240) says only, "Wanting to show the love He had for [Francis], the Lord impressed on his members and his side the stigmata of His most beloved Son."[18] *The Legend of the Three Companions*, also written in the 1240s, calls the imprinting of the *stigmata* "a unique privilege." Francis ardently "wanted to be crucified," like Jesus, and as he prayed, the crucified seraph appeared. According to this account, the seraph's features "were clearly those of the Lord Jesus." When the vision ended, Francis found the marks of crucifixion on his body. "Until his death" Francis was "unwilling to divulge God's sacrament." Since he couldn't conceal the marks totally, the *stigmata* "became known to at least his intimate companions."[19]

---

[15] Englebert, *Saint Francis*, 314.
[16] Thomas of Celano, *Life of St. Francis*, FA:ED 1:265.
[17] Thomas of Celano, *Life of St. Francis*, FA:ED 1:265.
[18] *Anonymous of Perugia*, FA:ED 2:58.
[19] *Legend of the Three Companions*, FA:ED 2:108.

According to Thomas of Celano's second Francis biography, *The Remembrance of the Desire of a Soul* (written between 1245 and 1247), Divine Providence guided the disclosing of the *stigmata* to Francis's closest brothers. The marks were after all "on parts of the body that were plainly visible and could not be hidden."[20] One day a brother saw the marks on the feet and said, "What is this, good brother?" "*Mind your own business!*" Francis replied.[21]

Later the same brother, who was caring for Francis, asked for his tunic so he could wash it. Seeing blood on the inside, he asked Francis whose blood it was. Francis pointed to his own eye and said, "Ask what this is, if you don't know it's an eye!"

Francis always tried to divert attention from the *stigmata*. He started wearing woolen socks to hide the protruding nails. His close brothers learned to look away whenever Francis had to uncover the wounds for any reason.[22]

Throughout his life, Francis had various mystical experiences— most profoundly, the *stigmata*. But he was not a mystic. His life was mostly "mundane," that is, of this world (*mundus*), filled with the daily unmystical stuff of life. His mystical experiences came not as the normal and most basic reality of his life, but rather as high points of *confirmation* that his very literal, very physical following of Jesus Christ was precisely what Jesus wanted. Francis was not a mystic who reluctantly endured the intrusive stuff of daily life, but a very human, very physical and natural person whose range of truly human experience *included* the mystical.[23] Or, as Chesterton put it, "This element of the supernatural did not separate him from the natural; for it was the whole point of his position that it united him more perfectly to the natural. It did not make him dismal or dehumanised; for it was the whole meaning of his message that such mysticism makes a man cheerful and humane."[24]

Angel of the Sixth Seal?

In the decades after Francis's death, Francis's *stigmata* began to take on prophetic and apocalyptic significance. As we will see shortly, the popular writings of the monk Joachim of Fiore heightened interest in

---

[20] Thomas of Celano, *Remembrance*, FA:ED 2:335.

[21] Thomas of Celano, *Remembrance*, FA:ED 2:335 (italics in the original).

[22] Thomas of Celano, *Remembrance*, FA:ED 2:335.

[23] See Bernard McGinn, *The Flowering of Mysticism: Men and Women of the New Mysticism (1200–1350)* (New York: Crossroad Publishing, 1998), esp. chap. 2, "Early Franciscan Mysticism and the Synthesis of Bonaventure."

[24] G. K. Chesterton, *St. Francis of Assisi* (Garden City, NY: Image Books, Doubleday [1924], 1957), 144.

the prophetic significance of Francis and his movement. In Book Five of his *Tree of the Crucified Life of Jesus* (1305), Ubertino da Casale cited the increasingly popular idea of six ages of the church (based loosely on the six days of creation in Genesis 1), and of Francis's apocalyptic role. Key Scriptures were Revelation 6:12, where the Lamb opens the sixth of seven seals, and 7:2, which speaks of "another angel ascending from the rising of the sun, having the seal of the living God."

Preachers and writers started identifying Francis as the Angel of the Sixth Seal. Francis was the promised one through whom God was now bringing to a climax his world-historical salvation plan. Ubertino claimed that Bonaventure himself "was fully convinced that the blessed Francis was the angel of the sixth seal." John the Revelator "actually had Francis, his form of life, and his Order in mind," and "saw Francis in spirit," foreseeing "the fraternity of his sons, who were perfect imitators of Christ," claimed Ubertino.[25] Those who believed this claim quite naturally saw Francis's remarkable *stigmata* as sign and proof that Francis was indeed this promised sixth angel of the Apocalypse, herald of a new age of the Spirit.[26]

---

[25] Ubertino da Casale, *The Tree of the Crucified Life of Jesus*, Book Five, FA:ED 3:149.
[26] See chapter 18.

15

Song of the Creatures

After encountering the seraph and receiving Christ's wounds in his own body, Francis made his painful way back from Mount LaVerna to the Portiuncula. This was still his favorite spot. Then, despite impaired health, he made a preaching tour through Umbria and The Marches. He also went to visit Clare at San Damiano, learning she was ill.[1]

It was probably in the spring of 1225 at San Damiano that Francis composed his memorable poem, *The Canticle of the Creatures*. Regis Armstrong writes,

> Almost blind and completely helpless, his body racked in agony, Francis lay in a little darkened cell. In those long hours of interior and exterior darkness, he endured severe temptations of despondency. Yet during one of these moments of discouragement, the Lord assured him that he would enjoy heavenly glory and this inspired this canticle of joy that will always characterize Franciscan spirituality.[2]

The song is often called *The Canticle of Brother Sun* because it begins praising God for "Brother Sun." The poem in fact celebrates a wide array of God's earthly creatures, including "our Sister, Mother Earth." Today many people call it *Canticle of the Creatures*.[3]

---

[1] Omer Englebert, *Saint Francis of Assisi*, 2nd English ed., trans. Eve Marie Cooper (Chicago: Franciscan Herald Press, 1965), 395.

[2] Regis J. Armstrong, Introduction to The Canticle of Brother Sun, in Regis J. Armstrong, OFM Cap., ed., *The Lady: Clare of Assisi: Early Documents* (New York: New City Press, 2006), 15; Ingrid J. Peterson, OSF, *Clare of Assisi: A Biographical Study* (Quincy, IL: Franciscan Press, 1993), 391.

[3] Copies now on sale in Assisi title it *The Canticle of the Creatures*.

Francis gloried in all his fellow physical creatures. He certainly did not suffer from what Richard Louv in his book *Last Child in the Woods* calls "nature-deficit disorder."[4] When at the Portiuncula, despite his sufferings and near blindness, Francis could hear birds and crickets and insects. Sometimes on still nights he perhaps could hear the fervent serene chanting of Clare and her sisters at San Damiano, two miles up the rise toward Assisi. In daylight he could still watch birds and flowers, even with his impaired sight. The *Canticle* grew out of suffering, and yet from joy in creation and a sense of God's presence and his own great passion to praise the Lord. Francis was at one and the same time a man of effervescent joy and "a man of sorrows, acquainted with grief" (Isa. 53:3 KJV).

According to *The Assisi Compilation,* one night Francis prayed fervently, "Lord, make haste to help me in my illnesses, so that I may be able to bear them patiently." He felt the Lord heard him. God assured him of his help and of Francis's final rest in God's reign. Brother Francis, God said, "be glad and rejoice in your illnesses and troubles," for you are as secure now as you will finally be in the kingdom of God.[5]

Rising the next morning, Francis told his brothers, "I must rejoice greatly in my illnesses and troubles and be consoled in the Lord, giving thanks always to God the Father, to His only Son, our Lord Jesus Christ, and to the Holy Spirit for such a great grace and blessing." For God had given him, he said, "still living in the flesh, the promise of His kingdom."

In gratitude, Francis said, "I want to write a new Praise of the Lord for his creatures, which we use every day, and without which we cannot live. Through them the human race greatly offends the Creator, and every day we are ungrateful for such great graces, because we do not praise, as we should, our Creator and the Giver of all good."[6]

Francis Composes the Canticle

Francis sat on the ground, meditated a bit, and then began to sing. "Most High, all-powerful, good Lord." Spontaneously he composed the *Canticle*, words and melody, and taught his brothers to sing it.[7]

---

[4] Richard Louv, *Last Child in the Woods: Saving Our Children from Nature-Deficit Disorder*, rev. ed. (Chapel Hill, NC: Algonquin Books of Chapel Hill, 2008).

[5] *Assisi Compilation*, in *Francis of Assisi: Early Documents*, ed. Regis J. Armstrong, OFM Cap., J. A. Wayne Hellmann, OFM Conv., and William J. Short, OFM (New York: New City Press, 2001), 2:185 [hereafter FA:ED].

[6] *Assisi Compilation*, FA:ED 2:185–86.

[7] *Assisi Compilation*, FA:ED 2:186. Similarly Thomas of Celano, *Remembrance of the Desire of a Soul*, FA:ED 2:384–85; Arnaldo Fortini, *Francis of Assisi*, trans. Helen Moak (New York: Crossroad Publishing, 1992), 565–69.

And so, we have *The Canticle of the Creatures,* composed not in Latin but in the everyday Italian of the people:[8]

> Most High, all-powerful, good Lord,
> Yours are the praises, the glory, and the honor, and all blessing,
> To You alone, Most High, do they belong,
> and no human is worthy to mention Your name.
>
> Praised be You, my Lord, with all Your creatures,
> especially Sir Brother Sun,
> Who is the day and through whom You give us light.
> And he is beautiful and radiant with great splendor;
> and bears a likeness of You, Most High One.
>
> Praised be You, my Lord, through Sister Moon and the stars,
> in heaven You formed them clear and precious and beautiful.
> Praised be You, my Lord, through Brother Wind,
> and through the air, cloudy and serene, and every kind of
>   weather,
> through whom You give sustenance to Your creatures.
>
> Praised be You, my Lord, through Sister Water,
> who is very useful and humble and precious and chaste.
> Praised be You, my Lord, through Brother Fire,
> through whom You light the night,
> and he is beautiful and playful and robust and strong.
>
> Praised be You, my Lord, through our Sister Mother Earth,
> who sustains and governs us,
> and who produces various fruit with colored flowers and herbs.
>
> Praised be You, my Lord, through those who give pardon for
>   Your love,
> and bear infirmity and tribulation.
> Blessed are those who endure in peace
> for by You, Most High, shall they be crowned.
>
> Praised be You, my Lord, through our Sister Bodily Death,
> from whom no one living can escape.
> Woe to those who die in mortal sin.

---

[8] Jon M. Sweeney, *When Saint Francis Saved the Church: How a Converted Medieval Troubadour Created a Spiritual Vision for the Ages* (Notre Dame, IN: Ave Maria Press, 2014), x.

Blessed are those whom death will find in Your most holy will,
for the second death shall do them no harm.

Praise and bless my Lord and give Him thanks
and serve Him with great humility.[9]

This is the final version. People familiar with ancient Hebrew poetry will notice that Francis's *Canticle* sounds much like the biblical Psalms, or like Jesus's Beatitudes.[10] The poem embodies a similar parallelism, written in simple couplets, the second line expanding or clarifying the meaning of the first:

Praised be You, my Lord, through Sister Water,
who is very useful and humble and precious and chaste.

It is curious that although Francis especially loved birds and animals, he does not mention them in the *Canticle*. He focuses rather on sun and moon, fire and water, flowers and herbs. Perhaps he was on such familiar terms with birds that he never thought to include them in his song.

The *Canticle* was at first about a third shorter, ending in praises to God for "Our Sister Mother Earth." But then Francis learned of a dispute happening in Assisi between church authorities and the city's leaders. To resolve the quarrel, Francis added the verse about forgiveness and peacemaking. He sent some brothers to sing the *Canticle* before Bishop Guido and the mayor, Oportulo di Bernardo, as a way to reconcile the two.[11] Both Guido and Oportulo were friends and supporters of Francis. In fact, Mayor Oportulo's young daughter Agnese had joined Clare in her community at San Damiano. Both men were moved in hearing Francis's words through his simple brothers. The poetic peacemaking succeeded in bringing reconciliation.[12]

Only later on his deathbed did Francis add the stanza acknowledging "Our Sister Bodily Death." By then both Francis and the brothers knew the end was near. Francis said to the brother who was attending him,

---

[9] There are many editions in many languages. The Italian version is found in Fortini, *Francis of Assisi*, 566–67, 577, 602–3.

[10] Consider also Nehemiah 9:5–6, "Stand up and bless the Lord your God from everlasting to everlasting. Blessed be your glorious name, which is exalted above all blessing and praise.... You are the Lord, you alone; you have made heaven, the heaven of heavens, with all their host, the earth and all that is on it, the seas and all that is in them. To all of them you give life, and the host of heaven worships you."

[11] Introduction, *The Canticle of the Creatures*, FA:ED 1:113; *Assisi Compilation*, FA:ED 2:187–88; Fortini, *Francis of Assisi*, 577–80.

[12] Fortini, *Francis of Assisi*, 574–80. Fortini tells the story in considerable detail.

"If I am to die soon, call Brother Angelo and Brother Leo that they may sing to me about Sister Death." Angelo and Leo came and, "with many tears," sang the *Canticle*. Francis then added, right before the final benediction, his praise to God for Sister Death. "Blessed are those whom death will find in Your most holy will, for the second death shall do them no harm."[13]

"In this last period of his life," comments Fortini, Francis's "illnesses and infirmities were steadily growing worse. But always, even when he was suffering most intensely, it was enough for him to sing and have his brothers sing his song of joy for him to gain the strength to endure every pain."[14]

On first composing the *Canticle*, Francis taught all the brothers to sing it. He wanted the song used in gospel witness, and he had a plan.

Among all the brothers, Pacifico was the real poet. The others called him "King of Verses." Francis thought it would be wonderful for Pacifico and a small band of brothers to travel about with Franciscan preachers. After the sermon, the brothers would sing the *Canticle*. The preacher was to say, "We are minstrels of the Lord. All we want as payment is that you live true and godly lives." Francis wanted the brothers to be like the traveling troubadours who formed a ring in city plazas and sang songs of chivalry and true love, of brave knights and maidens fair. Francis himself often said, "What are the servants of God if not His minstrels, who must move people's hearts and lift them up to spiritual joy?"[15]

Francis knew the end of his earthly journey was nigh. He longed in his death to be united both with heaven and with the earth. He wanted to die naked, on the bare ground.

His brothers and many others around could see that Francis was failing. If anything, that realization increased his fame and his appeal and the feeling that a true saint was among them.

The Rise of Popular Praise Music

We can see Francis's *Canticle* in broader perspective. Francis loved to sing. As a youth, he sang the popular songs of the French Troubadours. Of course, he heard the heavy Latin liturgical music in sacred church

---

[13] This according to *The Assisi Compilation*, FA:ED 2:121. Also Englebert, *Saint Francis*, 338. "Second death" is a reference to Revelation 2:11, "Whoever conquers will not be harmed by the second death."

[14] Fortini, *Francis of Assisi*, 569. See *Assisi Compilation*, FA:ED 2:187–88; Fortini, 577–80 and sources cited there.

[15] *Assisi Compilation*, FA:ED 2:186. Similarly Fortini, *Francis of Assisi*, 569.

settings. But he wanted music in the language people spoke in their daily lives, whether Provençal in southern France or the emerging spoken Italian of his day.

So, he wrote his *Canticle of the Creatures* in the language of the people and wanted his brothers to sing it with him. According to the *Mirror of Perfection,* Francis sometimes "picking up a stick from the ground and putting it over his left arm, ... would draw another stick across it with his right hand like a bow on a viola or some other instrument. Performing all the right movements, he would sing in French about the Lord Jesus."[16]

It is curious that French seems to have been Francis's language of ecstasy—one might say, his way of speaking in tongues. For *The Remembrance of the Desire of a Soul* reports,

> Whenever he was
> filled with the fire of the Holy Spirit
> he would speak in French,
> bursting out in fiery words,
> for he could foresee
> that he would be honored
> with special reverence by that people.[17]

The birth of the *Canticle* is in turn the birth of a larger story. Francis can be seen as the father of popular praise music. He wrote and probably sang his *Canticle,* celebrating God and the Earth with its beauties and its creatures. Perhaps he spontaneously sang other songs as he walked along his way.

Francis's *Canticle,* his praise song, thus marks the beginning of popular praise music in the church. Soon groups of awakened Christians were singing praise songs (*laude*) in their own languages. By the end of the century, vernacular praise songs were being sung by groups of Christians, particularly by Third Order Franciscans—devout Christians, men and women, married and single, living ordinary lives, meeting together regularly to worship and praise and learn.[18]

---

[16] *Mirror of Perfection,* FA:ED 3:340.

[17] Thomas of Celano, *Remembrance,* FA:ED 2:252. Here again French probably means Provençal.

[18] *Lauda* songs were perhaps influenced, in form and style, by the songs of the troubadours. Some *lauda* songs probably already existed at the time of the first Franciscans, but the Lesser Brothers popularized them and influenced their focus and content. See https://en.wikipedia.org/wiki/Lauda_(song).

This was a key part of the renewal that spread from Francis and Clare to common folk awakened and inspired through the ministries of Franciscan brothers and Clare's sisters. Music was a big part of the Third Order movement. Together these awakened Christians sang out their spiritual praises.

Music and song have always been a vital ingredient in renewal and spiritual vitality. The New Testament church shared "psalms and hymns and spiritual songs, singing and making melody in [their] hearts to the Lord" (Eph. 5:19). Throughout history, renewal has been enriched not only by ancient psalms and hymns, but also by newly inspired spiritual music.

In Francis's day these songs were called *laude*, "praises." They became "the most important form of popular religious song in medieval Italy," notes the *Dictionary of the Middle Ages*. With simple structure and singable melodies, these songs celebrated common themes of spiritual life based on Jesus's birth, sufferings and death, and resurrection, rather than embodying liturgical texts. Some of course celebrated the Virgin Mary.[19]

The Franciscan movement is closely linked with the rise and spread of this kind of popular praise music. Francis himself was often celebrated in these songs. Francis's *Canticle of the Creatures*, "the first vernacular Italian poem," is one of the earliest examples of vernacular praise music.[20] The poem "is preserved in at least one source with staves for music," showing that it was sung, not just recited.[21]

"Throughout the Middle Ages, the connection between the *lauda* [songs] and the Franciscan friars was strong," notes Michael Long in the *Dictionary of the Middle Ages*.[22] The most prolific composer of such songs was Jacopone of Todi (1230–1306), himself a Spiritual Franciscan, who wrote more than a hundred such songs. "Jacopone had the figure and example of St. Francis ever before his eyes," writes Giulio Silano.[23]

"Jacopone is on fire with love and can never stop singing about it—the Love that will not let him go, that holds him in its embrace, that opens the door of heaven, and that brings the lover into the presence of

---

[19] Michael P. Long, "Lauda," *Dictionary of the Middle Ages*, ed. Joseph Strayer (New York: Charles Scribner's Sons, 1986), 7:38.

[20] Sweeney, *When Saint Francis Saved the Church*, x.

[21] Long, "Lauda," *Dictionary of the Middle Ages*, 7:38.

[22] Long, "Lauda," *Dictionary of the Middle Ages*, 7:38.

[23] Giulio Silano, "Jacopone da Todi," *Dictionary of the Middle Ages*, 7:34. Silano provides extensive information on Jacopone, noting the controversies he was involved in as part of the Spiritual Franciscans and the fact that he was imprisoned for some years (7:33–35).

the Beloved where alone he can find rest," writes Moorman.[24] "Under the influence of the poetry of Jacopone" and other writers, Moorman adds, "the friars brought home to people, in verse and prose, the facts of the human life of the Son of God, and especially his sufferings on the cross and those of his Mother beneath it."[25] Jacopone the Franciscan is now recognized as one of the greatest poets of his time, and his "*laude* remain among the greatest and most moving achievements of religious literature."[26]

Michael Long notes, "The melodies of the *laude* are in general quite simple." The songs seem at first to have been sung in unison, not harmony. Typically, there were several verses and a refrain, somewhat like gospel songs today.[27] Later polyphonic (multipart) praise songs (*laude*) developed.[28]

Francis's Song of the Creatures

This is the story of Francis's *Canticle of the Creatures*. Chesterton remarked, "the whole philosophy of St. Francis revolved around the idea of a new supernatural light on natural things."[29] Here was another way—a poetic and musical way—that Francis helped create and popularize a spiritual movement that spread across the lands.

---

[24] John Moorman, *A History of the Franciscan Order: From Its Origins to the Year 1517* (Oxford: Oxford University Press, 1968), 266.

[25] Moorman, *History of the Franciscan Order*, 399.

[26] Silano, "Jacopone da Todi," *Dictionary of the Middle Ages*, 7:35. Todi is a hilltop town about thirty miles southeast of Assisi.

[27] Long, "Lauda," *Dictionary of the Middle Ages*, 7:38.

[28] "Polyphonic *laude* for two or three voices were composed throughout the fifteenth century" (Long, 38). This was one of the influences leading to the development of oratorio music, such as Handel's *Messiah*.

[29] G. K. Chesterton, *St. Francis of Assisi* (Garden City, NY: Image Books, Doubleday [1924], 1957), 57.

16

Francis's Final Days

Francis knew the earthly stage of his life was nearly done. He wrote or dictated two key documents. One, "A Letter to the Entire Order," was probably intended for the General Chapter of 1226, which Francis couldn't attend. The other was his *Testament*.

As the Order grew, the pope broadened its authority. On December 3, 1224, Pope Honorius III gave the brothers permission to celebrate the Lord's Supper together. Up to this time Franciscans attended Mass in local parishes with the common people and preached when invited. As the brothers established their own dwellings, they had oratories for prayer, but not full liturgical services. More and more of the brothers were now priests, however. Honorius's bull *Quia populares* "granted [the brothers] the privilege of celebrating the full choral Eucharist and Divine Office in all of their houses, effectively letting them carry on liturgical prayer independently of the local church in the manner of monastic communities."[1] This was a momentous change in status and practice.

This may be what prompted Francis's "Letter to the Entire Order." He reminded the brothers of their vocation, their call from God. "Observe His commands with your whole heart and fulfil His counsels with a perfect mind," he wrote. For God "has sent you into the whole world: that you may bear witness to His voice in word and deed and bring everyone to know that there is no one who is all-powerful except Him." Francis went on,

---

[1] Introduction to Honorius III's bull *Quia populares* (1224), in *Francis of Assisi: Early Documents*, ed. Regis J. Armstrong, OFM Cap., J. A. Wayne Hellmann, OFM Conv., and William J. Short, OFM (New York: New City Press, 2001), 1:562 [hereafter FA:ED].

Kissing your feet, therefore, and with all that love of which I am capable, I implore all of you brothers to show all possible reverence and honor to the most holy Body and Blood of our Lord Jesus Christ in Whom that which is in heaven and on earth has been brought to peace and reconciled to almighty God.

Francis reminded the brothers of God's call to holiness and to unfailing obedience to the Rule. "I do not consider those brothers who do not wish to observe these things [to be] Catholics or my brothers," Francis wrote. "I do not even wish to see or speak with them until they have done penance. I even say this about all those who wander about, having put aside the discipline of the Rule." Francis knew not all the brothers were walking in obedience.

Francis exhorted especially those brothers who were leaders "to guard what is written [in this letter] carefully and to have it observed more diligently according to the pleasure of the all-powerful God, now and forever, as long as the world lasts."[2]

Francis's other major writing, *The Testament*, would prove keenly important in the years and centuries following his death. He dictated the final form of this short document toward the very end of his life in 1226.

Francis makes clear that this is his final heartfelt word to the brothers. It is definitely not "another rule," he says. Rather, "this is a remembrance, admonition, exhortation, and my testament, which I, little brother Francis, make for you, my blessed brothers, that we might observe the Rule we have promised in a more Catholic [i.e., faithful and universal] way."[3]

The first thing Francis mentions in his *Testament* is the way God led him to a transforming encounter with lepers. Now "what had seemed bitter to me was turned into sweetness of soul and body."[4] From that radical conversion sprang all that followed—including the Order, which now numbered in the thousands.

Francis is passionate. He encourages but also gives words of stark warning to brothers who were not following the Rule faithfully. He would never preach in a parish without the priest's permission, he notes. Priests must be respected, even if they were sinful, for they are guardians

---

[2] Francis, "A Letter to the Entire Order," FA:ED 1:116–21.
[3] Francis, *The Testament*, FA:ED 1:124.
[4] Francis, *The Testament*, FA:ED 1:124.

of the "most holy mysteries." Christ's body in the Eucharist is the only way, Francis felt, that God was physically visible in the world. "And we must honor all theologians and those who minister the most holy divine words and respect them."[5]

Francis insists that the Franciscan way of life, embodied in the Rule, was not his own idea. God showed me, he said, that I must "live according to the pattern of the Holy Gospel." And so, Francis elaborates,

> I had this written down simply and in a few words and the Lord Pope confirmed it for me. And those who came to receive life gave whatever they had to the poor and were content with one tunic, patched inside and out, with a cord and short trousers. We desired nothing more. We clerical [brothers] said the office as other clerics did; the lay brothers said the *Our Father*; and we quite willingly remained in [existing] churches [rather than our own structures]. And we were simple and subject to all.
>
> And I worked with my hands, and I still desire to work; and I earnestly desire all brothers to give themselves to honest work. Let those who do not know how to work learn, not from desire to receive wages, but for example and to avoid idleness. And when we are not paid for our work, let us have recourse to the table of the Lord, [that is,] begging alms from door to door....
>
> Let the brothers be careful not to receive in any way churches or poor dwellings or anything else built for them unless they are according to the holy poverty we have promised in the Rule. As pilgrims and strangers, let them always be guests there.[6]

In other words, Francis says, *Do what you promised.* Live faithfully according to Rule and obedience you first pledged.[7]

Francis continued to grow weaker. He had done all he could by word and example to keep the multitude of his brothers faithful. In his last months he dictated several short exhortations and teachings, including twenty-eight "Admonitions," many of which beautifully echo Jesus in his Sermon on the Mount.

---

[5] Francis, *The Testament*, FA:ED 1:125.
[6] Francis, *The Testament*, FA:ED 1:125–26.
[7] Francis, *The Testament*, FA:ED 1:126.

Francis concludes,

> Where there is charity and wisdom, there is neither fear
> nor ignorance.
> Where there is patience and humility, there is neither
> anger nor disturbance.
> Where there is poverty with joy, there is neither greed
> nor avarice.
> Where there is rest and meditation, there is neither
> anxiety nor restlessness.
> Where there is fear of the Lord to guard an entrance,
> there the enemy cannot have a place to enter.
> Where there is a heart full of mercy and discernment,
> there is neither excess nor hardness of heart.
> Blessed is the servant who stores up in heaven the good
> things which the Lord shows to him and does not wish
> to reveal them to people under the guise of a reward,
> because the Most High Himself will reveal His deeds to
> whomever He wishes.
> Blessed is the servant who safeguards the secrets of the
> Lord in his heart.[8]

Francis safeguarded many things in his heart that he never revealed,
only hinted at.

"Our Sister, Bodily Death"

Francis died at the Portiuncula the evening of Saturday, October 3, 1226.
He was about forty-four.

Francis had been traveling but, knowing the end was near, he asked
his brothers to bring him back to his beloved Portiuncula, the "little
portion" where his community of brothers was born.

It was now spring 1226, about six months before Francis's death. His
pain and suffering grew worse. He sometimes vomited blood and could
eat nearly nothing. According to Thomas of Celano, his "bodily warmth
gradually diminished, and each day he drew closer to his end. The doctors
were amazed and the brothers were astonished that the spirit could live
in flesh so dead, since with his flesh all consumed only skin clung to his
bones."[9] Francis wanted to return to Assisi, and especially the Portiuncula,

---

[8] Francis of Assisi, "The Admonitions," FA:ED 1:136–37.
[9] Thomas of Celano, *Life of St. Francis*, FA:ED 1:274.

to finish his earthly course. He recovered his strength a bit but was too weak to walk, so the brothers carried him.[10]

They took him first to Bishop Guido's place in Assisi. As he grew weaker, however, Francis "asked the brothers to carry him quickly to the place of Saint Mary of the Portiuncula. For he wanted to give back his soul to God in that place where ... he first came to know perfectly the way of truth."[11] Some of Francis's brothers gently carried him down to the Portiuncula on his sickbed. A crowd of townsfolk accompanied them.[12]

Word quickly spread that Francis was dying. More and more brothers gathered at the Portiuncula. There Francis, nearly blind, mostly rested and waited and endured his pain.

Francis's mind went to dear Clare, not far away at San Damiano. He often thought of her but seldom saw her. She was often in his prayers. The week Francis died, Clare herself was gravely ill. She feared she would pass before she could see Francis one last time. She sent word by one of the Franciscan brothers, sharing her anxiety.

Francis was deeply moved by Clare's message. Seeing her was impossible, though. Both were too ill. So, Francis sent Clare a consoling letter. He "absolved her from any failings, if she had any." Francis told the brother whom Clare had sent, "Go and take this letter to Lady Clare, and tell her to put aside all her grief and sorrow over not being able to see me now. Let her be assured that before her death, both she and her sisters will see me and will receive the greatest consolation from me."[13]

Francis now called his brothers and "blessed each one as it was given to him from above," says Thomas of Celano, "just as Jacob of old, the patriarch, blessed his sons."[14]

"Brother" Jacopa

Only men surrounded Francis at this time. Women were not permitted in the Portiuncula. But Francis made one exception.

Francis had a special friend in Rome, a noblewoman named Jacopa de Settesoli. Francis was so careful in his relationships with the other

---

[10] Thomas of Celano, *Life of St. Francis*, FA:ED 1:276.

[11] Thomas of Celano, *Life of St. Francis*, FA:ED 1:277. On Francis's brief stay at the bishop's residence in Assisi, see Arnaldo Fortini, *Francis of Assisi*, trans. Helen Moak (New York: Crossroad Publishing Co., 1992), 595–606.

[12] Fortini, *Francis of Assisi*, 604–5.

[13] *Assisi Compilation*, FA:ED 2:128–29. The account in *The Mirror of Perfection* (Sabatier ed.), FA:ED 3:357, is almost word-for-word the same.

[14] Thomas of Celano, *Life of St. Francis*, FA:ED 1:276.

sex that (it is said) he once declared that Clare and Jacopa were the only women in the world whom he knew by sight.[15]

Lady Jacopa was the well-to-do widow of a Roman knight. She was one of several devout men and women who adopted Francis's way of life and looked to him for guidance but without joining an order— precursors of the Francis Third Order (tertiaries), which began in 1221.[16] Lady Jacopa had a large home, part of the ancient Septizonium palazzo in Rome. There she sometimes provided hospitality for Francis and his brothers on their visits to the City.[17]

Francis seems to have met Lady Jacopa in 1212. She was then young— only about twenty-two, and of high-ranking Roman blood. Her husband's death left her with two young sons. Had she been childless, she might well have entered a convent. Now in her mid-thirties, Jacopa hurried to the Portiuncula to do what she could for Francis during his final days.[18]

Some days earlier, Francis had asked his brothers to send Lady Jacopa a note. "Brother Francis begs you to come at once, and bring with you a little ash-colored cloth, like the Cistercian monks beyond the Alps make, and also everything needed to make that special sweet confection for the sick that you used to prepare, and even more, candles for my funeral."[19]

Francis wanted Lady Jacopa there when he died. Thinking ahead to his funeral, he requested gray cloth for his tunic. And before he died, he wanted a final taste of the small almonds and honey confection she used to serve him in Rome.

One of the brothers was chosen as the messenger. Just as he was about to leave, the brothers heard a commotion outside—horses, voices, a "clatter of swords and armour." There before the Portiuncula was a company of knights and others, men and women, and Lady Jacopa herself. She arrived before Francis's message could be sent.

"Is he still alive?" she asked anxiously. He was, and he was asking for her, the brothers said.[20] Bending the rules, Francis named the lady

---

[15] Thomas of Celano, *Remembrance*, FA:ED 2:322. Lady Jacopa is mentioned above in connection with the portrait of Francis weeping, said to have been commissioned by her. Her name is variously given as Jacopa, Jacoba, and Giacoma.

[16] Omer Englebert, *Saint Francis of Assisi*, 2nd English ed., trans. Eve Marie Cooper (Chicago: Franciscan Herald Press, 1965), chap. 15, "The Third Order," 258–70.

[17] Fortini, *Francis of Assisi*, 527. In the sources, Rome is frequently known simply as "The City."

[18] Englebert, *St. Francis*, 259–60; Fortini, *Francis of Assisi*, 373, 527.

[19] My reconstruction based on the *Assisi Compilation*, FA:ED 2:121–22; Fortini, *Francis of Assisi*, 609 and 668 n. 5, and other sources.

[20] Fortini, *Francis of Assisi*, 609–10.

"Brother Jacopa" and called her in. "Blessed be God, who has brought our Brother Lady Jacoba to us!" he said. "Open the doors and bring her in. The decree about women is not to be observed for Brother Jacoba!" She had brought with her the very items he desired, plus incense for the funeral and a silk cushion for his head.[21]

Lady Jacopa arrived at the Portiuncula midweek, perhaps on the Wednesday. Seeing her, Francis revived a bit. Jacopa was afraid the noise of her armed escort might hasten Francis's death, so she offered to send her retinue back to Rome while she stayed to help care for Francis. But Francis said, "No, don't! I will depart on Saturday, and on Sunday you and all the others will return." And so, it was.[22]

Release

Francis wanted to hear again the stories of Jesus. He asked a brother to bring the Gospel Book and read the account in John beginning with chapter 13, "Now before the festival of the Passover, Jesus knew that his hour had come to depart from this world and go to the Father. Having loved his own who were in the world, he loved them to the end." For his own sake and that of his brothers, Francis wanted to hear again how Jesus washed the disciples' feet.[23]

As Francis grew weaker, he asked two of the brothers to sing the *Canticle of the Creatures*. Francis "as best he could broke into that psalm of David," Psalm 142, beginning "With my voice I cry to the Lord; with my voice I make supplication to the Lord."[24]

Francis was full of joy as death drew near. Ever the dramatist, Francis was consciously preparing for death. He asked his brothers to lay him naked on the bare earth. He would be the least Lesser Brother to the end.[25]

The brothers helped him out of his worn habit and laid him flat on the ground. He was giving back his life to Lady Poverty. "Once I am

---

[21] Thomas of Celano, *Miracles*, FA:ED 2:418.

[22] Thomas of Celano, *Miracles*, FA:ED 2:418; also Fortini, *Francis of Assisi*, 611.

[23] Thomas of Celano, *Life of St. Francis*, FA:ED 1:278. There is some confusion in Celano's text here between chapters 12 and 13 of John, as noted by the editors, FA:ED 1:278 n. a. See also Fortini, *Francis of Assisi*, 614.

[24] Thomas of Celano, *Life of St. Francis*, FA:ED 1:277.

[25] "We cannot overstate how profoundly that final act of nudity brings certain themes of [Francis's] life to a fitting conclusion. The idea of nudity is deep in the consciousness of all the great Christian mystics." Lawrence S. Cunningham, *Francis of Assisi: Performing the Gospel Life* (Grand Rapids, MI: William B. Eerdmans, 2004), 71–72.

dead," he told them, "allow me to lie there for as long as it takes to walk a leisurely mile."[26]

Francis's brothers now clearly saw the *stigmata* on Francis's prone body. For all but a few, this was the first time. To the brothers it "seemed he had just been taken down from the cross, his hands and feet pierced by nails and his right side wounded by a lance."[27]

Several ancient sources tell how during the evening, after vespers as Francis lay dying, a flock of Skylarks—Francis's fondest birds—circled above the Portiuncula, singing, heralding Francis's release.[28]

Francis's body was dead. His spirit had flown. Thomas of Celano says simply, "And then that most holy soul was released from the flesh, and as it was absorbed into the abyss of light, his body fell asleep in the Lord."[29]

Francis's skin, however, was "now shining white in its beauty," wrote Thomas. "All his limbs had become as soft and moveable as in childhood innocence. His muscles were not taut, as they usually are in the dead, his skin was not hard, his limbs were not rigid but could be easily moved back and forth." His limp body made the *stigmata* stand out even more.[30]

It is said one of Francis's well-known brothers "saw the soul of the most holy father rise straight to heaven over many waters. It was like a star but as big as the moon, with the brilliance of the sun, and carried up upon a small white cloud."[31] No journey through purgatory for Francis.

Francis died during the night Saturday, October third, the brothers keeping watch. They clothed him in the new gray tunic Lady Jacopa brought, the Lady's cushion under his head. Candles were lit for the vigil.

Crowds began converging on the Portiuncula from Assisi and the surrounding area. "Brother" Jacopa convinced the brothers to open the door and let people in so they could witness the event and see the *stigmata*. Farmers, peasants, shopkeepers and merchants, noblemen and women gazed at the body or knelt in prayer. Many witnessed the *stigmata*. Years later a Roman official named Giovanni Pennate told how,

---

[26] Thomas of Celano, *Remembrance*, FA:ED 388; also Fortini, *Francis of Assisi*, 611–12.

[27] Thomas of Celano, *Life of St. Francis*, FA:ED 1:280.

[28] *Assisi Compilation*, FA:ED 2:129; Fortini, *Francis of Assisi*, 615.

[29] Thomas of Celano, *Life of St. Francis*, FA:ED 1:278. To "fall asleep in the Lord" is a hope-filled New Testament phrase: Acts 7:60; 1 Cor. 15:6, 18; 1 Thess. 4:13, 15; 2 Pt. 3:4.

[30] Thomas of Celano, *Life of St. Francis*, FA:ED 1:280.

[31] Thomas of Celano, *Life of St. Francis*, FA:ED 1:278. Thomas does not give the brother's name "since he does not wish to glory in such fame while still living in the flesh."

as a boy at his mother's side, he saw the *stigmata* on Francis's body, even touched them.[32]

Dawn was breaking. "In the morning, all the people of the city of Assisi, men and women, with all the clergy, took the holy body from the place where he had died. With hymns and praises, all carrying tree branches, they carried him to San Damiano, at the Lord's will, in order to fulfil that word which the Lord had spoken through His saint to console His daughters and servants."[33]

The San Damiano chapel had a window with an iron grille that gave access to the sisters within the cloister. Through this window Clare and her companions normally received Communion from priests and occasionally heard sermons. Francis's brothers removed the grille and for an hour held his body up to the window so Clare and her sisters could see him and mourn together.[34]

The procession continued up the hill to Assisi. Francis's body was carried to the Church of Saint George, just inside the city wall, where Francis had learned his lessons as a child.[35] His body was buried and would remain there until transferred to the new nearby Basilica of Saint Francis in 1230.

Clare after Francis

With Francis dead, "Clare became the most conspicuous champion of the ideal of total abnegation and complete dependence upon God," as Moorman puts it. She fought for this total poverty tenaciously.[36]

Shortly before Clare's death Franciscan Brother Rainaldo visited her, encouraging her to be patient. Clare told him, "After I once came to know the grace of my Lord Jesus Christ through his servant Francis, no pain has been bothersome, no penance too severe, no weakness, dearly beloved brother, has been hard."[37]

---

[32] Thomas of Celano, *Miracles,* FA:ED 2:419.

[33] *Assisi Compilation,* FA:ED 2:129. Similarly, Thomas of Celano, *Life of St. Francis,* FA:ED 1:284–85.

[34] Thomas of Celano, *Life of St. Francis,* FA:ED 1:284–85; *Assisi Compilation,* FA:ED 2:129; Fortini, *Francis of Assisi,* 625.

[35] "His sacred body was buried with great respect in the oratory of blessed George alongside the walls of Assisi." *A Liturgical Legend [Account] in the Tradition of the Friars Preacher* (1268), Lesson VII, FA:ED 3:835.

[36] John Moorman, *A History of the Franciscan Order: From Its Origins to the Year 1517* (Oxford: Oxford University Press, 1968), 205.

[37] *The Legend of Saint Clare,* in *The Lady: Clare of Assisi: Early Documents,* 3rd ed., ed. R. J. Armstrong, OFM Cap. (Hyde Park, NY: New City Press, 2006), 316.

Clare grew more and more ill and was largely confined to her bed. Christmas was drawing near, one of her last. She longed to be with her sisters very early Christmas morning to celebrate the Nativity in the oratory but could not. Alone in her bed, she thought about the baby Jesus being born, "sorrowing that she could not participate in His praises." She sighed, "Lord God, look at how I have been left alone in this place for You!"[38]

Then she began to hear music and singing. She realized she was hearing the Franciscan brothers, their voices and musical instruments, at the Portiuncula more than two miles away. And she saw a vision of baby Jesus in the manger, she told her surprised sisters later.[39]

Clare outlived Francis by twenty-seven years, abiding the rest of her days with her sisters at San Damiano. She finally won papal approval of her Rule in the specific form she insisted upon from Innocent IV just a day or two before her death, as we saw earlier. She died at San Damiano on August 11, 1253, her sisters and some Franciscan brothers gathered near. Her body was taken first to the Church of Saint George, as Francis's body had been.[40]

Clare was gone, but her community kept expanding, inspired by Clare and by Francis as well. Moorman notes, "The fame and influence of St. Francis had made itself felt far and wide, and many were the women who wished to be associated with the new movement."[41] The community of Clares provided the means. *The Legend of Saint Clare* notes, "The fame of [Clare's] virtues filled the chambers of noble ladies, reached the palaces of duchesses, even the mansions of their queens. The highest of the nobility stooped to follow her footprints and left its race of proud blood for her holy humility."[42]

Among these women were Princess Agnes of Prague (known also as Agnes of Bohemia), Elizabeth of Hungary, and Salome of Krakow. Agnes (1211–1282), daughter of Queen Constance of Bohemia, turned down offers of marriage from three kings, including Holy Roman Emperor Frederick II, and entered the Order of St. Clare. Agnes built a hospital

---

[38] *Legend of Saint Clare*, 306.

[39] *Legend of Saint Clare*, 306. "This incident prompted Pope Pius XII to proclaim St. Clare the patroness of television" in 1958, notes the editor of *The Lady: Clare of Assisi*, 306 n. b.

[40] *The Versified Legend of the Virgin Clare*, in *The Lady: Clare of Assisi*, 250. Brothers Juniper, Angelo, and Leo were present at Clare's death, it appears. *Legend of Saint Clare*, 316.

[41] Moorman, *History of the Franciscan Order*, 208.

[42] *Legend of Saint Clare*, 290.

for the poor and financed the construction of a Franciscan residence and a Poor Clare monastery. She became known for her life of prayer, strict poverty, and good works, including mending lepers' clothes. Eventually she was declared a saint.

Princess Elizabeth of Hungary (1207–1231) was married at fourteen, widowed at twenty, and died at twenty-four. After her husband's death, Elizabeth joined the Third Order Franciscans and dedicated her life to good works, following Clare's example. During her brief life as a Franciscan tertiary, she built a hospital and she herself served there. She also was canonized as a saint.

Salome of Krakow (Salome of Poland, 1212–1268) was the daughter of the Duke of Krakow. At age three she was married to the seven-year-old son of King Andrew II of Hungary. Her husband died in 1241 from war wounds, and shortly thereafter Salome joined the Order of Poor Clares. She founded a monastery for the Order and also helped support the Polish Franciscans.[43]

All this occurred because one teenage girl, Clare, inspired by Francis, decided to dedicate her life unreservedly to following Jesus.

Most other Clare convents did not follow as strict a rule of poverty as did Clare's original community. "Except for San Damiano, other houses were expected to hold property like the monasteries of ... nuns" in other orders.[44] The pope and wealthy benefactors often donated or bequeathed land and buildings. In 1233 Pope Gregory IX gave the Clares (or Clarisses, as they are sometimes called) a hospital in Monza, near Milan, for their use.[45]

Gregory IX worried about the Clarisses. Some of their cloisters had almost no means of support. Becoming pope in 1228, Gregory began requiring new houses of Clares to accept property and the income often connected with it. New houses of Poor Clares were thus constituted under less severe conditions, with some degree of assured support. Gregory ordered the Clares in a convent near Perugia to "take a mill, lands, vineyards, oliveyards, and gardens in the name of the Holy See," so they would not be destitute. The sisters were much grieved by this, as they saw it as compromising their vows. The pope's reasoning, however,

[43] See Agnes of Prague, Elizabeth of Hungary, Salome of Krakow, in *Legend of Saint Clare*, 39–40, 290 n. b; Moorman, *History of the Franciscan Order*, 209–11, 222; Ingrid J. Peterson, OSF, *Clare of Assisi: A Biographical Study* (Quincy, IL: Franciscan Press, 1993), 163–68, 228, 295–96, 355; and other sources.
[44] Peterson, *Clare of Assisi*, 354.
[45] Peterson, *Clare of Assisi*, 354.

was that since the property was owned by the church, their vocation remained unstained.[46]

Moorman writes,

> Many houses of Poor Clares were, in fact, in great penury; and many of the sisters were hungry. At San Damiano itself, conditions were very severe, not only through voluntary abnegation and self-discipline but from sheer shortage of provisions. Gregory, therefore, felt bound to act, and pleaded with Clare to accept some possessions from him; but she would not yield.... She would not surrender the Privilege of Poverty even though they should all die of starvation. She herself was ill, an illness that lasted for nearly thirty years; but it in no way diminished her tenacity of purpose.[47]

Clare the Saint

As with Francis, many viewed Clare as a saint well before she died. Pope Innocent IV, who much admired Clare, said that "God comes down to perform on earth many different miracles through her and her prayers." He believed that people who asked for God's help through the "merits" of Clare received aid miraculously "because the clear merits of the virgin Clare were interceding."[48]

A mere two months after Clare's death, Innocent IV opened an inquiry into her life—the first step toward canonization. Three of Francis's brothers, Leo, Angelo, and Marco, were put on the commission charged with documenting Clare's life and witness. Testimonies of people who knew Clare were collected, especially from Assisi city officials and from Clare's own San Damiano sisters.[49]

The process was completed within two years. On August 15, 1255, Clare was officially enrolled among the saints of the church. In Assisi, the imposing Basilica of Saint Clare was constructed along the southeast edge of the city. The basilica's façade of alternating layers of sand-colored and pink-hued native stone looks new even today, eight centuries later. Clare's body was buried here in 1260 beneath the high altar.[50]

---

[46] Moorman, *History of the Franciscan Order*, 206.

[47] Moorman, *History of the Franciscan Order*, 206.

[48] Prologue, *Acts of the Process of Canonization*, in *The Lady: Clare of Assisi*, 142.

[49] Introduction, *Process of Canonization*, 139. Some of the testimonies were quoted in chapter 10.

[50] Peterson, *Clare of Assisi*, xxvi. With time the location of Clare's sarcophagus was forgotten, or the records lost. In the nineteenth century the sarcophagus was located

More communities of Poor Clares continued to spring up, not only in Italy but throughout Europe. Nearly one hundred fifty convents had already been founded by the time of Clare's death in 1253.[51] At century's end there were at least forty-seven Poor Clare communities in Spain alone. Others were founded in Moravia, Poland, Hungary, England, Croatia, Germany, France, and elsewhere. Some of these new convents had previously been Benedictine; moved by Clare's example and wishing to take her as their model, these nuns became Poor Clares instead of Benedictines. About forty years after Clare's death, sixty-four Poor Clares were massacred at Acre, Palestine, when the city fell to the Muslims near the end of the Crusades.[52]

In her book *Clare of Assisi: A Biographical Study*, Ingrid Peterson, a Sister of Saint Francis, asked in what sense Clare might be a model for women today. Peterson notes the resurgence of interest in Clare, prompted partly by careful reexamination of the early sources and partly by contemporary women's movements both within and beyond the church. Clare emerges as a woman who lived within medieval expectations but also constantly pushed against them. She wanted to follow Jesus as radically as Francis did. That wasn't fully possible, given the restrictions the church put on nuns. Had she been able to, Clare and her sisters probably would have traveled about and served people, saints and sinners, much as Francis did. He was their ideal. Yet "Clare resolved the tension between her vision and traditional ways of female monasticism" by focusing "on the benefits of asceticism, not on its renunciation" of material goods and of marriage. "Ascetical practices enable the Poor Ladies to follow in the footsteps of Christ, and to become co-workers of God," Peterson writes.[53]

Regis Armstrong, editor of *The Lady: Clare of Assisi: Early Documents*, notes that "Clare became the first woman to write a religious rule and, in so doing, inaugurated a totally new epoch for women in the life of the Church."[54]

Over the centuries since Clare, more communities of Poor Clares arose. Besides the original Order of Saint Clare, additional branches have

---

and on October 3, 1872, Clare's body was placed in the crypt of the basilica, where it remains today.

[51] Peterson, *Clare of Assisi*, 355.

[52] Peterson, *Clare of Assisi*, 355–56.

[53] Peterson, *Clare of Assisi*, 358.

[54] Armstrong, "Introduction," *The Form of Life of Saint Clare* (1253), in *The Lady: Clare of Assisi*, 106. See also Peterson, *Clare of Assisi*, 333.

included the Colettine Poor Clares (founded in 1410), the Capuchin Poor Clares (1538), the Sisters of Saint Francis (1849 in St. Francis, Wisconsin), the Poor Clares of Perpetual Adoration (1854), and others.[55]

Today Poor Clares throughout the world number more than 20,000. Their monasteries are found in seventy-plus countries and are affiliated with sixteen different suborders. Most Clare communities are small, numbering only a dozen or so, though some are considerably larger. The website of the Poor Clare Sisters of Spokane, Washington, says, "the Poor Clare charism is one of family and St. Clare guided us that small communities were much better to keep this family spirit than larger ones. So when a community gets to a certain number we usually start new ones rather than just keep getting bigger."[56]

Pope John Paul II told assembled religious leaders in Assisi on October 27, 1986:

> This is the permanent lesson of Assisi. It is the lesson of Francis who has incarnated for us an attractive ideal. It is the lesson of Saint Clare, the first one to follow him. It is an ideal of gentleness, humility, of a deep sense of God and of the duty to serve everyone. Saint Francis was a man of peace. Saint Clare was, par excellence, the woman of prayer. Her union with God in prayer sustained Francis and his followers, as it sustains us today. Francis and Clare are examples of peace; with God, with themselves, with all men and women in this world.[57]

And with Earth and all its creatures.

---

[55] https://en.wikipedia.org/wiki/Poor_Clares.

[56] Poor Clare Sisters, http://poorclare.org/blog/?page_id=36.

[57] Quoted in Peterson, *Clare of Assisi*, 358–59.

Part III

Movements of the Spirit

17

Francis Wins the Universities

When Francis died in 1226, Franciscans were impacting church and society mainly in two ways. One was in local parishes. The other was in the life of Europe's growing universities.

In the thirty years following Francis's death, Franciscans in university towns unexpectedly emerged as the scholarly elite of Europe. Together with the Dominicans (most famously Thomas Aquinas), these friars–scholars became leading thinkers, authors, and teachers. Within parishes, the Lesser Brothers increasingly took on pastoral roles, assisting local priests, as the papacy encouraged them to do. As a result, "the pastoral ministries of the Lesser Brothers continued to expand dramatically throughout the 1230s."[1]

The Creative Dynamism of the 1200s

This broadening ministry of the Lesser Brothers was part of the creative dynamism of the times. Art, architecture, and universities flourished. Europe was bubbling with new learning, making this an exciting time

---

[1] Introduction, "*Ordinem vestrum* of Innocent IV (1245)," in *Francis of Assisi: Early Documents*, ed. Regis J. Armstrong, OFM Cap., J. A. Wayne Hellmann, OFM Conv., and William J. Short, OFM (New York: New City Press, 2001), 2:774 [hereafter FA:ED]. This was also the time of Louis IX, King of France (1214–1270), known to history as Saint Louis. Louis was crowned king on November 8, 1226, only twelve years of age, just five weeks after Francis died. Louis demonstrated compassion for many poor people and today is honored as patron of the Franciscan Third Order. Moorman notes that the Franciscans "were greatly helped by the generosity of Louis IX who, it was said, would have liked to abdicate and join the Order as a simple friar." John Moorman, *A History of the Franciscan Order: From Its Origins to the Year 1517* (Oxford: Oxford University Press, 1968), 160. The Lesser Brothers in fact grew rapidly in France during this period.

for young scholars, that is, young men. Young women lived in a world mostly walled off from academic pursuits.

Today Gothic cathedrals are the most visible remains of the 1200s. Architecture was the outward and visible sign of deep currents changing society. Knowledge was exploding—astronomy, mathematics, linguistics, medicine, as well as architecture, as the Gothic cathedrals testify.[2] Many scholars were up-to-date on the latest scientific technology, using instruments such as astrolabes, advanced armillary spheres (showing the motion of the stars around the Earth), clocks of increasing sophistication, and the torquetum, a sort of early mechanical analog computer for calculating the positions of heavenly bodies. These and other instruments were constantly being improved as new discoveries were made.[3] Franciscan scholars together with their Dominican counterparts were part of this medieval knowledge explosion.[4]

Four main reasons explain the new flood of knowledge. First, highly sophisticated treatises from Persian, Indian, Greek, and Arabic scholars, many translated from Muslim sources, were becoming available in Latin translations—especially the works of Aristotle on mathematics, optics, anatomy, and cause and effect in the physical world.[5] Second, the gradual breakdown of feudalism, the rise of commerce, and the ongoing Crusades spurred a quest for knowledge and a thirst for education. Third and relatedly, modern universities began to develop. The numbers of young men congregating in university towns soon ran into the thousands.

The fourth reason was simply the ever-growing fund of knowledge. Monastic scriptoriums were busy turning out copy after copy of manuscripts, bound into books covering every conceivable field of knowledge, and in high demand. Well before the invention of the printing press, the profusion of scriptoriums in the 1200s produced thousands of beautifully bound hand-printed volumes.

---

[2] Jean Gimpel, *The Medieval Machine: The Industrial Revolution of the Middle Ages* (New York: Penguin Books, 1977).

[3] Seb Falk, *The Light Ages: The Surprising Story of Medieval Science* (New York: W. W. Norton, 2020).

[4] Gimpel, *Medieval Machine*, 174.

[5] Jim al-Khalili, *The House of Wisdom: How Arabic Science Saved Ancient Knowledge and Gave Us the Renaissance* (New York: Penguin, 2011). Plato's works were already known in Europe, but many of Aristotle's works were not. They became broadly available through Latin translations from Arabic translations from the Greek. See J. A. Weisheipl, "Science in the Thirteenth Century," in J. I. Catto, ed., *The Early Oxford Schools*, vol. I of *The History of the University of Oxford*, ed. T. H. Aston (Oxford: Clarendon Press, 1984), 436.

Hundreds of those busy skilled hands belonged to Franciscans. Many Lesser Brothers found their vocations in meticulously copying books hour by hour each day. Book production in turn sparked the growth of libraries and a lively book trade.[6]

The Quest for Universal Knowledge and Science

Scholars in the 1200s made discoveries in astronomy, mathematics, physics, and natural science.

How did all the new knowledge in multiple areas fit together? How could one integrate everything into one broad Christian worldview? An integrated Christian understanding: many scholars made this their quest, their pilgrimage, maybe their noble crusade. Scholars wanted to know how everything connected—theological inquiry in the broadest, "wholist" sense.[7]

Add to this dynamic scholarly context, then, the growing monastic orders—thousands of new Dominicans and especially Franciscans—and one begins to perceive the dynamism of the period. The 1200s, the 1300s, and on into the 1400s, birthed the Renaissance—and on its heels in northern Europe, the Protestant Reformation of the 1500s, and eventually the so-called Enlightenment in the 1600s.

Given this mix, it is easier to see how so many leading scholars, teachers, and writers were Franciscans and Dominicans. Understandably, the followers of Francis—he who wrote the *Canticle of the Creatures* and called rabbits and birds and the heavenly bodies his brothers and sisters—wanted to understand more deeply how the whole creation worked and fit together. Historian Seb Falk calls this period "The Light Ages," not the Dark Ages.[8]

It took a century for European universities to assimilate all this new knowledge into the seven liberal arts, the *trivium* (grammar, logic,

---

[6] The large library at the Cathedral of Notre Dame in Paris "lent many books" to patrons, as did many of the monastic abbeys, notes Walsh. In Paris "the library of the Sorbonne was ... open not only to the professors and students" of the university "but also to those interested in books and in literature who might come from elsewhere, provided they were properly accredited." James J. Walsh, *The Thirteenth: Greatest of Centuries* (New York: Catholic Summer School Press, 1907), 149, 153.

[7] The Greek word for knowledge is *gnosis*, but in Latin it is *scientia*. If you were a scholar—philosopher, mathematician, theologian—you were a scientist. The quest for universal science and universal knowledge thus meant the same thing. The more restricted English term "scientist" (as we use it today) wouldn't be coined for another six centuries. Richard Holmes, *The Age of Wonder: How the Romantic Generation Discovered the Beauty and Terror of Science* (New York: Pantheon/Random House, 2008), 449–50, 474.

[8] Falk, *The Light Ages.*

rhetoric) and *quadrivium* (arithmetic, geometry, music, astronomy). The liberal arts had to be reworked to accommodate the new science and philosophy flooding in mainly from the Muslim world.[9]

Clericalization and the Impact of Lateran IV

In such a world of new learning how could an order of poor, lightly educated Lesser Brothers possibly have any impact, let alone produce leading scholars?

Yet they did. One reason was simply the astonishing growth of the Franciscans. Francis's brothers were now everywhere throughout Europe. They were local. Communities of brothers sprang up in hundreds of towns, villages, and cities. Naturally they would interact with the other big movement of the time: the rise and spread of universities.

There was also another big factor, a set of developments within the Roman Catholic Church and its structures, not outside it. As it happened, the rise of Franciscan engagement in the universities coincided with the increasing clericalization of the Order. Scholars at the universities were nearly all ordained priests. And by now most Franciscans were priests.

This naturally posed day-by-day challenges to Franciscan poverty and servanthood. Francis wanted all brothers to be equal in status—a nonhierarchical brotherhood. But, of course, the clergy–laity division was deeply embedded in the church. Over time, clergy brothers came to be viewed as having the more important role; "lay" brothers were increasingly viewed as assistants and servants to clergy brothers. This was especially true at the universities.

The document *Exiit Qui Seminat* of Pope Nicholas III in 1279— half a century after Francis's passing—shows how deeply the clergy-laity divide was now entrenched among the Franciscans themselves. Nicholas noted "the fact that certain brothers are not engaged in study and sacred ministry, but are attached to the service of those brothers who are engaged in study or the divine services or the ministry." Despite their secondary status, however, the pope says, these brothers "are entitled to their support along with those at whose service they are."[10] The editors of *Francis of Assisi: Early Documents* remark, "Nicholas's acceptance of the clericalization of the Order is evident here. He cannot envision the

---

[9] Weisheipl, "Science in the Thirteenth Century," 438.
[10] Pope Nicholas III, *Exiit Qui Seminat* (1279), FA:ED 3:758.

legitimacy of lay brothers in the Order unless they are 'waiting on' the ordained brothers, who were now providing the principal work of the brothers in the church."[11] This is a long way from the spirit of Francis!

The growing number of priests among the Franciscans could, however, be a key to clergy reform within the church, Innocent III knew. The pope made this central to his agenda for the Fourth Lateran Council in 1215. Coming just as universities were rising, the council "marked the beginning of a new era in the pastoral life of the church," notes historian M. W. Sheehan. "When [the Lateran Council] called the direction of souls 'the art of arts' it made clear the purpose of the pastoral programme which its decrees laid upon bishops and clergy: *an informed laity instructed by a reformed clergy*."[12]

This was Innocent III's reform agenda. Innocent's dramatic encounter with Francis six years earlier shaped the pope's view of renewal. Innocent saw the reforming potential of the Franciscans as well as the Dominicans. These orders, Innocent believed, largely through the universities, would be key to reforming the clergy and thus the church.

To bring about such change the clergy must "be disciplined, educated, orthodox, and fitted by character and training for the direction of souls," notes Sheehan. "Popes and bishops seized upon the friars as agents of reform because of the moral force of their lives and their dedication to the cure of souls"—unlike many priests and scholars.[13] It was clear to Innocent that Franciscan and Dominican priests were most ready and able to fill the reforming role and were eager to help implement Lateran IV's decrees.

Soon both orders were doing that. They formed communities at the growing universities—Bologna, Paris, Oxford, Cambridge, and a number of others. Dominicans and Franciscans had full papal support—not only of Innocent III (who died in 1216) but also his successors. With time, Alexander IV (1254–1261) and Clement IV (1265–1268) even permitted friars to teach theology in their communities in towns that had no university. Remarkably, Franciscan and Dominican convents became in effect seminaries authorized to train and produce parish priests.[14]

---

[11] Pope Nicholas III, *Exiit Qui Seminat* (1279), FA:ED 3:758 n. b.

[12] M. W. Sheehan, "The Religious Orders 1220–1370," in *The Early Oxford Schools*, 193 (emphasis added).

[13] Sheehan, "The Religious Orders," 193.

[14] Sheehan, "The Religious Orders," 193.

Franciscans at the Universities: The Light Ages

Both Franciscans and Dominicans played a key role as well in the way
university education developed. Scholarship advanced rapidly among
Franciscans in the years following Francis's death. As more and more
Franciscans were priests, so more and more were or wished to be scholars.
Soon we hear of two famous monk-scholars at the University of Paris: the
Franciscan Bonaventure and the Dominican Thomas Aquinas.

Franciscan communities became intellectual centers in two ways. One
was the increased learning among Franciscans themselves, due partly to
the impact of the new universities and parish schools. The other way,
equally significant, was the attraction of serious scholars to the Franciscan
movement. Many young scholars who were not Franciscans saw that the
Lesser Brothers were serious, deeply committed Christians devoted to
worship and service, unlike many of the clergy and young university
students around them. And these poor brothers lived in sustainable and
joyful, if rather poor and rustic, communities.

Soon several scholars, some already well along in their studies, joined
the Order. The best known was Bonaventure of Bagnoreggio—the very
same Bonaventure who as a child was healed after his mother made a
vow to Saint Francis (as noted in chapter 5).

It wasn't just poor young scholars who were drawn to the Franciscans.
Brother Bernard of Besse, Bonaventure's assistant and traveling partner,
wrote after Bonaventure's death, "Bishops, abbots, archdeacons, and
established Masters of Theology entered the Order. So too did princes,
nobles, and innumerable others who were noted for their dignity, their
nobility, and their knowledge. They were the flower of nobility and
learning." Bernard went on, "Who could count the number of brothers
. . . who were approved and celebrated Doctors of Theology?"[15]

Many Franciscan scholars were also superb preachers. Franciscans'
goal was practical, pastoral, and missional, not just intellectual. The
Lesser Brothers longed to see deep church reform and spiritual revival.
Sheehan notes, "The studies of the friars were aimed at their apostolate
of peaching in the pulpit and instruction in the confessional. This
combination of learning and its practical application to Christian life
made them indispensable to those committed to making a reality of
[Lateran IV] decrees."[16]

---

[15] Bernard of Besse, *A Book of the Praises of Saint Francis*, FA:ED 3:63.
[16] Sheehan, "The Religious Orders," 193.

Franciscan Preaching

As Franciscan brothers became better educated, however, their preaching grew more doctrinal and less evangelistic. They were now pastors of the flock, assisting (sometimes opposed by) parish priests. Franciscan preachers now had to be examined by the order's minister general to be sure they were well prepared and doctrinally sound.[17] "Thus the friars began to exercise a pastoral ministry rather different from what they had originally set out to do, and one which impinged more and more upon the proper work of the parish priest," notes Moorman. "Here lay the seeds of trouble. So long as the friars were content, as Francis had been, with a humble ministry exercised in full co-operation with the parochial clergy, all was well. But as soon as the friars became popular not only as preachers but also as directors of souls, friction was inevitable."[18]

The result was conflict, not only at the parish level but also churchwide. Popes generally supported Franciscan preachers, seeing them as bringers of new life. But bishops in France and elsewhere complained of Franciscan interference (as they saw it). This, coupled with growing Franciscan influence at the University of Paris, birthed conflicts that persisted for years.

Moorman summarizes:

> By 1232 the Order was clearly entering upon a new phase. Francis had founded his brotherhood upon the three ideals of poverty, simplicity, and humility.... But after his death things were different. The centre of gravity moved to those who believed that the Order should develop in other ways. So poverty began to give place to security, simplicity to learning, and humility to privilege. The rising basilica [of Saint Francis] at Assisi, with the vast sums of money collected for it, the growth of the scholastic movement in the university towns, and the clashes with the [parish] clergy ... were all symptomatic of the new age.[19]

---

[17] Moorman, *History of the Franciscan Order*, 91.

[18] Moorman, *History of the Franciscan Order*, 94.

[19] Moorman, *History of the Franciscan Order*, 94. Moorman provides considerable information on Franciscan preaching during this period and on the rise and influence of several notable Franciscan preachers—Brother Anthony of Padua (later St. Anthony), John of La Rochelle, Berthold of Regensburg, Haymo of Faversham, and others. Haymo (an Englishman) "once preached with such compulsion at Saint-Denis near Paris that he was obliged to spend the whole of the next three days in hearing confessions," notes Moorman. "But it was in simple sermons to village congregations that the friars really

Brother Elias, now general minister, had been a prime supporter of Francis's canonization and the building of the great St. Francis Basilica (still today the most prominent edifice in Assisi). Elias had his own ideas about the direction of the Lesser Brothers. Elias claimed, rather dubiously, that because of ill health, he was unable to live the rigorous common life specified in the Rule and to which he initially had pledged himself.[20]

In fact, the whole tenor of the movement was changing. And yet Franciscan preaching in local parishes across Europe was having great impact. An example is Brother Berthold of Regensburg (c. 1220–1272), described as follows:

> While exhorting all to be content with their station in life, he denounces oppressive taxes, unjust judges, usury, and dishonest trade.... He is never dry, always vivid and graphic, mingling with his exhortations a variety of anecdotes, jests, and the wild etymologies of the Middle Ages, making extensive use of the allegorical interpretation of the Old Testament [typical of the time] and of his strong feeling for nature.... His style is clear, direct and remarkably free from cumbrous Latin constructions; he employed, whenever he could, the pithy and homely sayings of the peasants.[21]

Berthold was extraordinary, but such popular preaching was typical of the Franciscans; "a large number of his fellow friars ... made preaching their 'job' and exercised a great influence on their fellow men."[22]

Learned Franciscans

By the 1250s—that is, within twenty-five years of Francis's death—the Franciscan Order "had become one of the most learned institutions in the world," Moorman notes. Each larger convent had its own "lector" or "reader," tasked with teaching the brothers theology and especially with preparing those who would go on to university. Given these duties, lectors were assigned their own private rooms.[23]

---

excelled," where the brothers typically used the vernacular rather than academic Latin. Moorman, *History of the Franciscan Order*, 274–75.

[20] Moorman, *History of the Franciscan Order*, 94–95.

[21] Hugh Chisholm, ed., "Bertold von Regensburg," *Encyclopedia Britannica* (Cambridge: Cambridge University Press, 1911), 813. Quoted in https://en.wikipedia.org/wiki/Bertold_of_Regensburg.

[22] Moorman, *History of the Franciscan Order*, 276.

[23] Moorman, *History of the Franciscan Order*, 123.

The best students were sent on to university. Franciscans set up their own schools at Paris, Oxford, and other universities where especially apt brothers could live and enroll in university courses. Here the brothers were able to "take the full academic course, graduate as masters of theology, and so become lectors in other convents. Each convent was to look out for young men with the appropriate gifts and to start them on their training."[24]

In these ways Franciscans fully integrated themselves into Europe's rapidly growing university system. The appearance of Franciscan scholars was not ad hoc or by chance. It was planned, systematized, and carried out competently—something Francis himself, prophetic as he was, could hardly have envisioned. Yet these young scholars were indeed Franciscans, devout brothers devoted now to study.

The program was rigorous. All Franciscan scholars had to know Latin and have studied logic.[25] Brothers could go on to university only after three or four years at a Franciscan school. "They must be intelligent, healthy, well-spoken, peaceable, and of good report; and they must stay for at least four years" and return to their convent with "a satisfactory report on their work," notes Moorman.[26]

Franciscans first arrived in England in 1224; five years later they had a school at Oxford. By 1238 Franciscan lectors were teaching in their convents at Cambridge, London, Canterbury, Hereford, Leicester, and Bristol, as well as Oxford. Within three decades of Francis's death the brothers had founded schools at Gloucester (1246), Norwich (1250), and Northampton (1258). "Equally rapid progress was made in other countries, so that by 1250 there was abundant teaching and study of theology among the Friars Minor" throughout Europe. These schools were designed for the training of Franciscans themselves, but

---

[24] Moorman, *History of the Franciscan Order*, 123. Provincial chapters had final say as to which brothers went on to advanced study.

[25] This and many other stipulations are contained in The Constitutions of Narbonne, a 1260 compilation of official Franciscan regulations dating back to 1239. The Constitutions are the fruit of the Franciscan chapter held at Narbonne, France, in May 1260. Convoked by Bonaventure, this chapter is notable for a series of actions that significantly shaped and reshaped the Order. "The Constitutions [of Narbonne] are divided into twelve rubrics or chapters based on the Rule. They have served as a norm for all other Constitutions edited by the Order since that time." Raphael M. Huber, OFM Conv., *A Documented History of the Franciscan Order: From the Birth of St. Francis to the Division of the Order Under Leo X (1182–1517)* (Milwaukee, WI: Nowiny Publishing Apostolate, 1944), 152–53.

[26] Moorman, *History of the Franciscan Order*, 124.

eventually non-Franciscan priests also attended.[27] These developments show indirectly how widespread was the awakening among youth across Europe and how deeply society was changing.

The quality of Franciscan schools helps explain how, within a generation, many leading scholars at Oxford, Paris, and other universities were Franciscans and Dominicans (for the Dominicans were developing along similar lines).

Having schools within their own communities was not controversial. But when the Franciscans began forming their own schools at the universities, that sparked conflict with university authorities. Moorman explains,

> In the thirteenth century the universities were themselves young, ready to welcome genuine scholars but naturally jealous of their authority and of their rights. A *universitas* was a guild of teachers with its own rules and constitution and a closed membership. No one could claim to be a member of the guild without the consent of the regent masters, and no member could infringe the rules of the society with impunity. When, therefore, the friars, especially [Dominican] preachers and [Franciscan] Minors, began to arrive in the university towns and establish their own schools and appoint their own teachers, a problem was immediately created. What was the status of these newcomers? Clearly they were not members of the *universitas* since they refused to regard themselves as subject to university discipline. Indeed, ... each Order of friars was, in a sense a *universitas* of its own, [operating] ... entirely on its own authority. Two such independent and sensitive institutions could hardly hope to work happily together.[28]

Serious conflict between friars and the university arose first at Paris. Franciscans arrived in France about 1219, still during Francis's lifetime. Dominicans were already there and were in the process of setting up their own school at Paris. The Dominican school was structured much as was the university itself with scheduled lectures, disputations (formal academic debates), its own library, and various academic exercises. The Franciscans followed suit. Then in 1225, four doctors of the university

---

[27] Moorman, *History of the Franciscan Order*, 124.
[28] Moorman, *History of the Franciscan Order*, 124–35. Moorman cites H. Rashdall, *Medieval Universities of Europe* (A. B. Emden, 1936), 1:371, as a source.

themselves became Franciscans! Suddenly the Franciscan school had a respected faculty.

Both schools—Dominicans and Franciscans—were soon drawing young men to their classes and to their orders. Most of the students in the Franciscan school were thus also brothers, though some "seculars" (students not in religious orders) were admitted. The friars' schools, having their own means of support, charged much lower fees than did university masters whose livelihood depended largely on students' fees.[29] In other words, the friars provided just as good an education but at lower cost.

Franciscan education was given a big boost in 1236 when the leading theologian of the University of Paris and a prominent churchman, Englishman Alexander of Hales, himself took Franciscan vows.[30] Alexander was thus the first Franciscan to hold a university chair. Already an older man when he became a Franciscan, Alexander lectured only two years. But he had a formative influence on Bonaventure and several others.

University of Paris authorities were not at all happy with these developments. The university operated under the authority of the church, and thus specifically the Bishop of Paris. As it grew, the university struggled for more independence. Franciscans and Dominicans, however, were closely attached to the church and had the smile of the papacy. When conflicts arose, church authorities usually sided with the Franciscans and Dominicans and against the university. This only increased tensions.

At Paris, struggles between the university and the friars continued for decades. The situation at Oxford was different; from the first, the Franciscan school there was more integrated into the university structure. Still, conflicts did gradually arise as the Franciscan school grew in size and reputation.[31]

The focus of conflicts shifted over time. It got channeled into charges of heresy in the 1250s when some Franciscan brothers became fascinated with the apocalyptic ideas of the Cistercian abbot and Bible scholar Joachim of Fiore. Joachim's interpretation of Scripture became known generically as "The Everlasting Gospel" (a phrase from Revelation 14:6).

We will look more closely at Joachim later. The point here is that some Franciscans began promoting the idea that Franciscans were the herald of the New Age of the Spirit that Joachim prophesied—God's

---

[29] Moorman, *History of the Franciscan Order*, 125–26.

[30] Moorman, *History of the Franciscan Order*, 92, 131.

[31] Moorman, *History of the Franciscan Order*, 126–35. Moorman covers these controversies in detail in his chapter, "The Friars and the Universities," 123–39.

latter-day provision for a radical renewal of the church. In 1254, a
Franciscan brother, Gerard of Borgo San Donnino, popularized Joachim's
ideas in his book *Introduction to the Everlasting Gospel*. The university
soon condemned the book as heretical. Franciscans who subscribed to
Joachim's views were suspected of heresy.[32] By then the Franciscans were
well enough established, however, that the charge of heresy didn't stick.

The long dispute between the university and the friars (Dominicans
and Franciscans) continued into the 1260s and 1270s. It turned into a
"pamphlet war" in which "tracts continued to be written from both
sides."[33] Partisans of the university questioned the whole notion of
"evangelical poverty" or "apostolic poverty" as professed especially by
the Franciscans. But Thomas Aquinas, Bonaventure, and others came to
the friars' defense.[34]

The dispute heated up to the point that in 1255, the university formally
dissolved itself to elude church control—though the university continued
functioning. In 1261, the French bishop Jacques Pantaléon became Pope
Urban IV, and under his papacy Rome worked out compromises. The
university was permitted to put some restrictions on the friars. It excluded
friars from the faculty of arts and decreed that the Franciscan school could
have only one non-Franciscan university professor and the Dominicans
two. And so "little by little, the university managed to assert its authority,
until eventually a *modus vivendi* was reached."[35]

Meanwhile, the Franciscan schools at Paris and Oxford thrived. The
one at Cambridge was growing. The Paris school attracted renowned
scholars and enjoyed a broadening reputation. At this time only Paris,
Oxford, and Cambridge had faculties of theology, but the Franciscans
founded communities at several other schools that did not have
theology faculties.[36]

At Oxford, the Franciscan impact was almost immediate. Moorman
notes that when the Lesser Brothers arrived in 1224 (two years before
Francis's death), "Their manner of life was such as to make an immediate
and deep impression on the academic world, and many scholars and
teachers joined the Order."[37] Among these was Adam Marsh, still in his

---

[32] Moorman, *History of the Franciscan Order*, 115, 128.
[33] Moorman, *History of the Franciscan Order*, 129.
[34] Moorman, *History of the Franciscan Order*, 127–30.
[35] Moorman, *History of the Franciscan Order*, 131.
[36] The next university after Paris, Oxford, and Cambridge to establish a theology
faculty was Bologna, Italy, in 1364. Moorman, *History of the Franciscan Order*, 133.
[37] Moorman, *History of the Franciscan Order*, 133.

twenties, who became known for his work in theology and mathematics. One of his pupils was Roger Bacon, soon to become a renowned scholar.[38] Many Franciscan students continued as university professors. Some went on to become bishops or other church leaders.

Franciscan and Dominican theology teaching at Paris and Oxford caused tension, however, because the friars' schools were not under university control. The universities "were obliged to accept the presence in their midst of a number of independent religious colleges which provided teaching of a very high quality, attracted many students, and yet refused to accept the authority of the university," notes Moorman.[39]

At Oxford, the Franciscan provincial minister, Brother Agnellus of Pisa, in 1229 managed to secure the renowned Robert Grosseteste as teacher. Historian of science J. A. Weisheipl calls Grosseteste "the most important figure in Oxford science" at the time. "As an already mature scholar, he formulated clearly his scientific ideas," even as he was teaching the Franciscans. Then in 1235, he was appointed bishop of Lincoln, England's largest diocese.[40]

Grosseteste formulated an ideal of scholarship that sounds remarkably modern. He held that serious academic study involves four elements, Weisheipl notes: "the importance of optics and mathematics generally in the study of nature; the primacy of personal experience (*experimentum*) over authority; the usefulness of ancient languages for Christian scholarship; and the special role of experimental science and mathematics in understanding the Bible and in living the Christian life."[41]

Like other medieval scholars, Grosseteste was intrigued by what has been called "the metaphysics of light." Based on his knowledge of Scripture and early Christian writers, Grosseteste developed a whole theology-and-science of light. Like other scholars, Grosseteste saw Jesus Christ as "true light," the "light of the world" (John 1:9, 8:12)—the light through whom God the Father created all things. The Apostle Paul wrote in Colossians, Jesus "is the image of the invisible God, the firstborn of all creation; for in him all things in heaven and on earth were created, things

---

[38] Dom David Knowles, *The Religious Orders in England* (London: Cambridge University Press, 1948), 213–14.

[39] Moorman, *History of the Franciscan Order*, 133.

[40] Weisheipl, "Science in the Thirteenth Century," 440–41.

[41] Weisheipl, "Science in the Thirteenth Century," 443. This is Weisheipl's summary of Grosseteste's views as carried forward by Roger Bacon. Grosseteste was building upon earlier scientific work, but now influenced by Aristotle's newly available writings. Grosseteste was one of the earliest scholars to see the great significance of Aristotle's writings on science.

visible and invisible, whether thrones or dominions or rulers or powers—
all things have been created through him and for him. He himself is
before all things, and in him all things hold together" (Col. 1:15–17). So,
of course, both physical and spiritual light must have the same source
and at some level the same being.[42]

Grosseteste had a shaping influence on ensuing Franciscan scholars.
These included Thomas of York (c. 1220–c. 1269), who later led the
Franciscan school at Cambridge; Roger Bacon; and John Pecham, future
Archbishop of Canterbury.[43]

Throughout Europe, the Franciscans also established centers
at cathedral schools that had not yet developed into universities.[44]
Franciscan centers at universities and cathedral schools were of course
in addition to the scores of their communities established throughout the
many towns and cities of Europe. These each had their own stories and
impacts. But it is the names of the great Franciscan university scholars
that still resound today.

Doctor Subtle and Doctor Marvelous

Within a generation Roger Bacon (1220–1292), known as "Doctor
Marvelous,"[45] John Duns Scotus, "Doctor Subtle" (c. 1265–1308),
Alexander of Hales (c. 1185–1245), called "Doctor Irrefutable," John
Pecham (c. 1230–1292), Archbishop of Canterbury—all Franciscans—
had become some of Europe's most famous theologians. Also included
were the Catalan[46] philosopher, mathematician, and linguist Ramon Llull
(c. 1232–c. 1316), "Doctor Illuminatus," missionary to Muslims, and of
course Bonaventure (1221–1274), "the Seraphic Doctor."

We need to understand these scholars better if we are to grasp the
full impact of the Franciscan penetration of Europe's rising universities.
We will look briefly at Bacon, Duns Scotus, and Llull.

---

[42] Weisheipl, "Science in the Thirteenth Century," 444–45.

[43] Weisheipl, "Science in the Thirteenth Century," 450; Moorman, *History of the Franciscan Order*, 134.

[44] Moorman, *History of the Franciscan Order*, 138–39. Cologne for instance had no university until 1389, but the Lesser Brothers had a thriving school there from the mid-1200s.

[45] Not the famous later scholar, Francis Bacon (1561–1626), who also made contributions to the study and application of the "scientific method."

[46] Born on the Mediterranean island of Majorca, south of Barcelona, Catalonia (now part of Spain), Llull was a scholar in the Catalan language.

Roger Bacon, "Doctor Marvelous"

Roger Bacon especially shines. Historian Jean Gimpel calls him "the greatest scientist of his time and the first man really to have undertaken planned experimental research." Bacon himself wrote, "There are two modes of acquiring knowledge—namely by reasoning and experience. Reasoning draws a conclusion and makes us grant the conclusion but does not make the conclusion certain, nor does it remove doubt," so certainty of truth comes only "when the mind discovers it by the path of experience."[47] Bacon felt that Franciscan simplicity and the shared practices of spiritual disciplines deepened one's ability to comprehend truth. He wrote, "Virtue ... clarifies the mind so that a man may comprehend more easily not only moral but scientific truths."[48]

So much for the idea that experimental science emerged only with the Enlightenment four hundred years later!

Figure 17.1 Roger Bacon
(wearing Franciscan habit) conducting an experiment

---

[47] Gimpel, *Medieval Machine*, 192, 193. Gimpel quotes Bacon from Bacon's *Opus Majus*, vol. 2, p. 583.

[48] Roger Bacon, *Opus Majus* 2:171, as quoted in Stewart C. Easton, *Roger Bacon and His Search for a Universal Science: A Reconsideration of the Life and Work of Roger Bacon in the Light of His Own Stated Purposes* (New York: Columbia University Press, 1952), 74.

Bacon became a pioneer in experimental science. He embraced Grosseteste's fourfold ideal of Christian scholarship, with its emphasis on combining reason and experimentation. Bacon sought to apply this approach in his studies and to live it out personally. It became the basis of the reform program Bacon proposed to Pope Clement IV in 1268. Unhappily, Clement died just about the time Bacon submitted his complex proposal.

Bacon's great work, his *Opus Majus,* circulated widely. It may well have influenced Christopher Columbus's decision to sail west rather than east in order to reach India. Bacon calculated that the distance from Spain to India was much less than commonly thought.[49]

Bacon was interested in all aspects of knowledge and sought to integrate diverse areas systemically. Historian Charles Freeman in *The Reopening of the Western Mind* (2023) notes that Bacon "went beyond optics to show how mathematics informed every other discipline" and proved "that the speed of light is finite." Bacon maintained that "all experience was an illumination from God."[50]

Missions historian Kenneth Scott Latourette notes that Bacon, like Francis, "held Crusades to be a cruel and useless waste of time, and declared that the infidel should be converted, not attacked."[51]

Bacon is still studied today. Seb Falk in his 2020 book *The Light Ages* calls him a "scientific reformer." Bacon saw "reform of the sciences [as] an essential part of defending Christendom against existential internal and external threats."[52]

It is largely due to the contributions of Franciscan scholars like Bacon that Falk calls this period in medieval history "the light ages." Scholars considered light in all senses: as a physical phenomenon; as spiritual illumination; and in ways, physical and spiritual light were interlinked. Falk notes, "Franciscans were unusually interested in light, which they took as the means of God's work in the material world," recalling the cryptic beginning of John's Gospel. In God was life, "and the life was the light of mankind [John 1:4]."[53] Franciscans and others were eager to find the coherence between Jesus Christ as light, the light of creation (Gen.

---

[49] Gimpel, *Medieval Machine,* 196.

[50] Freeman, *Reopening of the Western Mind,* 225.

[51] Kenneth Scott Latourette, *The Thousand Years of Uncertainty: A.D. 500–A.D. 1500* [1938], vol. 2 of *A History of the Expansion of Christianity* (Grand Rapids, MI: Zondervan, 1970), 319.

[52] Falk, *The Light Ages,* 74–75.

[53] Falk, *The Light Ages,* 114.

1:3–5), and light as a physical phenomenon. This quest focusing on optics would lead in time to Isaac Newton's great discoveries in the 1600s and to ongoing discoveries today.

Francis himself in his *Canticle of the Creatures* sang of Sister Moon and of Brother Sun, "through whom You give us light." He celebrated Brother Fire, "through whom You light the night." Franciscan spiritual DNA passed along to new brothers Francis's own interest in light and in Creation, whether visible or invisible, scientifically explicable or not. Bacon, writes Liam Brophy, "carried Franciscan idealism into the realms of scientific knowledge, and with Franciscan originality helped science to an autonomous life of its own"[54]—autonomous, that is, in the sense of a distinct area of inquiry within the broader scope of theology, "queen of the sciences," which of course incorporates everything.

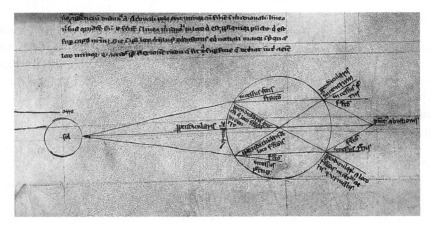

17.2 Roger Bacon optics diagram

Bacon's work continues to attract interest. "Scholarly evaluations of Bacon's contribution to science are still evolving," notes Freeman, "but he certainly deserves the accolade as one of the most imaginative and far-ranging minds of his time."[55] Freeman sees Bacon, Duns Scotus, and other Franciscan thinkers as key figures in the intellectual "reopening" that led to the Renaissance and beyond.

---

[54] Liam Brophy, *The Marvelous Doctor: Friar Roger Bacon* (Chicago: Franciscan Herald Press, 1963), 103.

[55] Freeman, *Reopening of the Western Mind*, 227.

John Duns Scotus, "Doctor Subtle"

Next to Bacon and Bonaventure, John Duns Scotus—still widely studied—is probably the best-known Franciscan intellectual.

John Duns Scotus came from the town of Duns, Scotland, where he was born in 1266. Franciscans had been active in the area since 1231, a mere five years after Francis's death. As a teenager John became a Lesser Brother. He was educated in a Franciscan *studium*, or study center, perhaps at Dumfries, Scotland. About 1280, when John was about fourteen, the brothers sent him to Oxford to study philosophy, normally an eight-year course. He was ordained as a priest about age twenty-five, probably while studying at Oxford.[56]

Scotus taught at Oxford, Cambridge, Paris, and finally at the Franciscan study house at Cologne, Germany. There he died in 1308 at age forty-two.[57]

While still at Oxford, Scotus "quickly developed a European reputation" for his brilliance and prolific output, even before he completed his master's degree.[58] He went to the University of Paris in the early fall of 1301, joining the community of some 160 Franciscans there. Vos writes, "John Duns—soon nicknamed *Scotus*—must have felt impressed in the scholarly capital of Europe which was already impressive around [the year] 1200 and by then the largest city in Europe."[59]

Scotus finished his doctorate in Paris in 1305. Young Franciscans, Dominicans, and others busied themselves making careful copies of Scotus's lectures and growing body of works, just as they did those of Aquinas and Albert Magnus.[60]

After only two years in Paris as a fully formed doctor of divinity, Scotus rather surprisingly went to the Franciscan school at Cologne, where there was no major university. He taught there only during the 1307–1308 academic year, for he died unexpectedly on November 8, 1308. His epitaph would become famous:

---

[56] Antoine Vos, *John Duns Scotus: A Life* (Kampen, the Netherlands: Summum Academic Publications, 2018), 31–57; E. A. Livingstone, ed., *The Oxford Dictionary of the Christian Church,* 3rd ed. (Oxford: Oxford University Press, 1997), 513. This article on Scotus summarizes Scotus's teachings and influence.

[57] Vos, *John Duns Scotus,* 178; P. Osmund Lewry, "Grammar, Logic and Rhetoric 1220–1320," in *The Early Oxford Schools,* 428; J. I. Catto, "Theology and Theologians 1220–1320," in *The Early Oxford Schools,* 506.

[58] J. M. Fletcher, "The Faculty of Arts," in *The Early Oxford Schools,* 385.

[59] Vos, *John Duns Scotus,* 118–20.

[60] Vos, *John Duns Scotus,* 101, 118–24; Walsh, *The Thirteenth: Greatest of Centuries,* 156–57.

Scotland brought me forth,
England taught me,
France received me,
Cologne holds me.[61]

Pope John Paul II, calling Scotus "a spiritual tower of faith," beatified Scotus during evening prayer at Saint Peter's on March 20, 1993.[62] Years earlier the Trappist monk Thomas Merton composed a poem honoring the great Franciscan:

Language was far too puny for his great theology:
But, oh! His thought strode through those words
Bright as the conquering Christ
Between the clouds of His enemies.[63]

J. I. Catto notes, "With Scotus the Oxford school of theology reached its zenith, for the first time it was the equal of Paris as a centre of original thought. [Scotus] was the first of the Oxford masters strongly to influence thought in the older university, and the critical, independent spirit of fourteenth-century Oxford begins with him."[64] Scotus's proofs for the existence of God became famous in the world of theology and philosophy.

Scotus viewed all knowledge, science, and learning as fundamentally one and coherent, finding their origin and unity in God's self-revelation. He was in effect reconciling the learning of the day with Franciscan spirituality. Like the brilliant church father Irenaeus in his theology of recapitulation a millennium earlier, Scotus sought to ground all knowledge and learning in Scripture and supremely in the incarnate Word, Jesus Christ.[65] Unlike the traditional view of "original sin," Scotus viewed sin as the privation of the good (of original justice) rather than as an infection passed on physically to ensuing generations.[66]

---

[61] Vos, *John Duns Scotus,* 178–79. *Scotia me genuit / Anglia me docuit / Gallia me recepit / Colonia me tenet.*

[62] Vos, *John Duns Scotus,* 179.

[63] Daniel P. Horan, OFM, *The Franciscan Heart of Thomas Merton* (Notre Dame, IN: Ave Maria Press, 2014), 100. Quoted also in Vos, *John Duns Scotus,* 180. Horan traces Scotus's shaping influence on Merton and his insights about the "true self," 95–116.

[64] Catto, "Theology and Theologians 1220–1320," 505.

[65] Eric Osborn, *Irenaeus of Lyons* (Cambridge: Cambridge University Press, 2001). Irenaeus was known and read in the Middle Ages (including his apocalypticism) but may not have had any direct or significant influence on Scotus. See Bernard McGinn, *Visions of the End: Apocalyptic Traditions in the Middle Ages* (New York: Columbia University Press, 1979, 1998), 18.

[66] Catto, "Theology and Theologians 1220–1320," 507, 511.

Catto notes, "Much of Scotus's fundamental thought was rooted in the Franciscan tradition."[67] Life as a Franciscan helped shape Scotus's theology both in its making and in its living. Scotus's writings are a more academically sophisticated way of saying what Francis himself taught. If Francis wanted one thing from theology, it was that it be practical, liberating, leading people to Jesus and salvation, not away from gospel truth.

Some people today may view scholars like Roger Bacon and Duns Scotus as bad examples of scholasticism—philosophers who delighted in highly abstract ideas and theories of no earthly value ("How many angels can dance on the head of a pin?"). This was an unfortunate stereotype. Scholars like Scotus and Bacon were at one and the same time astronomers, physicists, physicians, chemists, mathematicians, theologians, poets, historians, biblical scholars, and philosophers. For these were the days before academic disciplines got walled off from each other, as they are today. We best think of these scholars as *interdisciplinarians*. This period in fact—the high and late Middle Ages— laid the enduring foundations of today's academic disciplines.

Ramon Llull, "Doctor Illuminatus"

Ramon Llull (often anglicized as Raymond Lull) was an early Franciscan missionary to the Muslim world. He was born into a wealthy family on the island of Majorca in the Mediterranean and educated as a knight. Llull was born about 1232, just six years after Francis's death.[68]

At about age thirty, Llull experienced a remarkable conversion. One summer evening he was sitting alone in his room, humming a tune, and writing words to accompany it. Happening to look up, he saw a vision of Jesus Christ on the cross. Shocked, Ramon dropped the pen. The vision passed. But a week later this happened again. Then three more times Llull had the same experience. He later wrote in a poem,

> But Jesus Christ, of His great clemency,
> Five times upon the Cross appeared to me,
> That I might think upon Him lovingly,
> And cause His Name proclaimed abroad to be
> Through all the world.[69]

---

[67] Catto, "Theology and Theologians 1220–1320," 508.

[68] Moorman provides a profile of Llull. *History of the Franciscan Order,* 264–65.

[69] E. Allison Peers, *Ramon Lull, A Biography* (London: Society for Promoting Christian Knowledge, 1929), 21.

Llull began to lead a devout life and to write prolifically. He completed several books on religion and philosophy and traveled widely. He studied for a while at the University of Paris under Bonaventure.[70] His first major work, the *Book of Contemplation,* was written in Arabic as a missionary effort and was later translated into Catalan. In his philosophical writings Llull attempted to harmonize biblical revelation and the phenomena of the created order with each other and with the monotheism common to Judaism, Islam, and Christianity. He did this in part through an extensive use of diagrams and the widely known concept of "the great chain [or ladder] of being."[71]

A mystic and poet, Llull was also an accomplished scholar who wrote in Catalan, Latin, and Arabic. He made use of the vernacular as well as scholarly languages and is viewed today as one of the fathers of Catalan literature.[72] He had a brilliant and imaginative mind, and he felt called to win Muslims to Jesus Christ by persuasion rather than military crusades.[73]

In his sixties, Llull decided to profess as a Franciscan tertiary. This happened probably during a visit to Assisi. "Setting aside some of his property for his wife and children, Llull sold the remainder and gave the proceeds for the poor."[74]

Moorman in his *History of the Franciscan Order* notes that "among the [Franciscan] tertiaries [Llull] found the inspiration and companionship which he most needed; and this great mystic, missionary, and martyr became perhaps the most distinguished tertiary of the thirteenth, or indeed any other, century."[75]

---

[70] Moorman, *History of the Franciscan Order,* 248.

[71] Arthur O. Lovejoy, *The Great Chain of Being: A Study of the History of an Idea* (Cambridge, MA: Harvard University Press, 1976). The concept of "the great chain of being" and the related idea of "the principle of plenitude" were common to Greek, Jewish, Christian, and Muslim scholars and were known to Roger Bacon and Thomas Aquinas. See Lovejoy, 73–91, 100, 109–10.

[72] On a visit to Barcelona in 2016, I had the opportunity to visit a museum exhibit (in Spanish and Catalan) honoring Llull and his life and accomplishments. Llull's Franciscan connection was not highlighted in the exhibit, however.

[73] "His life goal was to preach the Christian faith and write books to convert unbelievers, persuade princes and popes to establish colleges for the training of missionaries to the Muslims, and give his life as a martyr." Alan Neely, "Lull, Raymund (*or* Ramon)," in Gerald H. Anderson, ed., *Biographical Dictionary of Christian Missions* (New York: Simon & Schuster Macmillan, 1998), 415.

[74] Latourette, *Thousand Years,* 322. See Peers, *Ramon Lull,* 131.

[75] Moorman, *History of the Franciscan Order,* 25. Moorman notes, "The Lullian literature is vast and shows no sign of coming to an end" (225). Interest in Llull's writings has grown over the years.

In his sixties and after his wife's death, Llull determined to travel to North Africa as a missionary, as he had long wished to do.[76] He sailed from Genoa to Tunis and at once began proclaiming the Christian faith and denying the claims of Islam. This landed him in prison, and he was soon deported. Then in 1307, now seventy-five, Llull sailed to Bugia, Algeria, further west along the North African coast, and tried again. When he started to preach, he was attacked by a mob. He would have been torn apart had not authorities arrested him.[77] His experience contrasts starkly with Francis's more prudent approach in Egypt about eighty-five years earlier.

Llull was imprisoned for about six months. When he could, even in prison, he held debates and discussions with Muslim leaders "who were amazed at his sincerity and constancy." But eventually he was again deported.[78]

Several years passed. Then at age eighty-two Ramon sailed again to Bugia, not expecting to return. This time he was more tolerantly received. He went on to Tunis, where he was now allowed to preach and hold debates and travel around to villages, as Francis had done in Italy. "For a few months, the holy old man with the long white beard became a loved and revered figure, and no opposition was offered to him. Indeed, he is said to have made a number of converts, and he continued to write books, one of which he dedicated to the Mufti of Tunis."[79] He felt called, however, to return to Bugia, where he had earlier been assaulted. As soon as he attempted to preach Christ, he was attacked and killed, perhaps stoned. He was then about eight-four.[80]

Missions historian Alan Neely writes, "Lull is significant for his extensive writings designed to persuade believers and non-Christians, especially Muslims, of the truth of the Christian faith; for the college established on Majorca for training missionaries in Arabic language and philosophy; and for his determined missionary efforts in the Muslim world."[81] Llull founded the first Franciscan missionary college at Majorca

---

[76] Moorman, *History of the Franciscan Order*, 224–25, 230.

[77] Moorman, *History of the Franciscan Order*, 231.

[78] Moorman, *History of the Franciscan Order*, 231.

[79] Moorman, *History of the Franciscan Order*, 231.

[80] Moorman, *History of the Franciscan Order*, 232. Accounts differ on details and dates and whether Llull was actually martyred.

[81] Neely, "Lull, Raymund," 415. There are several biographies of Llull including one by the Protestant Reformed missionary Samuel Zwemer (1867–1952), *Raymund Lull: First Missionary to the Moslems* (New York: Funk & Wagnalls, 1902).

about 1276, which focused primarily on the study of Arabic.[82] He was influential in promoting the study of Arabic at several European universities.[83]

The remarkable lives of Roger Bacon, Duns Scotus, Ramon Llull, and others like them give us a broader picture of the life and witness of Francis of Assisi.

Franciscan contributions to science, philosophy, and literature would only grow and expand in coming centuries. Many of the greatest scholars and scientists throughout history have been devout Jesus followers, and a surprising number of these were Franciscans. Lazaro Iriarte names more than thirty significant Franciscan scholars from the thirteenth, fourteenth, and fifteenth centuries, most largely unknown today. These include John of Marchena, "a cosmographer who worked in collaboration with Columbus" (along with several other Franciscans) and Cardinal Jimenez de Cisneros (1436–1517), founder of the University of Alcalá, who with a team of scholars published the monumental six-volume *Biblia Sacra Polyglotta* containing Scriptures in Hebrew, Aramaic, Latin, and Greek (including the Septuagint)—the first printed polyglot Bible.[84]

Another notable Franciscan was Luca Pacioli (c. 1447–1517), often called the father of accounting and bookkeeping. Pacioli was a brilliant mathematician who popularized the use of algebra and was a colleague and friend of Leonardo da Vinci.[85]

What Did Francis Think?

During Francis's lifetime, Lesser Brothers were winning reputations throughout Europe and beyond for their writings and scholarship. What did poor Francis make of this?

Watching the rising scholarship and relatedly the growing clericalization of his Lesser Brothers during his final years, Francis was of two minds. On the one hand, he believed priests and scholars should

---

[82] Huber, *Documented History,* 779. According to this source, the college lasted only about twenty years. Huber calls Llull "a great scientist, chemist, and alchemist" ("alchemist" here meaning a blending of chemistry and mysticism). Huber, 883.

[83] *The Oxford Dictionary of the Christian Church* notes that Llull's "one practical success was the decree of the Council of Vienne (1311–12) establishing *studia* of oriental languages in five universities." Livingstone, *Oxford Dictionary of the Christian Church,* 990.

[84] Iriarte, *Franciscan History,* 159–61 (quotation from p. 161).

[85] Walter Isaacson, *Leonardo da Vinci* (New York: Simon & Schuster, 2017), 201–6; see also Iriarte, *Franciscan History,* 161, 367.

be respected and honored. They had an authorized role in the church. On the other hand, Francis clearly saw the spiritual dangers of academia and of his Order becoming an elite ecclesial class. How could Franciscans faithfully continue to be "lesser brothers" if they were honored scholars?

As more and more students and professors were becoming Franciscan brothers, some of his companions asked Francis what he thought. Was he concerned that more and more brothers were devoting so much time to studying Scripture and philosophy?

Francis replied (as quoted by Bonaventure), "I am indeed pleased, as long as, after the example of Christ, of whom we read that he prayed more than he read, they do not neglect zeal for prayer; and, as long as they study, not to know what they should say, but to practice what they have heard and, once they have put it into practice, propose it to others. I want my brothers to be Gospel disciples and so progress in the knowledge of the truth that they increase in pure simplicity without separating the simplicity of the dove from the wisdom of the serpent."[86]

But Francis had his doubts. He knew scholarship meant books, which were expensive in this age before printing and all books hand-copied. And books meant libraries, and libraries meant universities and, often, status and power.

Also, tensions were rising among the Franciscans themselves. As they took on more and more scholarly and pastoral functions, some brothers felt the Franciscan Rule was too limiting. Pressure for relaxing the internal Franciscan disciplines began to build.

Brother Riccerio, "noble by birth and more noble by holiness" and much loved by Francis, is a good example. Francis was staying at the bishop's palace in Assisi due to his illnesses. One day, Brother Riccerio asked Francis his opinion about the present condition of the Order. Riccerio was himself a priest. He wanted to know what Francis thought about the direction the Franciscan community seemed headed. "I want to be sure of your intention and of your first and last wish," Riccerio said, "so that we, cleric brothers who have many books, may keep them although we will say that they belong to the religion [that is, the Franciscan order]?"

Francis replied, "I tell you, brother, that it has been and is my first and last intention and will, if the brothers would only heed it, that no brother

---

[86] Bonaventure, *Major Legend of Saint Francis*, FA:ED 2:612–13. This is Bonaventure's collage or summary of similar things Francis said on various occasions as quoted in Thomas of Celano, *Remembrance of the Desire of a Soul*.

should have anything except a tunic as the *Rule* allows us, together with a cord and underwear." In other words, strict adherence to the Rule, no compromises. It is striking that Riccerio freely admitted that he and other brothers had "many books" and that they freely fell back on the excuse that technically the books belonged to the Order, not to them personally.

Why then had Francis not strictly enforced the Rule on this point? In effect, he wanted to avoid conflict. Francis "did not want to argue," so he gave in to the brothers' wishes, "although not willingly," says the *Assisi Compilation*. For himself, however, to maintain fidelity to God's call, he would continue to obey the Rule strictly, both out of obedience and to teach the brothers by example. The Order now was in God's hands.[87]

Francis's original intention was that the brothers not own books or buildings at all. Over time, however, benefactors donated church buildings and residences. So, Francis wrote in his *Testament*, "Let the brothers be careful not to receive in any way churches or poor dwellings or anything else built for them unless they are according to the holy poverty we have promised in the Rule. As pilgrims and strangers, let them always be guests there."[88] In other words, use them if you must, but do not own.

Franciscan residences and centers in university towns gradually grew more elaborate—necessarily so, Franciscan scholars felt. Back in Assisi, Francis often told his brothers, "Here lies my pain and grief: those things which I received from God by His mercy with great effort of prayer and meditation for the present and future good of [our order], and which are, as He assures me, in accordance with His will, some of the brothers on the authority and support of their knowledge nullify and oppose me saying, 'These things must be kept and observed; but not those!'" Selective obedience! The *Assisi Compilation* adds that Francis, however, "because he feared scandal so much . . . permitted many things to happen and gave in to their will, in many things that were not according to his will."[89]

Francis was also very clear, always, that he did not want the brothers to hold church office. He emphasized this to Hugolino, Bishop of Ostia, the future Pope Gregory IX. "My lord," Francis said, "my brothers are called 'lesser' precisely so they will not presume to *become 'greater'* [Matt. 20:26]. They have been called this to teach them to stay down to

---

[87] *Assisi Compilation*, FA:ED 2:204–6; *Mirror of Perfection* (Sabatier ed.), FA:ED 3:255–56.

[88] Francis, *The Testament*, FA:ED 1:126.

[89] *Assisi Compilation*, FA:ED 2:212–13. Similarly, *Mirror of Perfection* (Sabatier ed.), FA:ED 3:265.

earth, and to follow the footprints of Christ's humility, which in the end will exalt them above others in the sight of the saints. If you want them to bear fruit in the Church of God," he told the bishop, "keep them in the status in which they were called and hold them to it."[90]

Every Franciscan was called to be a Lesser Brother. To be a great scholar and a Lesser Brother was a complex challenge. As an Order, the Franciscans would wrestle with this for decades—not only in Italy and throughout Europe, but eventually to the ends of the Earth.

---

[90] *Assisi Compilation*, FA:ED 2:148. Similarly, Thomas of Celano, *Remembrance*, FA:ED 2:342–43; *Mirror of Perfection* (Sabatier ed.), FA:ED 3:289. In the sources, these comments are part of a larger conversation Hugolino had with Francis and Dominic (founder of the Dominicans) when the two were the bishop's guests in Rome. Whether the exchange as presented is historically accurate, Francis's statement certainly expresses his views and preferences. The editors of *Francis of Assisi: The Founder* note, "This incident has not been recorded in early Dominican sources." FA:ED 2:148 n. a.

18

New Age of the Spirit?

The New Age of the Spirit has dawned! Earth's last chapter starts now! And the Little Brothers of Saint Francis are the sign, herald, and seal of the New Age!

This is what many Franciscans and others across Europe were saying and hoping in the 1260s. The Order continued growing rapidly. Prophetic voices, notably Joachim of Fiore, saw this growth in apocalyptic terms.

The Franciscans were growing not only in number but also in popularity, influence, and wealth. In the late 1200s, "assured of their important role in the Church and buoyed by their popularity, Franciscans embarked on a course of aggressive ministerial expansion. Large and impressive churches were built to accommodate the throngs of worshippers and to display God's blessings on the Order." New Franciscan church buildings were erected in Siena, Florence, Pisa, and London between 1289 and 1306. "To a great extent, this expansion was due to increased papal favor," expanding Franciscan permission to preach widely and to hear confessions. This inevitably "had an impact on the brothers' life-style" as they had larger and grander facilities, expanded financial support, and increasingly complex organization.[1]

These changes sparked criticism. Pope Clement V was very specific in *Exivi de Paradiso* of 1312, calling out Franciscan excesses. Clement named a dozen practices needing correcting: Maintaining "extensive gardens [and] large vineyards, from which they garner such quantities of vegetables and wine that they can put them up for sale."

---

[1] Editorial introduction to the bull *Exultantes in Domino* of Pope Martin IV (1283), in *Francis of Assisi: Early Documents*, ed. Regis J. Armstrong, OFM Cap., J. A. Wayne Hellmann, OFM Conv., and William J. Short, OFM (New York: New City Press, 2001), 3:764 [hereafter FA:ED].

"That they build churches and other buildings, or have them built, of such size, style, and costliness that they seem to be the abodes of the wealthy, not the poor.

"That the brothers in very many places also have so many church furnishings and so obviously expensive ones as to surpass ... even great cathedral churches." These brothers, "who have severed themselves from temporal possessions by such an exceptional renunciation [as specified in the *Rule*], must abstain from all that is or may seem to be incompatible with this renunciation."[2]

That the pope should need to make such an obvious point shows how far Franciscans had drifted—and how upset those brothers were who were determined to remain faithful to Lady Poverty.

Many Franciscans at the forefront of the Order's growing influence and popularity saw no problem. People were flocking to their churches and centers (some of which today could be called megachurches). More and more people thought the Franciscans were indeed the heralds of a new age of renewal.

Joachim of Fiore, whom we encountered earlier, was born in 1135, half a century before Francis. Becoming a Cistercian monk and eventually abbot, Joachim devoted much time to studying biblical prophecy. By his death in 1202, Joachim's ideas were sparking wide interest.

Joachim claimed the New Age was on the horizon. Many Franciscan brothers saw this as a true revelation. But other brothers said, No way! Definitely not. Maybe even heresy. Remember Francis! By 1250 and on into the early 1300s, Franciscans were battling clashing visions. This would lead more to division than renewal.

The Problem of Brother Elias

With Francis's death, the exponential growth of the Order, and the brothers' new scholarly and ecclesial roles, the nature of the Franciscan movement shifted quickly. Tensions grew between the rising number of scholarly Franciscans and the often less-educated brothers serving local parishes or leading contemplative lives in hermitages and small Franciscan communities, as we have seen.

Already in 1220, years before his death, Francis turned over leadership to others. He named Peter Catani as his successor (as noted in chapter 8). When Peter died just months later, Francis then turned

---

[2] Pope Clement V, *Exivi de Paradiso*, FA:ED 3:777–78.

to Brother Elias, a decision confirmed in the Chapter of 1221. Francis continued to be active by word and example, but Elias quickly picked up the administrative reins.

Six years later, in 1227—the year after Francis's death—John Parenti succeeded Elias. John served until 1232, but then Elias was reelected. Meanwhile during the intervening years Elias continued active in the Assisi area. "His little town, which he loved so much," Moorman writes, "was to be made one of the great centres of pilgrimage for the whole world, equal to such places as Rome, Jerusalem, and Compostela."[3] When Elias returned as minister general in 1232, he got his chance.

For nearly two decades—1221 to 1239—Brother Elias was the dominant Franciscan leader in and around Assisi. Officially he was minister general from 1221 to 1227 and from 1232 to 1239. But Elias, a born networker, had growing influence well before Francis's death and during the generalship of John Parenti (1227–1232).[4]

Capable as he was, Elias proved to be a problem. Many brothers soon distrusted him, believing he was betraying the very life to which they were called.

Elias came from a well-to-do noble family in the Assisi area. He had a winsome, persuasive manner and was highly capable and goal oriented. He was well educated, having attended the University of Bologna. He already had an established life by the time Francis began forming his community. He had been a mattress maker and a teacher, and perhaps served as Assisi's first consul or magistrate.[5]

Elias was thus not one of the very first brothers. Before he was a Franciscan he may have been married and had a son. Perhaps his wife then died, prompting him to seek out the Lesser Brothers. In the spring or summer of 1211 Elias became a Franciscan brother. Almost immediately his influence was felt.[6]

---

[3] John Moorman, *A History of the Franciscan Order: From Its Origins to the Year 1517* (Oxford: Oxford University Press, 1968), 85.

[4] Moorman, *History of the Franciscan Order,* 23, 84. John Parenti, a lawyer in Florence, was converted under Francis and together with his son joined the Order in its early days. A man of character and deep spirituality, John led the brothers ably for five years. See Rosalind B. Brooke, *Early Franciscan Government: Elias to Bonaventure* (Cambridge: Cambridge University Press, 1959), chap. 3, "The Character and Significance of John Parenti," 123–36.

[5] Arnaldo Fortini, *Francis of Assisi*, trans. Helen Moak (New York: Crossroad Publishing, 1992), 121. Or possibly it was Elias's father who was first consul. Brooke, *Early Franciscan Government*, 50–51.

[6] Fortini, *Francis of Assisi,* 121; Moorman, *History of the Franciscan Order,* 23, 96.

As minister general, Elias was an effective promoter of the Order as a well-run, far-flung organization. He encouraged young men to join, and as the Order grew, he formed more provinces. He urged new missions to far-off regions. He encouraged the brothers to study and to form new communities and ministries wherever they could.[7]

While Francis was alive, Elias behaved as a proper Lesser Brother. "But with Francis dead," Englebert writes, "he threw off all reserve. He never went anywhere save on horseback, dined at a separate table, ate choice viands, kept a special cook for his own use, and a dozen servants, dismissed and replaced [provincial ministers] according to his good pleasure, scattered and persecuted those [devout brothers who remained] faithful to the spirit of the Portiuncula, and, too occupied with his building projects and embassies to visit the transalpine provinces, he sent substitutes charged with imposing his will with an iron hand and carrying out his vengeances."[8] Elias seems to have seen himself as the Franciscan parallel to the pope. He acted virtually as supreme pontiff of the Order, endued with wide prerogatives Francis never intended. And yet Elias had been "a staunch friend, full of affection and tender care for the saint in his sickness and weakness. During the last months of Francis' life Elias was with him constantly, and knelt by him when he died."[9]

Elias promoted nonordained ("lay") Franciscan brothers to positions of leadership, including as provincial ministers, wanting to check the growing power of priests, scholars, and university professors within the Order. This was a way of increasing his own influence. He held only one General Chapter during his whole tenure! This meant there was no organizational check on his decisions.[10]

As soon as Francis was canonized in 1228, Elias pressed ahead in building the saint's two-level grand Basilica in Assisi. He encouraged large donations from wealthy patrons and "ordered levies upon the whole Order to complete the work."[11] The Lower Church was finished about the end of 1230, and work began immediately on the Upper Church. This was completed in 1236, though it was later further modified and made yet more ornate. Large cycles of frescoes by Giotto

---

[7] Omer Englebert, *Saint Francis of Assisi*, 2nd English ed., trans. Eve Marie Cooper (Chicago: Franciscan Herald Press, 1965), 250.

[8] Englebert, *Saint Francis*, 250. Englebert adds details.

[9] Moorman, *History of the Franciscan Order*, 96.

[10] Moorman, *History of the Franciscan Order*, 97–99.

[11] *The Chronicle of Brother Jordan of Giano*, in Placid Herman OFM, trans. and ed., *XIIIth Century Chronicles* (Chicago: Franciscan Herald Press, 1961), 64.

and others covered the walls and ceilings, as noted earlier.[12] At the far end of the massive basilica and down the steep hillside below, a large convent was built, "a magnificent home for the friars who served the church and kept the shrine."[13]

The Basilica of Saint Francis, dwarfing all church buildings in Assisi, was significant in several respects. Moorman writes,

> The whole structure marks a turning-point in the development of Italian architecture; but it also marks a crisis in the Order. If the Portiuncula, or San Damiano, or the rock-hewn caves [above Assisi where Francis often prayed] represent the poverty and humility of Francis and the early disciples, the great basilica represents the security and stability of the later days. The [basilica] has been described as 'the tomb of the Mendicant and the cradle of the Renaissance'. But it is more than the tomb of the Mendicant [Francis], for it is in a sense also that of his bride, the Lady Poverty.[14]

Whatever his good qualities, Elias thus began to undermine Franciscan simplicity. When he was elected, he told the brothers his health was poor and he wasn't able to lead the austere life of poverty that Francis taught. The brothers were shocked at Elias's self-indulgence. "He went about very little except to the houses of the great. In his own quarters he was surrounded by valets in livery." Whenever he traveled, he was accompanied by "a small retinue of chosen [brothers], all mounted on sleek horses." Elias claimed that in his position, he was not bound by Francis's Rule. "He lived in a luxurious manner, to the consternation not only of the brethren but of the world as a whole. The Order suffered as a result. The ideals of S. Francis were being dragged down."[15]

Bernardo, Francis's earliest companion, was especially appalled. One day Bernardo took plate and knife in hand and walked into Elias's dining room. Sitting down beside Elias, Bernardo said, "I think I'd like some of this good food."[16]

---

[12] Moorman, *History of the Franciscan Order,* 99, 278–79.

[13] Moorman, *History of the Franciscan Order,* 99.

[14] Moorman, *History of the Franciscan Order,* 99–100. Moorman is quoting from G. Golubovich, Biblioteca Bio-bibliografica della Terra Santa e dell'Oriente Francescano, 4 vols. (1906–27), 1:113.

[15] Moorman, *History of the Franciscan Order,* 100.

[16] Moorman, *History of the Franciscan Order,* 100.

Pressure gradually mounted for Elias to resign or be replaced. Two prominent Franciscan professors at the University of Paris, Alexander of Hales and John of La Rochelle, decided something must be done. Other brothers joined with them and began lodging complaints with the pope. English brothers meeting in provincial chapter in Oxford unanimously sent an appeal to Rome against Elias.[17]

Finally at Pentecost 1239, Pope Gregory IX—Francis's old friend Cardinal Hugolino, now about ninety-two—himself called a Franciscan General Chapter in Rome. Seven cardinals in addition to the Franciscans were present. Brother Thomas of Eccleston reports that "after a long consultation, brothers were chosen from the whole Order to provide for [its] reformation." This commission reported to the General Chapter, Pope Gregory presiding.[18]

Brother Haymo of Faversham and other brothers also reported their concerns about Elias. Some brothers defended him. Elias himself became angry and accused his critics of lying. He had never really pledged himself to the Rule, he said, and shouldn't be held to it.

The discussion grew heated. Pope Gregory silenced everyone. "This is not the way of religious," he said, and he sat silent for some minutes. The bishop of Ostia (later Pope Alexander IV) told Elias he should resign, but he publicly refused.

Finally, the pope spoke. He commended Elias for the good he had done and his devotion to Francis. But he was no longer acceptable to the brothers, Gregory said, and immediately removed Elias from office. "There was such immense and inexpressible joy" among the brothers that they "said they had never seen anything like it."[19]

Brother Albert of Pisa was elected to replace Elias.[20] Elias, however, went from bad to worse, amply proving his own character flaws. He traveled to the hilltop town of Cortona in Tuscany, where he had friends. He got involved politically in the affairs of Emperor Frederick II, whom Elias had known for some time, but whom Pope Gregory had excommunicated. He repeatedly visited the community of Clares in Cortona, which was against the Franciscan Rule. Albert of Pisa, the new general minister, ordered Elias to stop, but he refused. Elias

---

[17] Thomas of Eccleston, *The Coming of the Friars Minor to England* [c. 1258], in Herman, *XIIIth Century Chronicles*, 133.

[18] Eccleston, *Coming of the Friars Minor*, 154.

[19] Eccleston, *Coming of the Friars Minor*, 155.

[20] Moorman, *History of the Franciscan Order*, 101.

went to the court of Frederick II in Sicily, which made him subject to excommunication. Finally, Pope Gregory did excommunicate him.[21]

Concerned for both Elias and for the Order's reputation, Lesser Brothers tried to persuade him to repent and reconcile with the church. Elias refused, saying he did not want to lose the good graces of Frederick II. Finally, in the spring of 1253, Elias "fell ill and realized that his end was near. Then, and then only, did he show real signs of submission. He made his confession to the archpriest of Cortona, and on Holy Saturday he was absolved. He received the Blessed Sacrament on Easter Monday."[22] Elias died the next day, April 22, 1253. He was about seventy-two.

Elias was a capable and experienced leader, but he never fully shared Francis's spirit or vision. He was committed to Francis personally as a friend but not to his vision of discipleship. Elias oversaw the building of the St. Francis Basilica, perhaps reminding us of Jesus's words to the Pharisees: "You build the tombs of the prophets and decorate the graves of the righteous," while "inside you are full of hypocrisy and lawlessness" (Matt. 23:28–29).

Here is another *crucial issue of renewal*.[23] What happens when a movement falters? When leadership deviates from its own high calling? Unless the movement is functioning within a larger structure that holds it accountable, it can fail, betray itself. Yet if the broader authority is too heavy-handed or unsympathetic, its authority can squash the movement and its needed reforms.

For the Franciscans, linkage with the papacy was critical at several key points—above all, two: Pope Innocent III's initial approval of Francis and his Rule, and now in 1239, some thirty years later, when Brother Elias as general minister betrayed the very call and charism of the Lesser

---

[21] Moorman, *History of the Franciscan Order,* 101–2.

[22] Moorman, *History of the Franciscan Order,* 102–3. According to *The Deeds of Francis and His Companions,* Elias's own brother, who also was a Franciscan (though not a priest), appealed to Elias. His brother told him, "I am deeply saddened that you're excommunicated and will die without the habit outside the Order." Elias said his only hope was that his brother appeal directly to the pope, which his brother did. The brother "went from the Kingdom of Sicily to the pope and humbly asked, for the love of Christ and Saint Francis," to absolve Elias. "And it happened that, by divine permission and with the help of Saint Francis's prayers, the Lord Pope granted to that brother that, if he found Brother Elias alive, he should absolve him, on his behalf, from the excommunication and return the habit to him." Elias's brother returned and found Elias still alive. "Receiving the papal absolution, and with his habit returned, Elias passed to the Lord." Ugolino Boniscambi, *The Deeds of Blessed Francis and His Companions,* FA:ED 3:554.

[23] See chapter 20 on patterns of church renewal.

Brothers.[24] Fortunately the current pope, Gregory IX, was a man of insight and dedication who understood Francis and knew the church needed the Franciscans' renewing energy.

From Elias to Bonaventure

Four ministers general led the Order between 1239 and 1257—Albert of Pisa for just one year (1239–1240), the English brother Haymo of Faversham (1240–1244), Crescentius of Iesi (1244–1247), and John of Parma (1247–1257). Then begins the long tenure of Bonaventure of Bagnoreggio (1257–1274), later Saint Bonaventure.[25] Much as Francis was the most significant and formative leader until his death in 1226, Bonaventure was the most capable and shaping leader from 1257 till his death seventeen years later. Bonaventure's strong influence continued in the Order well into later decades.

Moorman notes,

> During the eighteen years from Elias to Bonaventure the Order was trying to find its level. It had to discover what its own nature was to be [now] and what was to be its relation to the rest of the Church. It had inherited from S. Francis an ideal which was only partially expressed in the official Rule, but which was supplemented on one side by the Testament and the memories of the saint preserved by men like Leo, Angelo, and Rufino, and on the other side by capitular decrees and papal pronouncements. The Rule was the only thing to which the friars were obliged to give their obedience and loyalty, but it needed a good deal of interpretation and expansion if it was to meet the needs of the day.[26]

The issue causing the most dissension within the Order was Francis's insistence on radical poverty. Everyone knew the brothers were called to total poverty, possession-lessness. But what did that mean in practice? This is ironic, because Francis was certainly clear as to what it meant— certainly in the Rule, and even more in his *Testament*. But as the Order grew and more and more brothers were scholars or took on other public

---

[24] As we have seen, the papacy (as long as it favored genuine reform) protected the Franciscans from university politics in Paris and appointed Franciscan brothers as missionaries to the Mongols and Chinese. On the other hand, some popes used the brothers for political purposes with which Francis would have been very uncomfortable and in support of military crusades against Muslims and heretics that Francis viewed as wrong-headed.

[25] Moorman, *History of the Franciscan Order,* 489.

[26] Moorman, *History of the Franciscan Order,* 116.

roles, absolute poverty was simply impossible. Scholars needed books and writing materials and stable residences.

Gregory IX and other popes recognized this. Some compromises and adjustments were needed; some already were being made. Gregory IX issued the bull *Quo elongati* in 1230 and Innocent IV issued *Ordinem vestrum* in 1245, both addressing questions of interpretation of the Rule and allowing some relaxations. Other papal pronouncements were also issued during this fifteen-year period. Gregory IX decreed that Francis's *Testament,* though it clearly expressed Francis's intention, was not binding. The brothers must not own property, said the pope, but others could hold it for them, for their use. The papacy itself could hold property for Franciscan benefit. Thus, the brothers could "use" things they needed without "owning" them—utensils, furniture, books, and so forth. Innocent IV in *Ordinem vestrum* went further, saying that representatives ("spiritual friends") outside the Order could hold money for the brothers, not only for "necessity" but also for "convenience." As Moorman notes, this "opened the door to all kinds of relaxations"; "necessities" was fairly clear, but just about anything could be a "convenience."[27]

The brothers themselves, dispersed in their many scattered provinces, debated how the Rule was to be interpreted in a range of diverse cases. Some argued the Rule should be interpreted in a "spiritual" more than literal sense. But what did that mean? In practice, a growing range of opinion developed as to what Franciscan poverty really meant. For many, this was a sincere quest. But with the Order's mushrooming growth, inevitably some brothers sought loopholes (as did Brother Elias) that would allow them to live in comfort and self-indulgence way beyond what Francis would ever have allowed. Such brothers began to tarnish the high public regard in which Franciscans were held, leading in time to the stereotypical figure of jovial, rotund, ale-loving Friar Tuck in the Robin Hood stories and other tales of lax friars in the late Middle Ages.[28]

Franciscan simplicity was further tarnished by the influx of money. Funds flowed to the Franciscans from three sources: indulgences, benefactions, and so-called Letters of Fraternity. In the 1240s, popes began granting indulgences to people who gave money to build friaries—remission of the penalties of sin in exchange for money donations or acts of penance. This evolved rapidly into a fundraising system. Popes granted indulgences for contributions to the building of Franciscan convents and schools.

---

[27] Moorman, *History of the Franciscan Order,* 117.
[28] See https://en.wikipedia.org/wiki/Friar_Tuck.

A second major money source was legacies, "pious benefactions." Wealthy people left money or property to the Franciscans in exchange for prayers to be said for them after they died.[29] Moorman notes that "whereas some of the friars were gratified at the easy way in which money was thus acquired, others were distressed at what seemed an obvious breach of the vow of poverty."[30]

The practice of Letters of Fraternity began about 1254. For a fee, a man or woman could arrange to be buried in a Franciscan habit and have the brothers pray for their souls after death. Like indulgences and benefactions, this practice spread across Europe. Many Franciscan communities were no longer poor.[31] Such practices among not only Franciscans but also other monastic orders of both men and women— fed in part by the doctrine of purgatory—led eventually to the corruption of many monasteries and to the mounting discontent that led to the Protestant Reformation in the 1500s.

Franciscan communities were looking more and more like the older religious orders. They grew increasingly status conscious. More distinguished brothers stopped taking their meals in the common refectory and began dining "in the infirmary or some other place where the ordinary rules and customs did not apply."[32]

In multiple ways, then, Franciscan communities and the daily practices of the brothers looked less and less like the fraternity of poor brothers that Francis originally created.

The Emergence of Bonaventure

Bonaventure of Bagnoreggio now played a key role. He became a Lesser Brother in 1243 at about age twenty-six while a student at the University of Paris.[33] We met him briefly as a child in chapter 5 and noted his leadership of the Franciscan Order in Chapter 18.

---

[29] In London in 1350, William de Trumpeton in his will left "[diverse] sums of money to religious orders in London and Cambridge for the benefit of his soul." Many benefactors left legacies to the Franciscans (and other orders), and often requested burial in the churches of the Lesser Brothers. See John R. H. Moorman, *The Grey Friars in Cambridge 1225–1538* (Cambridge: Cambridge University Press, 1952), 246–58.

[30] Moorman, *History of the Franciscan Order*, 119.

[31] See Moorman, *History of the Franciscan Order*, 119–20.

[32] Moorman, *History of the Franciscan Order*, 121.

[33] Ewert Cousins, "Introduction," in Ewert Cousins, trans. and ed., *Bonaventure: The Soul's Journey into God, The Tree of Life, the Life of St. Francis* (New York: Paulist Press, 1978), 2.

At Paris, Bonaventure's personal and academic star rose rapidly. He immersed himself in theology under the renowned Alexander of Hales. Alexander had himself become a Franciscan several years earlier.[34]

Bonaventure was licensed to teach in 1248 (Bachelor of Scripture) and began public lectures. He taught Scripture, producing his own *Commentary on the Sentences of Peter Lombard*, which became the basis of much of his teaching. He received his doctorate in theology in 1254 and was appointed head of the Franciscan school at Paris. Now a recognized university professor, his renown continued to grow.[35]

In 1257, at age forty, Bonaventure was elected Franciscan minister general, seventh in the line from Francis. This meant he had to resign his university position. But he still spent much time in Paris, "some of his best [theological] work being done during these years."[36] Moorman notes,

> In order to understand S. Bonaventure, it is necessary to remember that, besides being a distinguished philosopher and theologian, with a clear and penetrating mind, he was also a mystic and a saint. He was a peacemaker; and, as head of his Order, he knew that one of his chief responsibilities was to restore unity among the friars, and, if possible, convince the world that it was possible to be a theologian and a scholar and yet remain faithful to the ideals of St. Francis.[37]

Through his seventeen-year tenure as minister general, Bonaventure had a long-lasting shaping influence on the Order. His leadership finally ended with his death in 1274 at Lyon, France. Much of his tenure was occupied with resolving conflicts both within the Order and without. The internal conflict was the ongoing one about a more strict or more lenient interpretation of the Rule. But it involved also issues of eschatology and the apocalyptic teachings of Joachim of Fiore. The external controversies also concerned Joachim's teachings and relations between the Franciscans and the university.

Cousins notes that Bonaventure "favored a moderate position, attempting to be faithful to the ideals of Francis while developing the Order along institutional lines. In his interpretation of poverty,

---

[34] Cousins, *Bonaventure*, 3; E. A. Livingstone, ed., *The Oxford Dictionary of the Christian Church*, 3rd ed. (Oxford: Oxford University Press, 1997), 39.

[35] Cousins, *Bonaventure*, 6.

[36] Moorman, *History of the Franciscan Order*, 133.

[37] Moorman, *History of the Franciscan Order*, 245–46.

he allowed for adaptation and evolution as the Order expanded," promoting at once simplicity, spiritual depth, and profound learning. Bonaventure's leadership was so decisive that he is sometimes called the Order's second founder.[38]

Bonaventure once made an illuminating comment about his connection with Francis and the Rule. "I confess before God that what made me love Saint Francis's way of life so much was that it is exactly like the origin and the perfection of the Church itself, which began first with simple fishermen and afterwards developed to include the most illustrious and learned doctors. You will find the same thing in the Order of Saint Francis."[39]

Bonaventure's tenure as minister general marks a decisive transition in the Franciscan Order and ethos. The change was gradual, but it came to a head during his oversight. Bonaventure wrote his own biography of Francis, drawing on earlier sources and then suppressing earlier ones. He wrote two accounts of Francis, in fact: *The Major Legend of Saint Francis* and *The Minor Legend of Saint Francis* (both completed in 1263). He also wrote several sermons on Francis. His various writings on Francis run to some 257 pages in volume two of *Francis of Assisi: Early Documents*.

Bonaventure wanted his own interpretation of Francis to predominate, and it mostly did. He pictured Francis as the perfect embodiment of all the virtues of Jesus Christ, culminating in the *stigmata*. Francis's whole life, "from the time of his conversion, was adorned with the remarkable mysteries of the cross of Christ," Bonaventure wrote.[40] The editors of *Francis of Assisi: Early Documents* note that this focus on Christ's virtues manifested in Francis "are key to understanding Bonaventure's hagiographic hermeneutic."[41] Bonaventure's writings on Francis are indeed hagiographic: he highlighted and sometimes embellished Francis's life and actions and virtues. He did, however, base his writings on the early and more reliable sources and thus mostly avoided the extreme spiritualizing of much later writing on Francis.

---

[38] Cousins, *Bonaventure*, 6–7.
[39] Bonaventure, "A Letter in Response to an Unknown Master," in *Works of Saint Bonaventure: Writings Concerning the Franciscan Order*, introduction and trans. Dominic Monti (St. Bonaventure, NY: Franciscan Institute Publications, 1994), 54, quoted in Bonaventure, *Major Legend of Saint Francis*, FA:ED 2:621 n. a. Cousins also quotes this, but with his own translation from the Latin. Cousins, *Bonaventure*, 6.
[40] Bonaventure, *The Minor Legend of Saint Francis*, FA:ED 2:713.
[41] Editorial footnote to Bonaventure, *The Minor Legend of Saint Francis*, FA:ED 2:712. For this reason, I used Bonaventure's writings on Francis as a supplemental, never primary, source in writing about Francis's life.

Bonaventure did indeed become a great theologian, equal in stature to Thomas Aquinas, his Paris contemporary. Like Aquinas, Bonaventure's theology has organization and structure. He was fond of numbering and elaborating his points and insights. He never saw a simple truth he couldn't complexify, draw out, explain more deeply. But he didn't try to reconcile all theology with Aristotle's philosophy the way Aquinas did.

Bonaventure did have a great flair for complicating and "complexifying" simple things—of turning everything into a system, even (and especially) things mystical. He was brilliant, learned, and very clever. After his death he was soon declared a saint, for he led a godly life. But viewing Francis through Bonaventure's lens runs the danger of missing the very simplicity of Francis's life and Francis's focus on daily living, not only on the cross.

Not everything in life must be turned into a "deeper" or "higher" or more obviously "spiritual" truth. We will remember this when we later consider what we can learn from Francis today.

Order versus Division

After Bonaventure, the Franciscan Order was essentially the Order as Bonaventure conceived it. And yet across the Order's dozens of provinces, the Franciscan vision remained contested. Many brothers wanted the Order to stay just as it was under Francis—just as the Rule specified, without compromise or "gloss." This sentiment rang strong especially outside the university centers. The issue was, still, a strict or a more accommodating interpretation of the Rule. Debates and tensions were further complicated by the influence of Joachim's apocalyptic visions.

Controversy and disagreement among and between the various groups of brothers centered in several interrelated issues. These issues (as summarized by the editors of *Francis of Assisi: Early Documents*) come up repeatedly: "the practice of poverty, the role of learning, the pursuit of primitive observance, and the place of Our Lady of the Portiuncula"— that is, the centrality and moral authority of the original Franciscan center and community at Assisi.[42]

Joachim and the Three Ages

The apocalyptic ideas of Joachim of Fiore began to catch on throughout much of the church in the decades after Francis. Joachim died when Francis was just a child of about ten. But his dispensational interpretation

---

[42] Introduction, *A Collection of Sayings of the Companions of Blessed Francis,* FA:ED 3:110.

of history grew increasingly popular and influential as the Lesser Brothers were growing so rapidly.

In his *Harmony of the Old and New Testament* and other writings, Joachim worked out a theory of three ages of history. When in 1254 the Franciscan brother Gerard of Borgo San Donnino published his summary of Joachim's ideas in *Introduction to the Everlasting Gospel*, Joachim's ideas spread quickly within and beyond the Order.[43] Gerard identified the Franciscans themselves as the harbingers and firstfruits of the coming New Age.

The Old Testament was the age of the Father, Joachim said. The New Testament and the church comprised the age of the Son. We should expect a new age of the Spirit, an era of renewal. This new age was just now dawning. It would bring the full flowering of the gospel promise, a dispensation of love in which people enjoyed intimate fellowship with God. The church's monastic orders, filled with the Spirit, would play the leading role, largely replacing the church's hierarchy. Many people easily saw the growing Franciscan movement as the dawning edge of this New Spirit Age.

Joachim was inventive in his ideas and biblical mathematics. Citing several passages in Revelation, Joachim concluded that the New Age of the Spirit would begin around the year 1260. Working with patterns of twos and threes, sevens and twelves, Joachim proposed a theory of three great ages of history corresponding to the persons of the Trinity. The three ages would eventually lead to a final fourth: the age of Trinitarian consummation.[44]

Joachim said new religious orders would arise in the Third Age. These would convert the world and bring about a truly spiritual church (*ecclesia spiritualis*). Understandably, the Franciscans and Dominicans saw themselves as beginning to fulfill Joachim's prophecy. Many others, longing for church renewal and the full coming of Christ's kingdom, agreed.[45]

---

[43] Joachim was the abbot of an obscure Cistercian monastery who around the age of fifty received spiritual insights through which he elaborated views on the relationship between the two Testaments, the meaning of the Trinity, and the nature of history. Later he founded his own Order of St. John (San Giovanni) at Fiore in a remote mountain plateau in Calabria.

[44] For a summary of Joachim and his influence, see Howard A. Snyder, *Models of the Kingdom* (Nashville, TN: Abingdon, 1991), 30–33.

[45] Few of Joachim's ideas were really new. Joachim's genius lay in combining two eschatological traditions: that of seven ages of history corresponding to the six days of creation plus a final day of rest, and the Cappadocian tradition that saw God's kingdom as having somewhat different modes in history corresponding to the different Persons of

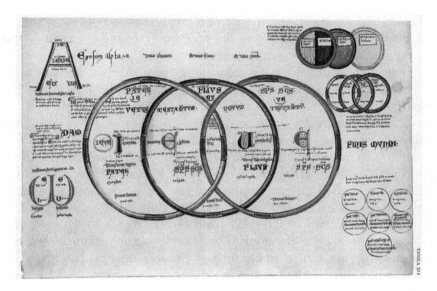

Figure 18.1 Joachim of Fiore: Ages of the Father, Son, and Holy Spirit

Thomas Aquinas refuted Joachim's ideas in his landmark *Summa Theologica*. But Joachim's fellow Florentine, Dante Alighieri (c. 1265–1321) in his *Divine Comedy* pictured Joachim in paradise.[46]

The Split: Spirituals versus Conventuals

Rising tensions within the Franciscan Order led eventually to a decisive split. The critical years were 1291 to 1312.

Bonaventure worked hard to keep the brothers together, but after his death groups of brothers grew farther apart. The main area of difference was still the interpretation of the Rule of Francis and of his *Testament*.

---

the Trinity. "Joachim's great idea was to identify the seventh day of world history with the kingdom of the Spirit. The great 'sabbath' of history, before the end of the world, and the kingdom of the Spirit mean the same thing," writes Moltmann. Jürgen Moltmann, *The Trinity and the Kingdom: The Doctrine of God*, trans. Margaret Kohl (San Francisco: Harper & Row, 1981), 204. John Phelan in *The Millennial Kingdom of the Franciscans in the New World* provides a comprehensive summary of the apocalyptic views of Joachim of Fiore in the context of the Franciscan controversies, Columbus's discoveries, and the role of the Roman Church and of Christian monarchs. John Leddy Phelan, *The Millennial Kingdom of the Franciscans in the New World*, 2nd ed., rev. (Berkeley: University of California Press, 1970), 14–15.

[46] David L. Edwards, *Christianity: The First Two Thousand Years* (Maryknoll, NY: Orbis, 1997), 259.

Should there be strict, totally literal interpretation, as Francis clearly intended, or accommodation to the necessary demands of schools and universities and priestly parish ministry?

There was a sociological dimension to the divide. On one side were the brothers serving mainly in cities, universities and local parishes, and mostly residing in their own monasteries or convents. These came to be called Conventual Franciscans (today, OFM, Conv., Order of Friars Minor Conventual)—"conventual" from the word "convent."

The other group consisted of brothers living mostly in small communities in or near towns, or in more remote hermitages. These brothers venerated the earliest days of the Order and insisted on strict observance of the Rule and *Testament*. They came to be called Spirituals, Zealots, or Observants.[47] They led austere lives devoted largely to prayer, fasting, and service to the poor. When Bonaventure as minister general tried to suppress earlier biographies of Francis, the Spirituals resisted. They prized highly the earliest writings about Francis and the first brothers.[48]

Brothers who opposed the relaxation of the Rule lived primarily in three areas: Tuscany, the Marches of Ancona northeast of Assisi, and Provence, the region in southeast France bordering Italy and the Mediterranean. In a few places, Franciscan authorities imprisoned some of the Spirituals for insubordination or for extreme or heretical views.[49]

Many Franciscan brothers, not only those who came to be called "Spirituals," were alarmed at the drift of the Order from its original poverty and simplicity. Brothers who had joined the Order years earlier wrote manuscripts recalling the first days and critiquing the movement's direction. Jabs at more educated brothers appear often in these accounts.[50]

But some of the more educated Franciscans were troubled, too. Peter John Olivi (1248–1298) was one. Olivi sharply criticized the growing worldliness and laxness of many Lesser Brothers. Moorman summarizes Olivi's views: "How could the world fail to regard the friars as insincere if, while declaring that they were the champions of poverty, they built

[47] "Spiritual Franciscans": see Lawrence S. Cunningham, *Francis of Assisi: Performing the Gospel Life* (Grand Rapids, MI: William B. Eerdmans, 2004), 126.

[48] Thus it happened fortuitously that "a few of the copies [of the early biographies] earmarked for destruction escaped. A number have been found, and these constitute the basis of every serious biography of St. Francis." Englebert, *Saint Francis*, 35.

[49] Moorman, *History of the Franciscan Order*, 191. Moorman discusses these developments in detail.

[50] Boniscambi, *Deeds of Blessed Francis*, FA:ED 3:526.

large churches and convents, employed proctors and bursars to look after their financial affairs, and lived lives of comparative comfort and security? And the same was true of the Church as a whole. Materialism was the cancer poisoning the body of Christ, and must be eradicated," Olivi felt.[51]

The third volume of *Francis of Assisi: Early Documents* gives a full overview of the struggle between the Spirituals and the Conventuals:

> The Spirituals were convinced, first of all, that Francis's cherished poverty did not consist simply in the renunciation of ownership, but in actually living with a severely restricted use of material goods. They decried the growing academic and clerical professionalization of the Order, which was establishing a caste system in the brotherhood. . . . With their slogan that the *Rule* must be observed "to the letter, without a gloss," they saw themselves as prophets calling the Order back to living as true Lesser Brothers. In return, the provincial ministers by and large viewed the Spirituals as self-righteous malcontents who were standing in the path of progress, criticizing other brothers who were providing essential pastoral services to the contemporary church. [Because of their perceived disobedience,] the Spirituals were harassed, even persecuted, by many superiors.[52]

Papal power was on the side of the Conventuals, for most of the changes had come by papal decision or with papal approval. Moorman notes, "The Spirituals must have known that they would be regarded as heretics, and that the Inquisition was both busy and powerful." He concludes, "The story of the Spirituals is a tragic one" that "could only lead to a division of the family of St. Francis."[53]

The Darkest Days

Controversies and struggles persisted for decades. Some Franciscan general ministers sided with the Spirituals; others sided with the Conventuals. Division deepened. Popes, such as Boniface VIII (pope 1294–1303) and Clement V (pope 1305–1314), tried to resolve differences by instituting reforms to address the worst abuses. But these proved ineffective, for they didn't go to the root issue. Moorman notes

---

[51] Moorman, *History of the Franciscan Order*, 197.
[52] Introduction, "Constitution *Exivi de Paradiso* of Pope Clement V (1312)," FA:ED 3:767–68.
[53] Moorman, *History of the Franciscan Order*, 192.

that as long as one party "wanted to go back to the poverty and insecurity of the early days, and another ... wanted the Order to play its part in the life of the Church by having large convents and learned friars supported by papal privileges and the security which came from endowments and rents, there was little hope of unity."[54]

The darkest days came during the papacy of John XXII, 1316–1334. John—a legal scholar and capable administrator—was seventy-two when elected pope and reigned into his early nineties. In dealing with the Franciscans, he was more a reactionary than a healer or innovator.

John XXII might be called the very embodiment of an institutional rather than charismatic view of the church.[55] He was far from the spirit of Francis. He wrote, "Great is poverty; greater is chastity; but the greatest good of all is obedience if it is strictly kept."[56]

All this occurred during the nearly seventy years that the papacy was based at Avignon, Provence (southeastern France).[57] Confronted with the troubles within the Franciscan Order, and much besides, John XXII decided it was time to put an end to Franciscan infighting and its causes, as he saw them. "From his white castle in the Rhone valley he soon had his fingers in every pie in Europe," including political conflicts.[58]

Addressing the question of "apostolic" or "evangelical" poverty, the pope declared that in fact Jesus and his apostles were not totally poor, having no possessions at all, as the Franciscans held. Franciscans should stop pushing that idea. Also, the idea that all the Franciscans' buildings and other property really belonged to the church, not to the brothers, was meaningless, a mere ruse. In his bull *Ad Conditorem* of 1322, John XXII said the papacy would no longer hold claim the ownership of Franciscan property so that the Lesser Brothers could use it without legally possessing it. This was just a way of getting around the Franciscan Rule.

This meant ownership of the property the Franciscans were using now passed to the Order itself, in direct violation of Francis's Rule. The papally

---

[54] Moorman, *History of the Franciscan Order*, 204; see 193–204.

[55] See chapter 20.

[56] John XXII, *Quorundam exigit* (1317), quoted in Moorman, *History of the Franciscan Order*, 311.

[57] Avignon, on the Rhône River about seventy miles north of the Mediterranean coast, was the residence of the papacy from 1309 to 1377.

[58] Friedrich Gontard, *The Chair of Peter: A History of the Papacy*, trans. A. J. and E. F. Peeler (New York: Holt, Rinehart and Winston, 1964), 318. I am here mostly bypassing the political disputes in which the pope declared it his prerogative to settle all such questions.

authorized Later Rule (*regula bullata*) of 1223 stated in its first provision that the Lesser Brothers are to live "in obedience, without anything of one's own."[59] This had been Francis's rule and practice from the beginning. John XXII's new provision, revoking earlier papal bulls, stunned many Franciscans. It meant that "at least officially, Francis would no longer serve as a prophet for a poor church," note the editors of *Francis of Assisi: Early Documents*.[60] In response to this and other papal acts, some Franciscans and some political leaders questioned whether John XXII was really a legitimate pope. Maybe he was a heretic, even the anti-Christ.[61]

In early 1317, John XXII called several Franciscan leaders to Avignon for questioning. Some Spirituals had started wearing shorter, tighter habits to distinguish them from the other Franciscans. They themselves were the true followers of Francis, they insisted, maintaining the standard of absolute poverty. John XXII demanded an end to this; all Lesser Brothers must wear identical habits. He put Michael of Cesena, Franciscan general minister, and a number of other brothers under house arrest until they agreed to submit fully.[62]

Twenty-five of the arrested brothers refused. John XXII turned the dissidents over to the church's Inquisitor for Provence, Michael Monachus (Michael le Moine)—ironically, himself a Franciscan. Most of the arrested brothers were Spiritual Franciscans. John XXII had already prejudged the case, calling these Franciscans *pseudofratres*, pseudo-brothers or false brothers, and heretics. Michael must deal with them accordingly.[63]

In the inquisition that followed twenty submitted, but five refused. One of these, finally recanting, was imprisoned for life. The remaining four were condemned to death and burned at the stake at the Marseilles central market on May 7, 1318.[64] We know their names: Jean Barrau,

---

[59] "The Later Rule," FA:ED 1:100.

[60] Editorial introduction to the Constitution *Cum Inter Nonnullos of John XXII*, FA:ED 3:789.

[61] Gontard, *Chair of Peter*, 322.

[62] Moorman, *History of the Franciscan Order*, 311.

[63] David Burr, *The Spiritual Franciscans: From Protest to Persecution in the Century after Francis* (University Park: Pennsylvania State University Press, 2001), 197.

[64] Moorman, *History of the Franciscan Order*, 311; Burr, *Spiritual Franciscan*, 204–6; M. D. Lambert, *Franciscan Poverty: The Doctrine of Absolute Poverty of Christ and the Apostles in the Franciscan Order 1210–1323* (London: SPCK, 1961), 215; David Saville Muzzey, *The Spiritual Franciscans* (New York: American Historical Association, 1907), 37. In pronouncing sentence, Michael the Inquisitor said the four brothers were guilty of heresy in not submitting to the pope and in claiming that his orders contradicted Jesus's words in the Gospels. Burr, *Spiritual Franciscans*, 205.

Deodat Michel, Pons Rocha, and Guillem Sancton—all apparently Spiritual Franciscans from the Provence area.[65]

"The fires kindled at Marseilles were a signal for the extermination of the Spiritualists [*sic*] throughout Provence. We hear of burnings at Narbonne, Montpelier, Toulouse, Lunel, Lodvère, Carcassonne, Cabestaing, Béziers, Montréal." In fact, "Franciscan inquisitors alone burned one hundred and fourteen of the zealots in a single year (1323)."[66]

In my mind, this is the lowest point in the whole Franciscan saga. Here is Francis's vision turned upside down: deadly conflict with the institutional church (embodied in the pope), Franciscan fighting Franciscan, some brothers even (like the Dominicans) serving as inquisitors and political pawns of the papacy, some promoting the crusades.[67] This period, the 1300s and 1400s, was in fact the height of inquisition fervor in Europe.

Like all professed Christians of the time, Franciscans were immersed in a culture where church and state were wed, even if the union was stormy and even violent. In such a situation it was hard for anyone to imagine that the church would *not* have to force infidels to submit to the Christian faith if they would not do so voluntarily. An infidel or heretic was defying both church and state and thus, people reasoned, God himself. And God had given the state the sword and the fire.[68]

---

[65] Burr, *Spiritual Franciscans,* 204–06.

[66] Muzzey, *Spiritual Franciscans,* 37.

[67] Several Franciscan preachers promoted the crusades in their sermons, often perhaps "more out of obedience to the popes" than from conviction, suggests one author. One of these brothers was Guillaume of Cordelle, who "preached the crusade in France from 1235 on," notes Benjamin Kedar. To recruit young men to join the crusades through one's sermons was known as "preaching the cross"! See Benjamin Z. Kedar, *Crusade and Mission* (Princeton, NJ: Princeton University Press, 1984), 139; Christopher T. Maier, *Preaching the Crusades: Mendicant Friars and the Cross in the Thirteenth Century* (Cambridge: Cambridge University Press, 1994); D. L. d'Avray, *The Preaching of the Friars: Sermons Diffused from Paris before 1300* (Oxford: Oxford University Press, 1985). Burr finds it "most striking" that the inquisitor, Michael, himself a Franciscan, maintained "that the Franciscan rule is distinct from the gospel and is thus subject to modification by the pope. In saying this, he seems to be putting asunder what had been joined together by Francis in the opining lines of the rule and by Nicholas III in *Exiit qui seminat.*" Burr, *Spiritual Franciscans,* 205.

[68] Dante Alighieri in his *Paradiso*, speaking in the voice of Bonaventure, said Francis's "family" that had "followed his footprints, has now turned back: its forward foot now seeks the foot that lags." Franciscans were divided over the Rule, "either given to escaping it our making it too strict." Dante Alighieri, *The Divine Comedy, Paradiso* Canto XII, quoted in FA:ED 3:891.

New Currents of Reform

By the 1300s, few Franciscans were living the life of strict poverty that Francis made an essential mark of the Order. But growing numbers of brothers were feeling the Order must reform, must return to the radical dynamism of its first days.

John Moorman notes, "The main problem which faced the Order of Friars Minor in the fourteenth and fifteenth centuries was how to carry out necessary reforms without dividing the Order."[69] Since most Franciscans had now drifted some distance from the strictness of the original Rule, brothers who sought a more radical following of Francis could easily be suspected of heresy.

But in 1334, Brother John de Valle, a committed Francis follower, together with three other brothers founded a new, strict Franciscan hermitage at Brugliano. This was a remote place two-thousand-plus feet up in the mountains east of Assisi, near the border between Umbria and the Marches of Ancona. The brothers lived a strict and simple life, much devoted to prayer and service.[70]

When Pope Clement IV found out about this, he initially opposed it, thinking the brothers were schismatics and heretics. But the brothers persisted, and the community gradually grew. Eventually Clement granted the brothers' request to occupy four small Franciscan hermitages, the one at the Carceri near Assisi and three others. Each was to have twelve friars.[71]

The incoming pope, however, Innocent VI, opposed this fledgling movement. He considered these Franciscan brothers schismatics. The little community's privileges were revoked, some brothers imprisoned, and the movement died. One of the brothers, however, Paul of Trinci, still wanted to see reform, to see the Lesser Brothers return to their earlier discipline.[72] Paul spent several years at the Franciscan friary at Foligno. Finally in 1367, he got permission from the new Franciscan minister general, Thomas of Frignano, to return to Brugliano and "revive there the life of poverty and austerity."[73]

---

[69] Moorman, *History of the Franciscan Order,* 369.

[70] Lambert, *Franciscan Poverty,* 246; Moorman, *History of the Franciscan Order,* 369.

[71] Moorman, *History of the Franciscan Order,* 370.

[72] "Deeply attached to an ideal of asceticism and simplicity, he was disturbed to find his fellow friars so easy-going, and he began to yearn for the reforms which were so long overdue." Moorman, *History of the Franciscan Order,* 371.

[73] Moorman, *History of the Franciscan Order,* 372.

Brother Paul was now nearly sixty. For a while he lived alone, but eventually other brothers, also longing for reform, joined him. They called themselves "the brethren of the family of the observance." The community continued to grow and a "movement for the strict observance of the Rule began to spread." In 1373, Pope Gregory XI gave his support and designated ten small convents for the use of this new movement—the Carceri and nine others.[74]

Gradually the reform movement picked up momentum. The Franciscan community at San Damiano joined in 1384. By 1389 the new movement counted twenty-one convents in Umbria, the Marches, and in Rome. Some Franciscan communities in Tuscany and elsewhere also joined, and in 1415, the pope gave the reform movement possession of the Portiuncula itself. By this time the Observants (as they were now called) counted thirty-five communities in Italy, all small but devout. The brothers were "inspired by the desire to recreate the conditions in which the early friars had lived and to observe the Rule, both in the letter and the spirit, as it had been dictated by S. Francis."[75]

This was the birth of the Friars of the Observance. Similar movements arose in Spain, France, and elsewhere.[76] The emergence of parallel movements throughout the scattered Franciscan provinces, all desiring a return to the strictness and devotion of the earliest Franciscans, testifies to the widespread sense that the Order had drifted far from Francis and to a widespread thirst for reform.

In the early 1400s, the movement was strengthened through the ministries of several brothers "of outstanding ability and holiness of life," three of whom were later declared saints: Bernardino of Siena, John of Capistrano, and James of the March.[77] Space does not permit more than a brief sketch, but their remarkable stories are all part of the dynamism of the Franciscan movement.

Bernardino of Siena (1380–1444) worked among the poor and became a superb preacher, scholar, and reformer. For "twenty-six years he was constantly on the move, tramping from place to place in Italy in order to preach," traveling with a small band of brothers. Like many of his day, however, his sermons were laced with anti-Semitism.[78] Bernardino

---

[74] Moorman, *History of the Franciscan Order,* 372.
[75] Moorman, *History of the Franciscan Order,* 372–73, 377.
[76] See Moorman, *History of the Franciscan Order,* 377–83.
[77] Moorman, *History of the Franciscan Order,* 374.
[78] Moorman, *History of the Franciscan Order,* 457, 463.

is among other things the patron saint of advertisers and of public relations—probably not something Francis could have envisioned![79]

John of Capistrano (1386–1456) was born in southern Italy. He studied at the University of Perugia and later was appointed a judge. He soon earned a reputation for humanity and a sense of justice.[80] Through a series of crises, including imprisonment, he was converted and became a Lesser Brother and eventually a notable preacher. "The son of a soldier," Moorman writes, John displayed "a certain love of conflict which spurred him on to attack the enemies of the Church, wherever and whatever they might be"—in particular, heretics and Muslims.[81] In this respect John was quite unlike Francis. He got himself "appointed an inquisitor to hunt out and destroy the nests of heretics in the Marches of Ancona."[82] Like Bernardino of Siena, he condemned Jews, which tended to reinforce Europe's already present anti-Semitism.

In 1776, Spanish Franciscans founded the San Juan Capistrano Mission in southern California. The mission became famous for its architecture and for the return of a flock of Cliff Swallows each March after wintering in Argentina. The return of the San Juan Capistrano swallows, prompting an annual festival, may remind us of Francis asking swallows to keep still while he preached.

James of the March (c. 1392–1476) was born into a poor family in the Marches of Ancona. As an adult he studied law, but soon decided to join a religious order. Passing through Assisi, he stayed overnight with the Lesser Brothers at the Portiuncula. This was shortly after the Franciscans there had adopted the stricter Observant discipline. James was so impressed with the brothers' fervor and devotion that he decided to stay. He became a novice in 1416 at the age of about twenty-five. He began preaching in 1422 and from then on preached almost every day for the next forty years.[83]

James's preaching proved popular, drawing large crowds. Church authorities named him an inquisitor to help ferret out heretics. He was also something of a scholar and encouraged scholarship among

---

[79] See also Raphael M. Huber, *A Documented History of the Franciscan Order: From the Birth of St. Francis to the Division of the Order Under Leo X (1182–1517)* (Milwaukee, WI: Nowiny Publishing Apostolate, 1944), 254, 280, 319, 347–65, 379.

[80] Moorman, *History of the Franciscan Order,* 376.

[81] Moorman, *History of the Franciscan Order,* 466.

[82] Moorman, *History of the Franciscan Order,* 466.

[83] Moorman, *History of the Franciscan Order,* 467, 473.

the brothers. James "relaxed his standards of poverty to allow him to collect books" for his library.[84] Like Franciscan university professors two centuries earlier, James discovered that Francis's strict rule against owning anything at all clashed with the necessary life of a scholar.

Inspired by Bernardino, John of Capistrano, James of the Marches, and others, Observant Franciscans continued to grow and expand. In general, Observant Franciscans, with their stricter discipline, tended to be centered more in small convents and remote hermitages than in the larger cities and in university communities. Much of their popular preaching, however, was in urban centers.

Observants and Conventuals

As the decades rolled on, the situation with the Franciscans gradually changed. Observant and Conventual Franciscans continued their ministries. Eventually the Roman Church formally acknowledged the existence of two distinct groups. This occurred at the Council of Constance in 1415. For another century the two groups functioned uneasily as officially one Order. Finally in 1517, Pope Leo X called a Franciscan General Chapter in Rome to try to sort things out once and for all. That again proved impossible. So, from then on, by the pope's decision, the Spirituals or Observants were called Friars Minor of the Regular Observance, or just Friars Minor of St. Francis. The Conventuals were given the designation Friars Minor Conventual (OFM Conv.).[85]

Moorman in his *History of the Franciscan Order* treats both the Conventuals and the Spirituals sympathetically. Both meant well. The Conventuals "believed in progress and development."[86] Spirituals, however, "felt that it was their special duty to save the Order from a betrayal of the trust which S. Francis had laid upon them." Moorman concludes, "These were men of clear vision to whom compromise meant betrayal. Everywhere around them they saw change and, as they thought, decay—the Order now very different from what it had been in its origin, the friar no longer a homeless evangelist and preacher, but secure, privileged, well housed, well fed, and given every opportunity for learning and study."[87]

---

[84] Moorman, *History of the Franciscan Order,* 473, 477.
[85] https://en.wikipedia.org/wiki/Order_of_Friars_Minor_Conventual.
[86] Moorman, *History of the Franciscan Order,* 191.
[87] Moorman, *History of the Franciscan Order,* 192.

The Capuchins

Like all movements, Franciscans thus struggled through a variety of conflicts, divisions, and reforms over centuries as they proliferated and diversified. Lesser Brothers were after all subject to the same wars, epidemics, and struggles that touched others. And yet despite struggles and setbacks, the number of Franciscan brothers and sisters continued to grow and spread.

One of the most important reforms was the rise of the Capuchins in 1525. Officially they were named the Order of Friars Minor Capuchin (OFM Cap.). This was a true reform. The main founder, Matteo Bassi (1495–1552), an Italian Observant brother in the Marches of Ancona, wanted to return to Francis's original Rule and practice.[88]

At first church authorities tried to suppress the new order, fearing it was too radical. The brothers went into hiding, and the Capuchins were briefly an underground movement. They were given shelter by a group of Camaldolese monks high in Italy's central mountains. The Camaldolese were an order of hermits founded and recognized by the church some two hundred years before Francis. The new Franciscan group adopted the hood (cappuccino) of the Camaldolese and the practice of wearing a beard, and came to be known as Capuchins.

After three years, in 1528, Pope Clement VII did recognize the Capuchins as a legitimate branch of the Conventual Franciscans but with their own provincial vicar under the authority of the Franciscan minister general. The Capuchin Rule required poverty and simplicity, a life as close to that of Saint Francis as possible. Their monasteries owned nothing and maintained supplies for only a few days at a time.

Capuchin communities were to remain small (twelve or fewer), were sustained by begging, and were forbidden to touch money, just as Francis had specified. The brothers were always to walk barefoot. The Capuchins main ministry was preaching and serving the poor, and their preaching grew immensely popular throughout Europe and beyond.[89] The Capuchins incidentally lent their name to Cappuccino coffee, named after the brown color of their habit.

---

[88] Iriarte covers the history of the Capuchins in detail. Lazaro Iriarte, *Franciscan History: The Three Orders of St. Francis of Assisi*, trans. from Spanish by Patricia Ross (Chicago: Franciscan Herald Press, 1982), 195–225.

[89] Iriarte, *Franciscan History*, 281.

Controversy and Division; Rebirth and Reform

In this chapter we saw conflicting currents converging and dividing. Was the church in deep trouble? Was a New Age of the Spirit dawning that would reform or perhaps replace the church?

Could Lesser Brothers keep faithful to the rigorous discipleship Francis embodied? What was the place of learning and scholarship, and the role of needed power and authority? How much was authentic Franciscan life a matter of the Rule, and how much of conscious and personal choice? How much of fidelity to the past, and how much of new visions of the future, perhaps like Joachim's?

In his story of *Reform and Division in the Medieval Franciscan Order*, Duncan Nimmo goes into these matters in detail. Nimmo divides this span of roughly two centuries into three periods: from Francis to 1323, from 1323 to 1378, and from 1378 to 1528. The underlying issue concerned more strict or more lenient observance of Francis's Rule and *Testament*. The issue took different forms at different stages. The papacy always played a role, and the universities were often part of the picture.

Nimmo summarizes the situation as of 1528, when the Capuchins were officially recognized. The emergence of the Capuchins meant that the Franciscans were now divided into "three separate families identified by different standards of observance." This was "the culmination of the composite issue of reform and division which ... had preoccupied the Order continuously almost from its beginning." Though the movement continued dynamic and growing, still its "internal dissensions ... tarnished its public reputation and marred its efficacy."[90]

As a movement, the Lesser Brothers were not, it turned out, immune to the difficulties that have troubled movements all down through history.

Renewal movements can go bad in several ways. They can be co-opted by the institutional church, get tied up in church politics, and become agents of church authority, thus undercutting their redemptive witness. Or a movement can move in the opposite direction: withdraw totally from society, and form small isolated communities and cease to provide the spark and ferment of renewal. Both these can happen at the same time, in fact.

Both these patterns are common in history, and both happened with the Franciscans. "The temptation of many Spirituals [was] to retreat

---

[90] Duncan Nimmo, *Reform and Division in the Medieval Franciscan Order: From Saint Francis to the Foundation of the Capuchins* (Rome: Capuchin Historical Institute, 1987), 646.

into hermitages, rather than engage in the preaching ministry," note the editors of *Francis of Assisi: Early Documents*.[91] At the other extreme, the Franciscan Order got drawn into the Inquisition. Franciscans were also co-opted by the pope to support the Crusades—preaching and raising money, and in some cases accompanying Crusaders on their campaigns. "Constantly appealing for money for the Crusade," Moorman writes, Franciscans "realized that they were losing the goodwill of their own supporters upon whom they depended for their expansion and new building." The Franciscan scholar Roger Bacon "declared that force of arms can never convert, it can only exterminate and, in so doing, leave much hostility and resentment behind," notes Moorman.[92]

The Inquisition was a problem and a snare. In the 1240s, within twenty years of Francis's death, popes began appointing Franciscans as inquisitors to ferret out heretics. In 1258, Pope Alexander IV assigned the Franciscans to head up the Inquisition throughout major sections of northern and central Italy.[93] Like supporting the Crusades, however, this role undercut the Franciscans' redemptive ministry. In France the first Franciscan inquisitor, Stephen of Saint-Thibéry, was assassinated in 1242. "Not always the best of men were appointed, the temptations to graft and dishonesty were very great, and several inquisitors had to be removed," notes Moorman.[94]

Following Francis as Francis followed Jesus was not easy. It required fidelity to Francis's spirit and heartfelt fidelity to the Franciscan Rule. Many brothers did stay true, despite the temptations and struggles, the attractions of right or left. Even when brothers or the Order itself were unfaithful, still the shining example of Poor Francis shone before them.

Brother Francis and Genghis Khan

Francis knew from the start that his parish was the world. He understood this intuitively, and it was confirmed also by dreams and visions. His mission with his brothers was to the ends of the Earth. Little surprise then that the mission would take Franciscans into the very realm of Genghis Khan and his successors far to the east in Mongolia and China.

Francis's calling was in effect threefold: leave the world and follow Jesus, see God's glory in the world God created, and win that world to Jesus. Francis's calling was a synthesis of these three.

---

[91] FA:ED 3:878 n. a.
[92] Moorman, *History of the Franciscan Order*, 301.
[93] FA:ED 3:879 n. a.
[94] Moorman, *History of the Franciscan Order*, 303.

Francis expressed this global vision many times. Once Bishop Hugolino of Ostia (future Pope Gregory IX) questioned Francis about his big vision. Lesser Brothers were already serving in distant lands. Some had died. Hugolino asked, "Why did you send your brothers so far away to die of hunger and to [face] so many other trials?"

Francis replied in "great fervor of spirit," "Lord [Bishop]," he said, "do you think that the Lord sent the brothers only for these regions? But I tell you in truth that the Lord chose and sent the brothers for the benefit and salvation of the souls of all people in this world. They should be received not only in the land of believers, but also in that of non-believers, and they will win over many souls."[95]

So it happened. The Franciscan impact in the 1200s reached far beyond Europe and to the world. Franciscans "carried their message to the ends of the earth."[96] The fourteenth-century brother Ugolino Boniscambi wrote, "The brothers ... longed to go into foreign Provinces, that they might be pilgrims and strangers in this world, and citizens with the saints in the household of God in heaven."[97] Within a hundred years of the Order's founding Franciscans could be found ministering not only in Continental Europe and the British Isles but also in North Africa, China, and India. Eventually the Franciscan mission would reach every continent.

In the late 1400s, Franciscans played a strategic role in the European discovery of the Americas. Franciscans often accompanied colonial expeditions. Brothers carried out missionary work in several regions in North, Central, and South America, and also in Japan. Franciscan expansion during this period was similar to that of the Dominicans and later the newly established Society of Jesus (Jesuits), founded by the Spaniard Ignatius Loyola in 1534. The earliest Franciscan mission beyond Europe and North Africa, however, was the Lesser Brothers' pioneering work among the Mongols in the Far East, and here the Franciscan story intertwines with that of Genghis Khan.[98]

* * *

---

[95] *Mirror of Perfection* (Sabatier ed.), FA:ED 3:310. Similarly, *Assisi Compilation*, FA:ED 2:216.

[96] Jean Dunbabin, "Careers and Vocations," in J. I. Catto, ed., *The Early Oxford Schools*, vol. I of *The History of the University of Oxford*, ed. T. H. Aston (Oxford: Clarendon Press, 1984), 604.

[97] Boniscambi, *Deeds of Blessed Francis*, FA:ED 3:545.

[98] See chapter 19.

In 1300, about seventy-five years after Francis's death, Pope Boniface VIII proclaimed a Jubilee Year. This was a first. Never before had the Roman Church mounted such a celebration. The Jubilee, based loosely on jubilee-year provisions in Leviticus 25, was a church festival and potentially a time for spiritual restoration after years of confusion and conflict.

Pope Boniface watched as thousands of pilgrims converged on Rome at Christmastide 1299, anticipating the new century. Everyone visited Saint Peter's tomb, especially, and other sacred spots. Seeing the crowds, Boniface thought a great Jubilee would be fitting. He would grant pilgrims a "plenary indulgence"—complete remission of sins— upon satisfying certain conditions. Every pilgrim must visit the basilicas of the Apostles thirteen times, make confession, and take Communion. Residents of Rome could be given the same full indulgence after their thirtieth visit. Folks unable personally to undertake the pilgrimage could receive the indulgence if they paid the expenses of others.[99]

The Florentine artists Cimabue and Giotto and the poet Dante were among the many Jubilee pilgrims to Rome.[100] Great Jubilee celebrations meant new artwork and new commissions! This opened opportunities for painters and sculptors throughout Christendom. Giotto and others created multiple artistic work for the Jubilee.[101]

The Jubilee Year did little to really renew the church. Then in 1346 bubonic plague—the Black Death—began its relentless sweep across Europe. As many as one in four people died.

Yet the Franciscan mission went on. Lesser Brothers ventured further and further, bringing many thousands to faith in Jesus Christ around the globe and sparking renewal in local parishes across Christendom.

Thus, the Franciscan Order grew into a global missionary movement. The Mongol mission bore some fruit and opened new contacts between the Roman Church and the Far East. The story of Franciscan impact involved both Genghis Khan and his descendants in the East and Christopher Columbus on his voyages west. East and west, north and south, the life of Francis and the expanding Franciscan mission played a

---

[99] Gontard, *Chair of Peter,* 304.
[100] https://en.wikipedia.org/wiki/Jubilee_in_the_Catholic_Church#First_Christian_ Jubilee.
[101] Lauren Arnold, *Princely Gifts and Papal Treasures: The Franciscan Mission to China and Its Influence on the Art of the West, 1250–1350* (San Francisco: Desiderata Press, 1999), 58–59.

role also in the development of art and culture. And for the first time, a Franciscan was pope!

Yet the story is filled with ironies, contradictions, contested questions as to who the Franciscans were, what they achieved, and what they were called to be—what their authentic charism really was and should be. For the Franciscans, this was a time of contested vision, of spirit versus structure, and a time of clashes between apocalyptic promise and institutional stability.

19

The Franciscan Story of
Genghis Khan and Christopher Columbus

The last chapter showed the missionary heart of the Franciscan movement and the ways this embodied the charism and vision of Francis himself. Francis's vision was global even before people really understood Earth as a globe. The good news must reach to the ends of the earth.

It is not really surprising, then, that mission would take Franciscans into the very realm of Genghis Khan and his successors far to the east in Mongolia and China, and that in the 1400s it would extend to the New World, the Americas. This chapter tells both these largely untold stories: Genghis Khan in the thirteenth and fourteenth centuries, and Christopher Columbus in the fifteenth. These stories further illuminate the dynamics of the Franciscans as a movement.

The Mongols Are Coming

Genghis Khan and Francis were contemporaries. Genghis, one of the most fearsome conquerors in human history, was born about forty years before Francis but he died in 1227, within a year of Francis's death.

Born in Mongolia, six thousand miles east of Italy, Genghis Khan never heard of Francis, nor had Francis heard of the great Mongol ruler. Yet the day would come when Francis's Lesser Brothers would meet Genghis's heirs. Mission historian Samuel Moffett writes that Franciscan brothers, "with the same utter disregard of their own safety" that Francis demonstrated, would "become the first Europeans to preach to the Mongols and the Chinese."[1]

---

[1] Samuel Hugh Moffett, *A History of Christianity in Asia*, vol. 1, *Beginnings to 1500* (New York: HarperSanFrancisco, 1992), 390. See also 406–9.

Franciscans organized their missions work into various regions, or "vicarages," each headed by a brother designated a "vicar." Three of these districts were dedicated to work among the Mongol peoples to the east. Another focused on Morocco and two encompassed areas of eastern Europe.[2] Franciscan missionaries who were priests were sometimes appointed bishops in the areas they served. In 1233, for example, a Franciscan was made bishop of Fez, Morocco. Another Franciscan bishop was appointed in Morocco in 1246, thus establishing precedents for Franciscans in episcopal roles.[3]

Franciscan missionaries also worked among Turkish-speaking peoples in southern Asia. In the late 1200s, some traveled on to China, following the routes of European merchants and traders. In about 1290, the Franciscans organized their eastern mission work into two vicarages, northern Tartary and eastern Tartary ("Tartary" being the vast area extending from eastern Europe all the way to the Pacific Ocean).[4]

The Rise of Genghis Khan

It was the rise of Genghis Khan and the rapid expansion of the great Mongol Empire that made the Western church look east. In a period of mere decades, Mongols conquered territory all the way from China and the Pacific to the Mediterranean and eastern Europe.

Genghis Khan managed to unite scattered nomadic Mongolian tribes and then expand his command through a remarkable series of conquests south and west. By 1215, he had captured Peking (Beijing) and extended Mongol dominion over Manchuria and most of northern China. He then turned his attention toward the West.

In the spring of 1222, thousands of Mongol horsemen appeared suddenly in southeastern Russia. A Russian chronicler wrote, "For our sins, unknown tribes came, none knows who they are or whence they

---

[2] Kenneth Scott Latourette, *The Thousand Years of Uncertainty: A.D. 500–A.D. 1500* [1938], vol. 2 of *A History of the Expansion of Christianity* (Grand Rapids, MI: Zondervan, 1970), 324. Latourette relies here on a work by Lemmens, *The Pagan Missions of the Late Middle Ages* (in German).

[3] Latourette, *Thousand Years*, 325.

[4] Moffett, *History of Christianity in Asia*, 1:456. Huber traces the history of the missionary vicarages, or "vicariates." Raphael M. Huber, OFM Conv., *A Documented History of the Franciscan Order: From the Birth of St. Francis to the Division of the Order under Leo X (1182–1517)* (Milwaukee, WI: Nowiny Publishing Apostolate, 1944), 762–84. The Vicarage of Northern Tartary was established by 1287 and encompassed Mongolia and adjoining regions. The Vicarage of Cathay (China), established in 1291, included India and much of Central Asia. The Vicarage of Eastern Tartary included Georgia, Armenia, and Persia. Huber, *Documented History*, 767–69.

came—nor what their language is, nor of what race they are nor what their faith is—God alone knows who they are and when they came out."[5]

The Mongols conquered through sudden attack and the systematic slaughter of men, women, and children. Mongol forces had several advantages: swift plains horses, light gear, and tested tactics. European cavalry and foot soldiers were no match. When a defending army came out to meet them, the Mongols would fall back, feigning retreat. Soon the heavier European horses, weighed down by soldiers' weapons and heavy armor, would tire, and the Mongols would counterattack. The attackers had stronger bows that could send volleys of specially designed arrows beyond the range of the Russian and European soldiers' weapons.[6]

Who were these people? Mongols were neither Muslims nor Christians, though there were pockets of Nestorian Christians among them. Mongols in general adhered to an animistic faith in which they worshiped Tegri (Heavenly Father) and Umay (Earth Mother, goddess of fertility). Worship practices included shamanism and ancestor worship. The Mongol armies invaded the West and Middle East during the period of the Crusades, just when Christians and Muslims were fighting each other over control of the Holy Land. But now (as Moorman writes), "both Christendom and Islam had to reckon with a common enemy in the Mongol empire of the East." After conquering much of China, Genghis "sent his armies careering into northwest India and on through Afghanistan into Georgia, the Caucasus, and south Russia."[7]

Genghis's forces withdrew after about fifteen years, then returned in force in 1237. Now led by Genghis's grandson Batu, the Mongol hordes "swept right across Russia nearly to the Baltic, slaughtering all who stood in their path."[8] Advancing further, in 1240 the Mongol forces "destroyed Kiev, the mother of Russian Christianity, and put all its people to the sword."[9] From there the Mongols moved on into Poland and Hungary.

---

[5] Quoted in Christopher Dawson, ed., *The Mongol Mission: Narratives and Letters of the Franciscan Missionaries in Mongolia and China in the Thirteenth and Fourteenth Centuries* (New York: Sheed and Ward, 1955), xii, from *The Chronicle of Novgorod*.

[6] Jack Weatherford, *Genghis Khan and the Making of the Modern World* (New York: Broadway Books, 2004), 139–42. "The mounted princes of Russia sat astride their massive warhorses with their shiny javelins, glistening swords, colorful flags and banners, and boastful coats of arms. Their European warhorses had been bred for a massive show of strength—to carry the weight of their noble rider's armor on the parade ground—but they had not been bred for speed or agility on the battleground" (141).

[7] John Moorman, *A History of the Franciscan Order: From Its Origins to the Year 1517* (Oxford: Oxford University Press, 1968), 232.

[8] Moorman, *History of the Franciscan Order*, 232.

[9] Moffett, *History of Christianity in Asia*, 1:406.

To Christians in the West, the Mongol conquests represented a terrible threat but also an opportunity. Moffett writes,

> As the *pax Romana* had prepared the way for the work of the apostles in the first century, so now in the thirteenth a *pax Mongolica* opened doors for Catholic missions across Asia to the half of the world beyond Constantinople. Never once in the century and a quarter from the first Catholic mission to Mongolia in 1245 to the fall of the Mongol dynasty in 1368 was there not at least one cross-Asiatic artery open for trade and cultural interchange between East and West.[10]

The Roman Church began to wonder if the Mongols could be enlisted to help defeat Muslims in the Middle East. Nothing came of this, but it entered into the complex calculations of the papacy.[11]

This opened a whole new chapter in Franciscan history: a mission to the east, the Lesser Brothers serving among the Mongols. A remarkable story began to unfold. Four Franciscan brothers were central to the Mongol mission: John of Piancarpino (c. 1185–1252), William of Rubruck (1220–1293), John of Montecorvino (1247–1328), and John of Marignolli (1290–1360). These brothers were sometimes celebrated merely as travelers and explorers by people who had no idea they were Franciscan missioners.

Brother John of Piancarpino

The Franciscan Order itself quickly recognized the Mongol invasions as a new missionary challenge and acted. Their first missionary to Mongolia was John of Piancarpino, an Italian born near Perugia. Moorman in his *History of the Franciscan Order* calls John "a great evangelist and missionary, a man of big ideas, always anxious to push on to new fields."[12]

Pope Innocent IV appointed John as his emissary to the Mongol court. The pope sent a letter to the Mongol ruler to see if he could develop friendly, peaceful relations between the Mongols and the church. Initially John of Piancarpino was thus more of an envoy than a missionary. As Moffett writes, "The missionaries were given two commissions: a

---

[10] Moffett, *History of Christianity in Asia,* 1:406.

[11] Moffett, *History of Christianity in Asia,* 1:406. Moffett notes that "the possibility of an alliance, far East and far West against the Muslim center, held out such hope of a last, great victorious Crusade that the wish proved stronger than the counsels of reality" (406).

[12] Moorman, *History of the Franciscan Order,* 162.

political one, to avert further onslaughts on Christendom by the invaders, and a spiritual one, to preach Christianity to them that they might be converted."[13] This was in 1245, about two decades after the deaths of both Francis and Genghis Khan.

Over the next hundred years, the Roman Church (principally the papacy) sent at least seven missions to the Far Asia. A couple of the missionaries were Dominicans, but the rest were all Franciscans. The famed travels of Marco Polo took place in the latter part of this period, principally between 1271 and 1295.[14]

John of Piancarpino and his partner Brother Benedict of Poland set off barefoot for Asia in the spring of 1245, knowing they would have to travel thousands of miles. The brothers took the northern route through what is now Ukraine, heading for the court of Batu, the Mongol ruler in Russia.[15] John wrote that he and Brother Benedict "feared we might be killed by the Tartars or other people, or imprisoned for life, or afflicted with hunger, thirst, cold, heat, injuries and exceedingly great trials almost beyond our powers of endurance—all of which, with the exception of death and imprisonment for life, fell to our lot in various ways in a much greater degree than we had conceived beforehand."[16] John was already an experienced missionary, but as Dawson writes, "We cannot fail to be impressed by the courage of this disciple of St. Francis who, at the age of sixty-five, without any knowledge of oriental languages or any resource except his faith, embarked on this tremendous journey to the heart of the barbarian [*sic*] world."[17]

Before long the two brothers were taken into custody by a Mongol outpost. They were then relayed from one outpost to another, continuing east. They came to the base of Mongol General Batu, north of the Caspian Sea. Batu decided to send the pair further east across the plains to the Great Khan himself. "They were then forced to ride, at enormous speed, through the great Steppes [flat unforested grasslands or prairies] for some thousands of miles at a pace which would have exhausted and killed men of much stronger physique."[18] Historian Christopher Dawson wrote, "And so they continued month after month for thousands of miles

---

[13] Moffett, *History of Christianity in Asia*, 1:406–7. Given the thinking of the time, the "political" and "spiritual" missions were viewed as totally intertwined, two aspects of one goal: Christianization of the world.

[14] Moffett, *History of Christianity in Asia*, 1:407.

[15] Moffett, *History of Christianity in Asia*, 1:407.

[16] Dawson, *Mongol Mission*, 3.

[17] Dawson, *Mongol Mission*, xv.

[18] Moorman, *History of the Franciscan Order*, 233.

... without rest or intermission. It would have been an ordeal for the toughest of horsemen, but for an elderly clergyman who was extremely fat and in poor health, it is one of the most remarkable feats of physical endurance on record."[19]

The two Franciscans and their escort finally reached the Mongol capital, Karakorum, Mongolia, about seven hundred miles northwest of present-day Beijing. John and Benedict arrived in July 1246, just in time to witness the enthroning of Guyuk (c. 1206–1248), another grandson of Genghis Khan, as the new Great Khan.

The brothers were astonished to find several Nestorian Christians in the khan's court. "The khan's personal clerks were Nestorians, and a Nestorian chapel, placed in front of the royal tent, resounded with the sound of public chants and the beating of tablets loudly announcing the appointed hours of Christian worship," notes Moffett.[20]

Brothers John and Benedict delivered the letter from Pope Innocent IV. They remained and waited until November, when Guyuk finally sent back his reply. The two Franciscans then made the arduous journey back to Europe during the cold winter of 1246–1247, often sleeping overnight in the snow.[21]

In his letter to Innocent IV, Guyuk Khan struck a tone of condescension. The pope was the one who should submit to the Great Khan, Guyuk said, not the other way round. He found the pope's letter "impudent." The Mongols themselves were God's agents. "How could anybody seize or kill by his own power contrary to the command of God?"[22]

Brothers John and Benedict eventually reached Europe and delivered their report and Guyuk Khan's letter to the pope. They had made no converts. Their venture was more a papal diplomatic mission. Still they, along with later Franciscan missionaries, fulfilled the task given them. Dawson notes that these brothers were in fact "disciples of St. Francis of the first generation who possessed the genuine Franciscan spirit of simplicity and poverty and self-abnegation. But above all they give an absolutely first-hand authentic account of the first contact between Western Christendom and the Far East."[23]

---

[19] Dawson, *Mongol Mission*, xvi.

[20] Moffett, *History of Christianity in Asia*, 1:408, citing John of Piancarpino's "History of the Mongols" as published in Dawson, *Mongol Mission*, 68.

[21] Moorman, *History of the Franciscan Order*, 233.

[22] Dawson, *Mongol Mission*, 85. Guyuk Khan's letter is found on pages 85–86 of this book.

[23] Dawson, *Mongol Mission*, vii.

In 1247 and 1248, further exchanges between the Mongol rulers and the pope took place. This time the pope used some Dominicans as envoys. Guyuk Khan died, however, probably assassinated, in 1248. After a period of turbulence his cousin Mongke (another of Genghis Khan's grandsons) became the fourth Great Khan.[24] Mongke Khan expanded the Mongol Empire further, conquering southeastern China and to the west, Persia and Baghdad by deploying two of his brothers with fresh Mongol armies. Meanwhile the Mongols sent envoys to Europe, one to the pope and one to King Louis IX of France (Saint Louis).[25]

King Louis and others in the West had heard that there were some Christians among the Mongols. The son of Batu, the Mongol ruler in Russia (and another grandson of Genghis Khan), was rumored to be a Christian. Intrigued, King Louis decided to send an envoy to Russia to investigate.

Brother William of Rubruck

The embassy of Brother John and Brother Benedict set the stage for the more extensive missionary work of the Franciscan William of Rubruck (1220–1293). In 1253, King Louis sent William along with another Franciscan, Bartholomew of Cremona, as his messengers to the Mongol court in Russia. Louis ordered William to keep a detailed account of his journey and mission. As a result, we now have a narrative running over two hundred pages in a modern published English edition. Christopher Dawson called William's report "one of the most living and moving narratives in the whole literature of travel, even more direct and convincing than that of [Venetian merchant] Marco Polo [1254–1324]."[26]

Brothers William and Bartholomew sailed to Constantinople, then on through the Bosporus into the Black Sea. From there they set off by land for the Mongol court, traveling with some assistants and four carts of fruit, wine, and other gifts. They eventually arrived at the court of Batu. He in turn sent the delegation on to the Great Khan at the Mongol capital in Karakorum, Mongolia, where Brothers John and Benedict had been earlier.

The journey across the vast steppes took several months. The brothers did find some evidence of Christian influence, as well as Muslim. En route

---

[24] Jack Weatherford narrates the transition in his book *Genghis Khan,* 164–67.

[25] Dale T. Irvin and Scott W. Sunquist, *History of the World Christian Movement,* vol. 1, *Earliest Christianity to 1453* (Maryknoll, NY: Orbis Books, 2001), 456.

[26] Dawson, *Mongol Mission,* xxii–xxiii; also Moffett, *History of Christianity in Asia,* 1:409–14.

they passed through a Christian village, and in the Mongol capital itself found a few Syriac Christian churches. They also discovered a scattering of European Christians who had been enslaved by Mongol traders. One of the Great Khan's wives, they discovered, was herself a Christian.

Brother William contacted Christians as he could and reported that he baptized six children of European Christians.[27] Most of the Christians whom William and Bartholomew encountered or heard about were the fruit of the East Syrian (Nestorian) Christian mission to China way back in the 600s. William and Bartholomew came from faraway Europe, however, not Syria.

William and Bartholomew found Karakorum to be a cosmopolitan and tolerant place, religiously speaking. The brothers encountered Buddhists, Muslims, Taoists, and Christians all present in the capital. Jack Weatherford notes that "the small city of Karakorum was probably the most religiously open and tolerant city in the world at that time. Nowhere else could followers of so many different religions worship side by side in peace."[28]

Christian influence was particularly strong at the Mongol court. Several of the Mongol rulers had Christian wives. Mongol rulers sometimes chose wives from among the peoples they conquered. Four of Genghis Khan's sons took Christian wives when Mongol forces conquered the Kereyid and Naiman tribes of northern Mongolia—tribes that had been largely Christianized centuries earlier by East Syriac (Nestorian) Christians.[29]

A sort of female Christian subculture seems to have thrived within the Mongol ruling families. Particularly influential was Queen Sorkaktani (Sorkhoktani), a woman captured from the Kereyid tribe. Wed to Genghis Khan's son Tolui, Sorkaktani raised her four sons (Mongke, Hulegu, Khublilai, and Arik Boke), as best she could, with Christian values.[30]

The two Franciscan brothers with their simple habits and bare feet proved to be a curiosity to Eastern Christians and non-Christian

[27] Irvin and Sunquist, *History of the World Christian Movement*, 1:457. This and many more aspects of William's journey are given in detail in Brother William's account as published in Jack Peter Jackson, ed., *The Mission of Friar William of Rubruck: His Journey to the Court of the Great Khan Mongke, 1253–1255* (Indianapolis, IN: Hackett Publishing, 2009).

[28] Weatherford, *Genghis Khan*, 135.

[29] Jackson, *Mission of Friar William*, 122. The Naiman were a Turkic people. William of Rubruck mentions four central Asian tribes as Christian: the Naiman, Kereyid (Kerait), Merkits, and some of the Uighurs. See Weatherford, *Genghis Khan*, 135–36; Moffett, *History of Christianity in Asia*, 1:409–11.

[30] Moffett, *History of Christianity in Asia*, 1:409.

Mongols alike. Following the Franciscan Rule, the brothers went barefoot except in the coldest winter weather. William writes that one winter morning "the tips of my toes froze, with the result that I could no longer go around barefoot."[31]

The Franciscans apparently arrived in Karakorum in early April 1254. After some days they were called before Mongke, now the Great Khan. Brother William explained why they had come. He made it clear that though they were sent by the French king, they were missionaries, not diplomats. Their mission was "to preach the work of God and to instruct men to live by His will," the brothers insisted.[32]

Later, on May 30, 1254, the eve of Pentecost, the Great Khan arranged a sort of interreligious debate to be held before him. Mongke Khan was aware of Chinese Buddhists, Muslims, Eastern Syrian Christians. Now Brother William was presenting the Western understanding of the Christian faith. Irvin and Sunquist give a good summary:

> Representatives from each of the various faith communities (Western Roman Catholic, Eastern Syriac Orthodox, Muslim, and Chinese Buddhists) were told to write down in advance a basic statement of their faith.... [T]hree judges (a Christian, a Muslim, and a Buddhist) were selected from among the court scribes to referee the conversation. The participants were enjoined on pain of death to show respect for one another's religions.
>
> It is a remarkable scene that the Franciscan described. Gathered before the most powerful military ruler then living on earth, inside his lavish tent, were representatives of several of the world's faith traditions, invited to engage in an interreligious debate for the benefit of the great khan. The debate opened with the questions of whether the world was created and what happens after death. William says he quickly shifted the discussion to the nature of God, arguing for the priority of the question of a creator. The Chinese disputed the notion of there being one God, uniting Muslims and Christians against them. More points followed concerning the nature of the one true God. The east Syrians then took over, making the case for the Trinity and incarnation.[33]

---

[31] Jackson, *Mission of Friar William*, 175.

[32] Dawson, *Mongol Mission*, xxi. ("Work" is the correct word here, not "word.")

[33] Irvin and Sunquist, *History of the World Christian Movement*, 1:458. See similarly Moffett, *History of Christianity in Asia*, 1:412–13.

At the end William reported with some disappointment, "Everybody listened without challenging a single word. But for all that no one said, 'I believe, and wish to become a Christian.' When it was all over, the Nestorians and [Muslim] Saracens alike sang in loud voices, while the [Buddhists] remained silent; and after that everyone drank heavily."[34]

Brother William proved knowledgeable and astute in debate, focusing on the gospel and quoting or referencing Scripture. He noted that "a great many people were present, as each party had summoned the wiser men of their nation, and many others too had gathered."[35]

The day after the debate—Pentecost Sunday—Mongke Khan summoned William for a final conversation. William was now free to return home, the Khan said. But first he would explain to William his own beliefs. The Mongol rulers believed God had given them the commission to conquer and unite the world under their rule and laws.[36] (The Great Khan didn't mention that they often conquered by subterfuge, proclaiming peace but then betraying it, nor that they fully expected to grow ever richer by looting or taxing the peoples they conquered.)

The Franciscans had by this time delivered their letter from King Louis to the Great Khan, given repeated clear witness to their faith, and engaged in extended dialogue with people of diverse religious views. Over the cold winter months, William continued his writing, describing in detail the culture and customs of the Mongols. Now they had the Great Khan's leave to return home.

William began his journey west in early July 1254.[37] Brother Bartholomew seems to have remained in Karakorum when William set out for home. According to one report, Bartholomew was too weak for the strenuous journey, so Mongke Khan gave him permission to remain among the Mongols and promised to provide for him.[38]

The trek back would take William a good year. He returned by a somewhat different route, arriving at the Mediterranean coast rather than going to France, since he learned King Louis was at this time on

---

[34] Jackson, *Mission of Friar William*, 235.

[35] Jackson, *Mission of Friar William*, 231. William's account is found on pages 226–35.

[36] Irvin and Sunquist, *History of the World Christian Movement*, 1:458; Moffett, *History of Christianity in Asia*, 1:412–13. Moffett calls William's exchange with the Great Khan "a remarkable interview that has no parallel in any other surviving accounts of personal Christian conversation with the great Mongol khans" (412–13).

[37] According to Jackson, *Mission of Friar William*, xiii. Moffett gives the date as July 10, 1253 (Moffett, *History*, 1:413).

[38] http://www.silk-road.com/artl/carrub.shtml.

a crusade against the Muslims. William reached the Mediterranean Sea safely in June 1255. He was able to attend the Franciscan chapter meeting in Tripoli, north Africa, on August 15.[39]

Brother John of Montecorvino

Back in Europe, William of Rubruck's account sparked heightened interest in the Mongol world and in Christian mission east to Mongolia and China. One result was that Pope Nicholas IV (pope, 1288–1292, the first Franciscan pope) sent letters to three of the principal Mongol leaders—including Khubilai (Kublai Khan), another grandson of Genghis Khan and brother of Mongke. Khubilai became the Great Khan in 1260 and ruled for more than thirty years. He had to battle his younger brother Arik Boke for four years—this marking the beginning of the fragmentation of the Mongol Empire. But Khubilai Khan went on to found the Yuan dynasty in China, ruling as the first Yuan emperor until his death in 1294.[40]

Pope Nicholas IV commissioned the Italian Franciscan John of Montecorvino (1247–1328) to carry his letters to Mongolia and China. The pope had received from Khubilai Khan an envoy—Rabban Sauma, a Nestorian Christian monk—bearing a request from the Great Khan for more Christian monks. The pope wrote to Khubilai Khan that he was sending "our beloved son, brother [John of Montecorvino], with his fellows of the Order of Minors."[41] John became the first Roman Catholic missionary to serve in China proper, as distinct from Mongolia.[42]

Brother John traveled east through Persia, spending some months in India before journeying on to China. With his cross-cultural experience and varied background, he was arguably one of the most culturally savvy missionaries in Christian history.

Arriving in the new Mongol capital, Zhongdu (now Beijing), in 1294, Brother John found that Khubilai Khan had just died.[43] John was

---

[39] "Chronology of Rubruck's Mission," in Jackson, *Mission of Friar William*, xi–xv. According to this chronology, William had his final audience with the Great Khan on May 31, 1254, started his journey west in July, reached Cyprus on June 16, 1255, and traveled on to Tripoli to attend the Franciscan chapter meeting.

[40] Arthur C. Moule, *Christians in China before the Year 1550* (London: SPCK, 1930; reprint, New York: Octagon Books, 1977), 268–69.

[41] Pope Nicholas IV, letter of Khubilai Khan, 1289, quoted in Lauren Arnold, *Princely Gifts and Papal Treasures: The Franciscan Mission to China and Its Influence on the Art of the West, 1250–1350* (San Francisco: Desiderata Press, 1999), 43.

[42] Moffett, *History of Christianity in Asia*, 1:456.

[43] Khubilai Khan had moved the Mongol capital from Karakorum to Zhongdu in

befriended, however, by the new khan, Timur, Khubilai's grandson. Timur gave John freedom to pursue his mission work, and John did so with considerable success. In 1303, another Franciscan, Arnold of Cologne, arrived to help. Within two years, the pair won a thousand converts. John learned the Mongolian language sufficiently to translate the New Testament and Psalms into Mongolian (or perhaps into Uyghur, the language commonly used by the Mongol rulers at this time).[44]

John built what is thought to be the first Catholic church building in China in 1299. By 1305 he had built a second. He had the walls of the edifices decorated with Old and New Testament scenes, employing local craftsmen to turn the interior walls into a visual "Bible of the Poor."[45]

In letters he wrote in 1305 and 1306, John reported having baptized six thousand Mongols in Beijing. Pope Clement V thereupon appointed him archbishop of Beijing and sent more Franciscan brother-priests to help him. Several of the Franciscan brothers were martyred en route, but others arrived safely.[46] Thus, John and his colleagues were able to expand the work south over a thousand miles into Fujien Province, even building a cathedral in Quanzhou, a coastal city across the straits from present-day Taiwan.[47]

The focus on erecting church buildings and on ordained clergy raises the question as to how far the Franciscans had already lost the original servant vision of Francis. The Franciscan mission success aroused opposition from the Nestorian (East Syriac) Christian community. Francis's original community in Assisi was raised up to live radical

---

1272. The Mongols called the new city Khanbalik (City of the Khan), but its Chinese name was Zhongdu. The city eventually grew into modern-day Beijing. At its center, Khubilai built The Forbidden City, which Weatherford describes as "a miniature steppe created in the middle of the Mongol capital" where "the royal family and court continued to live as Mongols." "While Khubilai and his successors maintained public lives as Chinese emperors, behind the high walls of their Forbidden City, they continued to live as steppe Mongols." Weatherford, *Genghis Khan*, 199.

[44] Gerald H. Anderson, ed., *Biographical Dictionary of Christian Missions* (New York: Simon & Schuster Macmillan, 1998), 334. Dawson notes, "When the Western missionaries speak of Tartars it is impossible to say whether they mean Mongols or Turks," as they did not distinguish the two from each other. Similarly, when John of Montecorvino says he translated Scriptures "into the 'Tartar' language he may mean Uighur or Jagatay or Mongol." Dawson, *Mongol Mission*, xxxiii n. 1. (Jagatay was a Turkic language once widely spoken in Central Asia.)

[45] Susangeline Y. Patrick, "Art as a Pathway to God: A Historical-Theological Study of the Jesuit Mission to China in the Late Ming and Early Qing Dynasties (1552–1773)." Ph.D. diss., Asbury Theological Seminary, 2020, 44. See Moule, *Christians in China*, 180.

[46] Dawson, *Mongol Mission*, xxxiv; Moule, *Christians in China*, 173.

[47] Anderson, *Biographical Dictionary of Christian Missions*, 334.

Christ-like evangelical poverty and in this way to renew the church. It was neither designed nor equipped to be a church-planting and institution-building order.

In fact, most of the Franciscans' work largely collapsed when the Mongol dynasty fell in 1368. John himself died in Beijing about 1328.

John Moorman, however, in his *History of the Franciscan Order* notes that

> the story of the Franciscan mission to the East in the first century or so after the death of S. Francis is a story of great enterprise and great devotion. It demanded of those who took part in it high qualities of courage and endurance, for the dangers were many and the tax on a man's physical and moral strength was heavy. Perhaps only friars could have undertaken such work, for they were inspired and fortified by a great love of souls, and had learned to travel light while about their Master's business. Francis had taught his friars to be reckless; and those who set out to visit the Tartars or to cross the Gobi Desert could take little thought for the morrow.[48]

Historian Christopher Dawson gives this assessment of these intrepid Franciscans:

> If there had been more men of similar courage and faith to carry on this work in the same spirit, the whole history of the world, and especially of the relations between Europe and the Far East, might have been changed. But at least a beginning was made, so that the story of the expansion of medieval Christendom is not to be found only in the bloody history of the Crusades or in that of the forcible conversion of the [non-Christian] peoples of Eastern Germany and the Baltic provinces [but also in this Franciscan witness].[49]

Brother John of Marignolli

In 1338, Pope Benedict XII received an embassy from the Mongol ruler of the Yuan Dynasty in China. The visitors asked the pope, in behalf of Christians in the Mongol court, to send some spiritual guides to nurture the Christian community in China, since the much-loved John of Montecorvino had died about ten years earlier. In response, the pope sent

---

[48] Moorman, *History of the Franciscan Order,* 238–39.
[49] Dawson, *Mongol Mission,* xxxv.

several priests, including the Franciscan John of Marignolli (Giovanni di Marignolli). The pope also sent the khan a gift of large French warhorses (probably two steeds) and other gifts. The delegation arrived at the Mongol capital, Beijing, four years later, in 1342.[50]

John of Marignolli and his colleagues found that much had changed since the days of John of Montecorvino and the earlier Franciscans. Mongol rulers were assimilating to Chinese culture and language. Some had married Chinese wives. The elite among the Mongols were studying and excelling in Chinese scholarship, literature, and art. In time, it would be Chinese culture—more advanced in learning and the arts than was the traditional Mongolian nomadic culture—that would predominate. This was the lively milieu in which John of Marignolli would labor and witness.[51]

The gift horses that Brother John and his companions brought from the West created a sensation. Chinese history and literature had stories about large warhorses that the Chinese had acquired from an enemy people in central Asia during the reign of Emperor Wu Di (140–87 BC) more than a thousand years earlier. From these sources arose the tradition in Chinese art of the Heavenly Horse, a horse of mythic power. When Brother John of Marignolli arrived with two Western warhorses, the Mongols viewed them as positive portents and as tribute horses—that is, gifts signaling submission on the part of the sender.

The size and type of the horses so impressed the Mongols that they immediately connected them with the Heavenly Horse of Chinese history and folklore. One of the horses, it is reported, was eleven and a half feet long and six feet, eight inches high. It was black all over except for white hind hooves. A painting by Zhou Lang from 1342 titled *The Heavenly Horse* commemorates the arrival of this European gift horse. The painting is found today in the National Palace Museum, Beijing.[52]

John of Marignolli "was completely unaware that the simple presentation of such a creature to the Emperor of China was perceived by those at court as the Pope's acknowledgement [of the Emperor's] suzerainty over the entire west," Arnold writes. John hoped the positive reaction by the Mongol ruler might be a sign of his eventual conversion.[53] It was a case of cultural miscommunication.

---

[50] Arnold, *Princely Gifts*, 95.
[51] Arnold, *Princely Gifts*, 97.
[52] Arnold, *Princely Gifts*, 102–5; Moule, *Christians in China*, 255–57.
[53] Arnold, *Princely Gifts*, 105.

John began his return to Europe in 1348, after only six years in China. He and his colleagues seem to have left no permanent fruit. Brother John carried with him a request from the Mongol emperor for more Franciscan brothers—a request never fulfilled.

"Marignolli was escaping a country on the brink of dynastic upheaval," writes Arnold—the fall of the Yuan Dynasty twenty years later. But "he was also re-entering a Europe on the verge of social cataclysm," for "Europe was about to be plunged into a dark crucible of its own that would change it forever—the first visitation of the Black Death"—the bubonic plague pandemic that reached Europe right at this time.[54]

The Mongol Mission and Italian Art

An intriguing aspect of the Franciscan mission to the Mongols involves the exchange of works of art—another easily overlooked dimension of Brother Francis's long shadow.

The legacy of Franciscan East–West exchanges can be traced in the appearance of Mongol and Chinese influences in Western art. Weatherford notes, "The Franciscans had the closest ties of any European group to the Mongol court." And in Assisi, "artists borrowed themes and techniques from the Chinese and Persian art brought in by the Mongols" on their visits to the West.[55]

Art historian Lauren Arnold tells the remarkable story in her book, *Princely Gifts and Papal Treasures: The Franciscan Mission to China and Its Influence on the Art of the West, 1250–1350.* Arnold displays dozens of examples documenting the exchange of art gifts between Christian leaders in the West and Mongol and Chinese rules in the East. Arnold traces Western influences on Chinese and Mongolian art as well as Eastern influences on art and artists in the West such as the master painter and architect Giotto di Bondone (c. 1257–1337), sometimes called the founder of Renaissance art. Giotto painted many of the scenes in the Basilica of Saint Francis in Assisi.[56]

---

[54] Arnold, *Princely Gifts*, 107. The plague pandemic, later called the Black Death, spread rapidly across Europe from 1346 to 1353 at a time when the Franciscans were still growing and spreading.

[55] Weatherford, *Genghis Khan*, 237.

[56] Giotto and Susannah Steel, *Giotto: The Founder of Renaissance Art—His Life and Paintings* (London: Dorling Kindersley, 1999); Eric Newton and William Neil, *2000 Years of Christian Art* (New York: Harper & Row, 1966); H. W. Janson, *History of Art* (New York: Harry N. Abrams, 1962, 1970), 267. Janson speaks of "the revolutionary new style of which Giotto is the greatest exponent" (267).

Pope Nicholas IV, the first Franciscan pope, issued a bull in 1288 shortly after receiving several art gifts from a Mongol envoy to the papal court. His bull called for repairs and renovation to the Basilica of Saint Francis in Assisi. The two-level basilica was still being completed and decorated. The Franciscans were instructed now to "repair, consolidate, enlarge, and adorn the church according to their judgment."[57] As Arnold notes, "The princely gifts from China had arrived just as one of the greatest projects in the history of western art—the decoration program of the Upper Church at Assisi—was getting underway with a Franciscan at the helm of Latin Christianity."[58]

Many of the resulting frescoes, painted by Giotto and others, show the influence of Franciscan contact with China. Arnold and others credit the first Franciscan pope, Nicholas IV, with this extraordinary tribute to Francis.[59]

The selection of Giotto, master of fresco painting, is noteworthy in several respects. This was the late 1200s, two centuries before the Italian Renaissance, which would make Michelangelo, Leonardo da Vinci, and other artists globally famous. The early Renaissance centered in Florence, one hundred miles northwest of Assisi, the area where Giotto was born.

Giotto was already renowned when he was commissioned about 1296 to decorate much of the Basilica of St. Francis in Assisi.[60] He in fact represents a key turning point between the Christian art that preceded him and those artists who would follow and bring the Italian Renaissance to full flower. "Giotto's portrayal of human emotion and sculptural form revolutionized art," notes the National Geographic Society volume, *The Renaissance: Maker of Modern Man.*[61]

Giotto's art pictures the created order more the way Francis himself saw it: wondrous, and capable of moving us to praise God and care

[57] Bull of May 15, 1288. Reg. Vat. 44, fol. 9r; Bullarum Franciscanum 1798, p. 23. Quoted in Arnold, *Princely Gifts*, 38.

[58] Arnold, *Princely Gifts*, 38.

[59] Arnold, *Princely Gifts*, 38. These "twenty-eight stories from the life of St. Francis [constitute] the most important part of the decoration of the Upper Church." P. M. Della Porta, E. Genovesi, and E. Lunghi, *Guide to Assisi History and Art*, trans. Mary O'Bringer and Julia Perry (Assisi: Editrice Minerva, 1992), 69.

[60] In response to Pope Nicholas IV's appeal, Giotto seems to have been commissioned to paint numerous frescoes in the Basilica of Saint Francis in 1296 by the Franciscan Minister General, John of Murrovale. "The narrative cycle is inspired by the *Legenda Maior* of St. Bonaventure." Porta, Genovesi, and Lunghi, *Guide to Assisi History and Art*, 69.

[61] Merle Severy, ed., *The Renaissance: Maker of Modern Man* (Washington, DC: National Geographic Society, 1970), 395.

for his creatures.[62] Art historians rarely draw attention, however, to the role that the Franciscan Mongol mission played in artistic depictions of Francis and his influence. "Certainly, Giotto and his contemporaries were aware of China; it is reflected in their work," notes Lauren Arnold, and she gives several examples. The Chinese and Mongol impact is seen for instance in the portrayal of silk fabric backgrounds in nearly all the frescoes. The backdrop of fabrics, Arnold suggests, is suggestive of the fact that Francis's father was a cloth merchant and importer. In the scene of Francis and his brothers appearing before Pope Innocent III, the background is a richly decorated hanging silk fabric.[63]

Arnold notes the irony in the pope's lavish provision for the Basilica of Saint Francis. Through gifts and artistic commissions at Assisi, Rome, and elsewhere, "Pope Nicholas IV aggressively continued his enrichment and beautification of the Church Universal, knowing that his role as Pope superseded the strong desire of his own order to play down the problem of material wealth. Ignoring his order's discomfort, with clear intent pope Nicholas IV melded the fervent apostolic vision of St. Francis with his own vision of a church resplendent, worshipping God with all that the world had to offer," commissioning Giotto and several other artists. Thus "the first Franciscan pope, the nemesis of iconoclasts within his own order, insured that the spiritual message of St. Francis would resonate through the ages."[64]

The Franciscan missions to the East also played a broader role in the history of East–West relations and in the history of Christianity, Arnold suggests. For "it is the Franciscans—the travelers, the missionaries, the map makers, the writers, and the patrons of the arts—who first took us to China and then brought China back to us in the west." Today "the faces of Tartars ... gaze out at us from the works of Giotto" and others, "silently attesting to the impact that China had on the visual imagination of the fourteenth century."[65]

---

[62] I have found nothing about Giotto's personal faith nor any evidence that he was personally influenced by or maintained any connection with the Franciscan brotherhood.

[63] Arnold, *Princely Gifts*, 39–40. Chinese influence can be traced as well, Arnold argues, in some of Giotto's landscapes in the Basilica of Saint Francis in Assisi, in the shape of the trees in Giotto's *St. Francis Preaching to the Birds*, and in other elements. Arnold presents examples and comparisons showing these and other influences. *Princely Gifts*, 121–25.

[64] Arnold, *Princely Gifts*, 40–41.

[65] Arnold, *Princely Gifts*, 154.

Nicholas IV, First Franciscan Pope

The story of the Mongol mission soon becomes the story also of Pope Nicholas IV (mentioned earlier). An Italian and a Franciscan, Nicholas was elected pope in 1288 and reigned for only four years. He died in April 1292, at age sixty-four. Never had a Lesser Franciscan brother been chosen to lead the Roman Catholic Church. By this time, however, Jerome of Ascoli (who became Nicholas IV) was a well-known church leader.

Jerome was born in the city of Ascoli Piceno, in the Marches of Italy, in 1227 and became a Lesser Brother early, as a young man. When Bonaventure died in 1274, Jerome was unanimously chosen to succeed him as general minister. Diplomatically gifted, Jerome was soon appointed Pope Gregory X's representative in negotiations with the Eastern Church. In 1288 he was elected pope and took the name Nicholas.[66]

So now—seventy-eight years after the founding of the Order and sixty-two after Francis's death—one of Francis's little Lesser Brothers had become Supreme Pontiff. Was this the great triumph of the Franciscan movement and its unique charism? Or its great betrayal? This is certainly not what Francis wished or envisioned. It is closer to what he feared. Francis was very alert to the subversive appeal of status and ecclesiastical power. For their part, however, church officials concerned about the vitality and integrity of the church saw Franciscans as a potential font of renewal. Devout Lesser Brothers were proving themselves fruitful in ministry and skillful in leadership across Christendom. Perhaps a Franciscan pope could infuse new life into the whole ecclesiastical structure and bring much-needed reform.

It was a conundrum. A perennial conundrum and paradox, in fact. Whenever in history the church groans and cries out for renewal, those best equipped to answer—the ones most prepared to provide capable spiritual leadership—are often serving at the margins, often unheralded and unknown, with no desire to lead the larger church.

Nicholas IV embodied this paradox. He brought skill, experience, and integrity to the papacy. On the other hand, he led the church in doing the very things Francis warned against: raising monuments, elevating the status of the Order, favoring the clergy, and in general making the Lesser Brothers greater.

This is a prickly issue of church renewal to which we will want to return later.

---

[66] "Miscellaneous Franciscan Sources," in *Francis of Assisi: Early Documents*, ed. Regis J. Armstrong, OFM Cap., J. A. Wayne Hellmann, OFM Conv., and William J. Short, OFM (New York: New City Press, 2001), 3:803–6.

Christopher Columbus's Debt to Francis

Christopher Columbus was a Franciscan wannabe.

In 1492 and again in 1493, Columbus took Franciscan brothers with him on his earliest voyages to America. Franciscans had earlier befriended and helped Columbus, and he himself greatly admired Saint Francis. At some point Columbus became a Third Order Franciscan. But his spiritual ideals always struggled with his hunger for fame and honors and for seafaring adventure.[67]

Columbus's voyages came at a momentous time in history—for Spain and for the world. In 1492, Spain finally defeated its last Muslim Moors. The same year, as Columbus was trying to win Spanish backing for his westward adventure, King Ferdinand and Queen Isabella issued an edict demanding that all Jews convert to Christianity or leave the country within three weeks. They must leave all gold and silver behind. Fourteen ninety-two is thus a landmark year: Spain's expulsion of the Jews, its defeat of the Moors, and Columbus's first westward voyage.[68]

Columbus admired Saint Francis. The Franciscan brother Juan Pérez was his friend and soon became a key figure in the explorer's life. Like several other navigators, Columbus had become convinced he could reach India by sailing west across the Atlantic. For years he had been unable to secure the needed financial and government support. This is where Juan Pérez enters the picture.[69]

Columbus was in Portugal with his five-year-old son Diego, seeking the king's support for his enterprise. Failing in that, in 1485, he and Diego sailed to Spain, hoping King Ferdinand and Queen Isabella would sponsor his quest. The monarchs were in Seville, southern Spain, at the time, so Columbus and his son sailed round from Lisbon to the Spanish port of Palos to reach Seville.

Starting up the Rio Tinto toward the city, "Columbus noted on a bluff the buildings of the Franciscan friary of La Rábida. These suggested a solution of his first problem, what to do with Diego" while he drummed up support for his venture, writes historian Samuel Eliot Morison.

---

[67] Laurence Bergreen, *Columbus: The Four Voyages* (New York: Viking Penguin, 2011), 229. Moorman writes, "It is, indeed, probable that Christopher Columbus, who owed so much to the friars, was a member of the [Franciscan Third] Order." Moorman, *History of the Franciscan Order,* 561.

[68] David Boyle, *Toward the Setting Sun: Columbus, Cabot, Vespucci, and the Race for America* (New York: Walker, 2008), 133–38, provides a good summary.

[69] Pérez's dates are uncertain, but he died before 1513.

Franciscans were famous for hospitality, and often ran schools for boys. Maybe Columbus could enroll his son there.[70]

Christopher and young Diego walked to the monastery and were given a warm welcome. The brother who greeted them happened to be Antonio de Marchena, an astronomer of some note. Columbus arranged for Diego to stay at the monastery and discussed with Antonio his dream of sailing west across the Atlantic.

Brother Juan Pérez, now head of the friary, was also intrigued by Columbus's proposed venture. Pérez himself had a great interest in astronomy and navigation. The la Rábida friary in fact maintained a school for navigators, and Pérez had built a small observatory. Brother Antonio was also immediately interested in Columbus's proposed trans-Atlantic voyage.[71]

The la Rábida friary was located about 125 miles northwest from Gibraltar and only about sixty miles downriver from the important city of Seville—strategically placed for navigation purposes. The brothers there "were knowledgeable enthusiasts about the latest developments in geography" and "had strong links with explorers around the world and kept their ears to the ground" regarding new ventures in exploration, notes David Boyle. Columbus no doubt picked up important intelligence of what other navigators were planning.[72]

Brother Juan Pérez himself came from the nobility. Before he was a Franciscan he served as accountant to the Queen of Spain. His spiritual hunger, however, led him to the Franciscans. Queen Isabella wanted him to stay at court as personal confessor, but that life did not suit Pérez. The queen permitted him to retire to the la Rábida friary.

Brothers Juan and Antonio could see Columbus was deeply discouraged. He could find no sponsors for his big venture. But the comradeship of the Franciscans seemed to spark new hope and spiritual life in Columbus. The explorer became "increasingly religious, saying his prayers with an almost trancelike devotion. He had forsaken swearing . . . and constantly reminded himself that, though he believed he had enemies everywhere, he must not hate them. . . . Only the monks seemed to remain the least bit supportive" of his dreams.[73]

---

[70] Samuel Eliot Morison, *Admiral of the Ocean Sea: A Life of Christopher Columbus* (Boston: Little, Brown, 1942, 1970), 80.

[71] Boyle, *Toward the Setting Sun*, 66, 96, 122.

[72] Boyle, *Toward the Setting Sun*, 96.

[73] Boyle, *Toward the Setting Sun*, 121–22.

Interaction with the Lesser Brothers at la Rábida thus affected not only Columbus's navigational plans but also his whole worldview. David M. Traboulay explains,

> Franciscan influence helped shape Columbus's religious vision. [Franciscans] were in the vanguard of missionary activity in the Canary Islands and Portuguese West Africa in the late fifteenth century. The Franciscan convent of La Rabida ... was especially active in this work and was highly regarded at the Spanish court. At La Rabida Columbus found support for his project both from scientific and politico-religious points of view.[74]

Columbus remained at la Rábida for some time. Juan Pérez encouraged him and eventually successfully intervened with the Spanish crown on his behalf.[75] Thus, Columbus's encounter with Pérez "was a turning-point in the history of discovery," notes Moorman, "for the friar immediately became interested in [Columbus's] plans ... and was able to put him in touch with those who could help him most. From that time onwards, Columbus did not look back. An expedition of three ships was fitted out and sailed on 3 August 1492."[76]

Columbus with his three ships, the *Santa Maria* (the largest ship, Columbus in command), the *Niña*, and the *Pinta*, sailed downriver past the la Rábida friary, where young Diego now was, as they headed out into the Atlantic. It was a little before sunrise on Friday, August 3; the la Rábida brothers above probably were chanting prime their early morning prayers. The ships sailed on, the ebbing tide sweeping them away from the coast.[77]

While at sea, Morison writes, Columbus as "a pious Christian, faithful in his religious duties, ... kept a book of hours in his cabin, and whenever possible said his prayers in private at the appointed hours, as he had learned to do when staying at La Rábida"—observing them as near as he could determine time while at sea.[78]

By the end of 1492, in just a matter of months, Columbus reached the New World. He made landfall first on some small islands and

---

[74] David M. Traboulay, *Columbus and Las Casas: The Conquest and Christianization of America, 1492–1566* (Lanham, MD: University Press of America, 1994), 9.

[75] Boyle, *Toward the Setting Sun*, 133–39.

[76] Moorman, *History of the Franciscan Order*, 578. Negotiations with Ferdinand and Isabella took nearly three months; Brother Juan Pérez "acted as Columbus's attorney" at the Spanish court. Morison, *Admiral of the Ocean Sea*, 104.

[77] Morison, *Admiral of the Ocean Sea*, 158–59.

[78] Morison, *Admiral of the Ocean Sea*, 171.

eventually set up a base on the island of Hispaniola (present-day Haiti and the Dominican Republic). Crossing the Atlantic was not as long or as hazardous as many thought.

Columbus returned to Spain and immediately began planning a return voyage. He made his second journey in 1493. Juan Pérez himself was one of about half a dozen Franciscans accompanying him.[79] When the expedition landed in Hispaniola, Pérez, a priest, reportedly celebrated the first Mass in America on December 8, 1493.[80]

In the end, Columbus made four trans-Atlantic voyages. On the second voyage some twelve hundred people, men and women, crossed the Atlantic in a fleet of seventeen ships, enough people to establish a colony.[81] A number of Franciscans went as evangelists. The brothers were distressed, however, when they realized that many of the "Christians" who arrived in the New World killed or enslaved the native peoples. Columbus himself eventually came to support slavery. Slave-trading the indigenous Taino people, he concluded, was economically necessary for the Spanish colony to prosper.

Columbus was morally conflicted, though. He admired the Franciscans and wanted to be like them. At some point he apparently became a Third Order Franciscan brother, as noted, and at times even dressed like a Franciscan. The priest Bartolomé de las Casas, a Dominican friar sympathetic to Columbus, called him "a great devotee of Saint Francis." In 1497, as Columbus was working to arrange a third voyage to America, Las Casas says, Columbus "dressed from this time on in brown, and I saw him in Seville ... dressed almost identically as a Franciscan friar."[82]

But Columbus never experienced a deep spiritual transformation—a real conversion, like Francis. He seems always to have been torn between piety and ambition: between spiritual questing and the hunger for

---

[79] Lazaro Iriarte, *Franciscan History: The Three Orders of St. Francis of Assisi*, trans. from Spanish by Patricia Ross (Chicago: Franciscan Herald Press, 1982), 323.

[80] https://en.wikipedia.org/wiki/Juan_Pérez_(friar). This article states that "when the second expedition reached Hispaniola, Pérez celebrated the first Mass in the New World at Point Conception on 8 December 1493, in a temporary structure.... He also became the guardian of the first friary which Columbus ordered to be erected in Santo Domingo. There all trace of him is lost. Whether he returned to La Rábida or died in America is uncertain." See also Zephyrin Engelhardt, "Juan Perez," *Catholic Encyclopedia*, vol. 11 (New York: Robert Appleton, 1903), https://en.wikisource.org/wiki/Catholic_Encyclopedia_(1913)/Juan_Perez.

[81] Bartolomé de las Casas, *The Only Way*, trans. Francis Patrick Sullivan, ed. Helen Rand Parish (Mahwah, NJ: Paulist Press, 1992), 12.

[82] Quoted in Bergreen, *Columbus*, 218. See also 229.

fame and riches. His conscience troubled him because of his inhumane treatment of the native peoples he encountered and attempted to rule. Earlier in Spain he had fathered a son out of wedlock.[83] Wearing the Franciscan habit seems to have been a form of penance, trying to atone for his sins.[84]

Crossing the waves, Columbus became interested in biblical prophecies and apocalyptic passages, especially those that could be interpreted as foreseeing the discovery of America. Perhaps he himself, Columbus, "Christ-bearer" (Christopher), was playing a key role in God's larger plan for the world. He made extensive notes on these matters and a year or so before his death wrote *The Book of Prophecies,* attempting to correlate biblical prophecies with Christ's return and Columbus's own discoveries. He argued that the Christian faith must spread through the whole world and a final Crusade must liberate Jerusalem from the Muslims, so Jesus can return there.[85] Bergreen writes, "The *Book of Prophecies* reflected Columbus's circumstances of the moment, serving as [a defense of his life] and announcing to his critics at court and to posterity that everything he did, all the violence, all the lives lost, was done according to a larger plan."[86]

In his own mind, Christopher Columbus was a Christian missionary.

Had Christopher undergone the deep conversion Francis and his first brothers did two centuries earlier, the whole later history of the Americas might have been different and immeasurably better—much more humane and peaceful—less exploitive.[87]

---

[83] Morison, *Admiral of the Ocean Sea,* 83–85, gives details. This was Ferdinand, younger half-brother to Diego. Columbus could have married the mother, Beatriz Enriquez de Harana, for his first wife had died. He did not, Morison suggests, because it was not to his social advantage.

[84] Bergreen, *Columbus,* 218, 229, 232.

[85] In his letter to Ferdinand and Isabella introducing his *Book of Prophecies,* Columbus reveals his apocalyptic vision. "Columbus seemed certain that the world was rapidly coming to an end. The gospel had therefore to be preached to all the peoples of the world. He said that the Holy Spirit had inspired him in his enterprise of the Indies. He insisted in this letter that the Holy Spirit would help in the project to liberate Jerusalem.... Columbus's mindset belonged to a Franciscan spiritual tradition of the thirteenth and fourteenth centuries, particularly the tradition influenced by Joachim of Fiore. For Columbus, 'the discovery of the Indies, the conversion of all the gentiles, and the deliverance of the holy sepulcher were considered to be the three climactic events which foreshadowed the end of the world.'" Traboulay, *Columbus and Las Casas,* 10, summarizing and quoting from the analysis of John Leddy Phelan, *The Millennial Kingdom of the Franciscans,* 2nd ed. (Berkeley: University of California Press: 1970), 19.

[86] Bergreen, *Columbus,* 295.

[87] Toward the end of his third voyage, in 1500, Columbus was put in chains due to

Christopher Columbus died on May 20, 1506, in Valladolid, Spain, where he owned a house. He was only fifty-four. He suffered increasing health problems, including rheumatoid arthritis and near blindness. Franciscan brothers tended him at the end. The explorer died wearing a Franciscan habit and initially was buried in the local Franciscan monastery. His son Diego wanted his remains interred at a Poor Clares convent on the island of Hispaniola, but this never happened.[88]

Figure 19.1: Christopher Columbus and his son Diego at the Franciscan Friary of Santa Maria de la Rábida, Spain *(Eugene Delacroix, 1838)*

Despite the tragedies, violence, and scandals of Spanish conquests in America, the Franciscan mission itself "made considerable progress," according to Moorman. By 1500, Lesser Brothers "claimed to have

---

charges of torture and mutilation in his administration of Hispaniola. He was freed by Isabella and Ferdinand when he arrived back in Spain. See, among others, Boyle, *Toward the Setting Sun*, 262–63. Columbus later kept his chains as a sign of his suffering and penance. Columbus "never quite lost his affection for the chains. They had become a symbol for him, of his own failures, or perhaps of the sins he regarded as being committed against him. For the rest of his life he kept them on his mantlepiece and, in his will, he asked to be buried with them" (Boyle, *Toward the Setting Sun*, 273).

[88] Bergreen, *Columbus*, 362–63; Boyle, *Toward the Setting Sun*, 306–9.

baptized 3,000" people of the indigenous population, apparently on the islands of Hispaniola, Cuba, Jamaica, and Isabela.[89] The first Roman Catholic bishop of Hispaniola was himself a Franciscan, Garcia de Padilla.[90]

Franciscans in the Americas were divided, however, about the indigenous peoples. Many agreed with the Dominican priest Bartolomé de las Casas that "the true and only way" to win people to faith in Jesus Christ was by friendship, not violence—the way of peace, "a gentle, coaxing, gracious way." Jesus himself modeled and taught "one way, one way only, of teaching a living faith, to everyone, everywhere, always," Las Casas wrote—"a way that wins the mind with reasons, that wins the will with gentleness, with invitation."[91]

Las Casas articulated what Francis himself believed and practiced but never set down in writing. By this time, however, almost three centuries after Francis, the Lesser Brothers were divided about forced conversions. Some prominent Franciscans—Bishop Juan de Zumárraga (1468–1548), first bishop of Mexico, Marcos de Niza (c. 1495–1558), Franciscan missionary in what is now the State of Arizona, and the French brother Jacobo de Tastera, a colleague of Bishop Zumárraga in Mexico—opposed the use of force. But most Franciscan missionaries now supported violence, war, and even torture if necessary to "Christianize" native peoples.[92]

---

[89] Moorman, *History of the Franciscan Order*, 578–79.

[90] Huber, *Documented History of the Franciscan Order (1182–1517)*, 445.

[91] Las Casas, *The Only Way*, 68. Las Casas titled his work *On the Only Way of Calling All People to a Living Faith*.

[92] Helen Rand Parish, "Introductory Note" to Addendum II in Las Casas, *The Only Way*, 196; see also 216.

20

Patterns of Renewal

This seems to be a law:

The greater the abuse in the church, the more radical reformers must be.

Yet the more radical a movement is in its founding, the more it will struggle in its second and third generations. On the other hand, if a movement is not radical at its founding, its second and third generations will have little or no vitality to pass on to next generations.

A complex conundrum. Is there a solution?

Yes.

The Franciscan movement was unique, though not totally so. If we step back, widen the lens, and view all church history, patterns of renewal and decline emerge. It will help us learn from Francis if we view him and his movement in this broader lens before focusing finally on the little poor man himself.

This chapter views the Franciscan movement in three ways. First, a snapshot of Franciscans today—the fruit of Francis's witness after eight hundred years. Second, we set Francis's movement alongside other movements in church history, looking for patterns, differences, and lessons. Finally, we trace insights for church and world today.

The Franciscan Legacy

Throughout all Christian history, perhaps no movement has renewed itself more often and more genuinely than the Franciscans—no movement at all, except for the Christian church itself.

Through ups and downs the dynamic spiritual witness of the Franciscans continues. Many Franciscan brothers and sisters serve all around the world. Thousands more Christian believers—Roman Catholics,

Protestants, Jesus followers in other traditions—look to Francis for inspiration and instruction. Francis is still the spring of spiritual renewal and personal guidance. New Francis books continue to tumble off the presses—like the novel *Chasing Francis: A Pilgrim's Tale*, about a young Evangelical pastor's discouragement and then discovery of Francis.[1]

Pope Francis keeps pointing to *il poverello*. On Francis's feast day on October 4, 2020, Pope Francis signed his second encyclical, *Fratelli tutti* (*Brothers and Sisters All*) on Francis's tomb in Assisi. The pope lifts up Francis as our model of mutual love and acceptance, just as he did in his earlier encyclical on climate change and inequality, *Laudato sí*. The pope cites Francis as our inspiration in caring for the earth and its creatures with joy, celebration, action.

On November 15, 2021, Pope Francis told the General Chapter of the Order of Secular Franciscans (OFS), "With this Franciscan and secular identity of yours, you are part of the outbound church. Your favourite place is to be in the midst of the people, and there … to give witness to Jesus with a simple life, without pretension, always content to follow the poor and crucified Christ, as did Saint Francis."[2]

Today, tens of thousands of Francis's brothers and Clare's sisters in many lands continue their ministry. They testify to the ongoing, frequently reborn spirit of Francis and Clare.[3]

There are many Franciscan branches in both Roman Catholic and Protestant confessions. The total number of Franciscans in all three orders and in all organizations and regions and traditions throughout the world numbers perhaps several million.[4]

---

[1] Ian Morgan Cron, *Chasing Francis: A Pilgrim's Tale* (Grand Rapids, MI: Zondervan, 2013).

[2] https://ciofs.info/2021/11/17/pope-francis-tells-ofs-may-you-be-men-and-women-of-hope/.

[3] As of 2013, according to the official *Annuario Pontificio* (Pontifical Yearbook), membership in the principal male Franciscan orders was as follows:

Order of Friars Minor: 2,212 communities with 14,123 members (of which 9,735 were priests)

Order of Friars Minor Capuchin: 1,633 communities with 10,786 members (of which 7,057 were priests).

Order of Friars Minor Conventual: 667 communities with 4,289 members (of which 2,921 were priests).

Third Order Regular of Saint Francis: 176 communities with 870 members (of which 576 were priests).

This totals a little over 30,000 Franciscan brothers, about two-thirds being priests. https://en.wikipedia.org/wiki/Franciscans.

[4] https://en.wikipedia.org/wiki/Secular_Franciscan_Order. Some of the best-known

Franciscans and Other Movements

Church history is as much the story of renewal movements as it is of doctrines, councils, and institutions. It is the story of people leading or being caught up in movements of new life.[5]

History can be the story also of bad movements that do a lot of harm.

Looking broadly at renewal movements, we discern patterns. Each movement is unique, but not totally. Movements exhibit remarkably similar characteristics when examined and compared. It is a little like spiritual and social DNA.

Let us examine the Franciscan movement through a renewal-movement lens and see what we find.

Key Marks of Renewal Movements

Renewal movements are usually seen in one of two ways. Some see renewal movements as troublesome insurgencies—folks unwilling to respect established authority and submit to recognized leaders. Call this the *institutional view*.

Others see things quite differently. A renewal movement is a sign of hope—a signal things can be better. Old things can become new. Fresh leaders with new life and energy can make things better for everyone. Dry bones can live again; old wine in new wineskins. We'll call this the *charismatic view* because it draws hope from new people with new gifts.

I discuss these two contrasting viewpoints elsewhere. Institution versus charism, structure versus spirit, tradition versus innovation, stability versus shakiness, dry roots versus new shoots. The hierarchical Roman Church struggling with radical Christ-like community that somehow attracts thousands of youth.[6]

Franciscan tertiaries down through history have been Joan of Arc, Thomas More, John Bosco, Pope John XXIII, Dante Alighieri, Vasco da Gama, Miguel de Cervantes, Franz Liszt, Louis Pasteur, Coventry Patmore, Antonio Gaudí (architect of the Sagrada Família Basilica in Barcelona), and John Michael Talbot. However, the connection or attraction of some of these to Francis of Assisi is tenuous at best.

[5] In previous books I have looked at the dynamics of various church renewals throughout history.

[6] The *institutional* and *charismatic* perspectives and related dynamics are discussed further in Howard A. Snyder, *Signs of the Spirit: How God Reshapes the Church* (Grand Rapids, MI: Zondervan, 1989), 270–75, and Howard A. Snyder, *The Radical Wesley: The Patterns and Practices of a Movement Maker* (Franklin, TN: Seedbed Publishing, 2014), 144–52, as well as quite thoroughly in other literature, both Christian and not, that deals with social movements in history. The extensive work of sociologist Rodney Stark is especially useful here: *The Rise of Christianity: A Sociologist Reconsiders History* (Princeton, NJ: Princeton University Press, 1996) and many other books. See

Two quite different perspectives. But the point here, and the point with Francis, is this: *it is not either/or.*

Francis saw this from day one. This was key to his genius. He felt it as he felt the first drawings of the Spirit. It was already there in the words of Jesus Christ from the San Damiano cross: "Go rebuild my house, which as you see has fallen into ruin." Not "flee my house" or "destroy," but "rebuild."

Francis saw this. Fortunately, so did Innocent III, who could have quashed Francis and turned him and his little band into heretics—an old pattern in church history then and since. Innocent III knew painfully that the church needed saving, even if he and Francis had diverging views as to what this meant.

Francis saw the both/and perspective and built it firmly into his Rule. Respect for the church and commitment to its central doctrines—above all, to Jesus Christ, the Incarnate Word.

In fact, the old and the new, the institutional and the charismatic, can be joined—held together. Often, they aren't. Right at this point the Franciscan experience helps us today. There is a Saint Francis way to renew the church: to combine institutional structure and charismatic energy.

This is important, because both sides here—the institution and the insurgency—embody truths needed for the ongoing health and witness of the church.

The two poles can be held together. To do this in practice, it helps to see how it can be done in theory, that is, as concept as well as incarnation.

A Franciscan-Shaped Model for Today

Jesus said, "Every scribe who has been trained for the kingdom of heaven is like the master of a household who brings out of his treasure things old and new" (Matt. 13:52 KJV, modernized). Francis did it. How can it be done now?

Drawing on Francis and his movement, we can trace a model.[7] The model must assume the value of some form of the institutional church

---

also Gregory F. Leffel, *Faith Seeking Action: Mission, Social Movements, and the Church in Motion,* chap. 3, "Social Movements: An Interpretive Framework" (Lanham, MD: Scarecrow Press, 2007), 45–77; and Alan Kreider, *The Patient Ferment of the Early Church: The Improbable Rise of Christianity in the Roman Empire* (Grand Rapids, MI: Baker Academic, 2016). The literature is vast and growing because it touches on multiple aspects of culture and cuts across several academic disciplines.

[7] On the value of models in theology and history, see Avery Dulles, *Models of the Church* (Garden City, NY: Doubleday, 1987); cf. Avery Dulles, *Models of Revelation* (Doubleday, 1985). Also Howard A. Snyder, *Models of the Kingdom* (Nashville, TN: Abingdon, 1991); Howard A. Snyder, *Yes in Christ* (Toronto: Clements Academic, 2011), especially chap. 11, "Models of Church and Mission" (221–58).

as well as the need for repeated renewal through distinct renewal movements.

The challenge is to conceive of a renewing structure that brings new life to the larger church without either compromising its own vitality or splitting the church. We must presuppose a structure that can be seen as normative, that is, whose appearance and impact are viewed not as aberration or threat but as part of the creative working of God's Spirit in the church. This is not to imply that the decline of the church is ever "normative," but only that, given conditions of decline, one may hope for and anticipate certain patterns of renewal.

The Franciscan movement offers such a model. Franciscans embodied the key elements described below. Helpfully, these characteristics can be illustrated from other renewal movements, too.[8] At some points they parallel the "six areas where Francis's life and message most transformed the Christian message and resurrected the original spirit of Christianity" highlighted by Jon Sweeney in his book *When Saint Francis Saved the Church*.[9]

Why did the Franciscan movement take off and have such a deep and self-renewing impact? Ten reasons, ten marks of genuine renewal:

1. *The renewal movement "rediscovers" the gospel.* Francis rediscovered the gospel heart. More accurately: The Holy Spirit awakened Francis to the meaning and power of the Good News.

This is how renewal happens. One or a few people discover, in both experience and concept, new power in the Christian faith. This upends their perception of the nature of the faith or of its essential core, leading to a new model or paradigm of the gospel and of the church (a "paradigm shift") for their time and place.

If a movement is authentic to Francis and the gospel, this means that renewal begins with a real encounter with Jesus Christ through the Holy Spirit. But, of course, there are other sorts of encounters and movements and spirits. Whether such a "rediscovery" is true to Scripture or not is in each case an open question to be weighed. Some "rediscoveries" may be heretical or bogus. This was the big fear in Francis's day, when "heretics" aplenty could be found.

---

[8] This formulation of the marks is based up Snyder, *Signs of the Spirit*, 276–81, further revised and adapted in light of studying the Franciscan movement and Saint Francis himself.

[9] Jon M. Sweeney, *When Saint Francis Saved the Church: How a Converted Medieval Troubadour Created a Spiritual Vision for the Ages* (Notre Dame, IN: Ave Maria Press, 2014), 18–19, 31–131.

A new movement's nucleus, its initial renewal cell, consists simply of those who have gained this altered experience and/or perception of the faith. Renewal movements are made up primarily of those who have found the new *experience,* this new social reality, probably with varying levels of understanding. Beyond the central core, usually there are some folks on the fringes who have had a *conceptual* conversion but not yet the new experience. That is, they really like the idea but haven't yet been touched inwardly.

The first Franciscan brothers were transformed by meeting Francis and making the same radical commitment to poverty, community, and service (a "life of penance") that Francis visibly embodied before them.

This sort of gospel discovery or rediscovery is an essential factor in renewal movements. It will be central in any model that "works" today. And Francis would, of course, say not just any new spiritual experience, but a life-upturning encounter with the living Jesus, not just with his image or icon or cross.

Genuine renewal movements nearly always begin when a few people by God's grace rediscover the heart and power of the good news of God's kingdom. This is the most important.

2. *The renewing movement thrives as an* ecclesiola—a "little church" within the larger church.[10] The movement embodies a smaller, more intimate expression of the church. It sees itself not as exclusively the true church but as a subform of the church that is necessary to the life of the larger body and that in turn needs the larger church in order to be complete. The movement understands itself as necessary not merely because of a perceived lack in the larger church but also because of a conviction that the Christian faith can be fully experienced only in some such "subecclesial" or small-church form.

Francis felt this intuitively; it took a bit of time to work out in his mind. Brothers gathered around him before he quite realized what was happening. Energy of community was released! And God soon revealed to Francis through visions and other ways that a great movement was aborning.

3. *The renewing movement uses some form of small group structure.* A vital renewal movement is an *ecclesiola* not in some vague or general sense; it takes on a specific small-group form within the local congregation. It is an *ecclesiola* in two senses: both as a network within

---

[10] Discussed further in Snyder, *Signs of the Spirit,* esp. 35–39, 257–62.

the church at large and in the more restricted sense of a movement expressing itself in specific small communities within local congregations. The size and structure of these small groups varies, but generally they consist of a dozen or less persons meeting regularly once a week at least.

This is a consistent pattern across many movements. Small-group life developed quickly among the Franciscans. It demonstrated unusual power and depth because of the radical commitment Francis modeled and expected. Francis put very little firm structure in place, so size varied considerably from place to place. But there was very high self-awareness, self-identity as a distinct new community and servant body—people with a passion to serve and to praise and to awaken the church.

The most consistent structures throughout the Franciscan movement were the canonical hours of prayer and shared meals together, with time for informal conversation and perhaps singing or gardening or caring for lepers. Another crucial structure was the network of hermitages, built on forms of small-group encounter.

Word spread quickly in the church: Francis and his brothers were a new kind of community where God's Spirit was working.

4. *The renewal movement has some structural link with the institutional church.* This is crucial. If the renewal community is to have a revitalizing impact without sparking division, it must be firmly linked to larger church structures. With medieval Franciscans, this was life-and-death critical in avoiding the lethal charge of heresy.

Renewal movements always kindle controversy. Folks who have experienced the "new thing" of God's Spirit, and those who have not (or not yet), see things quite differently. This is inevitable and often leads to conflict. Whether the conflict is resolved peacefully or instead leads to serious, maybe irrevocable division depends largely on relations between the new movement and existing church authorities and structures.

As we saw in chapter 17 especially, Franciscans ran into sharp conflict with both church and university authorities as Franciscan scholars grew more influential. The papacy intervened. At the same time, however, increasingly sharp division arose *within* the Order over how strictly to interpret and observe Francis's Rule. Here again the papacy had to intervene, to act as referee and supreme court. The struggle between the main body of the Order and the Spirituals became so heated, even violent, that the church finally divided the Order in two, the Conventuals and the Friars Minor of the Regular Observance (chapter 18).

Despite the disputes, the Roman Church managed to keep the great majority of the Franciscan movement—and thus Francis's renewing energy—*within* the church, where it continued as a spiritual force for good and continues still.

Volume three of *Francis of Assisi: Early Documents* provides full details on the relationship between the Franciscan Order and the papacy over more than a century.[11] The popes did not always agree. Their declarations discuss and debate the proper understanding of poverty and the inherent complexities in the idea that the Franciscans really *owned* nothing—that all its books, buildings, gardens, vineyards, vestments and investments, and so forth really belonged to the church. The brothers merely made "fair use" or "poor use" of them. Was this not a distinction without a difference? Was it not in fact a fiction and perhaps even hypocrisy? Critics thought so.

The editors of *Francis of Assisi: Early Documents* note that by the time of Pope Nicholas III's important decree *Exiit Qui Seminat* in 1279, "vast changes ... had taken place among the Franciscans," especially over the prior three decades; "the Lesser Brothers were now a major institution within the church, with an important role to play in its pastoral ministry and with corresponding organizational needs." Pope Nicholas, sympathetic to the Franciscans, wanted to make their ministry "as easy as possible for the brothers to fill, but without betraying their distinctive way of life." Nicholas essentially followed the path Bonaventure traced earlier. Like Bonaventure, "Nicholas was convinced that the Lesser Brothers filled a providential role in God's history of salvation, but he also knew that their favored place in the Church was dependent on their living the 'apostolic life' of poor Gospel preachers" rather than being absorbed into the church's powerful, socially elite, and wealthy hierarchy.[12]

---

[11] The volume includes the full text of papal bulls and other decrees regulating the Franciscans. *Francis of Assisi: Early Documents*, ed. Regis J. Armstrong, OFM Cap., J. A. Wayne Hellmann, OFM Conv., and William J. Short, OFM (New York: New City Press, 2001) [hereafter FA:ED].

[12] Introduction, "Constitution *Exiit Qui Seminat* of Pope Nicholas III (1279)," FA:ED 3:738–39. The text of *Exiit Qui Seminat,* which runs to twenty-five pages in this edition, shows how elaborate and complex Franciscan organization and ministry had become, how intertwined they were with the church's formal institutions, and the fundamental questions all of this therefore raised in figuring out how Francis's Rule might be upheld with integrity.

The history of the Franciscan interrelationship with the institutional church is thus extremely complex. But the essential insight is simple enough: fruitful renewal movements thrive through forming some functional tie with the institution. An agreement between the movement and the institution is mutually sought and agreed upon. This can mean ecclesiastical recognition as a religious order, as with Francis; ordination of renewal leaders; or some other organizational linkage, official or informal.

At the very beginning, Francis fully and wisely achieved this link by gaining papal approval. We noted especially the key role of Cardinal Hugolino (later Pope Gregory IX). Hugolino befriended Francis, believed in him and his vision, and did all he could to guide it within acceptable channels. Francis's personal friendship with Hugolino kept the burgeoning movement from deadly attack, on the one hand, and potential collapse, on the other. The relationship between Francis and Hugolino was always push/pull, a sort of ongoing negotiation bathed in love and the limits of workable expectations.

At crucial times later, the papacy protected the Franciscans when they were under attack. Sometimes popes used the brothers for political purposes to which Francis would have objected. Church authorities enlisted Franciscans in support of military crusades against Muslims and heretics—armed efforts that Francis viewed as wrong-headed.

Effective movement leaders who win acclaim in the larger church become saints. Those who do not are often declared heretics. Francis and the Franciscans, on the one hand, and Peter Waldo and the Waldenses, on the other, are the two classic examples from the Middle Ages, virtually paradigms of this institution–movement dynamic. And there have been many others.

The institutional link with the renewing body can take varied forms. It can mean official recognition of and liaison with the renewal body, as wisely happened in the twentieth century in Roman Catholic accommodations to the Catholic charismatic renewal. The link can be organizational and official, informal and personal, or both. But if it fails, the renewal movement ceases to have the full impact it would otherwise have within the institutional church—though it may spark some new form of the church, which in time develops its own institutional forms.

5. Because it sees itself not as the total church but as a necessary part of the church, *the renewal structure is committed to the unity, vitality and wholeness of the larger church.* It is focused first on the life of that branch of the church that forms its most immediate context (for example, a denomination or a theological or ecclesiastical tradition). But renewal

movements generally also have a vision for the universal church and a concern for church unity and united witness.

Francis never doubted that he was a *churchman*, even in an often corrupt or self-focused church. His sacramentalism was deep and strong, reinforced by a more-than-sacramental sense of God's marvelous creation. More than sacramental—for the birds and trees, flowers and sheep and rabbits, rivers and stars were not just *signs* of God's grace. They *were* God's grace, God's love incarnate in his creation, like and yet distinct from God's incarnation in Jesus. "Praised be You, my Lord, through our Sister Mother Earth, who sustains and governs us, and who produces various fruit with flowers and herbs," Francis sang.

Within this larger church frame, Francis was ready to respect the role of priests and prelates, even those he knew were corrupt. He trusted in the Lord God who had called him to be faithful and unambiguously prophetic by his very manner of life.

6. *The renewal structure is mission focused.* It senses keenly its special call and mission, which is conceived in part as the renewal of the church and in part as witness to the wider world. Renewal movements stress practical ethics, striving to combine faith and love; and belief with everyday life.[13]

Francis said this over and over, emphatically, in different ways. It began with his call and never lessened. "Go, rebuild my house, which has fallen into ruin." As far as Francis was concerned, he had received his mission in the very words of Jesus, and he never wavered: Proclaim the good news of God's reign! "Cure the sick, raise the dead, cleanse the lepers, cast out demons. You received without payment; give without payment" (Matt. 10:7–8). As far as Francis was concerned, his call was as broad and deep as that of Jesus—in unquestioning obedience. This he gave to his brothers by word and deed, and they caught the vision.

With Francis and his brothers, the sense of a world mission—all peoples, all tribes, all lands, every language everywhere—was especially strong, and it expanded as Europe's explorers sailed out around the globe.

7. *The renewal movement is especially conscious of being a distinct covenant community.* It knows it is not the whole church. It senses its

---

[13] This aspect, as well as some of the others described here, is part of the emphasis of the "mission groups" pioneered decades ago by the Church of the Savior in Washington, DC. See Gordon Cosby, *Handbook for Mission Groups* (Waco, TX: Word, 1975); Howard A. Snyder, *The Community of the King* (Downers Grove, IL: InterVarsity Press (2004), 176–80; Snyder, *Yes in Christ,* 221–46.

own incompleteness. But it sees itself as a visible form of the true church. It does not attempt or intend to carry out all the functions of the church but is a restricted community of people voluntarily committed to each other. Based on a well-understood covenant, it has the capability of exercising discipline, even to the point of exclusion, among its members.[14]

As a community, the renewal movement prizes face-to-face relationships, mutual responsibility, and interdependence. It especially stresses Scriptures that speak of *koinonia*, mutual encouragement, and admonition within the body—a "one-another" community. It sees itself as a primary structure for experiencing the more intimate, relational aspects of the church.

This was a strength of Francis's movement. With its radical commitment to Jesus, the gospel, and the world, Franciscan sense of deep covenant community was very strong. Covenant community was deeply infused into Franciscan DNA from their first small face-to-face nucleus. It could not be otherwise, given the initial sell-all call to join Francis's life and share round-the-clock routines and disciplines. Further, this was explicit, written down in the Rule. There was no ambiguity at first—until new communities of brothers expanded into the schools and universities and grew geographically more remote. As time passed, the first generation blended into the second and then the third. We traced this as we saw the Franciscan story unfold.

8. *The renewal movement provides the context for the rise, training, and exercise of new forms of ministry.* Small communities are incubators of leadership. Out of the experience of community comes a practical emphasis on the gifts of the Spirit and the priesthood of believers. This consciousness combines with the natural need for leadership within the movement and the outward impulse of witness and service to produce both the opportunity and the enabling context for new forms of ministry. New leaders arise not through the more restricted, established ecclesiastical channels (typically, education and ordination, restricted to males), but through practical experience and the shared life of the group.

---

[14] These are part of a movement's existence as an *ecclesiola* (point 2, above). The renewal movement takes on many of the functions of "church," body of Christ, but in an organic, relational way rather than through hosts of rules and regulations. Renewal movements thus often demonstrate similarities and parallels with believers' churches or Anabaptist churches within the broad Protestant world. See the section "Catholic Anabaptist Typology" in Snyder, *Signs of the Spirit*, 54–61.

This happened quickly with the Franciscans. On the one hand, there were endless needs: lepers to tend; poor folks to feed and perhaps shelter; farmers harvesting grain; towns to visit and evangelize; parish priests who needed help; men, women, young folks awakened and inspired by the Franciscan witness who sought out the brothers for counsel and spiritual direction. On the other hand, there were abundant resources. The diversity of the brothers' talents and gifts and in some cases education, and the very dynamic of the *charism* of the Holy Spirit, awakened a widening spectrum of ministries and ministers. Naturally, this was complicated, as we have seen, by the fact that a growing number of priests entered the Order, men accustomed to priestly authority and prerogatives.

Serving as an incubator for new workers and new ministries, the renewal group provides both opportunities for leadership and service, and also a natural environment for leadership training. Partly for this reason, a disproportionately high number of future church leaders often comes from the ranks of a renewal movement.

Popes and prelates early saw the potential of the Franciscans in this regard. They wanted to make them bishops and cardinals and in time, even pope. From the beginning, Francis sternly warned against this. But the force was irresistible as the number of brothers mushroomed, served effectively, gained more education, and preached and taught with distinction.

9. *Members of the renewal movement remain in close daily contact with society, especially with the poor.* Renewal movements vary widely here, as you'll see if you review the history of any three or four movements in history. But if there is one mark above others that shines through the Franciscan brothers, this is it. Here was the heart of the earliest Franciscan communities; and the later fading of this close daily fellowship with the poor was the biggest point of conflict in the hundred years following Francis's graduation to the heavenly realms.

Some renewal movements arise primarily among or appeal directly to the poor. Others do not. Compare the early Franciscans with the twentieth-century charismatic movement. Many of the first Franciscans were not at all poor, but they made a radical, decisive turn to the poor. They celebrated this as they gladly embraced Lady Poverty. The early Methodist revival five hundred years later in England was largely a movement of the poor and lower classes, even though led by Oxford scholars. But the modern charismatic was more a movement of the middle and upper classes, especially in Europe and North America. In this sense, it resembled Continental Pietism in the seventeenth and eighteenth centuries—a renewing movement that spread among the more or less stable Lutheran populace in Germany, Scandinavia, eastern North America, and eventually beyond.[15]

In general, movements that appeal to and spread among the poor are both more radical and more socially transforming than those that do not. The extent of social impact varies of course, depending on the specific cultural context and other factors.[16] Much of the unique power of the Franciscan movement is based here. Sociologically speaking the Franciscan movement consisted mainly of youth and of poor and marginalized folk. These are sectors of society with little stake in the status quo, who are ready to see things change, and who can be awakened or "conscientized" to make change happen.[17]

10. Finally, *the renewal structure maintains an emphasis on the Spirit and the Word as the basis of authority.* Often dynamic movements are both Christological and pneumatological. They stress the norm of Scripture in the life of the Spirit, Spirit and Word, maintaining both, usually in some tension with the traditionalism of the institutional church. If a movement veers to the right or the left here it will become either a highly legalistic sect or an enthusiastic cult liable to extreme or heretical beliefs.

Here is *a key strength of the Franciscan movement*, though it might not at first appear so. From the beginning of this book, we have noted Francis's commitment to and actual immersion in the Scriptures—the Gospels of course but also in much of the New Testament and a good deal of the Old, Psalms and the prophets, especially. This commitment was of course grounded in the church's liturgy and prayers. But it went well beyond this. Francis emphasized the Spirit as well as the Word, often using orthodox Trinitarian formulations. He had a great love for the

---

[15] See Snyder, *Signs of the Spirit*, esp. chaps. 3 and 4. The Moravian movement primarily under the leadership of Count Nikolaus von Zinzendorf began largely within German Lutheranism but after 1727 spread rapidly and grew into a dynamic worldwide missionary movement.

[16] See chapter 12, "The Pentecostal Renewal of the Church," in Snyder, *Yes in Christ*.

[17] See, for example, Paulo Freire, *Pedagogy of the Oppressed*, trans. Myra Bergman Ramos (New York: Herder and Herder, 1972); Frances Fox Piven and Richard A. Cloward, *Poor People's Movements: Why They Succeed, How They Fail* (New York: Vintage Books, 1979); and William Dale Morris, *The Christian Origins of Social Revolt* (London: George Allen & Unwin, 1949), which mentions the Franciscans.

Virgin Mary. But this accent supported rather than clashed with the Spirit and Word focus. We notice as well that virtually all the earliest authentic writings on Francis embody this Spirit and Word balance.

A healthy renewal movement stresses the Spirit and the Word as the ultimate ground of authority. But within limits it also recognizes the authority and traditions of the institutional church. Francis clearly and intentionally did this from the beginning—from the day when he, Bernardo, and Peter Catani looked for guidance in the Gospels, to the day Francis and the brothers set out to consult the pope, to the day ailing Francis lay naked on the earth and returned his life to his Maker.

For the Franciscans, this grounding in Spirit and Word meant struggle. Movement and institution seldom rhyme. They look at the world and the Gospel differently. In disputes, often the pope became the arbiter. Yet the Franciscans nearly always found ways to accommodate to papal tinkering with the Rule, even if some defected at the margins.

In Sum ...

Here is a model of renewal that sees a normative role both for the institutional church and for a reforming movement and structure. No actual renewal movement perfectly fits this pattern. But the model is useful in comparing and assessing various renewal movements, past, present, and future.

This model of renewal can include, at least conceptually, not only renewal movements that stay within the institutional church but also the believers' churches (early Anabaptists) or other groups that become independent sects. The model can include many of the medieval "heretical" sects, at least those whose only heresy was to separate from Rome. At this point of course most Catholics and Protestants still divide. However, the model helps us understand why such groups become independent, what the underlying issues are.

Here's a bigger point: If one understands "church" in a broad enough frame to include all the people of God in the various communions, all those who confess Jesus Christ as Savior and Lord, then various independent churches and sects may be seen as *ecclesiolae* (smaller churches) within the great Church of Christ, even though they are independent of any particular ecclesiastical structure larger than themselves.

All the points of this model can easily be illustrated from the histories of the many Catholic and Orthodox religious orders, various charismatic movements, and multiple Protestant and evangelical "awakenings" of past and present, including Continental Pietism, the Moravian Brethren, and Methodism. The pattern traced here emerges quite consistently down through history. Looking at the pattern systematically as a model clarifies some of the reasons renewal happens the way it does. Or why it doesn't. It suggests important points where the flow of new life can be either choked or nourished, either by action of the movement itself or by reaction of the larger church body.

This model is useful both as a hypothesis in understanding church renewal and as a resource for others concerned or involved with renewal. The more we learn from the past of the human and divine processes in renewal, the more helpful we may be as agents or coworkers in renewal ourselves. Perhaps we can avoid being barriers to the flow of the Spirit.

All this presupposes of course that at the most fundamental level God remains sovereign and his Spirit moves in the church in God's own time and way. But God tells us not to be like the horse or mule, which have no understanding. Seek wisdom and knowledge of his ways that we may be useful and willing instruments in his hands (Ps. 32:9). God invites us to cooperate with him in the work of renewal. His acts in history offer clues we do well not to ignore.

Lawrence Cunningham in *Francis of Assisi: Performing the Gospel Life* offers a fine summary of several of the things I have highlighted above:

> What one sees at close range with respect to the Franciscan *religio* is a microcosm of the larger problem within all institutional religion. One could say that the persistent problem of Catholicism has been to somehow balance fidelity to the gospel with the need for some kind of institutional coherence. The most fruitful way the problem has been handled, when recognized, has been to constantly refine the institutional weight of structures against the sources of the faith in an ongoing process of what the French call *ressourcement*. This demands a firm understanding that Christianity in general and any of its particular manifestations, such as religious movements, are not perfectionist sects but ongoing attempts to strive toward the demands of the gospel itself.
>
> As far as we can tell, Francis tried very hard to do what he had originally set out to do: preach penance, live by the gospel demands, and, as occasion demanded, tend to the growth of the movement he had inspired. One thing is very clear: he did not act as the "head" of an order. There is no evidence that he

stopped his wandering ways, his times of retreat, or his care for the immediate needs of the day. Indeed, while he was obedient to the letter, the adoption of the Rule of 1223 did very little to change his own way of life. His anxiety concerned those who would subvert that way of life for others. It seems clear that Francis held on to his way of life, and the Franciscan *religio* was taking on a life of its own as it grew. Even the charismatic power of Francis's life and witness could not change that.[18]

Unlikely Twins: Francis of Assisi and John of Oxford

Looking backward and forward in history, we see no one quite like Francis. Yet we do find people, both women and men, whose lives rhyme with his. Clare of Assisi, of course, in Francis's own day.

As the spark of a new movement, Francis can insightfully be compared with Dominic of Spain, founder of the Dominicans. Or Francis can be contrasted with highly organized Ignatius Loyola of the Jesuits (himself strongly influenced by Francis), or Bernard of Clairvaux and the rise of the Cistercians, or of course Benedict of Nursia and the Benedictines. Or maybe Thomas Merton, who admired Francis and himself nearly became a Franciscan.[19] Or we could compare Francis to Teresa of Ávila, Catherine of Siena, or maybe Dorothy Day (1897–1980), cofounder of the Catholic Worker Movement.

Instead, I would set Francis of Assisi alongside John Wesley of Epworth half a millennium later. Unlike Francis, Wesley lived a long life (1703–1791), twice that of Francis.

The contrasts are many. Francis was Catholic; Wesley, Anglican. Francis was lightly educated; Wesley was an Oxford scholar—more like a Franciscan academic in the generation after Francis. Wesley was briefly married, Francis never was. Wesley was an ordained priest, wrote many books, traveled to America, and intentionally maintained a disciplined regimen of good health—diet, exercise, sleep—and wrote about that. None of this was true of Francis. Also, notably, Francis lived in the age before the printing press; Wesley lived afterward.

---

[18] Lawrence S. Cunningham, *Francis of Assisi: Performing the Gospel Life* (Grand Rapids, MI: William B. Eerdmans, 2004), 71.

[19] Daniel P. Horan, OFM, *The Franciscan Heart of Thomas Merton* (Notre Dame, IN: Ave Maria Press, 2014). Theologically, Merton was especially attracted to the Franciscan scholar John Duns Scotus.

Yet both founded movements—the Franciscans, the Methodists.

The big differences between Francis and Wesley are precisely what make the similarities so striking. Saint Francis and John Wesley are alike in a dozen ways.

1. Both Francis and Wesley were transformed by Jesus's call and dedicated their lives to serving and proclaiming the gospel. And the primary motive was love—love for God and for all people, whoever or wherever they were. Wesley's constant theme was the love of God and "faith working through love" (Gal. 5:6) in Christians' lives. Both experienced and taught a love for all people—"disinterested love for all mankind," as Wesley put it—a love not based on self-interest.

Wesley showed the spirit of Francis when he said the "necessary fruit" of experiencing God's love in Christ is "the love of our neighbour, of every soul which God hath made."[20]

2. *Both Francis and Wesley viewed the Bible as authoritative and sought faithfully to live out its precepts and promises.* Though a scholar, Wesley was famously "a man of one book," the Bible. Francis fed on Scripture and sought its guidance in forming his community. He loved to hear the Bible read, especially the Gospels.

3. *Both Francis and John Wesley felt especially called to the poor*—to be with them, minister to and among them. In this book we have traced Francis's similar call. Fulfilling this vocation was the reason both Wesley and Francis traveled so widely.

In the spring of 1739 Wesley was asked to preach outdoors to a crowd of coal miners—a radical thing, he thought. Wesley preached to the miners and to himself: "The Spirit of the Lord is upon me, because he has anointed me to bring good news to the poor. He has sent me to proclaim release to the captives and recovery of sight to the blind, to let the oppressed go free, to proclaim the year of the Lord's favor" (Luke 4:18–19).

To reach plain people, both Wesley and Francis used plain speech, simple words. Wesley made a point of this, as did Francis, who "preached to the simple, in simple, concrete terms, since he knew that virtue is more necessary than words."[21]

---

[20] John Wesley, Sermon 18, "The Marks of the New Birth," in *The Bicentennial Edition of the Works of John Wesley,* ed. Frank Baker (Nashville, TN: Abingdon Press), 1:426.

[21] Thomas of Celano, *Remembrance of the Desire of a Soul,* FA:ED 2:318.

4. *Francis and Wesley both saw the necessity of small covenant community. Both created structures to let it happen so seekers could grow wide and deep.*

To build communities of committed discipleship, Francis wrote his Rule. Wesley had his *General Rules,* summarized in three points: "*First,* do no harm, avoiding evil in every kind—especially that which is most generally practiced. *Second,* do good, being in every way merciful after your power, as you have opportunity doing good of every possible sort and as far as possible to all people. *Third,* attend upon all the ordinances of God," including public worship, the Lord's Supper, family and private prayer, "searching the Scriptures," and fasting or abstinence.[22]

Wesley though created more detailed and prescriptive structures than did Francis—the band, the class meeting, the society, others. Quite different from Francis. Yet the key dynamic was the same: deep, intimate, energized face-to-face communities of people committed to Jesus and each other. Wesley's early Methodist communities involved both men and women, both single and married—in Francis's case, they were communities of men while Clare formed parallel communities of women. In reality, Franciscan tertiaries (Third Order Franciscans) were much like the early Methodists. Both involved married and unmarried women and men who lived normal lives in society.

5. *Both Francis and Wesley sought to live perfect lives of holy discipleship the way Jesus taught and showed.* In Francis's day, this was called "evangelical perfection," "evangelical poverty," and similar terms, as we have seen. In Wesley's time, common terms for this ideal Christian life were "Christian perfection," "entire sanctification," "holiness," and similar terms. In both cases the goal was the same: follow Jesus the way Jesus taught, empowered by the Holy Spirit—the power of the life of God within.

6. *Both Francis and Wesley were firmly committed to a life of good works.* Do whatever good you can, as the Spirit guides and opportunities arise. Francis watched over his brothers, leading and encouraging them in self-giving service. This was an essential Methodist commitment as well. Wesley said the true love of God was shown in "being 'zealous of good works'; the hungering and thirsting to do good, in every possible kind,

---

[22] Summarized from John Wesley, "The Nature, Design, and General Rules of the United Societies," *Bicentennial Edition of the Works of John Wesley,* 9:70–73. The three rules are found in slightly different form in various places.

unto all men; the rejoicing to 'spend and be spent for them,' for every child of man, not looking for any recompense in this world, but only in the resurrection of the just."[23]

7. *Both Francis and Wesley were churchmen. Both were committed to the church and especially the Eucharist.* The Lord's Supper is God's self-giving for us in Jesus Christ based on his atoning death on the cross. Theologically, Francis's and Wesley's conception of Holy Communion was somewhat different, of course—Wesley would not have subscribed to the doctrine of transubstantiation. Yet both men saw the Eucharist as a mystery of grace, more than a remembrance—a means by which God conveys grace to us through Jesus Christ by the Spirit.

Both Francis and Wesley therefore partook of the Eucharist whenever they could. As an old man, Wesley published a sermon on "The Duty of Constant Communion" with the text, "Do this in remembrance of me" (Luke 22:19). The Eucharist was a constant emphasis of Wesley, as it was of Francis.[24]

With both Francis and Wesley, their sacramentalism reinforced rather than detracting from intimate, informal Christian fellowship. Community and Communion go together, part of the interweaving ecology of grace within the one church of Jesus Christ.

8. Relatedly, *both Francis and Wesley loved and lived the liturgy.* We saw how Francis and his brothers faithfully followed the canonical hours—even, as best they could, when traveling. Wesley was similar. Wesley always had with him the *Book of Common Prayer*, and he used it daily. His Sunday preaching was generally based on the lectionary. Both Francis and Wesley understood the church's liturgy as a means of grace and organizing time. Yet their worship was often spontaneous, not solely liturgical.

9. *Wesley and Francis both loved and reveled in God's created order.* Here is an especially pointed likeness conjoining the two. Wesley loved to visit gardens and walk out of doors—both were walkers as much as possible! Francis and Wesley both cared about animals. They saw themselves under God as stewards of the created order.

---

[23] Wesley, Sermon 18, "Marks of the New Birth," 1:427.

[24] Wesley, Sermon 101, "The Duty of Constant Communion," *Bicentennial Edition of the Works of John Wesley*, 1:428–39. The sermon is a reworking of a "discourse" he wrote fifty-five years earlier.

Wesley wrote a multivolume work, condensing the research of others, explaining and celebrating *The Wisdom of God in Creation*. One of Wesley's great sermons is *The New Creation* (Sermon 64), with the text, "Behold, I make all things new" (Rev. 21:5 KJV). Like Francis in his *Canticle,* Wesley saw the beauty and intricacy of creation as a cause for praise and for the hope of final healing and restoration.

Wesley (like others in his time) said God gives us two books: the Book of Scripture and the Book of Nature (Creation). He said "the world around us is the mighty volume wherein God hath declared himself"; "the book of nature is written in a universal character," consisting "not of words, but things, which picture out the Divine perfections. The firmament every where expanded, with all its starry host, declares the immensity and magnificence, the power and wisdom of its Creator." Wesley concluded, "Thus it is, that every part of nature directs us to nature's God."[25]

10. *Both Francis and Wesley were passionate for the renewal of the whole church.* Francis's explicit vision and mission was to repair, rebuild, extend, and enliven the church, as Jesus called him to do. Soon the Roman Church from the pope on down broadly recognized this—though certainly Francis, like Wesley, had his critics and detractors.

Like Francis, Wesley saw the gaping need for renewal and reform in Anglicanism and beyond. His late sermon *The General Spread of the Gospel* (Sermon 63) lays out an inspiring vision of the world transformed, using Isaiah 11:9, "The earth shall be full of the knowledge of the Lord, as the waters cover the sea" (KJV). Wesley said "it is as easy to [God] to convert a world as one individual soul." He foresaw that God would in time fulfill "all his promises; until he hath put a period [an end] to sin and misery, and infirmity, and death; and re-establish universal holiness and happiness, and [cause] all the inhabitants of earth to sing together, 'Hallelujah! The Lord God omnipotent reigneth!'"[26]

11. *The lives of Francis and Wesley were marked by joy, by song, by music.* Both were poets and loved to sing. Francis saw his brothers as God's Troubadours. Wesley, as an Oxford student, loved to sing and later

[25] John Wesley, *A Compendium of Natural Philosophy, Being a Survey of the Wisdom of God in the Creation,* "A New Edition," ed. Robert Mudie, 3 vols. (London: Thomas Tegg and Son, 1836), 2:370, 371.

[26] John Wesley, Sermon 63, "The General Spread of the Gospel," *Bicentennial Edition of the Works of John Wesley,* 1:490, 499.

composed hymns. He translated German hymns and edited, published, and helped promote hundreds of his brother Charles's many hymns. Wesley wrote rules for Methodist singing and an essay, "Thoughts on the Power of Music."[27] Methodists do not, like some, sing "in a slow, drawling manner," Wesley said; "we sing swift, both because it saves time, and because it tends to awaken and enliven the soul."[28]

Francis did not reflect systematically on singing the way Wesley did, but he recognized its power. But both men loved music, loved to sing, and saw music as a form of both worship and evangelism.

12. Finally, *both Francis and Wesley had a world vision.* Both clearly expressed this and lived into it.

Francis had a vision of "all peoples, races, tribes, and tongues, all nations and all peoples everywhere on earth, who are and who will be," knowing God and walking in his ways, as he wrote in the Earlier Rule.[29] His brothers were to go throughout the world preaching the gospel. And they did. Francis told his early followers, "My dear brothers, let us consider our calling because God has mercifully called us not only for our own good but also for the salvation of many. Therefore, let us go through the world, encouraging and teaching men and women by word and example to [repent of] their sins and to remember the Lord's commandments, which they have forgotten for such a long time."[30]

Wesley, criticized for not staying put in just one Anglican parish, famously said, "The world is my parish."[31] As for the Franciscans, Esser wrote, "Their 'cloister' is the wide world, where they seek to serve the Kingdom of God by a life of poverty."[32]

Wesley sent one of his preachers, Francis Asbury, to evangelize North America—which Asbury did, with remarkable and enduring fruitfulness. In the century following Wesley, Methodists, like Franciscans, were famed

---

[27] John Wesley, *The Works of John Wesley,* 3rd ed. [1872] (reprt., Peabody, MA: Hendrickson Publishers, 1984), 8:318–19, 13:470–73.

[28] John Wesley, "Reasons against Separation from the Church of England," 1758, *Bicentennial Edition of the Works of John Wesley,* 9:340.

[29] "The Earlier Rule," FA:ED 1:84.

[30] *Anonymous of Perugia,* FA:ED 2:42.

[31] Wesley said, "I look upon *all the world as my parish*; thus far I mean, that in whatever part of it I am, I judge it meet, right, and my bounden duty to declare unto all that are willing to hear the glad tidings of salvation." Letter to a "friend," March 28, 1739[?], in *Bicentennial Edition of the Works of John Wesley,* 25:616 (emphasis in the original).

[32] Cajetan Esser, OFM, *Origins of the Franciscan Order,* trans. Aedan Daly and Irina Lynch (Chicago: Franciscan Herald Press, 1970), 57.

for their evangelistic, church-planting, educational, and philanthropic work around the globe.[33]

Other parallels between Francis and Wesley could be flagged. Wesley, though he published widely, refused to accumulate wealth. He wrote of "the danger of riches," reminding us of Francis. Both stressed simplicity and ignored social convention where it would compromise their witness. Both Francis and Wesley preached widely to crowds out of doors, not restricting themselves to church buildings. Both were keenly disappointed when some of their followers were unfaithful to their calling.

These are the biggest Francis-Wesley parallels. The two men were, however, starkly different in personality. Their temperamental differences encourage us now. God uses all kinds of people. In personality and temperament, Wesley was more like the Franciscan scholar and leader Bonaventure. He was also in some ways like Hugolino (Pope Gregory IX), who loved Francis and helped guide his fledgling movement. Francis in turn was temperamentally more like John Wesley's younger brother Charles, the poet and hymnwriter, than he was like John.

The point of this comparison is not the past, however. It is the future. The characters of these two, St. Francis and John Wesley, rhyme with the marks of renewal movements noted earlier. This we would expect, given their passion to walk in God's ways. As we peer into coming years, we can expect God will move again in ways like what we see in these patterns from the church's story prior to us. These insights and parallels guide and encourage us in our shared discipleship today.

These are the patterns we see in renewal movements. They hold promise for the church and for the personal following of Jesus today, as we will see in the next chapter.

"Be Faithful unto Death, and I Will Give You the Crown of Life"

The risen Jesus Christ speaks to the church at Smyrna, "Be faithful until death, and I will give you the crown of life" (Rev. 2:10).

Nothing can keep a saint or a living church or a dynamic renewal movement from going wrong other than God's providential governance. The history of renewal movements does, however, suggest three big things that can help God's people be faithful unto death.

---

[33] See, for example, David Hempton, *Methodism: Empire of the Spirit* (New Haven, CT: Yale University Press, 2005); Darrell L. Whiteman and Gerald H. Anderson, *World Mission in the Wesleyan Spirit* (Franklin, TN: Providence House Publishers, 2009).

First, Structure

In the story of Francis and his brothers and of many religious orders, structure plays a big role, like the bones in the human body. Movements that remain most vital over time maintain structure that is organic rather than highly institutional, flexible and adaptive as circumstances change, and resilient over time, renewing itself as do the cells in our body.

Second, Tradition

Traditions are forms of life that help carry vitality from one generation to the next. In a vital church or renewal movement, there are traditions of ways of living, of liturgy and worship, of firm doctrinal commitments, and of workable ways of resolving conflict: these help keep communities of Jesus followers faithful in their discipleship.

Third, Memory and Story

Jesus's disciples tell and retell the stories of God's faithfulness over time, of crises faced and conquered, of humble servants who showed what it means to be a lesser sister or brother in the way of Jesus. Memory and story are preserved through books and documents and pictures, through the stories of "heroes" and "saints," through historical perspective that helps guard against exaggeration and hagiography. Vital, God-honoring movements welcome thorough open research into their living but checkered past.

Over time, renewal movements, like all social movements, rise and fall, surge, and eventually recede. So it was with Francis and his Lesser Brothers.

Yet in a broader sense, the Franciscan movement never really did decline overall to any substantial degree. There was ebb and flow, lessening but then resurgence—if not in one place, then in another. In its spiritual impact, Francis's movement keeps growing, spreading, diversifying, as life often does, and as God early on showed Francis in dreams and visions.

Francis and the Future

In a sermon commemorating Francis's life on October 4, 1255, Bonaventure told the assembled Franciscan brothers,

> Saint Francis can say to us: Learn from me to be meek and humble, that is, to be Lesser Brothers. Although it is not for everyone to take the habit and profess the *Rule* of the Lesser Brothers, it is necessary

for everyone who wants to be saved to be a lesser brother in the sense of being meek and humble. As the Lord himself teaches: "Unless you turn and become like children, you will never enter the kingdom." (Matt. 18:3)[34]

The final chapter of this book asks what it looks like to follow Jesus the way Francis did. Some will want to take that path. Like Francis and his brothers, like Clare and her sisters, they will be blessed in doing so.

Not everyone will feel that call, though. Many of us admire Francis—a saint from centuries past who still inspires and instructs. But maybe this is not our own call or path. Even so, Francis and his movement hold lessons for everyone. God promises and desires *fullness of life* for everyone everywhere at all times. And reflecting on the full Francis story, we find lessons that can help anyone anywhere, anytime.

---

[34] Bonaventure, "The Evening Sermon on Saint Francis," FA:ED 3:517.

21

Lessons in Lesserness

We can never consider Francis at arm's length—only in an embrace.

In this final chapter, let's ponder the abiding lessons Francis offers. As we do, we will be thinking of our personal lives, lives together as church, and the encompassing realms of society and culture.

Perhaps we should start by pondering the ways Francis is and is not like us. Then we will see if Francis can help light our way.

Francis the Saint

Francis was a small man, barefoot, weak-looking, often shabbily dressed in his simple patched tunic and hood. If he weren't a saint, he would be an embarrassment. With eye problems and other health issues and frequent fasts he often looked sickly, especially in his later years.

A story in the *Little Flowers* tells how Francis once went begging with Brother Masseo, a large, good-looking man. Masseo got good food while Francis—"such a worthless-looking man and small of body"—got only "a few mouthfuls and some little pieces of dry bread." Masseo was offered whole loaves.[1]

Such was Francis. Until he opened his mouth to speak or pray or sing.

The key is that Francis was totally sold out to God. Francis was wholly focused on Jesus and his passion and on uncompromising obedience to Jesus's call.

Francis was also astute in discerning gifts and character. This helped extend and reproduce his witness. One day Francis preached "a

---

[1] *The Little Flowers of Saint Francis*, in *Francis of Assisi: Early Documents*, ed. Regis J. Armstrong, OFM Cap., J. A. Wayne Hellmann, OFM Conv., and William J. Short, OFM (New York: New City Press, 2001), 3:587 [hereafter FA:ED].

wonderful and great sermon about most holy humility." He taught the brothers that "the greater the gifts and graces God gives us, the more we must be humble, because without humility no virtue is acceptable to God." After the sermon, Francis "with very great charity" assigned each brother his particular responsibility.[2]

We can emulate Francis and learn from him. He quickens our pulse. Writers often liken him to Jesus. Some call him "second Christ" or "little Christ."

Francis was not Jesus though, and sometimes he erred.

Francis Was Wrong

Can we criticize a saint? Surely not, least of all Francis, the Lesser Brother and embodiment of Jesus *par excellence*.

Francis seemed to have the capacity to be absorbed in God—in prayer, praise, song, meditation, contemplation, often ecstasy. He was so absorbed as to be oblivious to things around him, even cold or physical pain. Only minimally and often reluctantly did he care for his own physical needs. Commendable, certainly, but this disregard unquestionably impaired his health and shortened his life. In time it also led to controversy and division.

Are we allowed to say Francis was wrong? To raise questions and criticisms?

Of course. Francis thought so. Like the Apostle Paul, Francis felt he was the worst of sinners, least of saints. He considered it a wonder worthy of endless worship that God loved him and showered him with such blessings undeserved, meritless.

Francis was only human, not really Jesus, and he knew it. And he was a man of his time. If he had virtues and visions, he also had blind spots and blurry eyes.

Francis inspires. But before we set off to follow him into lesser brotherhood or sisterhood, we should pause to ponder some limits to his vision. Francis would not mind. From this angle Francis's virtues shine even brighter. He got so much right! —whether viewed through history or the light of Scripture. We will ponder the things he got remarkably right shortly, but first, the problems.

1. *Francis put an extreme emphasis on poverty, suffering, and self-denial.* In Francis's day, "evangelical" or "apostolic poverty" was idealized in unhealthy ways. Such an extreme view of poverty is hard

---

[2] *Little Flowers*, FA:ED 3:586.

to reconcile with the New Testament. If you study the lives of the first apostles in the Gospels, Epistles, and Acts, you find that poverty was not their big focus. Jesus's apostles and other disciples, women and men both, were actively engaged in society. Some were married and had families. The Gospel accounts center on preaching and healing, prayer and worship, traveling and leading, but very little on poverty.

The problem is, Francis took his model of Christian living not from the whole of the New Testament but from a few passages in the earliest days of Jesus's ministry when Jesus chose and then deployed the Twelve and later the Seventy. This was consistent with ideals of spirituality in his day.

In other words, Francis's biblical model was not the full New Testament gospel but some select passages through which God clearly called him to his mission—these Scriptures filtered through medieval ideas of spirituality.

Consciously or not, Francis was drawing on a tradition of so-called apostolic life—*vita apostolica*—that by 1200 had become the glistening high road for those who devoted themselves fully to following Jesus. By Francis's time, "apostolic" meant not preaching and mission, as in the New Testament, but poverty and simplicity—"the life [supposedly] led by the apostles themselves," as Marie-Dominque Chenu writes, including "abandonment of all private goods in favor of the common life."[3]

This was the ideal that inspired existing monastic communities. Francis grew up with this ideal. It was the air he breathed.

Many in Francis's day, especially people who knew Scripture and history, realized this idealization of poverty was not the New Testament focus of discipleship. In fact, in the late 1200s and early 1300s big theological debates broke out at the University of Paris precisely on this point. Hand-copied pamphlets upholding and decrying so-called apostolic poverty flew back and forth as the growing influence of Franciscans in university affairs was contested.[4]

Francis's stress on poverty was often combined with extreme forms of self-denial or self-inflicted suffering. Francis warned his brothers

---

[3] Marie-Dominique Chenu, *Nature, Man and Society in the Twelfth Century*, trans. Jerome Taylor and Lester K. Little (Chicago: University of Chicago Press, 1968), 203–6. "The text which inspired this mode of life was the classic description of the first Christian community at Jerusalem in Acts 4:32, a text expressing the evangelical ideal for all time.... Such was the claim." Chenu, 206.

[4] We saw this in chapter 17.

against excessive austerity, but he himself practiced radical self-denial and self-abasement. Brother Bonaparte told of a time when Francis and some brothers were staying as guests in someone's home. "When Saint Francis sat down at the table, he used to pour ashes or cold water or something else like that over his food, making it virtually tasteless." This really upset the cook, who worked hard to prepare good meals. Francis told him, "You do well, [working] with a good intention; but I too do with a good intention what I think I should do." Other early accounts tell similar stories.[5]

Francis at times practiced extreme asceticism toward his body, though maybe not so much as later hagiography claimed. In hagiographic writing, isolated or occasional incidents are often pictured as though they were constant practice.

According to Thomas of Celano, Francis "said it was impossible to satisfy necessity," even of food or sleep, "without bowing to pleasure. He rarely or hardly ever ate cooked foods," and if he did, he deliberately spoiled the taste. If he was invited to a meal at the home of a prince or noble, he "would taste some meat in order to observe the holy gospel [Luke 10:7–8]. The rest, which he appeared to eat, he put in his lap, raising his hand to his mouth so that no one could know what he was doing. What shall I say about drinking wine, when he would not allow himself to drink even enough water when he was burning of thirst?"[6]

Thomas claims also that when sleeping, Francis "refused to use a straw mattress or blankets" and "would often sleep sitting up, not lying down, using a stone or a piece of wood as a pillow" so as to deny himself comfort.[7]

That was then, the Middle Ages. What about today?

Here the question is discipleship and spirituality for Christians now, not then. If we want to walk in Jesus's steps as Francis did, we will note carefully what Jesus taught and did. We look at the Messianic promises in the Old Testament and how Jesus fulfilled them, and their meaning now. We will study what Jesus taught his disciples and the mission he gave. We will note what the Bible teaches about the created order and God's covenant with the land and Earth's place in discipleship and in the reconciliation of "all things."

---

[5] *A Book of Exemplary Stories* (c. 1280–1310), FA:ED 3:801.

[6] Thomas of Celano, *Life of St. Francis*, FA:ED 1:227. This is clearly an exaggeration or overgeneralization.

[7] Thomas of Celano, *Life of St. Francis*, FA:ED 1:227. See similarly *A Life of Saint Francis by an Anonymous Monk of a German Monastery* (c. 1275), FA:ED 3:852.

We will, in other words, accept Francis's challenge to follow Jesus Christ fully, no compromise. But we take up the challenge with, we hope, a more biblically rounded view of evangelical poverty and with eyes alert to today's challenges.

The New Testament offers no evidence that Jesus despised or spoiled food. Quite the contrary! He often dined with various folks, so much so that the Pharisees noticed. Surely the gospel call is not to extreme asceticism or self-punishment but to discipline and moderation in all things. "So, whether you eat or drink, or whatever you do, do everything for the glory of God" (1 Cor. 10:31). This is not to deny of course that Christ may call some to more extreme forms of self-denial.

It doesn't seem credible that Christ would call his bride to such levels of self-denying self-abasement that the body actually cannibalizes itself— Jesus Christ, who was called a glutton and winebibber, who fasted at times and feasted at others and apparently kept himself physically fit. He did say that when the bridegroom was absent, his friends would fast. But the tone of the Gospel is that we prudently care for our bodies. "Do you not know that your body is a temple of the Holy Spirit within you, which you have from God, and that you are not your own? For you were bought with a price; therefore glorify God in your body" (1 Cor. 6:19–20).

Certainly, you can imagine times of tragedy or bereavement or great agony or intercession when the body is in trauma and suffers or is neglected. Of course—or perhaps you can imagine a bereft bride starving herself to near death out of loss and grief.

But Jesus is *alive*! We live the suffering and death and crucifixion, but also the joy and freedom and limitless hope and assurance of resurrection.

The first course correction then in following Francis is to adjust the view of poverty to make it more biblical, yet no less radical.

2. *Francis largely ignored the need for organizational structure.* A second question about Francis's vision arises here. Compare the Franciscans with the Benedictines and especially the later Jesuits. Francis's skimpy design looks like a limitation and a failing.

Was it really, though? The very freedom and flexibility, the relative freeform life of the brotherhood, was a magnet to many. The Franciscans were as *un*structured as the church bureaucracy was structured.

Franciscan commitment was totally radical. Renouncing everything, 100 percent, giving everything away. Total commitment to Jesus Christ and to the brotherhood—that was enough, Francis felt. The initial and lifelong Christ-first covenant would carry them through to the end.

Francis knew full well what he was doing. He was not so naïve as he might appear or as some of his contemporaries thought. He well knew how Benedictines and Augustinians were structured. He didn't want that. He wanted a much more open, fluid, egalitarian, freeform, radically hierarchy-less community. All would truly be "lesser brothers" on the same lesser plane. Francis steadfastly refused even to consider adopting the rules of other orders. That would be unacceptable, a treacherous step away from the simplicity and radical call of Jesus. It was not what Jesus did.

Francis knew the difficulty of maintaining such radical open community over time. He was very clear, even emphatic, in his writings and especially his *Testament*. This is why Francis insisted that his radical Rule be followed "without gloss," without shade of compromise. He demanded that

> the minister general and all other ministers and custodians be bound through obedience not to add to or take away from these words. And let them always have this writing with them together with the Rule. And in all the chapters which they hold, when they read the Rule, let them also read these words. And I strictly command all my cleric and lay brothers, through obedience, not to place any gloss upon the Rule or upon these words saying: "They should be understood in this way." But as the Lord has given me to speak and write the Rule and these words simply and purely, so shall you understand them simply and without gloss and observe them with a holy activity until the end.[8]

This would be enough. More structure or rules would just complicate.

And was Francis not right? Was Francis not here fully following Jesus, "nakedly following the naked Christ"? Doing just as Jesus did with the Twelve and other disciples, and finally on the cross? Jesus after all failed to give his followers much structure.

Yet in applying Francis's lessons and example today we must pay attention to organizational dynamics. Here we can learn from contemporary culture and from human and nonhuman animal organization. We can gain insights from anthropology and ecology, even as Franciscan scholars in the 1300s were beginning to do. We can learn from other renewal movements, too, as we saw in the previous chapter.

The point is simple: On the one hand, be aware of the importance of structure and structural assumptions, both formal and informal. On

---

[8] Francis, *The Testament*, FA:ED 1:127.

the other, follow Francis's example of 100 percent commitment to Jesus Christ in every area of life if we would be radical Jesus followers in the Francis mode.

Lessons for Everyone

What have I learned from Francis? I meditate and ask myself.

Francis is so fascinating partly because he is such an enigma still today. And he still offers lessons for everyone. Here are several clues all can apply in our lives if we find that Francis inspires as well as puzzles us. They offer as well a path for churches seeking a deeper, broader life and witness.

1. *Discover community.* In the Francis story, we see how a group of men, banded together, were energized to life, excitement, vision, and good works. That is the dynamic of community. Clare and her sisters discovered the same. Community generates energy. It takes someone like Francis or Clare, however, to "sanctify" that energy and turn it in positive directions, both for the inward and the outward journey.

2. *Love all creatures.* All living things are sacred because life comes from God. And God has an "everlasting covenant" with all Earth's creatures, the Bible says (Gen. 9:14–16). The glory of God is seen in all life-forms, even if it is distorted or hidden or in some way corrupted.

Francis loved all creatures. He marveled at them. When he saw them suffering or enslaved, he wanted to free them.

We become more fully whole and alive, more a part of life, when we love all creatures, partner with them, learn from them, protect their homes and habitats. Surely Francis teaches this.

3. *Learn to be lesser.* In the Francis story, we find the strange appeal and the surprising elevation of choosing to be lesser. As we have seen, the call to lesserness is a call to servanthood.

Lesserness is also a call to courtesy. In Francis day, the courtly "age of chivalry," *courtesy* was a much-sought virtue. To be mature, virtuous, chivalrous, was to be courteous. The way of lesserness is the way of courtesy, graciousness. It is a call to live graciously with all, be courteous with all, and to live for the poor so we can be more truly human and a blessing, not a curse.

4. *Live God's Word.* Francis's words and acts breathed the accents of Scripture. He lived his life as a response to Jesus. He sang psalms of praise. He understood the truth, "the word of God is living and active,

sharper than any two-edged sword, piercing until it divides soul from spirit, joints from marrow; it is able to judge the thoughts and intentions of the heart" (Heb. 4:12).

The point is not so much to believe, to agree, but rather to do, to perform, to live God's Word. Jesus said after all, "Why do you call me 'Lord, Lord,' and do not do what I tell you?" (Luke 6:46).

The way to life is to live God's Word.

5. *Find joy in suffering.* Here is an amazing truth, proved over and over in human experience and supremely in Jesus's own life. Jesus "for the sake of the *joy* that was set before him endured the cross, disregarding its shame" (Heb. 12:2). A deep spiritual and psychological truth: Joy defeats pain. Joy can overwhelm pain, turning suffering into surprising joyousness.

How else do we explain Francis? He suffered dreadfully for long periods; he endured pain. Yet he rose above this. How else do we explain the paradox of Francis, who would be cheerful, even joyous and light-hearted, even as he suffered in his eyes and in his stomach? Suffering was surrounded and overwhelmed and captured by joy, grace, love, self-giving.

So often it is true: those who suffer deeply love deeply. Pain may perhaps be endured, but it can be transcended. Joy, well placed, is stronger than pain. Francis shows we can learn to live above and beyond pain and distractions through prayer and mental/spiritual disciplines. It is possible! Many have learned this down through history, either voluntarily or of necessity. Francis shows how.

6. *Cherish church connections.* Surrounded by pain or shrinking meaning, we tend to neglect the very links that nurture us. Like an arm or a truth not exercised, connections with other truth-seekers and truth-walkers wither and die if not stretched and strengthened.

Much of the genius of Francis's life lives here. He reconnected nominal believers with the church. Even where the church was corrupt or decayed, Francis and his brothers offered living connecting cells and sinews that brought life to people in need.

Even churches that are mostly meaningless, spiritually void, often have a remnant where life lives and where bonds flourish. Connect or reconnect, and you may find life and living water.

7. *Go deep in prayer.* Prayer begins with reaching out to God. It is not a matter of right words or even pure thoughts and motives. Prayer

arises out of need or out of gratitude. We pray because being alone is not enough.

Wherever it begins, prayer grows and goes deep. It may be only a tender shoot, a shallow root, a weak pursuit for something beyond us as we realize that to be alone in the world is deadening or makes us vicious. So, we pray.

When we reach out to God with open heart, we find God already reaching for us. Fingers and faith meet. If we suffer or serve others, or if we feed on the Word and maintain church connections, there will be much to pray about and many motives for praise.

All accounts of Francis's life and of Clare and their brothers and sisters stress the vitality of prayer. Sometimes in exaggerated ways, accounts tell of Francis's brothers being caught up in ecstasy, lifted from the ground, having visions, conversing with Christ, losing all count of time. This was true of some, not others, for we are all different. But we all need prayer just as we all breathe and at times rest.

Prayer is the breath, the oxygen and nitrogen that supply life as we walk on God's Earth.

8. *Love the liturgy.* If we walk the path of truth, we see footprints, find well-trodden paths. For the path of truth is an ancient way. Travelers before us have left marks and signposts, maybe prayers, testimonies, and songs. Added together, these are called the church's *liturgy.* Liturgy in various forms is the record of the church's journey through time, often codified in forms of prayer and song and readings that offer profound words to help us pray and praise and grow.

I can and must pray in my own words. But the thing I love about liturgy is that it often says better than I can what I really mean or really need. Plus, it is not just me, or you. Liturgy is "of the people"—that is, it is the public property of God's people, so to speak.

This gives us a both/and, not either/or, walk with God in the world. Our own efforts and cries and prayers blend with those of the *communion of saints,* the vast numbers of folks in many cultures and in many lands who have walked and proved this way.

Liturgy helps us pray with a broader lens, a wider view—to remember in prayer important things we often forget.

9. *Find and live your gift.* As a self-centered youth, Francis showed the gift of hospitality. Often, he was the center of group life. But really it was all for his own sake—till he met Jesus and hugged a leper.

Transformed by Jesus and given mission, Francis discovered gifts of leadership, of teaching and preaching, of discipling, of humor and song. He discovered the gift of inspiring others. This was his *charism*, his grace-gift.

Francis constantly discerned people's gifts, sensed their call, sent them out usually two by two to preach or serve, perhaps to sing. Descriptions of Francis's early brothers point out the sundry gifts and graces and particular sensitivities among them.[9]

Thus, the brothers found their gifts. Some could garden and some could sing. Some could preach and some could dream. Some could go deep in theology and philosophy and the rising sciences, leaving legacies that still nurture us.

This call to service, this finding your central mission, was a great part of the power of the Franciscan Third Order as well. Tertiary orders channeled people's creativity into mission in the midst of everyday life—open doors to servanthood that "has been an inspiration to innumerable crowds of ordinary married men and women; living lives like our own, only entirely different," as Chesterton put it.[10]

We each receive a *charism*, a gift for ministry. The Apostle Paul said each of us has been "given grace according to the measure of Christ's gift" (Eph. 4:7), that is, given in abundant measure so we can serve and bless others. Peter agreed. We should be "good stewards" of God's grace and serve others with whatever gift (*charisma*) we have received. Maybe it's speaking; maybe it's serving. But the aim is "that God may be glorified in all things through Jesus Christ" (1 Pt. 4:10–11).

This is radical. It means you, you yourself, have a calling from God unique to you. You are uniquely empowered by Jesus through the Holy Spirit. No one can take this from you, though authorities or circumstances may limit it.

The doctrine of the gifts of the Spirit is the most radical, socially unsettling of Christian doctrines because it means that *anyone* God touches—poor or rich, powerless or powerful, weak or strong, woman or man, old or young, Black or White, impaired or whole, unauthorized

---

[9] For example, Arnald of Sarrant, *The Kinship of Saint Francis* (1365), FA:ED 3:680–93. Though hagiographic in drawing close parallels between Francis's early brothers and Jesus's twelve apostles, this source does show the diversity of gifts among the brothers.

[10] G. K. Chesterton, *St. Francis of Assisi* (Garden City, NY: Image Books, Doubleday [1924], 1957), 113.

or authorized, can serve and lead supernaturally. The gifts come from Jesus, who is full of grace and the Spirit. The New Testament stresses that gifts function best *in community* in order to build one another up and extend Jesus's witness in the world and avoid extremes (1 Cor. 14:1–31).

Francis and his brothers saw this and did it. Serving through our giftedness is authentically Jesus-like, authentically Francis-and-Clare-like. We don't find this calling and *charism* on our own, though. We need help. In addition to the Holy Spirit and the Bible, we need community, just as Francis taught. God gives his gifts *to the body*, the community, not to lone travelers. Gifts are given so each of us can serve others and be blessed and enriched in so doing. As we walk in God's ways, we should expect both to receive and to give—not only grow in grace, but help others grow in ways that each one can, each in our own unique ways.

10. *Trust God's future*. We look ahead to days to come—days and events and people still unknown to us—and trust all into God's hands. This is what the church calls *eschatology*, the matter of last and ultimate things, wrapped in mystery yet not needlessly ominous to us, for we trust God's power and character, justice and lovingkindness, and above all Jesus's victory.

Joshua in the Old Testament told the Israelites just before he died, "Not one thing has failed of all the good things that the Lord your God promised concerning you; all have come to pass for you, not one of them has failed" (Josh. 23:14). We can trust God and his covenant promises so long as we remain covenant faithful. Whatever our situation or station, we walk into the future with hope, trust, and joy.

Trust God's future, for the Lord God is already there and in his good providence will care for us, even if floods rise and mountains fall. "Trust in the Lord with all your heart, and do not rely on your own insight. In all your ways acknowledge him, and he will make your paths straight" (Prov. 3:5–6). "Trust in the Lord and do good; dwell in the land and enjoy safe pasture" (Ps. 37:3 NIV).

Francis believed this and lived and proved it to and through his final earthly hours.

11. *Forgive joyfully*. Francis saw no point in bearing grudges or withholding pardon. He made plain the way he wanted his brothers to live; while he could, he held them accountable. But he joyfully forgave when anyone in or out of his order turned from evil and walked the way of peace and justice.

For Francis, to forgive was not a burden. It was a joy. A brother or wanderer had been restored! He had the joy of the father welcoming back the prodigal. For in the end, Francis trusted his Savior and Lord, Jesus Christ.

When we joyfully forgive, we renew joy and freedom in ourselves. We become the liberated, not the victim or the oppressed one carrying the weight of others' crimes or failures.

12. *Shun extremes.* We live in an age of extremes. We may be pushed and pulled out of the perfect path into far-off ways that lead us astray. If we daily nourish our roots and reflect on God's promises, we find the path of perfection, the path Francis sought.

For "the path of the righteous is like the light of dawn, which shines brighter and brighter until full day" (Prov. 4:18).

Here, admittedly, Francis's advice was better than his life. As we saw, Francis went to extremes in his stress on poverty and embrace of suffering, especially regarding himself. Even here, though, Francis warned the brothers against extreme asceticism, against inflicting unnecessary pain on their bodies (as we noted in chapter 7).

A very few pious hagiographers say Francis wore a painful, irritating horsehair shirt next to his skin. The most trusted sources say no such thing. When Francis's simple tunic was removed so he could lay naked on the earth as he died, no hair shirt or metal manacle was found.

Francis shunned extremes in doctrine and liturgy, embracing established church tradition.

13. *Sing joyously.* Francis was a joyful troubadour. He loved songs and singing; he often went singing on his way, even when suffering. Joyful singing blocked out suffering, as it can do.

Young Francis knew the songs of his age—songs based on the *Romance of the Rose* and *Reynard the Fox* and the Knights of the Round Table, as we saw. Francis was poet and singer and dramatist. "As he saw all things dramatically, so he himself was always dramatic," said Chesterton; "a poet whose whole life was a poem."[11]

Francis saw the beauty of God and the bounty of creation. He lived the joy of life, celebrated creatures great and small—especially the sun above and the larks below. He also noticed fish and fireflies, flowers and flowing streams. So, the creatures noticed him—saw him as one of their

---

[11] Chesterton, *Saint Francis of Assisi*, 89.

own, perhaps. Birds would stop singing if he asked them and sometimes flock around or settle on him. There seems no reason to doubt this— some of us have known people with unusual affinity for wild creatures, a capacity and sensitivity the creatures themselves sense and respond to in kind.[12]

Even knocked into a snow drift, Francis rose singing. Thomas of Celano says, "Exhilarated with great joy, he began in a loud voice to make the woods resound with praises to the Creator of all," singing away in French.[13]

Francis was a living metaphor—all the more because he was flesh and blood and could bleed as well as make music.

14. *Follow Jesus steadfastly.* It was all for the sake of Jesus—his life and resurrection, and especially his sufferings for us. This is what moved Francis. He would weep long and bitterly over the sufferings of Christ. Yet like a lark, he would rise in song for the new life he received on Jesus's account.

The way to life is to walk in Jesus's ways and learn from him. This joyful certainty never faded for Francis, and his brothers caught the contagion.

Following Jesus steadfastly: this of course is number one. It is the clue and key and power of the others things we learn from Francis. This echoes what we said earlier about first things in following Francis's way.

Again, the starting point is not *what one believes* about Jesus. People who open-heartedly or searchingly look to Jesus feel a magnetic drawing. They follow perhaps from afar; they feel themselves drawn closer and step by step their lives change. Transformation is the journey. Jesus said, "If you continue in my word, you are truly my disciples; and you will know the truth, and the truth will make you free" (John 8:31–32). Try and see!

Following Jesus like Francis Did

We are not Francis, but Francis has lessons for everyone.

This closing summary is not for the merely historically curious or for those happy with shallow discipleship. This is for those who want to be Jesus followers like Francis was—just as radical. If our heart prompts us, we can follow Jesus the way Francis did, now, in our own time, not going back centuries.

---

[12] See, for example, the remarkable story of Sally Carrighar in her memoir *Home to the Wilderness: A Personal Journey* (Boston, MA: Houghton Mifflin, 1973).

[13] Thomas of Celano, *Life of St. Francis*, FA:ED 1:194.

The way is simple, yet most profound. That is Francis, after all. His profundity was his simplicity—his willingness to take Jesus at his word no matter what.

This translates beautifully into our day. All distills into four key steps.

1. *Jesus 100 percent.* Jesus is the Way. He is the Truth, the Light.

Francis quoted Jesus's words from John 14:6 ("I am the way, and the truth, and the life") and said, "Let us, therefore, hold onto the words, the life, the teaching and the Holy Gospel of him who humbled himself to beg his Father for us and to make his name known saying: 'Father, glorify your name and glorify your Son that your Son may glorify you.'"[14] Echoing Peter the Apostle, Francis said that Jesus by his life and self-sacrifice "[left] us an example, that we might follow His footprints."[15] Francis repeated this many times in multiple ways.

Francis says, if you want to know fullness of life, make Jesus your center. Francis proved this by experience. So have the thousands who followed him.

This is a conscious life decision. What you believe or do not believe about Jesus is not the point. The point is that Jesus's life was so full of grace, love, courtesy, surprises, and utter devotion to his Heavenly Father that still today he takes our breath away. Something deep inside says, "I too want that!"

So, make Jesus the center of your life. Worry not about doctrine. Time enough to ponder that later. Doctrine is not the point anyway, any more than it was in Jesus's earthbound days. Jesus said things like this:

> Come to me, all you that are weary and are carrying heavy burdens, and I will give you rest. Take my yoke upon you, and learn from me; for I am gentle and humble in heart, and you will find rest for your souls. For my yoke is easy, and my burden is light. (Matt. 11:28–30)

> I came that [you] may have life, and have it abundantly. (John 10:10)

> If you continue in my word, you are truly my disciples; and you will know the truth, and the truth will make you free. (John 8:31)

---

[14] Francis, "The Earlier Rule," FA:ED 1:81 (capitalized pronouns changed to lowercase).

[15] Francis, "Later Admonition," FA:ED 1:46, quoting 1 Pt. 2:21.

I am the bread of life. Whoever comes to me will never be hungry, and whoever believes in me will never be thirsty.... Everything that the Father gives me will come to me, and anyone who comes to me I will never drive away. (John 6:35, 37)

Try and see! Whatever your degree of faith or no faith, start following Jesus and see what happens. You may be an agnostic, a Muslim, a Hindu. It's OK if you're an atheist or a skeptic, Buddhist or libertarian. Give yourself to Jesus, and see if his word is true. You will find other strange people along the road, but all are headed in the same direction with the same quest: to follow Jesus.

2. *Accept the challenge of being lesser.* This may be the hardest step. Accept the challenge to be a lesser brother, a lesser sister.

Francis said that "the Lord has willed that [his companions] be called Lesser Brothers," part of the "little flock" Jesus mentions in Luke 12:32.[16] He founded the Order, Francis said, "upon a firm rock, the greatest humility and poverty of the Son of God, calling it the religion of 'Lesser Brothers.'"[17]

The point in following Jesus is not to be known or successful or scale a ladder. Certainly, it is not to become wealthy, powerful, influential. The point in following Jesus is to be lesser, so Jesus can be all and others can be lifted.

The night before his crucifixion Jesus showed what this means. "Jesus, knowing that the Father had given all things into his hands, and that he had come from God and was going to God, got up from the table, took off his outer robe, and tied a towel around himself. Then he poured water into a basin and began to wash the disciples' feet and to wipe them with the towel that was tied around him" (John 13:3–5).

Follow Jesus and commit to be lesser. Don't try to be "humble"; that's too vague, abstract, pious. Just pledge to be lesser in every way. That kind of behavior is social, cultural, often visible, and starkly countercultural. It is acting like Jesus who, "though he was in the form of God, did not regard equality with God as something to be exploited, but emptied himself, taking the form of a slave, being born in human likeness. And being found in human form, he humbled himself and became obedient to the point of death—even death on a cross" (Phil. 2:6–8).

---

[16] *Assisi Compilation*, FA:ED 2:204.
[17] *Mirror of Perfection* (Lemmens ed.), FA:ED 3:223.

As in Francis's day, few will do this. Yet many will do this. Enough to make a movement, light a spark, start a fire, like in the 1200s. The genius of Francis of Assisi was that he made people *aspire*, hunger and thirst, to be lesser. Clare inspired young women, even older ones, to be lesser, too. Hundreds and then thousands did; many still do.

Jesus said, "Whoever wishes to be great among you must be your servant, and whoever wishes to be first among you must be your slave; just as the Son of Man came not to be served but to serve, and to give his life a ransom for many" (Matt. 20:26–28).

To be lesser means being humble also in relationship to the planet, the Earth. To tend the garden, care for God's creatures as they minister to us. Being lesser means putting God's purposes and plans for people and the whole of creation ahead of our own purposes and plans. To be lesser beings means putting Earth's welfare and flourishing ahead of our own finances and conveniences and preferences and other priorities, as Robin Wall Kimmerer pictures so beautifully in *Braiding Sweetgrass*.[18]

I will serve God by being obedient to God's Word to care for the garden and help fulfill the implications of God's everlasting covenant with the earth. I will follow Jesus. Francis understood this. Jesus was his model and example. Being "lesser" was the most prophetic thing Francis and his movement could be in the context of his time. In no other aspect were Franciscans truly unique.

The call to be lesser in Christ, to serve lepers and flowers, is a call to identity and community, not anonymity and isolation. Here we find our true self, our identity in Jesus. Follow Jesus 100 percent through the joy of lesserness.

The call to lesserness is a deeper way to radical equality.

3. *Adopt basic spiritual disciplines.* This is essential. Undisciplined gifts produce chaos and discord. Undisciplined gifts spread confusion, as Paul showed in 1 Corinthians 12–14.

Francis led his brothers into a life of both freedom and discipline. Their days were shaped by the canonical hours in a joyful, not slavish, way. The brothers were to celebrate the Eucharist regularly as prescribed by the church, to follow the church's fasts, and periodically retreat into hermitages.

---

[18] Robin Wall Kimmerer, *Braiding Sweetgrass: Indigenous Wisdom, Scientific Knowledge, and the Teachings of Plants* (Minneapolis, MN: Milkweed Editions, 2013).

Francis based the brothers' disciplined life on the pattern of Jesus and the practices of the church. He wrote in the Earlier Rule, "For this reason let all the brothers, whether [priests] or lay, recite the Divine Office, the praises and prayers, as required of them."[19]

The New Testament shows that the gifts and fruit of the Spirit grow together in God's garden. What is the harvest? "The fruit of the Spirit is love, joy, peace, patience, kindness, generosity, faithfulness, gentleness, and self-control" (Gal. 5:22–25).

The fruit of the Spirit grows through spiritual disciplines. Like the Franciscans and Clares, we adopt specific consistent first-priority practices that nurture the promised tasty fruit. We care for the garden.

This is not complicated. Basic Christian disciplines go back to the birth of the Christian faith and further. They are rooted in Scripture. Psalms and Proverbs nurture our disciplines. All the classic disciplines are rooted in daily practices of prayer, Scripture, rest, community, worship, service, and communion with God's creation. Spiritual disciplines are about living a healthful daily rhythm.

Franciscan and Clare communities were sometimes extreme in their disciplines, unhealthily so. We learn from their plus and minuses, from Scripture and history, above all from Jesus.

Disciplines are essential because they structure our lives for good. Without spiritual disciplines our lives are either formless or dictated by foreign forces. These forces might be job, entertainment, government, habits, addictions, or the necessary quest for food, shelter, and security. In our day, spiritual disciplines *must* confront social media. Social media of various sorts structures our lives in toxic and addictive ways, if we let it. Internet apps and sites, like everything else, must be granted only limited space, must be put under a yoke.

4. *Live a sustainable ecosystem of worship, community, and witness.* The genius of the Francis movement was community. Franciscans were not hermits, though they used hermitages.

Francis, lover of creation and creatures, at a deep level understood *interdependence.* Or today we might say *lived ecology, reciprocity, symbiosis.* Being centered in Jesus meant connection with all creation. Birds and flowers reminded Francis of God's grace; God's grace saturated the beauty of creation and the ecology of its parts. Francis knew and sensed this. In the next generation, Franciscan scholars like Roger Bacon, Bonaventure, and Duns Scotus explored it theologically and philosophically.

---

[19] Francis, "The Earlier Rule," FA:ED 1:65.

Worship, community, witness! With Francis and his brothers, with Clare and her sisters, these three components thrived (most of the time) day by day. Roots must grow deep before trees grow tall: be nourished, spread wide, intertwine, for the tree to grow sweet fruit. This is what worship, witness, and community give.

Look closely at Francis and his brothers. Worship structures the day— the canonical hours. Community lends the dynamic of accountability and joy and sharing. We sing together, eat together, do chores together, pray together, serve others, deliberate and decide together. We perhaps garden together, watch birds and trees and flowers and rivers and seas together, and build things together.

We need such community today, adapted to our time. To live Francis-like joy, we will learn spiritual disciplines-in-community.

These four steps—Jesus focus, "lesser-ness," spiritual disciplines, the harmony of worship–community–witness—these put a wrap on all that has just been said. Learning from Francis means inhabiting a sustainable ecosystem in which worship, service, meditation, and prayer nurture each other in community.

This is how Francis helps us follow Jesus now. This is the profundity of simplicity, the depth of spirituality, the breadth of witness, and the height of worship and aspiration. This is what Francis found, what God's Spirit showed him. It renewed the church. It is the way to the kingdom. It can happen again.

Yet there is one more thing that, next to lesserness, may be hardest and highest: *bold faith—absolute trust*. This is the fifth thing maybe. Actually, it is the breathed-in air, the atmosphere of the whole Francis way, start to finish.

The church suffers chronically not from too much faith but from too little. Francis corrected this. His boldness was breathtaking. "Never was any man so little afraid of his own promises," Chesterton wrote. "His life was one riot of rash vows; of rash vows that turned out right."[20]

The only way to understand Francis is to look at Jesus. Jesus called disciples who didn't really believe God's kingdom could actually come *now*, in present time, at least not the way Jesus said. Jesus called them "little-faiths" (*oligopistos*, Matt. 6:30).

Bold faith, the kind Jesus births and calls us to, is audacious. It believes the unlikely and unbelievable, not because it is naïve or crazy or mentally impaired, but because it *trusts in God's promises*. Simply trusts God's Word. Promises like—

---

[20] Chesterton, *St. Francis of Assisi*, 42.

He shall judge between many peoples, and shall arbitrate between strong nations far away; they shall beat their swords into plowshares, and their spears into pruning hooks; nation shall not lift up sword against nation, neither shall they learn war any more; but they shall all sit under their own vines and under their own fig trees, and no one shall make them afraid; for the mouth of the Lord of hosts has spoken. (Mic. 4:3–4)

The wolf shall live with the lamb, the leopard shall lie down with the kid, the calf and the lion and the fatling together, and a little child shall lead them. (Isa. 11:6)

Do not fear, for I am with you, do not be afraid, for I am your God; I will strengthen you, I will help you, I will uphold you with my victorious right hand. (Isa. 41:10)

Do not be afraid, little flock, for your Father delights to give you the kingdom. (Luke 12:32 paraphrased)

This is what it looks like when God's people trust his promises and God's will is done on Earth as in heaven.

When we can't trust our own faith, we turn to Jesus. When we can't trust anything else, still we trust him. When we doubt doctrine, we trust his promises. That in turn gives us center and circumference, beginning and end, and thus all in between.

Francis teaches how to follow Jesus as fully as he himself did—in our own time yet in the Francis way. We learn to follow Jesus through (1) one hundred percent commitment to him; (2) accepting the challenge to be lesser; (3) growing spiritual disciplines; and (4) inhabiting an ecosystem of worship, community, and witness.

This covenant commitment is then energized by bold faith, absolute trust, a gift from God. This is all part of *being* the good news, the evangel, the Jesus Gospel.

There is nothing new here really, as there wasn't with Francis. All this is mere New Testament life. What is new and thoroughly Franciscan is *turning this into action now*: not just agreeing, not just saying an actionless mental *yes*.

Conclusion

We, today, are not Francis. Our century number is twenty-one, not thirteen. Yet still Francis impacts and impels us. Examining Francis in his own space and time, we perhaps see limitations and complexities. Yet through these, Francis's prophetic witness shines forth even more brightly. We feel the impact of his prophetic witness.

In this chapter we have alleged several things about the *poverello*. Francis's stress on poverty and suffering was extreme, compared with Jesus and what Jesus said and did. Francis largely ignored the need for organizational structure—yet this had some positive benefits, whatever the negative side. In some ways Francis's movement was hampered and distorted also through an overemphasis on "merit" and penitential acts, plus the growing emphasis on indulgences in his day.

Recognizing these possible limitations and then laying them aside—taking a second look at Francis—we distill a few steps, key dynamics, that can make Francis's radical discipleship real and compelling and socially impactful, fermentive, in our lives today:

- Jesus, one hundred percent! Whatever the cost.
- Welcoming the challenge to be *lesser*, serving others.
- Discerning our particular *charism* and calling through Jesus's help and grace.
- Adapting firm and freeing spiritual disciplines.
- Inhabiting a healthful ecosystem of worship, community, and witness.
- Wrapping all this in bold unflappable faith—zero trust in ourselves; audacious, daring faith in God; trusting Jesus to work in and through us by his Spirit the way God did with Francis.

Chesterton said Francis was "one of the strongest and strangest and most original personalities that human history has known"[21]—something we say above all of Jesus Christ. We are not Francis, and Francis was not Jesus. Francis helps us be like Jesus and within our own little sphere and beyond, and have a Jesus-like impact on our world.

We are all called to be lesser brothers and sisters—not by Francis, but by Jesus. Francis is our gentle reminder. We can be lesser.

---

[21] Chesterton, *St. Francis of Assisi*, 83.

Acknowledgments

This book owes much to many people—most of all of course to Francis and Clare themselves. I am indebted to all those who have offered encouragement, insight, advice, and research leads over the past dozen years. Several people, including my daughter and son-in-law Jerilyn and Sean Winstead, have read and given me feedback on various chapters, and also shared a week with me in Assisi in 2022. I am grateful to all who have helped make the book better.

I want to thank Bill Burrows, former Orbis Books publisher and longtime friend through the American Society of Missiology, for initially reviewing and encouraging my book proposal. At Orbis Books, Jon Sweeney, then with Orbis and himself the author of several books on Francis, saw the potential of my manuscript and gave it the green light. I thank Robert Ellsberg, Orbis publisher and editor-in-chief, for his efficient editing, astute advice, and patience with a fairly long manuscript, managing editor Maria Angelini for her expert guidance in preparing the manuscript for publishing, and Bernadette Price for excellent promotion.

Many friends and colleagues have encouraged this project and offered insights or advice. Thanks especially to Bruce Cromwell (himself a Francis scholar), David Bundy, Steve Seamands, Jonathan Raymond, Winfield Bevins, Darrell Whiteman, Joe Culumber, Nathan Smith, Alexei Laushkin, and Dawn Eden Goldstein. Professor Lawrence Cunningham, author of *Francis of Assisi: Performing the Gospel Life*, helped me early on through email responses to questions I raised.

I also acknowledge the inspiration I received from Pope Francis's *Laudato Si': Encyclical on Climate Change and Inequality: On Care for Our Common Home* (2015).

Above all, I am thankful to my wife Janice who was with me on that first visit to Assisi in 2003 and then on a longer stay in 2019. We walked to many of the Francis sites, and together enjoyed Italian salads and pastas she prepared after our visits to Assisi shops and street markets.

It has been a journey of discovery as I have sought to integrate new learnings from Francis and Clare and their continuing communities with my earlier studies of movements of God's Spirit.

Select Bibliography

Armstrong, Regis J., OFM Cap., *The Lady—Clare of Assisi: Early Documents,* 3rd ed. Hyde Park, NY: New City Press, 2006.

Armstrong, Regis J., OFM Cap., J. A. Wayne Hellmann, OFM Conv., and William J. Short, OFM, eds., *Francis of Assisi: Early Documents,* 3 vols. New York: New City Press, 2001.

Arnold, Lauren. *Princely Gifts and Papal Treasures: The Franciscan Mission to China and Its Influence on the Art of the West, 1250–1350.* San Francisco: Desiderata Press, 1999.

Bergreen, Laurence. *Columbus: The Four Voyages.* New York: Viking Penguin, 2011.

Boyle, David. *Toward the Setting Sun: Columbus, Cabot, Vespucci, and the Race for America.* New York: Walker & Company, 2008.

Brooke, Rosalind B. *Early Franciscan Government: Elias to Bonaventure.* Cambridge: Cambridge University Press, 1959.

Brophy, Liam. *The Marvelous Doctor: Friar Roger Bacon.* Chicago: Franciscan Herald Press, 1963.

Brown, Raphael, ed. and trans. *The Little Flowers of St. Francis.* New York: Doubleday, 1958.

Burr, David. *The Spiritual Franciscans: From Protest to Persecution in the Century after Francis.* University Park: Pennsylvania State University Press, 2001.

Catto, J. I., ed. *The Early Oxford Schools,* vol. I of *The History of the University of Oxford,* ed. T. H. Aston. Oxford, UK: Clarendon Press, 1984.

Chesterton, G. K. *St. Francis of Assisi.* Garden City, NY: Image Books, Doubleday [1924], 1957.

Cirino, André, OFM, and Josef Raischl, eds. *Franciscan Solitude.* St. Bonaventure, NY: The Franciscan Institute, St. Bonaventure University, 1975.

Cousins, Ewert, trans. and ed. *Bonaventure: The Soul's Journey into God, The Tree of Life, the Life of St. Francis.* New York: Paulist Press, 1978.

Cron, Ian Morgan. *Chasing Francis: A Pilgrim's Tale.* Grand Rapids, MI: Zondervan, 2013.

Cunningham, Lawrence S. *Francis of Assisi: Performing the Gospel Life.* Grand Rapids, MI: William B. Eerdmans, 2004.

Cuthbert, Father, OSF Cap. *Life of St. Francis of Assisi,* 3rd ed. London: Longmans, Green, 1948.

d'Avray, D. L. *The Preaching of the Friars: Sermons Diffused from Paris before 1300.* Oxford, UK: Oxford University Press, 1985.

Dawson, Christopher, ed. *The Mongol Mission: Narratives and Letters of the Franciscan Missionaries in Mongolia and China in the Thirteenth and Fourteenth Centuries.* New York: Sheed and Ward, 1955.

Easton, Stewart C. *Roger Bacon and His Search for a Universal Science: A Reconsideration of the Life and Work of Roger Bacon in the Light of His Own Stated Purposes.* New York: Columbia University Press, 1952.

Englebert, Omer. *Saint Francis of Assisi,* second English ed., trans. Eve Marie Cooper. Chicago: Franciscan Herald Press, 1965.

Esser, Cajetan, OFM. *Origins of the Franciscan Order,* trans. Aedan Daly and Irina Lynch. Chicago: Franciscan Herald Press, 1970.

Falk, Seb. *The Light Ages: The Surprising Story of Medieval Science.* New York: W. W. Norton, 2020.

Fortini, Arnaldo. *Nova Vita de San Francisco.* 2 vols. Rome: Bibliotheca Fides, 1969.

_____. *Francis of Assisi,* trans. Helen Moak. New York: Crossroad Publishing, 1992.

Francke, Linda Bird. *On the Road with Francis of Assisi.* New York: Random House, 2005.

Freeman, Charles. *The Reopening of the Western Mind: The Resurgence of Intellectual Life from the End of Antiquity to the Dawn of the Enlightenment.* New York: Alfred A. Knopf, 2023.

Gimpel, Jean. *The Medieval Machine: The Industrial Revolution of the Middle Ages.* New York: Penguin Books, 1977.

Gontard, Friedrich. *The Chair of Peter: A History of the Papacy,* trans. A. J. and E. F. Peeler. New York: Holt, Rinehart and Winston, 1964.

Herman, Placid, OFM, trans. and ed. *XIIIth Century Chronicles.* Chicago: Franciscan Herald Press, 1961.

Hoeberichts, J. *Francis and Islam*. Quincy, IL: Franciscan Press, 1977.

Horan, Daniel P., OFM. *The Franciscan Heart of Thomas Merton*. Notre Dame, IN: Ave Maria Press, 2014.

House, Adrian. *Francis of Assisi*. Mahwah, NJ: HiddenSpring [Paulist Press], 2001.

Huber, Raphael M., OFM Conv. *A Documented History of the Franciscan Order (1182–1517)*. Milwaukee, WI: Nowiny Publishing Apostolate, 1944.

Iriarte, Lazaro. *Franciscan History: The Three Orders of St. Francis of Assisi*, trans. Patricia Ross. Chicago: Franciscan Herald Press, 1982.

Irvin, Dale T., and Scott W. Sunquist. *History of the World Christian Movement*. Vol. 1, *Earliest Christianity to 1453*. Maryknoll, NY: Orbis Books, 2001.

Jackson, Jack Peter, ed. *The Mission of Friar William of Rubruck: His Journey to the Court of the Great Khan Mongke, 1253–1255*. Indianapolis, IN: Hackett Publishing, 2009.

Kedar, Benjamin Z. *Crusade and Mission*. Princeton, NJ: Princeton University Press, 1984.

Knowles, Dom David. *The Religious Orders in England*. London: Cambridge University Press, 1948.

Lambert, M. D. *Franciscan Poverty: The Doctrine of Absolute Poverty of Christ and the Apostles in the Franciscan Order 1210–1323*. London: SPCK, 1961.

Las Casas, Bartolomé de. *The Only Way*, trans. Francis Patrick Sullivan, ed. Helen Rand Parish. Mahwah, NJ: Paulist Press, 1992.

Lewis, C. S. *The Allegory of Love: A Study in Medieval Tradition*. Oxford: Oxford University Press, 1936, 1959.

Maier, Christopher T. *Preaching the Crusades: Mendicant Friars and the Cross in the Thirteenth Century*. Cambridge: Cambridge University Press, 1994.

Mancini, Giulio. *San Damiano: Recalling the Soul*. Assisi, Italy: Edizioni Porziuncola, 2009.

McGinn, Bernard. *The Flowering of Mysticism: Men and Women of the New Mysticism (1200–1350)*. New York: Crossroad Publishing, 1998.

_____. *Visions of the End: Apocalyptic Traditions in the Middle Ages*. New York: Columbia University Press, 1979, 1998.

McNamara, Jo Ann Kay. *Sisters in Arms: Catholic Nuns through Two Millennia*. Cambridge, MA: Harvard University Press, 1996.

Miller, Ramona, OSF. *In the Footsteps of Saint Clare*. St. Bonaventure, NY: The Franciscan Institute, 1993.

Moffett, Samuel Hugh. *A History of Christianity in Asia*, Vol. I, Beginnings to 1500. New York: HarperSanFrancisco, 1992.

Moorman, John R. H. *The Grey Friars in Cambridge 1225–1538*. Cambridge: Cambridge University Press, 1952.

_____. *A History of the Franciscan Order: From Its Origins to the Year 1517*. Oxford: Oxford University Press, 1968.

Morison, Samuel Eliot. *Admiral of the Ocean Sea: A Life of Christopher Columbus*. Boston: Little, Brown, 1970.

Moses, Paul. *The Saint and the Sultan: The Crusades, Islam, and Francis of Assisi's Mission of Peace*. New York: Doubleday Religion, 2009.

Moule, Arthur C. *Christians in China before the Year 1550*. London: SPCK, 1930; reprint, New York: Octagon Books, 1977.

Nimmo, Duncan. *Reform and Division in the Medieval Franciscan Order: From Saint Francis to the Foundation of the Capuchins*. Rome: Capuchin Historical Institute, 1987.

Peers, E. Allison. *Ramon Lull, A Biography*. London: Society for Promoting Christian Knowledge, 1929.

Peterson, Ingrid J., OSF. *Clare of Assisi: A Biographical Study*. Quincy, IL: Franciscan Press, 1993.

Phelan, John Leddy. *The Millennial Kingdom of the Franciscans in the New World*, 2nd ed., rev. Berkeley, CA: University of California Press, 1970.

Picard, Marc, OFM Cap. *The Icon of San Damiano*. Assisi, Italy: Casa Editrice Francescana, 2000.

Powell James M. *Anatomy of a Crusade, 1213–1221*. Philadelphia: University of Pennsylvania Press, 1986.

Riley-Smith, Jonathan, ed. *The Oxford Illustrated History of the Crusades*. Oxford: Oxford University Press, 1995.

Runciman, Steven. *A History of the Crusades*. Vol. 3, *The Kingdom of Acre and the Later Crusades*. Cambridge: Cambridge University Press, 1987.

Sabatier, Paul. *The Road to Assisi: The Essential Biography of St. Francis*, ed. Jon M. Sweeney. Brewster, MA: Paraclete Press, 2004.

Salmon, Dom Pierre. *The Breviary through the Ages*, trans. Sister David Mary. Collegeville, MN: Liturgical Press, 1962.

Schmucki, Octavian, OFM Cap. "The Illnesses of St. Francis of Assisi before His Stigmatization," trans. Sergius Wroblewski, OFM. *Greyfriars Review* 4:3 (1990), 31–61.

_____. "The Illnesses of Francis during the Last Years of His Life," trans. Edward Hagman, OFM Cap. *Greyfriars Review* 13:1 (1999), 21–59.

Smith, Charles Edward. *Innocent III: Church Defender*. Baton Rouge: Louisiana State University Press, 1951.

Snyder, Howard A. *Signs of the Spirit: How God Reshapes the Church*. Grand Rapids, MI: Zondervan, 1989.

_____. *The Radical Wesley: The Patterns and Practices of a Movement Maker*. Franklin, TN: Seedbed Publishing, 2014.

Sweeney, Jon M. *The Enthusiast: How the Best Friend of Francis of Assisi Almost Destroyed What He Started*. Notre Dame, IN: Ave Maria Press, 2016.

_____. *When Saint Francis Saved the Church: How a Converted Medieval Troubadour Created a Spiritual Vision for the Ages*. Notre Dame, IN: Ave Maria Press, 2014.

Thoman, Bret, OFS. *St. Francis of Assisi: Passion, Poverty, and the Man Who Transformed the Catholic Church*, 2nd ed. Charlotte, NC: TAN Books, 2018.

Thomas of Eccleston. *The Coming of the Friars Minor to England,* in *XIIIth Century Chronicles,* trans. Placid Hermann, OFM. Chicago: Franciscan Herald Press, 1961.

Traboulay, David M. *Columbus and Las Casas: The Conquest and Christianization of America, 1492–1566*. Lanham, MD: University Press of America, 1994.

Vauchez, André. *Francis of Assisi, the Life and Afterlife of a Medieval Saint,* trans. Michael F. Cusato. New Haven, CT: Yale University Press, 2012.

Vos, Antoine. *John Duns Scotus: A Life*. Kampen, the Netherlands: Summum Academic Publications, 2018.

Walsh, James J. *The Thirteenth: Greatest of Centuries*. New York: Catholic Summer School Press, 1907.

Weatherford, Jack. *Genghis Khan and the Making of the Modern World*. New York: Broadway Books, 2004.

Zwemer, Samuel. *Raymund Lull: First Missionary to the Moslems*. New York: Funk & Wagnalls, 1902.

Index

Abbey of St. Albans, England, 120
Abu Shama, Arab chronicler, 171
Agnes of Bohemia (Agnes of Prague), 219–20
Agnes, daughter of Assisi mayor; Poor Clare sister, 147
Agnes, Poor Clare sister, 137. *See also* Catherine (sister of Clare)
Ahmed, Mona, 160
Albert Magnus, 244
Alexander IV, Pope, 231, 258
Alexander of Hales, 237, 240, 258, 263
America, 106, 280, 283
  Christopher Columbus and, 280, 301–2
  Franciscan witness, 280, 306
Anthony of Padua, Brother (Saint), 96
Anabaptists, 321
Angel of the Sixth Seal (Apocalypse), 200–1
  and Francis's *stigmata*, 200–1
Angelo, biological brother of Francis, 91
Angelo Tancredi, Brother, 48, 51, 84, 126, 174, 196–97, 206, 221, 260
animals, 40–42, 205, 326
  animal stories and fables, 42
  at Greccio manger scene, 175
  care for, 177, 326, 347
Anonymous of Perugia, xv, 46, 50, 59, 65, 86, 87, 199
Anti-Christ, 271
anti-Semitism, 6, 274–75, 301
antiphonaries (choir books), 126
Antonio de Marchena, Franciscan astronomer, 302
Apocalypse, biblical book, 201. *See also* Revelation, biblical book of

apocalypticism, 201, 253, 265, 282
Arik Boke, grandson of Genghis Khan, 290, 293
Armstrong, Edward (ornithologist), 42
Armstrong, Regis, 142, 149, 202, 222
Arno River and valley, 49, 195
Arnold of Cologne, 294
Arnold, Lauren, 296, 298–99
art: Franciscan contributions to, 282
  East–West exchanges, 297
Asbury, Francis, 328
asceticism, xv, 38, 71, 87, 180, 336
Asia, Franciscan mission work in, 284
Assisi, xiv, 3–4, 14–16, 27, 33, 39, 42–43, 50–51, 56, 72, 97, 137–38
  class structure: *majores* and *minores*, 15–16
  disputes and conflicts, 205
  geography, 15–16
  microcosm of medieval society, 116
Assisi Compilation, 75, 172, 184, 185, 187, 190, 191, 197, 203, 251
astronomy, xiv, 228, 229, 230, 246, 302
Augustine of Hippo, 98
Augustinian Order, 337
Avignon, Provence, France, 270–71

Bacon, Roger (Franciscan), xiv, 239, 240–44, 246, 249, 279, 348
  "Doctor Marvelous," 241
  experimental scientist, 241–42
  reform program, 242
  work on light, optics, 243
Barbaro of Assisi, Brother, 48, 51, 154
Bartolomé de las Casas (Dominican friar), 304, 307
Basilica of Saint Clare, Assisi, 126, 141, 221

Basilica of Saint Francis, Assisi, 168, 169,
178, 218, 233, 256–57, 259, 297
architectural significance, 257
Chinese influence on frescoes, 298
Giotto frescoes, 297
Batu Khan, 285, 287, 289
beggars, begging, 11, 15, 53, 80
Benedict XII, Pope, 295–96
Benedict of Nursia, 75, 98, 117, 323
Benedict of Poland, Franciscan
missionary, 287, 289
Benedictines, Order of Benedict, 32–35,
55, 62, 66, 75, 86, 98, 107, 118,
143, 145, 337
Bergreen, Laurence, 305
Bernard of Besse, Brother, 47, 232
Bernard of Clairvaux, 98, 118, 323
Bernardo di Quintavalle, Brother,
44–52, 59, 84, 119, 135, 137,
257, 321
Berthold of Regensburg, Brother,
234–35
Bible, the, xv, 44, 111, 320
allegorical interpretation, 234
authority and norm, 320, 324
basis of spiritual disciplines, 348
Francis's knowledge of, xv, 111, 338
Biblica Sacra Polyglotta (Hebrew,
Aramaic, Latin, Greek), 249
birds, 10, 40, 160, 177, 195, 203,
205, 229, 317, 344, 348, 349
care for, 177, 347
Cliff Swallows, 275
Francis preaches to, 43
on Mount Laverna, 197–98
Skylark, 40–41
Black Death, 281, 297. *See also*
bubonic plague
Bologna, Italy, 7, 55, 91, 112, 116, 158
Bonaventure of Bagnoregio, xiv, 57,
89, 102, 165, 168, 180, 238, 244,
267–68, 315, 348
and Joachim of Fiore, 263
becomes Franciscan, 57, 232, 262
canonized, 260, 263
*Commentary on the Sentences of
Peter Lombard*, 263
hagiographic view of Francis,
110–11, 188, 201, 250, 264, 343
healing as child, 57

leadership, 89, 262–65
Major Legend of Saint Francis, 264
Minor Legend of Saint Francis, 264
mystic, 263, 265
scholarship, 232, 263, 265
"Seraphic Doctor," 240
suppresses earlier Francis
biographies, 268
view of *stigmata*, 264
Boniface VIII, Pope, 269
Book of Nature (Creation), 327
Boyle, David, 302
Brady, Ignatius, 127
breviaries, Franciscan use of, 125–26
Britain. *See* England
Brophy, Liam, 243
Brother Body, 181–83
as faithful friend, 182
care of, 182, 336
Brother Sun, Sister Moon (dir. Franco
Zeffirelli), 4, 60, 73
bubonic plague pandemic, 281, 297
Buddhists, 290, 291–92, 346
Buoncompagni the Rhetor, 120
Byzantine Christianity, 22. *See also*
Eastern Orthodox Church

Cairo, Egypt, 155, 157, 158, 170, 172
Cambridge University, 231, 235, 244
Canticle of the Creatures, 6, 40, 190,
202–9, 229, 243, 327
Francis composes and sings, 202–3
Italian vernacular, not Latin, 204
parallelism in, 205
sung as Francis neared death, 216
Capuchin Order, 183, 277–78
early opposition, 277
origin, 277
Capuchin Poor Clares, 223
Carthusians, 129
Cathars, 55, 61, 69, 85, 115
Catherine of Siena, 323
Catholic Worker Movement, 323
Catto, J. I., 245, 246
Celestine III, Pope, 60
Chapter of Mats, 95–97
charism, *charismata*, 110, 259, 282.
See also gifts of the Spirit
charismatic renewal, 316, 321
Chenu, Marie-Dominique, 69

Chesterton, G. K., 13, 31, 34, 52, 107, 132, 146–47, 191, 200, 209, 341, 343, 349, 351
China, Franciscan missions to, 279, 280, 283–84, 293
chivalry, 6, 8, 10, 31, 37, 51, 52, 338
Chronicle of Ernoul, 163, 165, 167
Cimabue, Florentine artist, 281
church, 38, 55
  Bride of Christ, 336
  ecosystem of worship, community, witness, 348–50
  renewal of, 55, 61, 108, 232, 278
Church of England (Anglican Church), 323
Cistercians, 55, 85, 118, 215, 254, 323
Clare of Assisi, xiv–xvi, 6, 15–18, 35, 70, 131–51, 203, 214, 215, 323, 325, 331, 338
  as abbess, 147–48
  ascetic extremes, 140, 143, 348
  canonization, 141, 147, 221
  Christ-likeness, 139
  compassion for poor, 133, 177
  first woman to write religious rule, 222
  hair shirts, 141–42
  illness, 140–42, 147, 214, 221
  insistence on Privilege of Poverty, 145–46
  joins Francis at the Portiuncula, 132, 134–35
  limitations as woman, 133
  meets secretly with Francis, 133
  Palm Sunday flight, 133–35
  prayer life, 141, 145, 150
  suffering, 141, 213
  Testament, 132, 141, 143
  wed to Jesus Christ, 140
Clarisses. *See* Poor Clares
Clement III, Pope, 60
Clement IV, Pope, 231, 242, 273
Clement V, Pope, 253–54, 269, 294
Clement VII, Pope, 277
Colettine Poor Clares, 223
Cologne, Germany, Franciscan school at, 244
Columbus, Christopher, 106, 242, 249, 281, 283, 301–7
  admiration for Francis, 301

buried in Franciscan habit, 306
first trans-Atlantic voyage, 303
Franciscan friends and colleagues, 249, 301, 306
Santa Maria, Niña, Pinta, Columbus's ships, 303
self-image as Christian missionary, 305
Third Order Franciscan, 301, 304
writes *Book of Prophecies*, 305
Commerce, commercialism, 16, 48, 52, 116, 228
community, 48, 338
  covenant commitment, 48, 318
  Franciscan, 48–49, 113–14, 119, 129
Considerations of the Holy Stigmata, The, 196–97
Continental Pietism. *See* Pietist Movement
Conventual Franciscans, 267–69, 276
conversion, 12–13, 30–31, 35–36, 80
courtesy, chivalry virtue, 169, 338
Cousins, Ewert, 263–64
creation, the, 40–43, 52, 326
  and New Creation, 327
  beauty and bounty of, 40, 42, 327, 343
  ecology of, 348
  God's "everlasting covenant" with, 335, 338, 347
  manifests wisdom, 327
  stewardship of, 326
creatures of Earth, xvi, 40–43, 53, 80, 202, 309
  care and protection, 309, 338, 347
  Francis's fondness for, 40–42, 202–3, 338
  noticed Francis, 343–44
Crucifix of San Damiano, 22, 30–31
Crusader armies described, 156–57
  camp followers, 156, 157
  numbers, 158
  weapons, 159, 171
Crusades, the, 5–6, 8, 31, 36–37, 51, 52, 61, 68, 116, 153, 222, 242, 272, 285, 295, 305
  as Christian piety, 69
  as prophetic of eschaton, 156
  cross symbol, 8, 158
  economic aspects, 6, 116

Crusades, the *(continued)*
  fifth, 5, 61, 69, 90–91, 152–72, 187
  fourth, 5, 61
  Franciscan involvement with, 272,
    316
Cunningham, Lawrence, 7–8, 16, 30,
    33, 58–59, 100–1, 180, 193, 196,
    322

Daily Office, 76, 77, 94, 125. *See also*
    Liturgy of the Hours
Damietta, Egypt, 90–91, 154–72,
    170–71
Dante Alighieri, xiii, 173, 267, 281
  describes Francis's Muslim mission,
    173
Dawson, Christopher, 287–89, 295
Day, Dorothy, 323
discipleship, xvi, 10, 18, 45, 68, 70,
    80, 133, 181, 250, 259, 336
Disease and History (Cartwright and
    Biddiss), 185
dispensationalism, 265–66
Divine Comedy (Dante), xiii, 173, 195
Dominic de Guzmán, 97, 323
Dominicans, 69, 98, 122, 125,
    227–29, 236, 244
Duns Scotus, John (Franciscan), xiv,
    240, 243–46, 249, 348
  academic reputation, 244–45
  doctorate at University or Paris,
    244, 246
  "Doctor Subtle," 244
  Franciscan education and influence,
    244
  proofs of God, 245

Earth, 40, 223, 228
  God's "everlasting covenant" with,
    335, 338
  Mother, Sister, 110, 202
Eastern Orthodox Church, 22, 300.
    See also Byzantine Christianity
ecclesiola (little church, small group),
    313–14, 321
ecology, ecological perspective, 106,
    277, 337
Egypt, 51, 90, 151, 155–72, 187, 248
Elias, Brother, 93, 98, 154, 254, 261
  abuse of authority, 256

as minister general, 98–100, 102,
    189, 234, 254–60
excommunicated, 259
Elizabeth of Hungary, Princess, 219–20
England (Britain), 5, 47, 83, 88, 222
Englebert, Omer, 60, 100, 133, 180, 256
eschatology, 113, 253–54, 342
Esser, Cajetan, 82–83, 106–7, 114–15,
    119, 122–25, 129–31, 328
Eucharist, 212, 218, 325, 326, 347.
    See also sacraments
evangelical awakening, 69, 321–22
evangelical poverty, 67–68, 238,
    270, 295, 325, 336. *See also vita
    apostolica*
Everlasting Gospel, the (Joachim of
    Fiore), 237

faith, 37–38, 349
  and works, 38
  Francis's faith, 37–38
  salvation by, 38
Falk, Seb, 229, 242
farmers, farming, 50–51, 53, 70, 80,
    319
fasting, 38, 71, 87, 91, 185, 325, 336
feudal age, feudalism, 3, 5–6, 15–16,
    114
Florence, Italy, 14, 16, 22, 49–50, 55,
    138, 253
Fonte Colombo hermitage, 99, 190
Fortini, Arnaldo, 9, 10, 20, 23, 27, 29,
    31, 37, 40, 45, 56, 68, 92, 144,
    157–62, 170, 206
Fourth Lateran Council, 61–62, 90,
    108, 125, 143, 168, 230–31
Francesco Pipino, chronicler, 159
Francis, Pope, 309
Francis of Assisi
  "Admonitions," 212–13
  adopts habit, 35, 65
  appearance, 112–3, 120, 332
  as Christ's troubadour, 5, 31, 327
  as leader, xiv, 107–8
  asceticism and austerity, 38, 72,
    180–81, 335
  call from God at Santa Maria degli
    Angeli, 36
  canonization, 105, 256
  Canticle of the Creatures, 6, 40, 190

care for brothers, 71, 74

cauterization of eyes, 189–93

charism, 8, 52, 107, 283, 341

conversion process, 8–10, 12, 19–31, 35–36, 72, 110

death, 105, 180, 206, 213–18, 227, 321

disrobes and renounces father, 28–30

dreams and visions, 8–9, 20, 37, 59, 63–64, 279

encounter with lepers, 12–14, 19, 30, 37

encounter with Pope Innocent III, 59, 62–63

example and model, 53–54, 92, 98, 107, 113, 279, 308–9

faith of, 37–38

final days, 210, 212–18

genius, xiv, 117–8, 130, 337, 339, 347

global vision, 152, 280, 283, 317

health and illness, 4, 8, 10, 36, 72, 93, 161, 172, 180–93, 332, 399

hearing before Bishop Guido, 27–31, 37

innovator, 106, 117–30

joy, 111, 186, 216, 327, 339

"Letter to Entire Order," 210

loss of eyesight, 187, 192

love of music and singing, 6–7, 31, 47, 206, 343

meets Sultan Malik al-Kamil, 163–65

naked at death, 216–17, 321, 343

personality and temperament, xii, 7, 52, 107

photophobia (aversion to intense light), 187–88, 190, 192

prayer life, 10, 11, 38, 40, 66

preaching, 39, 54, 66, 73–74, 96–97, 110–13, 117, 132, 194, 202

prisoner in Perugia, 4, 8, 36, 183

radical vision, 52–53, 63, 68, 85, 107, 109, 294–95

relinquishes leadership, 92, 187, 254

repairs San Damiano chapel, 24, 33–34, 37

Rule for Hermitages, 127

"second Christ," 333

stigmata, 102, 180, 194–200, 217, 218, 264

suffering, 53–54, 180, 203, 339

Testament, 12, 35, 121, 210, 211, 251, 260–61, 267–68, 278, 337

world parish, 279–80, 317, 328

Francis of Assisi: Performing the Gospel Life (Cunningham), 322

Franciscan Order, 56, 58–59, 64–65

as movement, xiv, xvi, 44–50, 68, 106–17

authorized to preach, 64–65, 70

buildings, 91, 253–54, 269, 294

changes after Francis's death, 233–34

chapters, 70, 85–89, 123–24, 127, 152, 194, 256

clericalization, 210, 230–31, 256, 319

co-opted to support Crusades, 279

community, 48–51, 70, 76, 113–14, 117, 127, 314, 318

dissension and division, 89, 91–92, 98, 101, 117, 250, 254, 265, 278

education and scholarship, 52, 100, 229, 232, 235

equality, 68, 79, 82–83, 87–88, 113–14, 230

fratres minores (little/lesser brothers), 15, 69, 79

growing public awareness, 48, 50–51

habit, 56, 65, 73, 79, 94, 120–21, 212, 251

herald of New Age of Spirit?, 237, 254, 266, 278

impact on universities, 227–30

joy, 50, 53, 71, 77, 124

manual labor, 80, 118, 212

missionary journeys, 82, 121–22

novitiate instituted, 79, 92–93

pastoral ministries, 227, 233, 250

prayer life, 53, 66, 70, 77–78, 125–27

preaching, 54, 233–34

provinces, 88–89, 94, 256

rapid growth, 44, 48, 69, 83–84, 89, 91, 105–17, 131, 162, 230, 253

reform and renewal within, 278–79, 308–9, 330

revisions in Rule, 93–94, 99, 152

Spirituals versus Conventuals, 267, 314

structure, structural innovations, 58, 70, 79–80, 83–90, 101, 106, 119–31, 330

Franciscan Order *(continued)*
vicarages (mission districts), 284
wealth increases, 253–54, 261–62
witness and impact, 50–51, 53–54
Francke, Linda Bird, 156, 170, 178,
187–88, 192
fratres minores. See Franciscan Order
Frederick I, Holy Roman Emperor, 73
Frederick II, Holy Roman Emperor,
73, 150, 172, 219, 258–59
Freeman, Charles, xiv, 242, 243
Friars Minor Conventual (OFM Conv.).
See Conventual Franciscans
Friars Minor of St. Francis. *See*
Observant Friars
Friars Minor of the Regular
Observance. *See* Observant Friars
Friars Minor. *See* Franciscan Order
Friars of the Observance. *See*
Observant Friars

Garcia de Padilla (Franciscan), first
Catholic Bishop of Hispaniola, 307
Genghis Khan, 279–81, 283–85, 287,
290
Gerard of Borgo San Donnino,
Brother, 238, 266
gifts of the Spirit *(charismata)*, 340–41,
351
Giles, Brother, 46–47, 49–51, 82, 83,
153
Gimpel, Jean, 241
Giotto di Bondone, artist, xiii, 168,
178, 256–57, 281, 297–98
Giovanni di Fidanza, 56–57. *See*
Bonaventure
glaucoma, disease of eyes, 188
Gontard, Friedrich, 60
Gothic cathedrals, xiii, 228
Greccio, Italy, Nativity scene at,
174–76, 192
Gregory IX (Hugolino), Pope, 109, 139,
145–46, 220, 251, 258, 260–61, 316
Gregory VIII, Pope, 60
Gregory X, Pope, 300
Gregory XI, Pope, 274
Greyfriars (English Franciscans), 120
Guido, bishop of Assisi, 20, 26–29,
37, 48–49, 56, 62, 75, 134, 140,
186, 205, 214

guilds, 3, 116, 177
Guillem Sancton (Spiritual Franciscan),
272
Guyuk Khan, 288

hagiography, 184, 264, 335, 343
hair shirts, 72, 141–42, 343
*Harmony of the Old and New
Testament* (Joachim of Fiore),
266
Haymo of Faversham, Brother, 258, 260
Heavenly Horse tradition in Chinese
art, 296
Henri d'Avranches, 14, 29, 113
heretics, heretical movements, 53,
55–56, 61, 85, 108, 115, 275,
268, 311, 312, 316, 321
hermitages, Franciscan, 68, 80, 99,
127–31, 186, 196, 254, 276, 314,
347–48
Hispaniola, Island of, 304, 306–7
Holy Roman Empire, 6, 72, 150, 172,
219
Honorius III, Pope, 90, 100, 105, 109,
112, 129, 145, 171, 210
Hugolino, bishop and cardinal (Pope
Gregory IX), 97–98, 100, 112,
280, 329

Ibn al-Farid, Sufi mystic, 166
Ignatius Loyola, 117, 280, 323
Illuminato of Rieti, Brother, 154,
160–61, 163, 167–68, 170
imitatio Christi, 68, 69
indulgences, 281, 351
Innocent III, Pope, 4, 6, 56, 59–64,
69, 72, 90, 162, 231, 311
approves Francis's early rule, 64,
70, 79, 90, 212, 259
power and influence, 60–61, 108
reform agenda, 61, 108, 231, 311
Innocent IV, Pope, 138, 219, 221,
261, 286, 288
Innocent VI, Pope, 273
Inquisition, the, 269, 271–72
institution versus charism, 65, 101,
270, 310–11
*Introduction to the Everlasting
Gospel, the* (Gerard of Borgo San
Donnino), 238, 266

Iriarte, Lazaro, 76–77, 79–80, 84, 88, 105, 249
Irvin, Dale T., 291
Islam, 5, 247. *See also* Muslims

Jean Barrau (Spiritual Franciscan), 271
Jerome of Ascoli, Brother (Pope Nicholas IV), 300
Jimenez de Cisneros, Brother (cardinal), 249
Joachim of Fiore, 200–1, 237, 253, 254, 263, 265–67
  Ages of Father, Son, and Holy Spirit, 266
  Franciscans and, 237–38, 266
  prophesies New Age of the Spirit, 237, 254, 266
Jacobo de Tastera (Franciscan), missionary in Mexico, 307
Jacopa de Settesoli, Lady, 192, 214–17
Jacopone of Todi (Spiritual Franciscan), composes *laude* songs, 208–9
Jacques Pantaléon, Bishop (Pope Urban IV), 238
James (Jacques) de Vitry, cardinal, 86, 107–8, 113–16, 120–22, 161–65, 167, 169
James of the March (inquisitor), 274–76
Japan, Franciscan missions in, 280
Jerusalem, 5, 17, 154–55, 157 170, 255
Jesus Christ, xiv–xv, 19, 30–31, 40, 52, 54, 58, 74, 79, 111, 140, 246
  as light, 242
  commissions apostles, 35, 44
  crucifixion, 22, 246, 309, 336, 346
  Francis and, xv, 30–31, 37, 111, 216
  as example, xv, 10, 37, 54, 59, 68, 80, 118, 250, 345, 348
  nativity, 176, 219
  proclaims kingdom of God, 54, 110
  resurrection, 22, 329, 336, 344
  sufferings, 10, 22, 37, 141, 181, 336, 344
  Way, Truth, Life, 345
Jews, 61, 247, 275, 301
John de Valle, founds strict new Franciscan hermitage, 273
John of Capistrano, 274–76

John of Marignolli (Franciscan missionary), 286, 295–97
John of Montecorvino (Franciscan missionary), 286, 293–96
  first Catholic missionary to China, 293
  translates and portrays Scriptures, 294
John of Piancarpino, Brother, 286–89
John Paul II, Pope, 223, 245
John Pecham, Brother (Archbishop of Canterbury), 240
John XXII, Pope, 270–71
Juan de Zumárraga (Franciscan missionary), first bishop in Mexico, 307
Juan Pérez, Brother, 301–3
Jubilee Year, 1300, 281–82
Julian of Speyer, Brother, 121–22, 164, 166

Karakorum, Mongolian capital, 288, 289, 291–92
Khubilai Khan, 290, 293
Kimmerer, Robin Wall, 347
kingdom of heaven, kingdom of God, 35–37, 39, 110, 121, 203, 317, 349
Knights of the Round Table, 6, 343
knights, knighthood, 8, 9, 17, 33, 36–37, 51, 52, 113, 206
knowledge, quest for, 229–30
Kublai Khan. *See* Khubilai Khan

La Rábida Franciscan friary, Spain, 301–3
Lady Poverty, 29, 40, 52, 122, 167, 216, 254, 257
Langton, Stephen, Archbishop of Canterbury, 60
Last Child in the Woods (Louv), 203
Lateran IV. *See* Fourth Lateran Council
Latourette, Kenneth Scott, 242
laude (praise songs), 207–9
LaVerna, Mount. *See* Mount LaVerna
leadership, 92, 107, 259, 318
Leo X, Pope, 276
Leo, Brother, xiii, 84, 99, 126, 196–97, 206, 221, 260
Leonardo da Vinci, 249, 298
lepers, leprosy, 12–13, 15

Lesser Brothers. *See* Franciscan Order
lesserness, 52, 68, 86, 332, 337, 351
Letters of Fraternity, 261–62
liberal arts: *trivium* and *quadrivium*,
    229–30
light, 239–40, 242–43
    Franciscan interest in, 242–43
    science of, 239–40, 243
Light Ages, The (Falk), 229, 242
Little Flowers of St. Francis, xv, 332
liturgy, 125, 320, 326, 340
Liturgy of the Hours, 49, 58, 66, 94,
    125, 140, 314, 326, 347
Lord's Supper. *See* Eucharist; sacraments
Lotario di Segni. *See* Pope Innocent III
Louis IX, king of France (Saint Louis),
    289, 292–93
Lucius III, Pope, 60
Lull (Llull), Raymond. *See* Ramon Llull

McNamara, Jo Ann Kay, 54–55
Magna Carta, xiii
malaria, 142, 184–87
    chronic, 184–85
    Francis and, 184–87
Malik al-Kamil, Muslim Sultan, 152,
    157, 161–69, 172, 187
manger scene at Greccio, 174–79
Marco Polo, 287, 289
Marcos de Niza, Brother, missionary
    in Arizona, 307
Marsh, Adam, Brother, 238–39
martyrs, Franciscan, 153, 173, 247,
    294
Mary, Virgin, 22, 34–35, 52, 142, 176,
    208
Masseo, Brother, 84, 196–97, 332
medieval society, 14–17, 30, 34, 82,
    128, 181–82, 222
merchants, merchant class, 5, 6, 15,
    30, 52
merit, 148, 221, 351
Merton, Thomas, 245, 323
Methodist movement, 124, 319, 321,
    324, 328–29
Michael Monachus (Michael le Moine),
    inquisitor, 271
Michelangelo, 298
mission structures, 317, 330
Moffett, Samuel, 283, 286, 288

Monastery of Saint Paul (Benedictine
    nuns), 135, 137
Mongke Khan, 289, 290, 291–92
Mongols, Franciscan mission to, 286
Mongol Empire, 284–85, 289
Mongolia, 279, 280, 281, 283, 286–94
Monte Casale hermitage, 80–81
Moorman, John, 88, 92, 153, 208–9,
    233–39, 247, 255, 363, 268–70,
    276, 279, 306–7
Morico the Short, Brother, 47, 51
Morison, Samuel Eliot, 301–3
Morocco, 153, 172, 186, 284
Moses, Paul, 166–80
Mount LaVerna, 127, 194–200, 202
movement dynamics, xiv, xv, 54–55,
    68–69, 103–31, 278
music, 230, 328, 343. *See also laude*
    songs; praise music
Muslims, 6, 51, 53, 70, 82, 90, 101,
    149–51, 222, 228, 230, 275, 301,
    346. *See also* Islam
mystery plays, 177–78

nakedness, spiritual significance, xvi,
    29, 216
Neely, Alan, 248
Nestorian Christians, 285, 288,
    290–92, 294
New Age of the Spirit, 237, 253–69, 278
Nicholas III, Pope, 230, 315
Nicholas IV, Pope, 293, 298–300
    first Franciscan pope, 293, 300
Nimmo, Duncan, 278
nobility, 6, 15, 49, 51, 67, 68, 87,
    112–13, 113
Normandy Chronicle, 113

Observant Friars, 274, 275–76, 314.
    See also Spiritual Franciscans
Offreduccio, Catherine (sister of
    Clare), 17, 137
Offreduccio, Clare. *See* Clare of Assisi
Offreduccio, Favarone (father of
    Clare), 17
Offreduccio, Ortulana (mother of
    Clare), 17
On the Road with Francis (Francke),
    156, 170, 178, 187–88, 192
Opus Majus (Roger Bacon), 242

Order of Friars Minor Capuchin (OFM Cap.). *See* Capuchins
Order of Friars Minor Conventual. *See* Conventual Franciscans
Order of Lesser Brothers. *See* Franciscan Order
Order of Preachers, 97, 122. *See* Dominicans
Order of Saint Clare. *See* Poor Clares
Order of Saint Damian. *See* Poor Clares
Order of Saint Francis. *See* Franciscan Order
Order of Secular Franciscans, 309
Origins of the Franciscan Order (Esser), 82, 106
Otto IV, king of Germany, 72–73
Oxford University, 231, 235

Pacifico, Brother (poet), 206
Patarini. *See* Cathars
peace, 39, 67–68, 74, 87, 110, 112, 223
Peking (Beijing), China, 284, 288
Pelagius, Cardinal, 162, 171–72
penance, 12–13, 33, 39, 64, 110, 127, 194, 211, 218, 261, 313, 351
perfection, ideal of, 71, 343
Peter Catani, Brother, 44–46, 51–52, 92–93, 119, 154, 254, 321
Peter John Olivi, Brother, 268
Peterson, Ingrid, 17, 132, 142, 145–48, 222
Philip the Tall, Brother, 48, 51, 133, 135, 137
Pica, mother of Francis, 4, 20, 26
Picard, Marc, 22
Pietist Movement, 320, 322
Pietro (Peter), priest of San Damiano, 21, 23–24, 33
Pietro di Bernardone (father of Francis), 4–6, 8, 15, 20, 24, 27–30, 116
Pons Rocha (Spiritual Franciscan), 272
Portiuncula, 34–39, 46–47, 50, 53, 58, 70, 74–76, 82, 85, 95–98, 132, 172–73, 199, 265
Poor Clares, 17, 51, 115–16, 137, 309
  as women's movement, 138
  cloistered, 140, 146
  extreme poverty, 221
  form of life, 139–43
  growth, 138, 146, 222

Rule, 139, 141
Poor Clares of Perpetual Adoration, 223
Poor Ladies of San Damiano, 70. *See also* Poor Clares
Poor Men of Lyons. *See* Waldensians
popes, papacy, 5, 55, 58–61, 69, 85, 227, 278, 314
  role in Crusades, 5, 69
  support of Franciscans, 108–9, 117, 253, 314, 316
poverty, xiv, 29–30, 37, 96, 148. *See also* Lady Poverty
Powell, James, 161
praise music, Franciscan origins, 207–8
prayer, 33, 40, 58, 76, 125, 127, 223, 339–40, 340, 349. *See also* Liturgy of the Hours
preaching, 54
  by example, 112
  Francis's preaching described, 110–12
Princely Gifts and Papal Treasures: The Franciscan Mission to China (Arnold), 297
Privilege of Poverty, 143–46
Protestant Reformation. *See* Reformation, Protestant
purgatory, 217, 262

Rabban Sauma, Nestorian monk and Mongol envoy, 293
Ramon Llull, Franciscan tertiary, 240, 246–49
  Book of Contemplation, 247
  "Doctor Illuminatus," 246
  education, 246–47
  knowledge of languages, 247
  martyr, 247–48
  missionary to Muslims, 246–47
Reform and Division in the Medieval Franciscan Order (Nimmo), 278
reform movements, 308
Reformation, Protestant, xv, 229, 262
Regula bullata (papally-sealed rule), 90, 100, 109, 124, 126, 174, 271. *See also* Rule of Franciscan Order
Regula non-bullata (rule without papal seal), 90, 124
Renaissance, the, xiv, xv, 30, 229, 243

*Renaissance: Maker of Modern
Man, The* (National Geographic
Society), 298
renewal movements, xv, 54–55, 68,
103, 108
  birth new forms of ministry, 318
  co-optation, 278–79
  Franciscans as paradigm, 278, 308
  models and paradigms, 312, 321
Reopening of the Western Mind, The
(Freeman), xiv, 242
Revelation, biblical book of, 266. *See
  also* Apocalypse, biblical book
Reynard the Fox, 6, 343
Rivo Torto, Franciscans stay at, 70–74
Robert Grosseteste (Franciscan
  scholar), 239–40
Roger of Wendover, chronicler, 105,
  120, 122, 171
Roman Catholic Church, 55, 59, 85,
  115, 230, 287, 321, 327
Romance of the Rose, 6, 343
Rome, Italy, 3, 6, 11, 14, 17, 56,
  59–62, 174, 255, 274
Rufino, bishop and martyr, 15, 22
Rule of Saint Clare, 143–47
Rule of Franciscan Order, 99–102, 212,
  254, 260, 278, 311, 318, 323, 347
  approved by Honorius III (*regula
  bullata*), 90, 100, 109, 174
  disputes over, 97–100, 187, 250,
  261, 265
  literal vs. "spiritual" interpretation,
  261
  relaxations and compromises,
  261–62, 268
Runciman, Steven, 155, 163–64, 172

Sabatier, Paul, 20, 50, 66
sacraments, 85, 87, 139, 210, 218,
  317, 325
Saint Peter of the Thorn chapel, 34, 37
Salome of Krakow (Salome of
  Poland), 219, 220
Salmon, Pierre, 126
San Damiano chapel, 20–31, 33–34,
  46, 75, 139–40, 218
  becomes motherhouse of Poor
  Clares, 137
  Francis and, 20–23, 33–34, 37, 46

cross (crucifix) of, 22, 30. *See also*
  Crucifix of San Damiano
Saint Nicholas church, Assisi, 45
San Giorgio (Saint George) church,
  Assisi, 7, 39, 74, 219
San Juan Capistrano Mission,
  California, 275
San Rufino Cathedral, Assisi, 3, 14,
  15, 18, 21, 46, 73, 75
Sant'Angelo di Panzo monastery, 137
Santa Maria degli Angeli chapel, 34,
  199, 214. *See also* Portiuncula
Santiago de Compostela, Spain, 17,
  186, 255
Saracens, 149, 153, 292. *See* Muslims
science, xiv, 42, 228–30, 243
  and theology, 243, 246
  experimental, 239, 241–42
  of light, 242–43
Schmucki, Octavian, analysis of
  Francis's illnesses, 183–89
Scripture. *See* Bible, the
Second Order of Saint Francis, 116,
  143. *See* Poor Clares
servanthood, service to others, 52, 87,
  213, 223, 338, 347
Sheehan, M. W., 231–32
Sisters of Saint Francis, 223
Skylark, 40–42, 217
small groups, small-group structures,
  313–14. *See also ecclesiola*
social movements, 55, 68, 103, 138,
  146, 222, 308
spirit versus structure, 282, 310, 330
spiritual disciplines, 142, 241, 339,
  347–48
Spiritual Franciscans, 267–69, 271.
  See also Observant Friars
  burned at stake, 271–72
Stephen of Saint-Thibéry, Franciscan
  inquisitor, 279
Summa Theologica (Thomas
  Aquinas), 267
Sunquist, Scott W., 291
Sweeney, Jon, 312
Sylvester, Brother, 46, 58
Syriac Orthodox Christians, 290, 291

Teresa of Ávila, 323
tertiaries, 116, 127, 215, 247, 325.

See also Third Order of Francis
theology, theologians, 212, 246
Third Order of Francis, 127, 139,
    215, 301, 325, 341
Thomas Aquinas, xiii, 227, 238, 244
Thomas of Celano, Brother, xv, 7, 10,
    28–29, 39, 67–68, 76, 82–83, 93,
    123, 175–76, 335, 343
    describes giving of *stigmata*, 198–99
    Francis's first biographer, xv, 7
Thomas of Frignano, Brother (general
    minister), 273
Thomas Eccleston, Brother, 125, 258
Timur Khan, 294
Traboulay, David M., 303
trachoma eye disease, 187–89
    cauterization as treatment, 189
    Francis contracts, 187–88
    photophobia (aversion to intense
    light), 187–90
transubstantiation, doctrine of, 61, 326
Tree of the Crucified Life of Jesus
    (Ubertino da Casale), 201
Trinity, the Holy, 203, 291, 320
troubadours, xiii, 4, 6, 31, 133, 206

Ubertino da Casale, 201
universities, xiii, 7, 52, 116, 227–30
    Franciscan impact on, 117, 236
    rise and growth of, 116, 227–28
    student communities at, 116–17
University of Bologna, 7, 60, 91, 112,
    116
University of Paris, 57, 60, 116, 231,
    235, 236, 244, 245, 258, 262
Urban IV, Pope, 238

Valdes, Peter. *See* Waldo, Peter
vita apostolica, 68, 79, 162, 270, 315.
    See also evangelical poverty
Vos, Antoine, 244

Waldensians, 55, 63, 85, 115, 316
Waldo, Peter, 55, 63, 316

Walsh, James, xiii, 116
Walter of Brienne, Count, 4, 8–9, 13
wealth, 53, 87, 261, 346
Weatherford, Jack, 290, 297
Weisheipl, J. A., 239
Wesley, Charles, 328, 329
Wesley, John, 323–29
    call to the poor, 324
    Christian faith and ministry, 324
    contrasts with Francis, 323, 329
    covenant community, 325, 326
    emphasis on Eucharist, 326
    "faith working through love," 324
    health and regimen, 323
    movement founder, 324
    music and song, 327–28
    parallels with Francis, 324–29
    preaching in public, 324, 329
    quest for holiness, perfection, 325
    structures for discipleship, 325, 330
    world parish, world vision, 328
When Saint Francis Saved the Church
    (Sweeney), 312
William of Ockham (Franciscan), xiv
William of Rubruck, Franciscan
    missionary to China, 286,
    289–93
Wisdom of God in Creation, The
    (John Wesley), 327
women, 17, 52, 67, 138
    followers of Francis, 115–16, 117,
    219
    ministry of 54–55
    movements of, 55, 138
    restrictions on, 54–55, 67, 133, 214,
    222

Yuan dynasty, China, 293, 295
    Khubilai Khan and, 293
    requests Christian teachers, 295

Zhou Lang (Chinese artist), 296

Previously Published in the
American Society of Missiology Series

1. *Protestant Pioneers in Korea,* Everett Nichols Hunt Jr.
2. *Catholic Politics in China and Korea,* Eric O. Hanson
3. *From the Rising of the Sun: Christians and Society in Contemporary Japan,* James M. Phillips
4. *Meaning across Cultures,* Eugene A. Nida and William D. Reyburn
5. *The Island Churches of the Pacific,* Charles W. Forman
6. *Henry Venn: Missionary Statesman,* Wilbert R. Shenk
7. *No Other Name? Christianity and Other World Religions,* Paul F. Knitter
8. *Toward a New Age in Christian Theology,* Richard Henry Drummond
9. *The Expectation of the Poor: Latin American Base Ecclesial Communities in Protest,* Guillermo Cook
10. *Eastern Orthodox Mission Theology Today,* James J. Stamoolis
11. *Confucius, the Buddha, and Christ: A History of the Gospel in China,* Ralph R. Covell
12. *The Church and Cultures: New Perspectives in Missiological Anthropology,* Louis J. Luzbetak, SVD
13. *Translating the Message: The Missionary Impact on Culture,* Lamin Sanneh
14. *An African Tree of Life,* Thomas G. Christensen
15. *Missions and Money: Affluence as a Western Missionary Problem ... Revisited* (second edition), Jonathan J. Bonk
16. *Transforming Mission: Paradigm Shifts in Theology of Mission,* David J. Bosch
17. *Bread for the Journey: The Mission and Transformation of Mission,* Anthony J. Gittins, C.S.Sp.
18. *New Face of the Church in Latin America: Between Tradition and Change,* edited by Guillermo Cook
19. *Mission Legacies: Biographical Studies of Leaders of the Modern Missionary Movement,* edited by Gerald H. Anderson, Robert T. Coote, Norman A. Horner, and James M. Phillips
20. *Classic Texts in Mission and World Christianity,* edited by Norman E. Thomas
21. *Christian Mission: A Case Study Approach,* Alan Neely
22. *Understanding Spiritual Power: A Forgotten Dimension of Cross-Cultural Mission and Ministry,* Marguerite G. Kraft
23. *Missiological Education for the 21st Century: The Book, the Circle, and the Sandals,* edited by J. Dudley Woodberry, Charles Van Engen, and Edgar J. Elliston

24. *Dictionary of Mission: Theology, History, Perspectives,* edited by Karl Müller, SVD, Theo Sundermeier, Stephen B. Bevans, SVD, and Richard H. Bliese

25. *Earthen Vessels and Transcendent Power: American Presbyterians in China, 1837–1952,* G. Thompson Brown

26. *The Missionary Movement in American Catholic History,* Angelyn Dries, OSF

27. *Mission in the New Testament: An Evangelical Approach,* edited by William J. Larkin Jr. and Joel W. Williams

28. *Changing Frontiers of Mission,* Wilbert R. Shenk

29. *In the Light of the Word: Divine Word Missionaries of North America,* Ernest Brandewie

30. *Constants in Context: A Theology of Mission for Today,* Stephen B. Bevans, SVD, and Roger P. Schroeder, SVD

31. *Changing Tides: Latin America and World Mission Today,* Samuel Escobar

32. *Gospel Bearers, Gender Barriers: Missionary Women in the Twentieth Century,* edited by Dana L. Robert

33. *Church: Community for the Kingdom,* John Fuellenbach, SVD

34. *Mission in Acts: Ancient Narratives in Contemporary Context,* edited by Robert L. Gallagher and Paul Hertig

35. *A History of Christianity in Asia: Volume I, Beginnings to 1500,* Samuel Hugh Moffett

36. *A History of Christianity in Asia: Volume II, 1500–1900,* Samuel Hugh Moffett

37. *A Reader's Guide to Transforming Mission,* Stan Nussbaum

38. *The Evangelization of Slaves and Catholic Origins in Eastern Africa,* Paul V. Kollman, CSC

39. *Israel and the Nations: A Mission Theology of the Old Testament,* James Chukwuma Okoye, C.S.Sp.

40. *Women in Mission: From the New Testament to Today,* Susan E. Smith

41. *Reconstructing Christianity in China: K. H. Ting and the Chinese Church,* Philip L. Wickeri

42. *Translating the Message: The Missionary Impact on Culture* (second edition), Lamin Sanneh

43. *Landmark Essays in Mission and World Christianity,* edited by Robert L. Gallagher and Paul Hertig

44. *World Mission in the Wesleyan Spirit,* Darrell L. Whiteman and Gerald H. Anderson (published by Province House, Franklin, TN)

45. *Miracles, Missions, & American Pentecostalism,* Gary B. McGee

46. *The Gospel among the Nations: A Documentary History of Inculturation,* Robert A. Hunt

47. *Missions and Unity: Lessons from History, 1792–2010,* Norman E. Thomas

48. *Mission and Culture: The Louis J. Luzbetak Lectures*, edited by Stephen B. Bevans

49. *Comprehending Mission: The Questions, Methods, Themes, Problems, and Prospects of Missiology*, Stanley H. Skreslet

50. *Christian Mission among the Peoples of Asia*, Jonathan Y. Tan

51. *Sent Forth: African Missionary Work in the West*, Harvey C. Kwiyani

52. *Mangoes or Bananas: The Quest for an Authentic Asian Christian Theology*, Hwa Yung

53. *Contemporary Mission Theology: Engaging the Nations: Essays in Honor of Charles E. Van Engen*, edited by Robert L. Gallagher and Paul Hertig

54. *African Christian Leadership: Realities, Opportunities, and Impact*, edited by Kirimi Barine and Robert Priest

55. *Women Leaders in the Student Christian Movement: 1880–1920*, Thomas Russell

56. *Traditional Ritual as Christian Worship: Dangerous Syncretism or Necessary Hybridity?*, R. Daniel Shaw and William R. Burrows

57. *Christian Mission, Contextual Theology, Prophetic Dialogue: Essays in Honor of Stephen B. Bevans, SVD*, edited by Dale T. Irvin and Peter C. Phan

58. *Go Forth: Toward a Community of Missionary Disciples*, Pope Francis, selected with commentary by William P. Gregory

59. *Breaking through the Boundaries: Biblical Perspectives on Mission from the Outside In*, Paul Hertig, Young Lee Hertig, Sarita Gallagher Edwards, and Robert L. Gallagher

60. *A Long Walk, A Gradual Ascent: The Story of the Bolivian Friends Church in Its Context of Conflict*, Nancy J. Thomas.

61. *The Missionary Spirit: Evangelism and Social Action in Pentecostal Missiology*, Jerry M. Ireland

62. *Christ among the Nations: Narratives of Transformation in Global Mission*, Sarita Gallagher Edwards, Robert L. Gallagher, Paul W. Lewis, and DeLonn L. Rance

63. *Virtuous Persuasion: A Theology of Christian Mission*, Michael Neibauer (Lexham Press)

64. *Christ Among the Classes: The Rich, The Poor, and the Mission of the Church*, Al Tizon

65. *Community of Missionary Disciples: The Continuing Creation of the Church*, Stephen B. Bevans